They and We

They and We

Racial and Ethnic Relations in the United States

Sixth Edition

Peter I. Rose

Paradigm Publishers

Boulder•London

Copyright © 2006 Paradigm Publishers.

Published in the United States by Paradigm Publishers, 3360 Mitchell Lane Suite E, Boulder, CO 80301 USA.

Paradigm Publishers is the trade name of Birkenkamp & Company, LLC, Dean Birkenkamp, President and Publisher.

Library of Congress Cataloging-in-Publication Data

Rose, Peter Isaac, 1933-
    They and we: racial and ethnic relations in the United States /
Peter I. Rose. — 6th ed.
        p. cm.
    Includes bibliographical references and index.
    ISBN 1–59451–205–1 (pbk.: alk. paper)
    1. Minorities—United States. 2. Discrimination—United States. 3. United States—Race rela-
tions. 4. United States—Ethnic relations. I. Title.
    E184.A1R72 2006
    305.8'0973—dc22

                                                                                    2005021804
Printed and bound in the United States of America on acid-free paper that meets the standards of the American National Standard for Permanence of Paper for Printed Library Materials.

Designed and typeset by Straight Creek Bookmakers.

10 09 08 07 06
5 4 3 2 1

For Hedy

Contents

Part III   Attitudes, Actions, and Minority Reactions

Preface

The first edition of *They and We* was completed in 1963, the year the Civil Rights Movement reached its zenith. "Black Power" was but a hushed whisper then. Few who listened to the Reverend Martin Luther King, Jr., address a quarter of a million black and white Americans assembled on the Mall in front of the Lincoln Memorial in Washington, D.C., on August 28, 1963, realized that he, his people, and their allies in the struggle—and their enemies—were about to enter a new era. The whisper was to become a roar.

Those days now seem light-years away. In the period immediately before the March on Washington, thousands had participated in a crusade of radical pacifism, a campaign involving a variety of nonviolent direct action tactics—marches, boycotts, sit-ins, and freedom rides—seeking to force the country to honor its own vaunted ideals and win for all the rights most white Americans took for granted. It was a difficult and uphill struggle. Although the costs were considerable, there were a number of significant victories. But several events that occurred a few months after the March on Washington led to a dramatic change in the tone, the temper, and the orientation of the movement.

The mounting frustration of militant blacks and many others confined to inner-city ghettos became painfully apparent to all members of society. Anger was expressed in a variety of contexts. Riots broke out in some cities. Within the civil rights organizations, many whites who had played key roles as organizers or foot soldiers were eased or pushed from positions of leadership; many African Americans (and Asian Americans and Latinos and Native Americans in their own fashions) foreswore the rhetoric of integration for the rhetoric of revolution.

In many ways the rhetoric was reified. In a real sense there was a revolution.

First, the members of the dominant white majority were told over and over that they, all of them, and not just "the southern bigots," were racists. A spate of new books hammered home the theme. Many black people who, for any number of reasons, had not organized themselves before began to add action to their verbal attacks. Demands were made, met, escalated, and often met again. A new litany began to be heard. Watchwords like "Freedom, Now" and "We Shall Overcome" were replaced by various new slogans that reflected the view tersely expressed in the warning: "Look out, whitey, black power gon' get your momma." Then there came a call for recompense. Ultimately, in what many saw as justified and others saw as a kind of racism-in-reverse, the pleas for admission and fairness became a call for special treatment to help those handicapped by the stigma of inferiority to improve their chances to run an equal race.

As the demands, particularly of college students, were beginning to be responded to by frightened faculties and baffled administrations (often liberal and therefore particularly susceptible to the accusations of the protesters), more conservative organizations began making their own concessions. For example, large industries increased the level of tokenism to include more African American and Latino workers, especially in places where they would be seen. Television networks and local stations began to employ them, too. In the beginning most of the new hires were assigned to do race-based "Minority Reports." (It would be several more years before they would begin to move more directly into mainline positions.)

The pressure tactics were quite successful. It was a revelation to some to see how many qualified "people of color" were actually available as potential students for Ivy League colleges, as workers in various Fortune 500 companies, as TV announcers and print media commentators when the threat of disruption loomed on the immediate horizon.

As disaffected members of the old civil rights movement were beginning to rally their troops for new assaults on the academy and the factory, the people on the street became involved, too. Some did it in organized fashion, others more spontaneously. Dozens of urban disturbances flared up in cities as different as New York, Detroit, Cleveland, and Los Angeles as poor folks joined in the burning and looting in a frenzied expression of frustration and bitterness and, for some, the sheer thrill of revenge.

Other people engaged in more carefully planned political activities, many of them centered on the issue of local or community control, particularly of schools. Still others simply took renewed pride in who they were, if not where they found themselves.

All this—the rhetoric, the organizing, the calculated attacks on the system, and the spontaneous outbursts—shook the entire nation. Many white Americans reeled in disbelief and then, in a variety of ways, they reacted.

Part of the response came from traditional reactionaries whose predominant theme was "We told you so." But more significant, and far greater in the numbers involved, was the response of those in two significant cohorts: white, Protestant, lower-middle-class and small-town "middle Americans," and working-class, predominantly Catholic and urban "white ethnics." The latter group, often but a generation or two from ghetto living themselves, began to feel that they, in particular, were being asked to pay for the sins of other peoples' fathers and mothers.

Backlash became a reality, though, save for widespread reaction to forced school busing, it was far less vicious than many had predicted. Even so, by the early 1970s the bookstores had another section to add to the one that shelved volumes by Maya Angelou, James Baldwin, Eldridge Cleaver, Angela Davis, Ralph Ellison, Franz Fanon, and on through the rest of an alphabetical list of black writers and writers on black subjects. The new shelf, not yet so long, included books with telling titles like Murray Friedman's *Overcoming Middle Class Rage,* Nathan Glazer's *Affirmative Discrimination,* Andrew M. Greeley's *Why Can't They Be Like Us?,* Louise Howe's *The White Majority,* Michael Novak's *The Rise of the Unmeltable Ethnics,* Peter Shrag's *Out of Place in America,* and many more with similar themes. That list was to grow much longer, especially in the 1990s and in the first decade of the new millennium. It would include two especially hard-hitting critiques: Arthur M. Schlesinger's *The Disuniting of America,* published in 1991, and Samuel P. Huntington's *Who Are We?,* published in 2004.

Parallel to the growing resistance to the pressures being exerted by black and brown and other minority Americans was a reexamination of their own places in the society, and their own histories as well. A new cadre of African American writers appeared. Many of them would form the vanguard of a powerful group of articulate activists, college professors, public figures, and celebrity intellectuals who began to have a heavy impact well beyond the confines of their base communities. In fact, the leaders and spokespeople for the Black Power movement and their emphasis on ethnic consciousness were largely responsible for identity politics and communalism becoming legitimized—then institutionalized—in what would later be known as "multiculturalism"—in a manner unprecedented in our history.

The period from 1963 to 1973 was quite a volatile one on the ethnic front. Yet, by the middle of the 1970s "race" was no longer a central issue, nor was American involvement in Vietnam, the war having ended in 1975. From that time through the rest of the decade, economics and energy concerns took center stage, dominating foreign affairs and also domestic debates.

This is not to say everything was settled in the realm of racial and ethnic relations. It wasn't. In fact, the energy crisis served to accentuate the plight of the poor who had the most to lose from rising prices and increasing shortages of fuel, to say nothing of the growing scourge of unemployment as the economy slowed and lay-offs became the order of the day.

At the same time, the general economic downturn led increasing numbers of middle Americans and white ethnics to take even more conservative stances regarding bread-and-butter issues. Concerned about where tax dollars were going, they railed against "give aways" to "welfare chiselers," who some styled "the undeserving poor." Many voiced the opinion that minorities seemed to get too much of the public funds and too many of the private positions and jobs. Court decisions gave additional support to those opposed to affirmative action and quotas, however "benign" they were claimed to be.

By the end of the 1970s, the strains of economic and political problems were deeply etched in the face of America. Unemployment reached a forty-year high and, as always, non-whites bore the brunt of the burden. Riots in Miami, Orlando, and Chattanooga in the summer of 1980 were an ugly reminder of the depth of hostility still extant in urban ghettos.

International conflicts influenced many domestic debates as well, and many began choosing sides over U.S. policies in southern Africa and the Middle East. Moreover, increasing numbers of citizens expressed resentment over the influx of hundreds of thousands of Cubans, Soviet Jews, and Southeast Asians who were seen not just as refugees from Communism but as potential usurpers of jobs and benefits of Americans.

With the depressed economic situation, the increase in racial tension, the rising tide of political conservatism, and a dearth of strong civil rights leadership, many feared that the gains made by minorities in the 1960s and 1970s would prove to be Pyrrhic victories. They were not far off the mark. One reason is that, for all the changes, including the implementation of affirmative action programs during the years of the Nixon administration, certain underlying structural characteristics of our society remained relatively constant. Among the most enduring of a long list of seemingly endemic traits was that of a nation that remained hierarchically divided in terms of social class.

While it is true that those in the upper echelons were better off than ever before (this was a time when a new and colorful term, *yuppie*—young, urban, profes-sional—took on special meaning) and increasing numbers of minority-group members were able to join the ranks of the middle class, often as the result of special efforts to assist them, many black and brown as well as white working-class Americans found they were treading water just to stay afloat in a highly turbulent economic sea. This was also true of the hundreds of thousands of resident aliens who, thanks to the Immigration Reform Act of 1965, had entered the country as immigrants looking for chances to benefit from the still widely regarded promise of the "American Dream." Like the many refugees being resettled in the U.S, they also often found themselves perceived of as interlopers poised to take jobs of those who claimed them almost as their birthright. Often the legal immigrants and the political refugees were grouped with illegal migrants or "undocumented aliens." In many circles, as it had been in the late nineteenth and early twentieth century, "immigrant" was becoming a pejorative word.

Then there were those others, who came to be known in the press and in the sociology classroom by the generic label "underclass"—many of them members of non-white minorities—who were found to be falling farther and farther behind. The social profiles of such truly disadvantaged African, Hispanic, and Native American people belied any claims, even by the most optimistic of political lead-ers, that dramatic progress had been made in dealing with one of the most basic domestic problems in our society.

The Reagan years, which began in 1980, were extended with the presidency of George H. W. Bush. Despite assurances that he would be a "kinder and gentler leader," Bush adhered to many of the policies that had turned away from the pro-gressive activities of the 1960s and 1970s, favoring instead a faith in "voluntarism." But even the attempt to ignite "a thousand points of light," Bush's expression for private initiatives, could not stem the tide of decay in the most devastated parts of society. Consequently, during the waning years of his one-term occupancy of the White House, the country was plagued with renewed calls for governmental action to address the needs of those most disadvantaged by past and continuing discrimination.

Bush was defeated. But it was not because of his racial policies—or lack thereof. Still, there was hope in the old civil rights circles that the new president, Bill Clinton, would be more sympathetic to the plight of the poor and the dispossessed, especially when he so pointedly selected cabinet members with liberal agendas, individuals who also, for the first time in history, did, as Clinton himself said, "look like America."

While some attempts were made to address the persisting grievances of minorities, women, and homosexuals, as well as poor whites, the constant sniping of the old centrist groups (those middle Americans and white ethnics) led to considerable equivocation and, eventually, retreat on many fronts. But even such acquiescence was not enough. In 1994, hundreds of Republicans were swept into office and took control of both houses of Congress, riding to power on the concerns of many who still opposed "welfarism" and "special treatment" of certain minorities, and who were firmly opposed to what they called "governmental interventionism." At the time of their victorious routing of the liberals, many of whom had been specifically targeted, the United States was still a deeply divided nation, separate and unequal in many quarters. The depth of the division became most clearly apparent in the fall of 1995 when, after a lengthy televised trial, African American former football star O.J. Simpson was found innocent of charges of murdering his ex-wife, Nicole, and her friend, Ronald Goldman. Both of the victims were white.

Poll data after the verdict was handed down revealed what those who had hoped for a color-blind assessment of the case most feared: opinion about the correctness of the jury's decision was directly correlated with "color." An overwhelming majority of African Americans thought the decision was justified. As for whether it was just, some claimed that "Whatever the truth, this was clearly a victory over a traditionally biased system of criminal justice." Most whites disagreed with both the verdict and the sentiment, some quite vehemently.

Almost immediately on the heels of the Simpson trial came both corroboration and contradiction. The "Million Man March" in Washington in 1995, organized and led by the Muslim leader Louis Farrakhan, provoked reaction that, while far more nuanced than those in response to the Simpson verdict, further pointed to a seemingly deepening chasm cleaving two major communities and influencing the general perceptions of white and black Americans. Yet there was mounting evidence that that may only be one side of the story.

Until he withdrew from consideration on November 8, 1995, former Chief of Staff of the Armed Forces, General Colin Powell, a black moderate and self-professed Republican, was the most popular challenger to Bill Clinton, who was gearing up to run for a second term in the Oval Office. Some argued that Powell, whose support was almost as strong among whites as it was among African Americans, was seen so favorably because it was felt that only someone like him could begin to bring the clearly estranged communities together.

Colin Powell did not run for president, but he did become the Secretary of State in the cabinet of the man who won the election of 2000, George W. Bush. A conservative by every measure but in his seemingly color-blind selection of high-ranking officials in his first administration, the second President Bush, like Ronald Reagan and like his father, still did little to address the continuing needs of minority communities. Indeed, in many ways he and the members of his administration set back the clock on civil rights and, after the momentous attacks on the twin towers of the World Trade Center and the Pentagon, on civil liberties as well.

Although he came into power with seemingly little interest in foreign affairs, after "9/11," he became preoccupied with them—and with asserting America's role on the world stage. His first term was dominated by military actions in Afghanistan and Iraq, and with "homeland security," prompted by the desire to stave off future attacks on the country, particularly by Islamic terrorists. One result of this was a growing fear in the ranks of American Muslims—many of Arab background, many others African American converts—that they would become the scapegoats seen as responsible for many of the country's problems. There was also fear in some Jewish circles that, as the war in Iraq failed to be the cakewalk predicted by Secretary Donald Rumsfeld and his neo-conservative colleagues, some of whom were Jewish, they too would become scapegoats.

In November 2004, after a protracted and, in many ways, very ugly campaign for the presidency, the conservative George W. Bush won a second term over the liberal senator from Massachusetts, John F. Kerry. Despite growing disillusionment with foreign adventures and many domestic matters, especially in the "blue" (heavily Democrat) states of the Northeast and the West Coast, the Republicans prevailed, not only keeping the presidency but strengthening their positions in both houses of Congress.

In his very brief, 22-minute inaugural address in January 2005, the President not only mentioned the word "Freedom" more than two dozen times, but he boldly stated that "our country must abandon all the habits of racism, because we cannot carry the message of freedom and the baggage of bigotry at the same time." His forceful words seemed to jibe with his personal proclivity toward color-blindness in appointments. His cabinet and senior staff were the most "multicultural" to that point in the nation's history. In addition to those of East Asian, South Asian, Hispanic, and African origins, Bush also appointed more women than any of his predecessors. But the jury remains out on how his rhetoric and actions in the White House will translate into greater opportunities for those with whom the likes of Condoleezza Rice, Alberto Gonzales, Elaine Chao, and Norman Mineta are identified.

It did not take long for a dramatic indication that such appointments are welcome but are hardly sufficient to effectively address the persisting dilemma linked to slavery's legacy and the plight of African Americans. No better example is to be found than in perceptions of the federal government's response to hurricane Katrina that hit Louisiana, Alabama, and Mississippi in early September 2005. A disproportionate percentage of those who suffered most from devastation and displacement were black and poor. Their plight dramatically increased long-held suspicions of ordinary African Americans about presidential empathy and the true commitments of the Bush Administration. This was most clearly evident in the results of a nationwide USA/Gallop Poll conducted a week after the calamity. In answer to the question "Do you think President Bush cares about black people?" 67 percent of whites said "Yes," compared to only 21 percent of blacks. These differences offer a stark reminder that racism, and the pervasive poverty that is often linked to it, remains one of the most divisive social issues in the United States. It pointedly underscores the belief of many people that we are a nation still divided, separate, and unequal.

While many significant changes in social policy and definitive gains on the "race relations front" have occurred in the nearly fifty years since I first began to write the first edition of this book, much of what was said about the character of American society and about ways of studying it then still seems appropriate. In that first edition, I sketched out the ways sociologists looked at what was then called "inter-group relations," at America's ethnic history, at some of the principal theories put forth to handle the flow of newcomers into the national polity, at prejudice and discrimination, and at minority responses.

The preparation of each subsequent edition has involved reassessment, revision, and, often, the introduction of new ideas and new information on such matters as "Black Consciousness" and its significance for African Americans and other non-white minorities, the challenge of minority assertiveness and its effect on the "resurgence of ethnicity" among other groups, debates over intelligence testing and affirmative action policies, political correctness, and multiculturalism. Preparation of the last edition once again involved a major overhaul of the text, including an expansion of the historical sections and those dealing with contemporary issues—such as "political correctness."

Much of this sixth edition of *They and We* follows the outline and the arguments of the preceding ones. But, in addition to new discussions of such concepts as "immigrants" and "refugees," an update of statistics cited and further interpretation of what they mean, and the introduction of fresh ideas and recent findings by social scientists and historians, what is most different here is the attention paid to four recent phenomena: the rise of anti-Americanism abroad and the stark reality for many of being placed in the role of stereotyped "minorities" on the world stage; the rebirth of nativism in this country as growing fear of what foreigners might bring with them—from secreted weapons to ideas and ideologies that run counter to those of the mainstream—that seems to shape both foreign and domestic policy; the rapidly changing demography (an overall doubling in the number of foreign-born in the past decade and the influx of dramatically increasing numbers of both legal and undocumented aliens in certain areas which, to some, gives legitimacy as well as license to the expression of such fears; and, 50 years after the landmark *Brown v. The Board of Education* of Topeka, Kansas, decision of the Supreme Court, a reconsideration of the status of African Americans, who, until recently surpassed by those in the broad cohort of Latinos, have long been our largest minority population.

Like all of its earlier versions, this new edition of *They and We* is not a blueprint for change. It is, rather, a guide for study and reflection. As explained in the preface to the original edition: while organized efforts to bring about a reduction in racial and ethnic tension represent an important part of contemporary life, and the tactics and strategies employed are a matter of great concern to many social scientists, including the author, they can only be introduced within the compass of this small book. It is hoped, however, that what is presented here will help to replace some of the popular misconceptions of the problems discussed and will thus serve as a basis for understanding, the first step toward change.

As I have five times before, I welcome the chance to thank many teachers, colleagues, students, and friends who have taught me, encouraged me, and offered assistance, advice, and criticism. There are many to whom I am deeply indebted, but I especially want to acknowledge ten individuals who had a special influence on my decision to become a social scientist and to pursue a research career that focused mainly on race, immigration, and the dilemmas of diversity in this and other countries: Nathan Goldman, Robin M. Williams, Jr., John P. Dean, Edward A. Suchman, Oscar Cohen, Alan Holmberg, Melvin M. Tumin, David Riesman, Milton M. Gordon, and Lawrence H. Fuchs. Each was, in a different way, both a mentor and a model. In addition, I extend my gratitude to three others: Charles D. Lieber, an editors' editor who commissioned me to write a small book on American minorities for a Random House series way back in 1960 and, later, as president of Atherton books, published my two-volume collection, *Americans from Africa*; the late Charles Hunt Page who, as a consulting editor at Random House, taught me much about writing and editing, and even more about sociology, and who remained a trusted adviser and close friend until his death in 1992; finally, Ely Chinoy, a superb social scientist, sensitive critic, and wonderful colleague at Smith College, whose untimely death thirty years ago I still mourn.

I also offer my appreciation for the support and guidance of Ted Caris, Arthur Strimling, David Bartlett, Philip Metcalf, Phillip A. Butcher, Peggy C. Rehberger, Jill Gordon, and Kathy Blake, editors at Random House and at McGraw-Hill, who each played a part in the publication of one or more of the first five editions of *They and We*. To that list, I add special thanks to Dean Birkenkamp and his staff at Paradigm Publishers who urged me to let them be the ones to bring out this new edition of my first book. After nearly fifty years of writing, editing, and sweating through the publication of a number of volumes, I am still awed by the intricacies of the work of publishers responsible for the final editing, production, and promotion of both trade books and texts.

Finally, in this year of our fiftieth wedding anniversary, I am pleased to repeat, once again, what I have written five times before. This book is dedicated to my wife, Hedy, who knows best what has been involved. Our daughter, Lies, and son, Dan, literally grew up with *They and We*. And now, as I write this (re)dedication, I hope that our teenage grandsons, Jordan Rose and Robert Rose, will come of age in a country and a world in which the dream of Martin Luther King, Jr., will finally be realized—that there will be a day when we will all be judged by the content of our character and not the color of our skin, and that all those "theys" will become part of an all-encompassing "we."

Peter I. Rose

PART I

CONTEXTS AND CONCEPTS

Chapter 1

Race, Ethnicity, and the Sociological Perspective

Reaping the Whirlwind

As a native of the area, I have been appalled by the wanton riots, the pillaging and the total disregard for law and order exercised by some members of the community the past few days. As a lifelong advocate of integration, I am deeply troubled, for I see in the streets of the city the acceleration of the "boomerang effect" that responsible civil rights leaders have so assiduously tried to avoid. But, as a social scientist, I am not at all surprised by what is happening. There have been changes, but in too many instances they have been token measures, which have done little to alleviate the basic malaise.

For years there have been warnings of the consequences of continued denial and exclusion, of the real possibility of violent upheaval, of dislocation and civil strife. And now the predictions are the frightening facts of daily life.

No one wins in these skirmishes. The police may succeed in maintaining or restoring order, but only at the expense of greater alienation and repeated charges of brutality (many real, many fabricated). The white community may say that this merely proves that blacks are unfit for entry into their *sanctum sanctorum,* but they do so only by failing to recognize that the hatred and deprivation which pervade the ghettos is not mainly the Blacks' problem but their own. The rioters may thrill at the power they wield as they run amok through the streets striking their blows for freedom as they give "whitey" his comeuppance, but even the satisfaction gained is short-lived and, too frequently, off target.[1]

3

These words might have been written in May 1992, when South Central Los Angeles went up in flames. They weren't. The quoted paragraphs, only slightly emended, are excerpted from a letter to the editor published by the author in the *New York Times* over forty years ago, on July 27, 1964, to be precise. They referred to what had just occurred in my hometown of Rochester, New York, in the area but a block from where my mother was raised and where her mother still lived. Many who lived through the events of the 1960s or read the numerous reports by the National Advisory Commission on Civil Disorders (also known as the Kerner Commission)[2] and others who studied similar events and their causes, then saw the same things happen again and again, had a sinking sense of déjà vu. We had been there before.

Political activists of the period when Rochester, Newark, Harlem, Detroit, Watts, and downtown sections of many other cities were burning—and the first edition of this book was published—used to sing an antiwar song in which each stanza ended with the refrain, "When will they ever learn? When will they ever learn?" The question remains appropriate to any number of persisting problems faced by those who live in this society—and those in many other societies as well.

Few matters of contemporary life are more in need of continuous investigation and assessment than the tensions and cleavages that exist between racial and ethnic groupings. One need look no further than the pages of a daily newspaper or a television screen to see evidence of this fact. The conflicts reported from distant places describe national rivalries, regional disputes, tribal warfare, sectarian hatreds, and campaigns of "ethnic cleansing." Daniel Patrick Moynihan described this as a kind of "global pandemonium;"[3] Robin M. Williams, Jr. refers to "the wars within."[4]

It is especially noteworthy in countries long under the yoke of the Soviet Union where the fall of communism often proved less an occasion for true democratic reform and more a time of return to bitter group-based politics and overt discrimination. At the time, Isaiah Berlin wisely noted, "Nationalism is not resurgent. It never died. Neither did racism. They are the most powerful movements in the world today."[5]

These movements are still evident on every continent and subcontinent. Many are based on demands for self-rule from long suppressed groups and marked by resistance of those in power to relinquish it. Most recently such strains against autocratic rule by those seeking autonomy have been notable not only in the former "Soviet bloc," the lands of Eastern and Central Europe, but throughout the Middle East (one thinks of the independence movement of Kurds in Turkey and Iraq; and the continuing struggles for dominance between Shiite and Sunni Muslims in Iraq), Africa (where the recent conflict in the Darfur region of the Sudan is only the most publicized of many), Central and South America (where native peoples struggle for recognition), and in various parts of South, East, and Southeast Asia (as between Buddhists and Hindus in Sri Lanka, ethnic Chinese and Malays in Malaysia). They are even to be found in Australia and New Zealand, where indigenous peoples, Aborigines and Maori, respectively, are increasingly active in asserting their rights.

In Canada and the United States, surely two of the most multiethnic nations in the world, the persistence of both "nationalism" and racism are clearly evident. In

Canada, a society that, like Australia, has institutionalized the idea of "multicultur-alism" as national policy and has often been characterized as a mosaic of distinct and separate peoples,[6] the strain best known is the continuing struggle by some in the French community determined to make the Province of Quebec a separate country, but it is also evident in mounting resistance to nonwhite migrants across the entire country, from the Maritimes to British Columbia.

In this country, continued discrimination—more subtle than in the past but nevertheless still extant—against African Americans, in both northern and south-ern areas, is only the most obvious case. Puerto Ricans, Dominicans, Mexican Americans, people from various countries in Asia and the Middle East, Native Americans, and other nonwhites are still subject to stereotyping and, too often, to differential treatment. So, too, are members of certain religious groups (especially Muslims) as well as political dissenters and dissidents, homosexuals, and women in every ethnic, religious, and racial category.

Although conflicts between those of different color, group membership, reli-gious affiliation, gender, and political orientation are global phenomena—and daily fare on television screens and the front pages of newspapers highlighting ethnic rivalry—this book is mainly about the house *we* live in. In looking at ourselves, the intention is to provide a framework with which to examine the character of a society built almost entirely by outsiders, voluntary migrants and those forced to come; a society in which diversity—whether celebrated or not—was endemic from the first confrontations native tribes had with one another and then with those who came from abroad.

From long before it became an independent nation, what we call "America" has been a multiethnic society and one that seems always to have been struggling to define itself in terms of this basic fact of social life. Throughout U.S. history political leaders and policy advisers have tacked back and forth between an iso-lationist and superpatriotic stance (often, ironically, called "nativist") and a more welcoming and tolerant one.

The former position is often expressed by the use of the word "American" as synonymous with the descendents of those who came on the Mayflower or the "Founding Fathers," folks who deemed themselves as the progenitors and guard-ians of the core culture as well as the turf itself. Their greatest fear seems to be contamination by alien ideas brought in by those of different backgrounds. Its most recent expression is to be found in the writings of the political scientist Samuel P. Huntington, whose latest book poses the question "Who are we?" then answers it by claiming the "we" to be white, Anglo-Protestants of English background—like himself![7]

The latter, far less monocultural position, is reflected in three things: an ideo-logical commitment to the spirit of asylum and openness ("A home for all God's children"), a belief that there is "strength in diversity," and a far more pragmatic attitude relating to the exploitation of those eager to come to the land of milk and honey thought to exist behind "the Golden Door."

Whatever the motivation of those who came (and continue to come), the results have been significant, not only for non-"Anglo-Saxon" European immigrants and their descendants but also for others, not least the growing number of Latino and Asian newcomers whose ranks have swelled in the past three decades through the liberalization of restrictive immigration policies.

It is important to pause to take note of the fact that those concerned with intergroup tensions often tend to overlook successes in the move toward true integration. There have been many, and not just for immigrants.

America's oldest minorities, native peoples and the descendents of African slaves, have also made considerable gains in the struggle for full participation, particularly through the results of the civil rights struggles that removed many of the legal barriers. But, even in acknowledging the accomplishments that have been made (often, it must be noted, because of the vigorous protests of those who demanded access to the opportunity structures enjoyed by those in the dominant groups), serious problems remain. As sociologists Douglas Massey and Nancy A. Denton clearly indicate in their detailed analyses of race relations in the United States, many fail to acknowledge what ought to be obvious to even casual observers, the persistence of segregation in many areas of American life.[8] Despite a number of dramatic improvements on a variety of fronts, our society remains a divided nation in which, as Andrew Hacker demonstrates, separation and inequality persist in too many sectors of the polity and the society.[9]

Although examples of the overt manifestations of intolerance in this country, as in so many others, are readily observed, the forces that create, maintain, perpetuate, or alleviate intergroup tensions are highly complex.

To understand such challenges, it is helpful to have a sense of the historical context in which group relations are shaped and to be able to define, discuss, and debate the meaning of such ideas as democracy, meritocracy, and the civic culture; such concepts as prejudice, discrimination, institutional racism, and group rights; such processes as assimilation, amalgamation, and accommodation; and such slogans and expressions as "Freedom Now," "Black Power," and "Why can't they be like us?" within a framework of sociological inquiry.

Why Sociological Inquiry?

Sociologists are primarily investigators of group life and intergroup interaction; they are social scientists concerned with the study of social relationships and varied patterns of social behavior. Sociologists share with other scientists the fundamental view that only through the orderly accumulation of empirical evidence and rigorous analysis can the realities of the physical and social world be revealed. The commitment is to the investigation, description, and analysis of what is, to social realities, not to what ought to be. Yet, in seeking to uncover the complexities of social life, for many there is the ever-present conviction that we may benefit from greater knowledge of the human condition. As Auguste Comte, the founder of sociology, put it: *Savoir pour prévoir et prévoir pour pouvoir*. From knowledge comes foresight, from foresight, power, the ability to influence others.[10]

Many sociologists have long strived to engage in value-free social science. Increasingly, however, more and more recognize the difficulties of maintaining strict neutrality in the face of behavior felt to be detrimental to the functioning of society or injurious to its members. In examining such phenomena as crime and delinquency, political upheaval, family disorganization, or racial and ethnic relations, they often walk a tightrope. They recognize that it is a difficult but necessary task to maintain the principle of scientific rigor.

They know it is difficult because they want to study such aspects of social life precisely because they are considered problems. But even for those—perhaps, especially for those—particularly sensitive to injustice, it is necessary to try to maintain objectivity in the collection of data and its assessment because, as the late Robert M. MacIver observed, "A moral judgment—no matter how much we may agree with it, cannot be a substitute for the proper study of causes."[11] (Put differently, we must avoid the tendency to think "My mind is made up, don't confuse me with the facts!").

Forthcoming

In the pages to follow both the analyses and reflections of sociologists, as well as historians and other researchers and commentators on the subject of racial and ethnic relations, will be introduced and discussed in a series of linked essays. Because it is necessary to have a common language to begin such a study, the next chapter, "Constructions of Reality," considers the definition and explication of several key sociological concepts. Chapters Three, Four, and Five offer a brief summary of the history of voluntary and involuntary migration to the United States and a critical evaluation of the theories and processes of adjustment and acculturation of those who came. The three succeeding chapters address the nature of prejudice, some of the ways groups of people have been treated—and mistreated—in this society, and the responses of those in "minority" communities. Chapter Nine addresses the politics of identity and the resurgence of ethnicity prompted in large part by the protests of those minorities. Chapter Ten examines the shifts from the "Civil Rights Compact" of the 1960s to the "Contract with America" of the 1990s and continuing debates over the impact of such matters as affirmative action, bilingualism, and immigration politics. The next chapter, called "Social Physics," zeroes in on reactions to the changes taking place in race and ethnic relations in the post–World War II era. Chapter Twelve offers a commentary on the meaning of multiculturalism. It is focused on competing ideas about American pluralism and the future. Finally, a very brief "coda" returns to the matter of integration, offering a last word of sorts.

If there is a leitmotif or theme running throughout the book it is not the achievements that have been the lot of many who came to American in search of a dream but the persistence of differentiation and discrimination based on the sort of dichotomous thinking that has long led many Americans, like people everywhere, to distinguish between others and themselves, between "they" and "we," and, often, to act accordingly. As shall be seen, the "they"—or the "other"—is sometimes a genuine rival for power, an entity that, in the words of the late Gordon Allport, has an "earned reputation."[12] More often it is a perceived or socially constructed threat to the established order, a targeted aggregate or group, often characterized by caricatured portraits, images that stress both difference and inferiority.

A subtheme is also woven throughout the pages to follow. It was already alluded to in the reference to Comte's formula: many of the distinctive and threatening traits one imagines others to have, and upon which one often acts, are based not on knowledge but ignorance or jealousy or fear. It is therefore important not only to understand societal divisions but to have a clear sense of their bases, their functions for those who maintain them, and the problems inherent in all systems of social stratification, be they based on such predominantly ascriptive or "assigned" (as opposed to achieved) characteristics as gender, race, religious affiliation, national origin, or what will soon be more clearly defined, ethnicity.

Notes

1. Peter I. Rose, "Letter to Editor," *New York Times* (July 27, 1964), p. 30.

2. *The Report of the National Advisory Commission on Civil Disorders,* U.S. Government Printing Office, Washington, D.C., 1968.

3. See Daniel Patrick Moynihan, *Pandemonium: Ethnicity in International Politics* (New York: Oxford University Press, 1993).

4. See Robin M. Williams, Jr., *The Wars Within* (Ithaca: Cornell University Press, 2004).

5. As quoted in Nathan Gardels, "Two Concepts of Nationalism: An Interview with Isaiah Berlin," *New York Review of Books* (November 21, 1991), pp. 19–23.

6. John Porter, *The Vertical Mosaic: An Analysis of Social Class and Power in Canada* (Toronto: University of Toronto Press, 1965).

7. See, for example, Samuel P. Huntington, *Who Are We? The Challenge to America's National Identity* (New York: Simon and Schuster, 2004).

8. See Douglas S. Massey and Nancy A. Denton, *American Apartheid: Segregation and the Making of the Underclass* (Cambridge: Harvard University Press, 1993).

9. Andrew Hacker, *Two Nations: Black and White, Separate, Hostile, Unequal* (New York: Scribner's, 1992)

10. Auguste Comte, *The Positive Philosophy,* Vol. I, pp. 22–21 (1896 edition) as quoted in Lewis Coser, *Masters of Sociological Thought* (New York: Harcourt Brace Jovanovich, Inc., 1971), p. 4.

11. Robert M. MacIver, *Social Causation* (Boston: Ginn, 1942), p. 148.

12. Gordon W. Allport, *The Nature of Prejudice* (New York: Addison Wesley, 1954), pp. 222–226.

Chapter 2

Constructions of Reality

Differentiation and Discrimination

Boys will be boys....
Some people are born to lead, others to follow.
The "white man's burden" is a heavy one.
Women have no aptitude for math or science.

In all societies individuals are differentiated by biologically and socially defined criteria. Everywhere people are ranked in hierarchical fashion, as superior or inferior, according to those attributes that are considered important. Even in the simplest, most isolated societies, where subsistence is apt to be the primary concern, distinctions are made on the basis of age, gender, and kinship ties and, often, on "character." More advanced societies, in addition to those methods of ranking, are usually divided into distinct social strata. Those higher on the scale have access to greater opportunities for wealth, prestige, and social control.

The discrepancies between those in superior and subordinate positions are generally quite evident. There is an obvious disparity in the lifestyles and material possessions of parvenus and peasants, gentlemen and yeomen, bosses and workers. No less significant is the differential access to political and economic power for those on top and those below. Such distinctions often account for intense feelings of intraclass identification and interclass rivalry. The rich and powerful seek to maintain their positions; those below try to raise themselves in the status hierarchy or, in some instances, to turn the entire system upside down.

Opportunities for improving one's position largely depend upon the socially defined nature of social stratification. Where a rigid caste system exists, there is little hope for individual advancement, for status is fixed by birth and marriage is endogamous (within the caste group).

In societies with a feudal social structure, placement is determined largely by heredity. The estate system, as it is also called, sometimes does provide limited channels for mobility and individuals are sometimes able to change their estate by royal decree, by marrying someone of higher status, by entering the clergy or military service, or by becoming artisans or tradesmen. Such a system has been most prevalent in agricultural societies, where status is directly related to the ownership and use of land.

In societies with socialist governments, heredity is largely replaced by party position as a basis for status. One thinks of the post–World War II changes in China, beginning with the civil war, the ousting of the "nationalist party," the Kuomintang, the development of the communist regime, and the subsequent "Cultural Revolution," all ostensibly designed to rid the society of its feudal character.

In industrial societies, where land tenure is relatively unimportant, wealth and income become the relevant measures of social position. In some such societies, an "open class system" is said to prevail. Ideally, every individual should be able to gain recognition based upon personal ability and performance, regardless of birth or previous condition of inequality. Although greater opportunities do exist for movement up and down the ladder of social mobility within the open class system, there is no society where individual merit is the sole criterion for determining status.

In the United States several already noted factors have long served to inhibit full realization of the traditional ideal of equal opportunity; not the least of these is membership in a particular group or cohort. Foreign-born persons, females, members of certain religious groups, individuals with dubious political affiliations, and, especially, those with dark skin have long been handicapped in their attempts to enjoy the advantages of the meritocracy, to advance strictly on the basis of personal ability. Many members of such groups have been categorically denied the right to fulfill their own potentialities in the "pursuit of happiness."

What the Swiss sociologist Kurt Mayer said about this society a half-century ago still pertains: "If the absence of estate-like characteristics makes the American class system unique, it is likewise true that the intrusion of racial caste-like features is almost without parallel in modern Western experience."[1]

It would be obvious, even to a Martian visiting the United States for the first time, that a critical aspect of placement in the status hierarchy of American society is keyed to color—and to gender as well. The Martian sociologist would note that most of the leadership positions and much of the power is held by white males. The double traits are related to perceptions deeply rooted in this culture.

Race and Culture

The words "culture" and "race" are widely misused and often misunderstood. Culture refers to the way people live; the rules they set for themselves; the general ideas around which they organize their lives; the things they feel are good or bad, right or wrong, pleasurable or painful. Cultural norms or standards for behavior are learned from those around us, relatives, teachers, friends, and, in recent times, from what is generically called "the media."

We often speak of "Western culture" as the principal source of the American heritage. This characterization, although hardly telling the whole story, is quite accurate for, despite many modifications, our social system is largely a product of European values and attitudes. Ideas from across the North Atlantic were replanted in the New World, providing a sort of seed corn for many of the assumptions that shaped the social contexts in which we are now living, especially those relating to race and race differences.

From ancient times to the present, people in various parts of the world have made the sorts of "we" and "they" distinctions mentioned in Chapter One. In the European minds that shaped much of the thinking and many of the practices in this country, the tendency has long been to divide the human species in terms of "racial" classifications, visually distinct, color-keyed categories, usually referred to as "white," "black," "red," "brown," and "yellow." David Hollinger recently has referred to the latter phenomenon as our "ethno-racial pentagon."[2]

Although today it is difficult to find those who belong to a "pure" race, and many would like to discontinue using the word altogether, many pundits, politicians, and ordinary people still find it useful to place humans into separate racial pigeonholes. Political, economic, and psychological considerations almost invariably combine to provide the motivation for doing this.

When it seems that everything else often has been grouped and packaged according to appearance or some other means of making distinctions, it is not illogical to find that many want to categorize people according to gross similarities. Moreover, it ought not be surprising that such external criteria as skin color; head form; facial features (like broad or narrow noses); stature; and color, texture, and distribution of body hair are used as criteria for such taxonomies. Indeed, although the use of the concept of "race" is one of the most discussed and debated issues, especially today,[3] some anthropologists, even adding the caveat about the rarity of "pure" groupings, still would be comfortable defining a race as "a statistical aggregate of persons who share a composite of genetically transmissible physical traits."[4] For the layperson, such conclusions make considerable sense. Why then all the fuss about making "racial" distinctions?

Surely, even today, using well-known ideal-type images, it is not difficult for observers to pick out an "Asian," "Caucasian," or a "Black" on a crowded street in San Francisco, Chicago, or New York. To do this they simply look at those they observe, mentally "measuring" them against a set of criteria associated with each category. A person with brownish-yellow skin, straight black hair, almond-shaped eyes, and a nose that seemed to lack a pronounced bridge would, most likely, be considered Asian or "Yellow." A person with whitish, pinkish, or ruddy skin; blond or brunette, wavy or straight hair; blue or green eyes; and a straight, hooked, or pug nose would fall in the category "White." A person with dark brown or brown skin, kinky or tightly spiraled black hair, brown eyes, a rather broad nose, and thick lips undoubtedly would be considered "Black."

Of course, if one were true to the scheme of using only specific criteria, not all would fit into the predetermined categories in the heuristic model. It is harder to categorize someone who has a straight, high-bridged nose, dark wavy hair, and a dark brown complexion. Yet, most Americans, regardless of background, would probably say such an individual "must be black." Why? Because in this society, like many others, racial designations are not merely simple ways of classifying people according to their genetic makeup. Rather, "race" is used for locating or placing people according to *culturally defined social positions.*[5] It is, in the words of Richard Delgado and Jean Stefancic, "not something that is objective, inherent, or fixed ... [races] are categories that society invents, manipulates, or retires when convenient." They continue:

> People with common origins share certain physical traits, of course, such as skin color, physique and hair texture. But these constitute only an extremely small portion of their genetic endowment, are dwarfed by that which we have in common, and have little or nothing to do with distinctly human, higher-order traits, such as personality, intelligence, and moral behavior. That society frequently chooses to ignore these scientific facts, creates races, and endows them with pseudo-permanent characteristics.... .[6]

The sociologist Rubén G. Rumbaut has suggested that race is merely "a pigment of the imagination."[7] His half-joking comment is quite accurate. But beneath the humor is an important lesson: race, as it is commonly used in our society, is a prime example of how concepts are socially constructed and then defined. Even those, such as geneticist Neal Risch, whose recent research notes a strong connection between self-identified race and genetically defined categories, say that even "while being genetically differentiable, [members of so-called racial groups] also differ for a large variety of environmental factors—socioeconomic, cultural, behavioral and so on."[8] Without putting it in so many words, Risch joins Rumbaut in implying a distinction between "race" and "racism." The latter concept refers to those who assume that there is a connection between looks and outlooks, between one's genetic makeup and the way one thinks and acts. And, going farther, implicit in the idea of racism is the assumption of group-based superiority and inferiority. This is most clearly manifest in the ways those said to belong in a particular pigeonhole are perceived and treated. As the English sociologist Paul Gilroy has stated: Despite "the founding absurdity of 'race' as a principle of power, differentiation, and classification, [it] must now remain persistently, obstinately, in view."[9] As any number of critics of old race theories contend, it may not be real but it is the omnipresent phantom that haunts all aspects of American life. Consider the case of those of "mixed" parentage.

American history is filled with instances of "race mixing." Most Mexican Americans are descendants of European Spaniards and indigenous "Indians;" Puerto Ricans, like Dominicans, are the offspring of white and black as well as "Indian" ancestors; and many American people whom we call black are actually very light-skinned. In fact, to find pristine Negroid types is very difficult in this country (as compared with almost any place in sub-Saharan Africa). Even so, until 1960, the

United States Census Bureau gave instructions to its enumerators to include the following criteria for designating Negroes: "In addition to persons of Negro and mixed Negro and white descent, this category includes persons of mixed American Indian and Negro descent, unless the Indian ancestry very definitely predominates or unless the individual is regarded as an Indian in the community."[10] Many non-white Americans long have been aware of the fact that racial labels mean something special. In the words of the old sardonic reproach,

> If you're white, you're right.
> If you're brown, hang around.
> But if you're black, brother,
> Get back, get back, get back.

If no cultural value were placed upon ancestry—whether "pure" or "mixed"—it would matter very little what one was called or under which rubric one was placed. But in a race-conscious society like the United States, those who are "colored" (as opposed to "white") have generally been put in inferior positions and treated accordingly. In almost every American town there has long been a close connection between the tasks people perform and the place in which they live, and the color of their skin. Menial work is disproportionately the province of "colored" citizens, the shabbier neighborhoods their disproportionate domain. White people have tended to have a greater percentage of better and more varied jobs and, in many instances, finer homes in better neighborhoods.

The sociological importance of such a correlation lies in the fact that it is culturally, not genetically, determined. There is nothing in their nature that predisposes nonwhites to lives of inferior status—nor whites to rule. There is much, however, in the social image of the nature of those so designated, which largely determines their places in the social hierarchy.

Defining Situations

> When men define situations as real they are real in their consequences.[11]
> —William I. Thomas

These words, written very early in the twentieth century, remain among the most quoted in the field of sociology. In jargon-free, straightforward language, the single sentence explicates the principle of the social construction of reality. We have already seen evidence of W. I. Thomas's principle about definitions of situations in regard to how individuals and groups are placed and regarded in status hierarchies based on class and "race."

Such placement is often internalized.

When given inferior positions in the social order, individuals often reflect in their attitudes and behavior the status imposed upon them.[12] Shingoro Takaishi, the Japanese writer, discussing the traditionally subordinate status of Japanese women, illustrates this quite clearly. "The education of our women was neglected, and her intelligence became more and more narrow owing to there being little or no chance for her to see things in the outer world. The next thing, which was bound to happen, was man's contempt and disdain for her narrow-mindedness and stupidity.[13]

In similar fashion, in the United States, members of certain "races," like women in Japan (and here, too) considered by many to have lower potentialities than others are given low-status, poor-paying jobs, and are denied equal opportunities for achievement. Excluded and often embittered, lacking in advantages and limited in their access to employment and schooling, they may in fact reflect in their behavior and attitudes the stereotypes held by those in dominant positions. This is a classic example of what Robert K. Merton called "a self-fulfilling prophecy.[14]

Migrating Populations

In the following chapter it will be noted that all Americans came from somewhere else, and this includes those we often think of as indigenous, those entitled to call themselves the only true Native Americans. In fact, our entire society has been built by migrants. Their motivations, however, have been (and continue to be) as varied as their origins and, as we hone the conceptual tools for analyzing relations between and among America's people, it is important to make some distinctions that are not only useful in demographic analyses but in understanding political tensions and persisting social issues.

The first distinction that deserves brief consideration is that between those peoples who go to new places voluntarily and those who are forced to do so. In the first instance, incentives for leaving home and moving to other territories include everything from those of nomadic hunters and gatherers who have little choice but to keep moving as they forage for food, to pilgrims searching for nirvana and religious zealots seeking converts, to adventures and explorers looking for new worlds to conquer, to settlers and those called immigrants, to labor migrants. The political scientist Samuel Huntington makes a distinction between two of the three largest types of voluntary migrants: the settlers and the immigrants.

"Settlers," he suggests, "leave an existing society, usually in a group, in order to create a new community. They are imbued with a sense of collective purpose.... . Immigrants, in contrast, do not create a new society." [15] Here Huntington is both correct and quite wrong. Motivations may vary—and there are differences between settlers and immigrants, but, as we shall see in Chapter Three, there is little question that many in the latter category do, indeed, create new societies and, when very different immigrants enter the same foreign territory at roughly the same time, as has happened in several periods of American history, they can dramatically transform what has already existed. This reality is often troublesome to those who wish to preserve what they see as the collective consciousness of those who claim propriety by having been among the first settlers.[16]

Members of each of these rather disparate groupings have one thing in common: they are attracted by hope of achieving something beneficial for themselves. The force is centripetal. Even those poor folks who cope with the scourges of poverty and are looking for ways of improving their lives and those of their families would rarely leave home if there were no thought of advantages provided at the end of their journeys. Not surprisingly, labor migrants depend most on promises real and imagined.

Although most voluntary migrations are quite benign in the intentions of the migrants, with few thoughts of hurting others, sometimes the motives are more Machiavellian: setting out to convert the "heathens," to conquer new territories, to colonize, or to capture slaves to bring back to the homeland.

Involuntary migrations are quite different. They are carried out by people forced to flee and those who are quite literally carried away. In the first case there are those who represent the obverse of all of the people mentioned above. They are rarely pulled in, instead they are those who have been expelled or are driven out by those who target them as threats to the society, subversives, enemies of the state. Such victims of persecution often seek asylum or refuge in other places. Such dispossessed and often displaced persons are known as "refugees" rather than "immigrants."[17]

The second case of involuntary migration, although not based on centrifugal, "push" factors, is as poignant and as pernicious. The classic example is African slavery.

It seems almost obscene to call those brought to the New World against their will "migrants" of any sort, yet they were. And like all migrants—voluntary and involuntary—the slaves from Africa brought with them all sorts of cultural baggage, values and beliefs and traditions, the characteristics we now associate with culture—and ethnicity.

Ethnic Groups

"Man [meaning humankind] is separated from man, not only by real or assumed physiological traits, but by differences of group traditions, national or regional or religious, that may or may not be associated with biological distinctions."[18] Groups whose members share a unique social and cultural heritage passed on from one generation to the next are known as ethnic groups. Ethnic groups are frequently identified by distinctive patterns of family life, language, recreation, religion, and other customs that cause them to be differentiated from others.[19] They often live, by choice or because of the requirements of others, in their own enclaves, ghettos, or neighborhoods. Above all else, members of such groups feel a consciousness of kind[20] and an interdependence of fate[21] with those who share their identity. Members of different ethnic groups may look very much alike (think of the Catholics and Protestants in Northern Ireland or the Hindus and Moslems in India) but have very different views of the world and of their roles in it.

In America, members of most ethnic groups or their ancestors have come from a common homeland, as in the case of Italian, Irish, and Mexican Americans. Not surprisingly, such groups were long referred to as "nationalities." Some ethnic group members, however, like Jews or Gypsies, joined by common traditions and experiences that cut across political boundaries, are frequently known as "peoples." And some who may come from different states but are treated as a singular entity may begin to see themselves as others see them, often turning negative impressions into positive and collective identity. This has certainly been the case of Americans who came from various parts of Africa and whose ancestors may have belonged to different and sometimes rival tribal entities.

In a nation made up of many cultural groups like our own, the intensity of ethnic identity or ethnicity is apt to be determined by the attitude of the members of the dominant members of society toward the "strangers" in their midst. This attitude, in turn, is often but not invariably dependent upon how closely the "newcomer group" approximates the characteristics of those in the cultural mainstream. Acceptance may loosen the bonds of ethnic identity, as in the case of Scottish and German immigrants to America; deep-rooted notions of the biological inferiority of certain groups—and reactions to such assumptions manifest in norms of conduct sometimes referred to as institutional racism—regardless of how close they seem to reflect dominant group values, may serve as a barrier to acceptance; rejection and subordination may strengthen them,[22] as among Mexican Americans or African Americans today.

Many sociologists have studied the relationship between membership in an ethnic group and social acceptance. They concur that "when the combined cultural and biological traits [of the ethnic group] are highly divergent from those of the host society the subordination of the group will be very great, their subsystem strong, the period of assimilation long, and the processes slow and usually painful."[23] (It should be noted that this widely expressed view is based on the assumption that "assimilation" is the goal of most minority peoples. As shall be pointed out, many voices recently have been raised seriously questioning the ideology that underlies what the critics would see as a classic case of liberal dogma.[24])

The Significance of Gender

"Racism" and sexism": the two terms, referring, respectively, to categorical discrimination against members of a particular "racial" category or against women based on assumptions of inferiority, frequently resound with a kind of connectedness as Gunnar Myrdal noted many years ago.[25] Both practices reflect ideological stances relating to notions of superiority and inferiority by those in positions of power and influence and treated accordingly.

For centuries, arguments, some already introduced, have been made explaining or justifying the treatment of those of different colors. The same has been true for women, also often relegated to second-class or lower status.[26] Their second-class status is reflected in the writings of many who wrote the "classics" that many consider the literary canon of the Western world. It is even more evident in practices that have kept women marginal in male-dominated societies.

Unlike racial groups, whose labels are so often socially defined ("a drop of Negro blood"), physiological and physiognomic differences between men and women are quite unambiguous. These differences are biological. And these determine much of gender identity. But there are also assumptions that have more to do with nurture than nature in the "assignment" of roles men and women are expected to play.

Almost invariably women have been seen as belonging to "the weaker sex" and the "distaff" partners in social and sexual relationships with men. Although there are exceptions, the pattern is almost universal. It is true in most of the societies of Africa, Asia, Europe, and Latin America as well as in North America.

In many places ruled by colonial powers—or in cultures that are legatees of European conquest and influence, like the United States—women of color are, or have been put, "in double jeopardy.[27] They carry a double burden.[28]

Explaining this phenomenon, Deborah King, writing on the dual and systematic discriminations of racism and sexism, has noted that "black women have long recognized the special circumstances of our lives in the United States: the commonalities we share with all women as well as the bonds that connect us to the men of our race. We have also realized that the interactive oppressions that circumscribe our lives provide a distinctive context for black womanhood. For us, the notion of double jeopardy is not a new one.[29] As Mary Church Terrell, the first president of the National Association of Colored Women, said in 1904, those for whom she spoke were handicapped "Not only because they are women, but because they are colored women."[30]

Add the dimension of "class," and one readily notes that many poor nonwhite women suffer a form of "triple jeopardy." One commentator, a black delegate to a convention of the National Organization for Women, also spoke of the relationship in very explicit terms: "Minority women share with all women the experience of sexism as a barrier to their full rights of citizenship ... the institutionalized bias based on race, language, culture and/or ethnic origin in governance of territories or localities has led to the additional oppression and exclusion of minority women and to the conditions of poverty from which they disproportionately suffer."[31]

"The effect of race, class and gender does 'add up'—both over time and in intensity of impact, but," Margaret Andersen and Patricia Hill Collins caution, "seeing race, class and gender only in additive terms misses the social structural connections between them and the particular ways that different configurations of race, class, and gender affect group experience."[32] These words offer a clue to the fact that there are and have long been strains in the movements to challenge racism and sexism in America, with not a few "women of color" arguing that they have little to gain from joining the feminist cause because racism is, or ought be, the most important priority.[33] Some go farther and say that strengthening the position of the males, especially in a society that tries to emasculate them or keep them in childlike dependency, is a principal goal. Evidence of this continuing conundrum is to be found in the latest statistics on the educational successes and failures of African American women and men.

According to a report released by the American Council on Education early in 2005, the number of African American, Hispanic, Asian American, and Native American students enrolled in college doubled in the decade from 1990–2000. But this good news was offset by some other facts. For African Americans the gender gap widened considerably—in the instance, it was not the women who were found to be falling farther and farther behind but black males in terms of percentages of high school graduates (43 as opposed to 56 percent) and in college enrollment (twice as many African American women attended college in the period than African American men), and college graduation rates showed the same discrepancy. Many explanations have been offered, with most pointing to such matters as inappropriate role models for young black males, broken homes, and bad school experiences where many are shunted off to special education, reinforcing the view that they are unfit for mainstream opportunities.[34]

Before leaving the subject, it should be quite clear to the reader that race, class, and gender *are* at once independent and interdependent variables relating to social differentiation and its institutionalization. Like definitions of race and class, sex roles, although partly related to biology, are most often culturally defined. Here, however, issues are made somewhat more complex owing to physiological factors, many of which, whatever their true distinctiveness, play into the hands of those who define status. The expectations of what men and women can and ought to do in different societies are strongly influenced by cultural factors. This point is made abundantly clear by Donna Gabaccia in her book, *From the Other Side: Women, Gender and Immigrant Life in the U.S,* published in 1995.[35]

In a middle section called "Foreign and Female," Gabaccia noted, "Demographically and culturally, women immigrants closely resembled men of their own backgrounds ... [at] work, at home and in their communities, however, their lives diverged from the men's: regardless of their exact origin, women's and men's responsibilities were more often complementary than shared."[36] These roles, which often are found to be significantly out of balance, with women still being subordinated despite the fact that they may be the primary caregivers, stabilizers, and agents of acculturation, are often "ethnically specific." Thus women in some societies may be far more involved in entrepreneurial activities than those in a neighboring one. And both expected and accepted roles are often carried into new situations.

Minorities

In 1932, Donald Young, writing about group relations in the United States, stated: "There is, unfortunately, no word in the English language which can ... be applied to all these groups which are distinguished by biological features, alike national traits, or a combination of both."[37] He proposed "minority," a term that had been used in a related but different context. Earlier, "minority group" had been applied to subsegments of European societies inhabited by conquered persons or those incorporated by annexation to another national group. Many persons of different ethnic background who lived under Soviet rule in the former U.S.S.R. represent such minorities.

Since Young's adoption, the term minority has been used by sociologists to refer to those groups whose members share certain racial or ethnic similarities that are considered to be different from or inferior to the traits of the dominant group and who are thereby "singled out for differential and unequal treatment."[38] In recent years the term has come to be applied in a related but more restricted sense. Since its implementation during the early years of the Nixon presidency, the U.S. government and its various agencies have taken to labeling as minorities only those in specified categories—African Americans, Asian Americans, Hispanic Americans, and Native Americans. In this book, although I will discuss the reasoning behind such arbitrary designations, and their implications for "affirmative action" policies, the term will be used in the less limited manner, as Donald Young intended.

Thirty years ago, Graham Kinloch suggested the mere existence of racial and ethnic minority groups raises a number of issues relating to their relationship to those in the dominant society in terms of social organization, patterns and mechanisms of social control, basic cultural values, levels of societal development, and indices of social change.[39] Of course, racial and ethnic groups are not the only ones "singled out for differential and unequal treatment."

Of late, many people have been categorized in similar fashion—women, children, the aged, the poor, the disabled, homosexuals, and various other groups labeled by some as social deviants, sometimes called "behavioral minorities."[40] Although fully cognizant of the problems encountered by those groups and the many similarities relating to their treatment—including the phenomena of being variously stigmatized, criticized, ostracized, and discriminated against in different ways—attention here will still be focused primarily on those originally considered by Donald Young, the members of racial and ethnic bodies.

Statistical underrepresentation does not, in itself, explain why a racial or ethnic group is considered a minority in the sociological sense. It is not even a necessary condition. Until the dramatic changes that recently took place in the Republic of South Africa, the black "minority" far outnumbered the white rulers. Prior to independence in Algeria the community of colonists was very small compared with the native "minority" group. For much of the nineteenth and twentieth centuries a limited number of Europeans dominated "minority" peoples in the East Indies (now Indonesia), the islands of the West Indies, most of Africa, and the entire Indian subcontinent. In many towns in the southern states of this country black people constituted the largest ethnic element in the population but remained a sociological minority.

Careful observers of the changing scene on the world stage note that neither dominant nor subordinate (minority) status is fixed or immutable. Not only is it possible that a majority group in one place may be a strategic elite in another (one thinks of Chinese on the mainland and in Malaysia) and a subordinate group in one country may itself be dominant in another. The position of Jews in Russia and in Israel, French Canadians living in New England and in the Province of Quebec, and "ethnic" Chinese in Jamaica, the Philippines, and Vietnam, compared to those in Taiwan or Singapore, are cases in point.

Still, in most Western societies the power-holding group is made up of persons having "white" skin and professing a belief in Christianity. In the United States the dominant group long consisted largely of white individuals of North European background who belonged to one of the Protestant denominations (people some-times referred to as WASPs—white, Anglo-Saxon Protestants). This "majority group" has traditionally been the determining element in public policy. In language, customs, and moral codes, these descendants of early settlers have set the standards for American behavior. Moreover, they have generally determined which groups are to be considered minorities and how each shall be treated.

A Culture of Inequality

Although the issues that concern us are hardly limited to our shores, there is still good reason for choosing the United States as the focal point for a study of racial and ethnic relations. Few nations can match the heterogeneous quality of American society. No other modern society can claim a history characterized so markedly by the importation of foreign ways and ideologies. All Americans (including the "natives") came from somewhere else. In this sense ours is literally a nation of immigrants.

The history of this country bears witness to the fact that the absorption and ac-commodation of many racial and ethnic groups has been an essential element in developing an elastic, ever expanding culture.[41] Ralph Linton once described the extent of "outside" influence when he wrote: "Our solid American citizen ... reads the news of the day, imprinted in characters invented by the ancient Semites upon a material invented in China by a process invented in Germany ... and as he absorbs the accounts of foreign troubles he will, if he is a good conservative citizen, thank a Hebrew deity in an Indo-European language that he is 100 percent American."[42]

In a recent social history of multicultural America, *A Different Mirror,* Ronald Takaki elaborated on the point, emphasizing the contributions not only of those who came but also of those already here:

> The signs of America's ethnic diversity can be discerned across the continent— Ellis Island, Angel Island, Chinatown, Harlem, South Boston, the Lower East Side, places with Spanish names like Los Angeles and San Antonio or Indian names like Massachusetts and Iowa.
>
> Much of what is familiar in America's cultural landscape actually has ethnic origins. An early Chinese immigrant named Ah Bing developed the Bing cherry. American Indians were cultivating corn, tomatoes, and tobacco long before the arrival of Co-lumbus.... . The "Forty-Niners" of the Gold Rush learned mining techniques from the Mexicans; American cowboys acquired herding skills from Mexican vaqueros and adopted their range terms—such as lariat from *la reata,* lasso from *lazo,* and stampede from *estampida.* Songs like "God Bless America," "Easter Parade," and "White Christmas" were written by a Russian Jewish immigrant named Israel Baline, more popularly known as Irving Berlin.[43]

The influence of many peoples in creating one nation is an idea that has gained considerable currency in recent years. Multiculturalism has become an alternative vision to more traditional ideas about the core character, the ideas and institutions of

American society. This is, however, but one side of the picture, for as the presence of newcomers has, in each generation, provoked the resentment and suspicion of those already here, so, too, is the notion that maybe, despite lip service long paid to egalitarianism, we are, or ought to be, seen as co-contributors regardless of race, creed, color, or national origins. That idea is, for some, still hard to accept.

America has not been—nor is it—immune from group hatred and discrimination. Throughout its history there have been those who have persisted in denying their fellow citizens the right to full participation in American life, who wished to maintain a society where the "right" skin color or religious preference or cultural heritage was considered to be an essential requisite to acceptance on an equal basis.

Gunnar Myrdal, the Swedish social scientist who came to study race relations in the 1940s, observed that the United States as a nation possesses a wide gulf between the democratic ideal of brotherhood and the overt manifestations of intergroup conflict.[44] The American creed of freedom and equality of opportunity for all has been so deeply embedded in the civic culture and its Sinaidic-like Bill of Rights continues to be challenged by the acts of many citizens. What Myrdal called "The American dilemma" remains evident, but the problems that beset minorities in this country are far more complex than the simple discrepancy between the national ethos and individual behavior. As the late Robert Merton suggested, the failure to recognize the intricacies of these problems tends so "to simplify the relations between creed and conduct as to be seriously misleading both for social policy and for social science."[45]

Between the prescription set forth in the Preamble to the Constitution and its first ten amendments and the actual behavior of many people, there exists a wide range of standards for behavior, which vary markedly from group to group, from place to place, and from time to time. The formal and informal policies of a region, state, and local community; the social, economic, religious, and political groups to which one belongs; the attitudes of parents, teachers, and peers; and the demands of particular intergroup and interpersonal situations all greatly influence the way in which individuals act toward others. Some of these complexities are analyzed in the following chapters.

But, before zeroing in on the promises and dilemmas of diversity in the United States, it is essential to realize that, today, even such introspection must be placed in a broader context. Although we will not be exploring in depth any of the racial and ethnic conflicts in other nations mentioned above, it must be acknowledged that, perhaps now more than at any time in our nation's history, for good or ill, we are a sort of template against which others measure themselves.

Genus Envy

In many parts of the world today "Yank" is a four-letter word—and not in just the literal sense. For many decades and in many places the society whose modal citizen is known by that snappy sobriquet has been a source of scorn, jealousy, and emulation. Since the collapse of communism and the ascension of the United

States to the status of "the world's only superpower," resentment of this country as well as grudging admiration for all things American have grown simultaneously stronger.

Citizens of this nation, regardless of origins, are all legatees and the majority are beneficiaries of a unique social and intellectual 225-year-old history. In a global sense, we are privileged members of an extraordinary, freewheeling political genus, America's consitutional democracy. Our country is seen by many in other lands as freewheeling, open, and pluralistic. It is not at all surprising that outsiders, especially those in totalitarian societies or those recently freed from the yoke of communism, and some trying to loosen the shackles of Islamic fundamentalism, have a good deal of "genus envy." They want what we have. To be sure, that is not limited to our Constitution and our creeds. They want our material goods, too. And many want to join us.

But sometimes these very same people, and others who are seen as our closest allies, have contradictory thoughts. They resent us for our success and decry us for our hypocrisy, especially when we claim to the world that we believe in the freedom of expression and in the rights of all, and then display a seemingly callous disregard for our own poor and infirm and those who come from different shores than those of the European continent.

Many are chagrined that, after rallying to our side when we were attacked on September 11, 2001, our government officials seemed to turn their backs on long loyal allies and began a flaunting of power that made us seem like bulls in the china shop of international affairs, personifying on a grand scale the crudest caricatures. The war in Iraq is the prime but not only example.

Yet, because of extraordinary successes at home and abroad, militarily, economically, and in McDonaldizing the world, it is not surprising that, more than any other nation, we have not only become the country others most love to hate but, ironically, the one whose culture many most desire to emulate. This is not true affection so much as a passionate eagerness not just for our soft goods and our hardware (most of which is American in name only, being manufactured elsewhere), but for the thing we often take for granted: our freedoms great and small.

These days there is ample evidence that, despite the cries of "Cultural Imperialism!" and the diatribes against pervasive globalization (read: American hegemony), arrogance abroad and persisting racism at home, many government leaders and industrial moguls, members of the bourgeoisie, mechanics and middlemen, workers and peasants in even the remotest parts of the world are taken with all manifestations of American spirit and enterprise, the popular culture and the technowizardry. They may decry the aggressive openness and rough-rider manners of the "Yanks," but they are also intrigued by them. They may laugh at the proclaimed piety of our politicians and denounce our seeming fetishes relating to sexuality and crime but are intrigued by the former and titillated by the latter. And, although criticizing the treatment of minorities in the United States, they will acknowledge that such people have many more chances for moving into the mainstream of society than those in similar straits in their homelands.

This love-hate relationship is the subject of a number of recent studies, including journalist Mark Hertsgaard's engaging and informative disquisition on America's image abroad, *The Eagle's Shadow*.[46]

Hertsgaard's book is grounded in the author's two decades of encounters and reflections while living overseas, and a six-month, September 11, 2001–straddling, earth girdling excursion. While en route the author spoke to poobahs and ordinary people in every part of the globe. *The Eagle's Shadow* is a revealing report on others' current views of American society and everything associated with it. It is also something more. The critique of our society by those outside it is complemented by Hertsgaard's own running commentary on how *he* sees the United States.

Using the advantage of having been away for so many years, like Henry James who also spent twenty years overseas, Hertsgaard scrutinizes the scene with the eyes of an outsider as well as those of an insider. And, as was James, he was often displeased by what he learned. Tending toward smugness and insularity, he suggests that the *Weltanschauung* (worldview) of most Americans is hardly worldly. It ends at water's edge. Even more troubling, people "not only don't know about the rest of the world, [they] don't care."

Hertsgaard captures the mixed and often confusing presumptions of those who see us from afar and often through Hollywood-tinted glasses, and offers a panoply of explanations why, as his subtitle succinctly states, "America fascinates and infuriates the world."

Early in his assessment Hertsgaard reminds his readers that Thomas Jefferson once said, "Every man has two nations, his own and France." The United States is today's France; for good or bad reasons it is everybody's primary reference group. Hertsgaard's book is organized around ten dialogues relating to sets of generalized images all starting with the words "America is . . . ": "America is parochial and self-centered . . . rich and exciting . . . the land of freedom . . . an empire, hypocritical and domineering . . . [a land of] philistines . . . the land of opportunity . . . self-righteous about its democracy . . . the future . . . out for itself." These assumptions/beliefs/values are interwoven throughout the text.

On a most recent trip, Hertsgaard visited many places on both sides of what he calls the "rich/poor divide." It started in South Africa where his 32-year-old driver, Malcolm, told him that every black township in South Africa has "two street gangs named for your country: 'The Young Americans' and 'The Ugly Americans.'" The former "dress like Americans"; the latter "shoot like Americans." Wealthy and dangerous, stylish bullies: that is how many there see us. And these are the views of our admirers! Others describe how ignorant we are, how wasteful, how corrupt—and corrupting—and yet even they tend to echo the words of the former environmental minister of the Czech Republic, Beldrich Moldan, whom Hertsgaard quotes: "You may like the United States or dislike the United States but you know it is the future."[47]

Writing about our society fifty years earlier, the sociologist Robin M. Williams, Jr., anticipated Beldrich Moldan's remarks as he identified and explicated the many contradictions in our creed and conduct that he, too, expected to be a model for others. In *American Society,* a sociological treatise far more academic and analytical than Hertsgaard's, Williams highlighted, then laid the groundwork for examining many of the same value conflicts that titled the journalist's chapters. Williams acknowledged that almost all of them had been first noted by French visitor Alexis de Tocqueville, in his famous two-volume *Democracy in America,* written in the 1830s.[48]

Discussing "Major Value Orientations in America,"[49] Williams listed such familiar blocks in the foundation of our collective character and the deep-rooted subjects of our early socialization: beliefs in "achievement," "success," "activity," "work," "efficiency," "practicality," "progress," "material comfort," "science" and "rationality" (but not, interestingly, "religiosity," though he did consider this in other parts of his book), "external conformity," and "nationalism-patriotism." In addition, he discussed several more that are clearly contradictory. One of these is the heavy emphasis Americans place on "humanitarian mores," the unselfish willingness, even eagerness, to aid and comfort those in dire straits, including people we hardly know. A modern day example is the incredible outpouring of concern and money by private citizens at the time of the great tsunami that killed nearly 175,000 people in countries around the Andaman Sea and Indian Ocean in late December of 2004.

Williams contends that such a value is rooted in the humanitarian and communitarian thinking of the French enlightenment, which contrasts sharply with an English philosophy with a French name, *laissez faire,* which did not stress man's relationship to his fellows but to the acquisitive instinct reflected in many of the values listed earlier, especially efficiency and practicality. Then there is the idea of "equality," which requires that "the individual must feel guilt, shame, or ego deflation where he acts in inequalitarian ways; and that there must be sanctions supported by the effective community for conformity or nonconformity."[50] But there is a difference between the well-entrenched American notion of the equality of opportunity (leading to various means to enhance access, as in the case of affirmative action policies) and the equality of condition, the latter the basis of much of Marxist ideology. Few Americans are aware of such critical distinctions.

"Equality" itself is often connected to the idea of "freedom," but they are clearly quite different and, in some ways, opposing concepts. The former implies some sort of leveling of the playing field; the latter the right to do one's own thing, to fly in the face of tradition. The prescient Tocqueville himself had stated that America had to face sooner or later a conflict of values described as a contradiction between the principle of freedom and the principle of equality. And we have not yet addressed the full implications of the distinction recognized nearly two centuries ago.

"Democracy" is a value we hold especially dear. It is one that encompasses not only the system of our government but the civic culture itself. It may be something we take for granted but, as we have learned time and again, most recently in Afghanistan and Iraq, it is a difficult thing to export and even harder to impose on others. It consists of a congeries of variables: "along with majority rule, representative institutions, and the rejection of the monarchical and aristocratic principles under which [American] society began, early American democracy stressed the reservation of certain 'inalienable rights' as unalterable by majority rule."[51] Almost all Americans proud of this value orientation may want to ask themselves how it jibes with another set of values, those on which we focus in the next ten chapters, values relating to "racism and related group-superiority themes.

Notes

1. Kurt B. Mayer, *Class and Society,* rev. ed. (New York: Random House, 1955), p. 30.

2. David Hollinger, *Postethnic America: Beyond Multiculturalism* (New York: Basic Books, 1995.)

3. See David L. Wheeler, "A Growing Number of Scientists Reject the Concept of Race," *The Chronicle of Higher Education* (February 17, 1995), 8–9, 15.

4. See, for example, Douglas G. Haring, "Racial Differences and Human Resemblances," in M. L. Barron (ed.), *American Minorities* (New York: Knopf, 1957), pp. 33–39.

5. For some further views on the use of the term "race" see Ashley Montague, "The Concept of Race," *American Anthropologist,* 64 (October 1962), 919–928; Juan Comas, "Scientific Racism Again?" *Current Anthropology,* 2 (October 1961), 303–340; Manning Nash, "Race and the Ideology of Race," *Current Anthropology,* 3 (June 1962), 285; and Marvin Harris, "Race," in the *International Encyclopedia of the Social Sciences* (New York: Macmillan, 1968), Vol. XIII, p. 263.

6. Richard Delgado and Jean Stefancic, *Critical Race Theory: An Introduction* (New York: New York University, 2005), p. 7–8.

7. Rumbaut has discussed this in many places, most recently in his essay "The Melting and the Pot: Assimilation and Variety in American Life," in *Incorporating Diversity,* Peter Kivisto, editor (Boulder, CO: Paradigm Publishers, 2005) , pp. 154–173.

8. See, for example, the results of recent research by Neil Risch and a team from the Stanford Medical School as reported in the *American Journal of Human Genetics.* See also, Jessica Zhang, "New Study Links Race and DNA Material," *The Stanford Daily* (February 4, 2005), 1–2.

9. Paul Gilroy, *Against Race Imaging: Political Culture Beyond the Color Line,* (Cambridge: Belknap Press of Harvard University Press, 2000), p. 42.

10. U.S. Bureau of the Census, 1960 Census of Population, Supplementary Reports, PC (S1)-10, Washington, D.C., September 7, 1962, p. 2.

11. See William I. Thomas, "The Behavior Pattern and the Situation," Publication of the American Sociological Society (Papers and Procedures), 1927, 1–13.

12. See Robert K. Merton. "The Self-Fulfilling Prophecy," *The Antioch Review,* 8 (Summer 1948), 192–210. Merton says, "The public definitions of a situation (prophecies and predictions) become an integral part of the situation and thus affect subsequent developments."

13. The original source of this quotation appears in the Introduction to Kaibara Ekken, *Greater Learning for Women,* and appears in David and Vera Mace, *Marriage East and West* (New York: Doubleday, 1960), p. 78.

14. The effect of this situation on the development of antiblack sentiments is, in part, the basis of Norman Podhoretz's controversial essay, "My Negro Problem—And Ours," *Commentary,* 35 (February 1963), 93–101. Also see "Letters from Readers," *Commentary,* 35 (April 1963), pp. 338–347.

15. Samuel P. Huntington. *Who Are We?* (New York: Simon and Schuster, 2004), p. 39.

16. See Peter I. Rose, "The Persistence of (An) Ethnicity," in Kate Delaney and Ruud Janssens (eds.), *Over (T)Here: Essays in Honor of Rob Kroes* (Amsterdam: VU University Press, 2005). Pp.

17. Peter I. Rose, Introduction to the section "Forced Out," in Peter I. Rose (ed.), *The Dispossessed: An Anatomy of Exile* (Amherst and Boston: University of Massachusetts Press, 2005), pp. 1–5.

18. Robert M. MacIver and Charles H. Page, *Society: An Introductory Analysis* (New York: Rinehart, 1949), p. 386. See also Robin M. Williams, Jr., *The Reduction of Intergroup Tensions* (New York: The Social Science Research Council, 1947), p. 42.

19. Max Weber, *Economy and Society,* Guenther Roth and Claus Wittich (eds.) (New York: Bedminster Press, 1968), pp. 387–398. For discussions of Weber's views of ethnicity, see Howard M. Bahr, Bruce A. Chadwick, and Joseph H. Stauss, *American Ethnicity* (Lexington, Mass.: D.C. Heath, 1979), pp. 4–6. See also Pat Shipman, *The Evolution of Racism: Human Differences and the Uses and Abuses of Science* (New York: Simon and Schuster, 1994).

20. See Andrew M. Greeley, *Why Can't They Be Like Us?* (New York: Dutton, 1971), pp. 120–121.

21. See Kurt Lewin, *Resolving Social Conflicts* (New York: Harper, 1948), Chaps. 10 to 12.

22. See, for example, J. Milton Yinger, "Social Forces Involved in Group Identification and Withdrawal," *Daedalus,* 90 (Spring 1961), 247–262; and Charles F. Marden and Gladys Meyer, *Minorities in American Society,* 2nd ed. (New York: American Book Company, 1962), p. 26.

23. Lloyd Warner and Leo Srole, *The Social System of American Ethnic Groups* (New Haven: Yale University Press, 1954), p. 286.

24. See L. Paul Metzger, "American Sociology and Black Assimilation: Conflicting Perspectives," *American Journal of Sociology,* 76 (January 1971), pp. 627–647.

25. Gunnar Myrdal, *An American Dilemma* (New York: Harper, 1944), pp. 1073–1078.

26. See Helen Hacker, "Women as a Minority Group," *Social Forces* 30 (1951), pp. 60–69.

27. Margaret Andersen and Patricia Hill Collins, "Preface" to *Race, Class and Gender: An Anthology,* 2nd ed. (Belmont: Wadsworth Publishing Company, 1995), pp. xi–xii.

28. See Yanick St. Jean and Joe R. Feagin, *Double Burden: Black Women and Everyday Racism,* (Armonk, NY: M.E. Sharpe, 1998).

29. Deborah K. King, "Multiple Jeopardy, Multiple Consciousness: The Context of Black Feminist Ideology," in Beverly Guy-Sheftall (ed.), *Words of Fire* (New York: The New Press, 1995), p. 294.

30. Mary Church Terrell, "The Progress of Colored Women," *Voice of the Negro,* 1:7, (July 1904), p. 292.

31. The commentator was Jane Addams. Her remarks are quoted in Vincent Parrillo, *Strangers to These Shores,* 4th ed. (New York: Macmillan, 1994), p. 506.

32. Andersen and Collins, op. cit, p. xii.

33. See the writings of bell hooks, especially, *Ain't I a Woman: Black Women and Feminism* (Boston: South End Press, 1981).

34. A summary of the American Council of Education's report appeared under the heading "Black Men Fall Behind," *USA Today* (February 16, 2005), p. 10A.

35. See Donna Gabaccia, *From the Other Side: Women, Gender, and Immigrant Life in the U.S., 1820–1990* (Bloomington: University of Indiana Press, 1995).

36. Ibid. p. xiii.

37. Donald Young, *American Minority Peoples* (New York: Harper, 1932), p. xiii.

38. Louis Wirth, "The Problems of Minority Groups," in Ralph Linton (ed.), *The Science of Man in the World Crisis* (New York: Columbia University Press, 1945), pp. 3–7. MacIver and Page state, "even when mere recognition of difference is all that marks the relationship between groups—an inevitable situation in complex society—there is a necessary antithesis between the 'they' and the 'we,' between in-group and out-group." See MacIver and Page, op. cit., p. 387

39. Graham C. Kinloch, *The Sociology of Minority Groups* (Englewood Cliffs, N.J.: Prentice-Hall, 1979), pp. 11–13.

40. For a more detailed discussion see Kinloch, op. cit., esp. pp. 33–46.

41. See, for example, Oscar Handlin, "Historical Perspectives on the American Ethnic Group," *Daedalus*, 90 (Spring 1961), 220–232. See also Maxine Seller, *To Seek America* (Englewood, N.J.: Jerome S. Ozer, 1977), pp. 1–13.

42. Ralph Linton, *The Study of Man* (New York: Appleton-Century-Crofts, 1936), pp. 326–327.

43. Ronald Takaki, *A Different Mirror: A History of Multicultural America* (Boston: Little, Brown and Company, 1993), pp. 15–16.

44. Gunnar Myrdal, *An American Dilemma,* op. cit, especially Chapter 1.

45. Robert K. Merton, "Discrimination and the American Creed," in Robert M. MacIver (ed.), *Discrimination and National Welfare* (New York: Harper, 1949), p. 99. See also Ernest Q. Campbell, "Moral Discomfort and Racial Segregation—An Examination of the Myrdal Hypothesis," *Social Forces,* 39 (March 1961), 228–234; Nahum Z. Medalia, "Assumptions on Race Relations: A Conceptual Commentary," *Social Forces,* 40 (March 1962), pp. 223–227. See also Andrew Hacker, *The Two Nations,* op. cit.

46. Mark Hertsgaard, *The Eagle's Shadow: Why America Fascinates and Infuriates the World* (New York: Farrar, Straus, and Giroux, 2002).

47. Ibid.

48. See Alexis de Tocqueville, *Democracy in America,* trans. by Henry Reeves as revised by Francis Bowen (New York: Vintage Books, 1945 edition).

49. Robin M. Williams, Jr. *American Society: A Sociological Interpretation* (New York: Knopf, 1951).

50. Ibid., p. 411.

51. Ibid., p. 433.

PART 2

ENCOUNTERS

Chapter 3

Natives, Settlers, and Slaves

Origins

In his famous poem "Song of Myself," Walt Whitman described the United States as a place populated by those "of every hue and caste."[1] Although a rather exaggerated characterization of this country in the nineteenth century, the portrait is much more accurate today. More than any other country, including other "immigrant societies," the United States is home to one of the greatest cross-sections of humankind ever assembled under a common flag.

Although a detailed description of the origins of the incredibly heterogeneous American people is not an aim of this volume,[2] a brief review of American racial and ethnic history and highlights of changes that have occurred since the days of the first settlement provide a baseline for understanding the contemporary scene. Here we begin the story by considering three major cohorts: the natives, the North European conquerors, colonists and settlers, and the African slaves.

The First Americans

It is often said about this country that "everyone came from somewhere else." The statement usually means everybody but the indigenous people. But they, too, should be included in the generalization. The ancestors of those often referred to today as "Native Americans" were once strangers themselves, migrants who crossed over from Asia and began to disperse in a southward and southeastward direction more than 20,000 years ago. For many centuries they were the sole inhabitants of the land taken over and, in time, overrun by Europeans.

It is estimated that in the days before the conquests began 1,500,000 people already occupied the territory now comprising the United States and Canada and that as many as 30 to 40 million people were living in the Western Hemisphere.[3] Hundreds of different tribal groups speaking many different tongues inhabited the forests, plains, deserts, and mountain ranges of the Americas. A wide range of culture patterns marked their differing social structures, and their political organizations were as varied as those of modern industrial societies.[4] Many, especially in Meso-America and in what later became known as Latin America, built and participated in complex, if autocratic civilizations, with politics and art forms that matched those of ancient Greece. Some, such as the Aztec, still existed when Spanish conquerors destroyed them in their quest for treasure and their zeal to convert them to Christianity. In North America there were also highly developed societies, rich in cosmologies, art, architecture, and agricultural practices. Some, like the Mayans, Toltecs, and Aztecs of Mexico were also highly authoritarian. Others, such as those federated in the Iroquois Nation of the Northeast, were far more democratic.

There never was a characteristic or single "Indian" culture of the kind frequently fictionalized by novelists and writers of Hollywood screenplays.

The vast majority of Native Americans did, however, share in common the fact that the conquerors—who often treated them as one people (claimed by many to have been misnamed "Indians" by Christopher Columbus, who thought he was somewhere else)—markedly influenced their customary ways. Many tribes were annihilated by genocidal policies. (Lord Jeffrey Amherst, who helped to settle the Pioneer Valley of Western Massachusetts, is reported to have distributed small-pox-laden blankets to the local natives in order, in his words, " to extirpate this execrable race.")

Many who did not suffer such blatant attempts to exterminate them were fated to die a slower death, a death of the spirit and the culture. They were made to suffer the humiliation of being dispossessed from their traditional areas of domain. In fact, from almost the first excursions to the New World, the natives were exploited and mistreated by whites who laid claim to their lands for their kings and countrymen, extorted the riches that lay above and beneath the soil, tried to convert them to Christianity and who, through bargain, barter, and brutal force, succeeded in taking over the vast territories that had been their homes for millennia.

In the early days of colonial rule, each group of settlers dealt with the Indians in its own way. Some tried to make treaties, others established trade relationships, and still others fought to maintain their holdings in Indian Territory. In 1754 a general policy was established by the British Crown that took decision and jurisdiction away from local communities and from the various colonial administrations. The tribes were recognized as "independent nations under the protection of the Crown; Indian lands were inalienable except through voluntary surrender to the Crown; any attempt by an individual or group, subject to the Crown, or by a foreign state, to buy or seize lands from Indians, was illegal."[5]

Attempts to implement this new policy met with strong resistance from many settlers. Some writers, reviewing the situation, have suggested that this conflict indirectly contributed to the American Revolution itself.[6]

As the frontier moved westward and homesteaders hungered for land for culti-
vation and grazing, the new American government vacillated between attempts at
bilateral negotiations with the members of the various Indian nations and outright
massacre or removal. What could not be accomplished by treaty—such as the
Congressional Indian Removal Act of 1830, which specified that consent of the
natives or their leaders was required by those to be moved to new territories—was
accomplished by military force. In the first half of the nineteenth century, thousands
of Indians from eastern states were transported, often under brutal conditions, to
the territories of the West. It is estimated that one-third of the Cherokees, who in
1838 were driven from their homes in North Carolina and Georgia, died en route
to Oklahoma. Their route is still referred to as the "Trail of Tears."

Then came the California gold rush, described by Pierre van den Berghe as "the
final phase of the territorial expansion of the United States by a process of land
encroachment and frontier wars between white settlers and a small number of Indian
groups. It took several more decades to beat the last remnants of the indigenous
population into total submission and to reduce the last Indian lands to the status of
human zoos for the amusement of tourists and the delights of anthropologists."[7]
Van den Berghe's bitter reflection suggests that few were any longer interested in
the fate of the original Americans, save for their own selfish motives. This is an
exaggeration—but only a slight one.

After the Civil War, attempts were made to resolve the "Indian problem" by
means of government reservations established for the alleged purpose of assimilating the now subdued and severely depressed Indians. In 1871, Congress ruled that
henceforth no tribe would be recognized as an independent power. Treaties were
abrogated and the native peoples became wards of the federal government.

Federal agents were to help the tribes adjust to reservation life and to farming. Yet, as
should have been foreseen, adjustment proved difficult since both land ownership and
agriculture were foreign ideas to a number of native peoples. Moreover, the programs
to educate them in efficient land utilization were woefully inadequate. The provisions
of the General Allotment Act of 1887 (also known as the Dawes Act) gave every male
Indian the right to a tract of land (40 to 160 acres) to be kept in possession and not sold
for 25 years. Because the property was to be divided equally among his heirs upon the
death of the landholder, however, each succeeding generation necessarily would have
less and less land to till. This situation provoked the comment: "Indians sometimes live
a long time, and when Old Charlie Yellowtail dies at the age of 99, the number of heirs
may be something little less than astronomical. Forty acres of land divided among, say
120 heirs, gives each just about enough room to pitch a tepee."[8]

The story of Wounded Knee was but one episode in a series of tragedies that ultimately spelled the complete subjugation and humiliation of proud Indian nations, in
this case the Sioux of the Dakotas. Plainsmen and hunters, the Sioux had been steadily
pushed onto reservations by government troops. In 1890, rumors of uprisings brought
the wrath of the cavalry. Black Elk, an eyewitness, described it as follows:

> Men and women and children were heaped and scattered all over the flat at the bottom
> of the little hill where the soldiers had their wagon-guns, and westward up the dry

gulch all the way to the high-ridge, the dead women and children and babies were scattered.... It was a good winter day when all this happened. The sun was shining. But after the soldiers marched away from their dirty work, a heavy snow began to fall.... . There was a big blizzard, and it grew very cold. The snow drifted deep in the crooked gulch, and it was one long grave of butchered women and children and babies, who had never done any harm and were only trying to run away.[9]

They couldn't, nor could many others. Reservation life created many problems of adaptation—and sheer survival—for the captive residents. Moreover, their removal from the mainstream of life had other consequences. For those in areas where the competition of truly emancipated native peoples would have constituted an economic threat (as in the northern plains states, the Pacific Northwest, or the desert areas of New Mexico and Arizona), reservations provided places for finally putting to rest any claims on the land. For missionaries and anthropologists they provided a locus for proselytizing and for research. For many other Americans the reservations began to be seen as living museums where part of our rich heritage was to be preserved in perpetuity.

Few non-Indians were aware of the true conditions of life in these places of perpetual internment, nor did they fathom the extent to which even the idea of preserving of traditional ways was undermined by paradoxical "assimilationist" policies that demanded the denigration of traditional ways and the adopting of new ones with no promise of where those who would undergo such resocialization might enjoy life in the new American mode. The tragic-farcical character of the whole charade was made clearly evident as more and more West Coast film makers and East Coast commentators romanticized the life of the Indian. No longer seen solely as objects of derogation, the "red men" came to be viewed as faithful companions (as in the case of Tonto, the Lone Ranger's loyal assistant), or as heroic, if still "primitive," people, living reminders of a glorious past. Early in the twentieth century, the "proud and resourceful" Indians were represented in names of children's camp units: Senecas, Cayugas, Mohawks, Oneidas, and Onondagas. They also became favored symbols and mascots of many college teams like the "Dartmouth Indians," often represented in crude caricatures of tomahawk waving, big-nosed, war-painted wild men. (They remain so even in this twenty-first century time of "politically correct" expression. The continuation of the tradition is most evident in the realm of professional sports. One need only think of the Washington "Redskins," Atlanta "Braves," Kansas City "Chiefs," and Cleveland "Indians.")

It wasn't until June 2, 1924, that the long-demeaned and then (sometimes) idealized original residents of the nation were even recognized as United States citizens. Four years later the Institute for Government Research published a report on "The Problems of Indian Administration," pointing out the dismal failure of assimilationist policy and setting forth bold recommendations. At last somebody seemed to be caring.

When John Collier became Commissioner of Indian Affairs in 1933, a new program was instituted to permit indigenous people to retain their traditions without the overwhelming imposition of "white" ways. The Indian Reorganization Act of

1934 also permitted Indians to sell their land to tribal members, establish tribal councils to manage local affairs, and incorporate into self-governing units. Since then progress has been very uneven. Here and there fallow lands have been irrigated and erosion halted. In some places education has been improved, especially with the long overdue closing of the assimilationist boarding schools. Birth rates increased dramatically and death rates declined as health and welfare problems began being dealt with more effectively through such government agencies as the Public Health Service, which took over medical services from the Bureau of Indian Affairs in 1955.[10] Yet, the same Bureau of Indian Affairs (a branch of the Department of the Interior, which also supervises national parks and wilderness areas) still maintains administrative control over most Native Americans, now numbering well over several million, the largest majority of whom live on reservations, two-thirds of them concentrated in the states of Oklahoma, Arizona, New Mexico, and the Dakotas.

The government's policies continued to vacillate significantly after the Reorganization Act more or less reversed the orientation of the Dawes Act. Although the general thrust has been toward greater self-determination for many, this has been a mixed blessing. For example, in the 1950s, attempts were made to terminate all special arrangements and obligations. If implemented, such plans would have meant the severing of all ties to the Federal Government and the loss of lands as well. They were never put into effect. However, a more positive approach was institutionalized in the Self-Determination and Educational Assistance Act of 1975, the terms of which gave tribal leaders the rights to allocate federal funds to serve the special needs of their peoples.[11] Even with this new and seemingly enlightened policy, there were difficulties—difficulties in communication between local agents and the bureaucrats in Washington, between younger and older Indian spokespersons, between traditional leaders and more radical ones, often including those involved in pan-Indian activities such as those of AIM, the American Indian Movement.

Over the years many young Indians thought it best to leave the reservations. The first major effort came during World War II, when many served in the armed forces, including a number of Navaho "code talkers" in the Marines who used their native language to baffle the Japanese. (Native Americans continue to have a high percentage of members in the military to this day).

Some of those who left the reservations over the years were among the best trained and the most success-oriented. They took their skills and talents with them, leaving a vacuum behind. But most of those who left were poor. Like other impoverished peoples, they frequently sought opportunities in urban centers. Yet, in spite of the fact that some were integrated into the general community or found employment in specialized trades (for example, the high-steel workers among the Mohawks of New York State), most of those who relinquished their status as wards of the government suffered the plight of other "colored" minorities. Figures are difficult to obtain but estimates suggest that in the early years of the twenty-first century as many Indians are living in cities as on reservations. Most urban Indians are concentrated in metropolitan areas on the West Coast, in the Southwest, and the Midwest. There are, however, as many as 15,000 in New York City, mostly East Coast natives but many from the West—"Hopi from Arizona, Navajo from

New Mexico, Creek from Oklahoma, Blackfoot from Montana, and others.... ."[12] Discriminatory practices in all of these places continue to limit severely opportunities for advancement and achievement.

For most of those who remain on the reservations life continues to be harsh. In spite of further improvements that have taken place since World War II, the first Americans—and this includes those long known as Eskimos, the Inuit people, and the Aleuts, native people of Alaska—remain members of a depressed minority situated in the bottom tenth of the economic hierarchy.

The 1970 Census of Population showed that the average Indian had but five years of schooling, that the family income was only $1,500 per year, and that the rate of unemployment was a miserable 45 percent. Some young Native Americans did not wait to see the 1970 census figures. They knew what was happening and many decided to fight. Following, and in many ways attempting to emulate, black militants, representatives of different tribal groups formed "Red Power" organizations as both cultural centers and bases for challenging the system that in their view did little of a positive nature and much that was destructive to Indian peoples.

In some areas the loose confederation of militants gained notoriety and limited success. Perhaps the most dramatic cases were the invasion and occupation of the abandoned island of Alcatraz and its empty prison buildings in 1970, the takeover of the Bureau itself in Washington in 1972, the two-month siege of Wounded Knee in 1973, and the bloody skirmish at the Red Lake Reservation in Minnesota in 1979 in which two Chippewa were killed in a confrontation with federal authorities. Other attempts to dramatize their cause, to bring all native peoples together, or to effect change have been less successful. One of the many reasons for this record is the important fact that Pan-Indianism was a rather new idea. Many Native Americans did not see themselves as brothers and sisters to members of distant (or sometimes even proximate) tribes. They were Navajo or Seminole or Cherokee or Sioux, not "Indians," often having very different notions of what they wanted and where they wanted to go. Still, there was a growing belief that all were owed reparations—of land, money, and respect. And for good reason. The 1980 Census showed that the problems of unemployment, poor health, exceedingly high instances of alcoholism, and a birth rate that is double the national average were still major problems—and despite evidence of pockets of improvement, the Census of 1990 showed little aggregate change, especially for those who continued to live on government reservations.[13]

Specific gains have been made, however. Over the past two decades a number of suits were filed to regain large tracts of land, especially in New England, in western and midwestern states, and in Alaska. In several celebrated cases in the late 1980s and early 1990s, 150-year-old treaties about fishing rights were recognized. In perhaps the best known one, sixteen recognized tribes in the state of Washington were, on the basis of previous agreements, finally assured the legal right to harvest shellfish from private beaches, state parks, and even in places where commercial oystermen have their beds. Others, by virtue of their special status, have been exempted from certain taxes and zoning regulations allowing them to further expand giant enterprises on their own lands. Two dramatic examples are in Mississippi and Connecticut. In the first case, members of the Choctaw tribe became primary employers with five car parts factories and other businesses. The second is in Ledyard, Connecticut, where casino gambling has made once-poor Mashantucket Pequot natives exceedingly wealthy. (Native American groups have established over 300 casinos in 26 states in addition to Connecticut.) Although these are clearly important economic breakthroughs, in many instances, settlements "out of court" have ended in "buying off" the Native American plaintiffs. Such a practice is an old story, going back to the time of the first encounters with Europeans.

According to the Census of 2000, nearly 2,500,000 people claimed tribal membership. In addition, half a million self-identified American Indians or Native Alaskans did not specify a particular tribe. But, of the others, the two tribes with the largest membership were the Cherokee and Navajo, each with more than 265,000 members. The Chippewa, Sioux, and an assortment of cross-border (Canadian or Mexican) groups numbered over 100,000. Information gathered since the 2000 Census has shown a rather bifurcated pattern.

Although many of the descendants of America's first peoples are still plagued by poverty, some have gained considerable ground on the economic front. Between 1990 and 2000, the average income of Native Americans increased by 30 percent. Moreover, the number of American Indian—and Native Alaskan–owned firms increased 84 percent between the years 1992 and 1997; the businesses were concentrated in four states, California, Texas, Oklahoma, and Florida, the home to three in ten Native Americans. Of industries classified by the researchers, most involve service of some sort.[14]

Despite these clearly positive signs, Native Americans still have a long way to go to achieve parity with their fellow citizens. In a projection reported early in 2005, economists estimated that the per capita income of America's native population would not reach that of other Americans for at least five decades!

But, perhaps, greater public awareness of the continued struggles of the natives first encountered by European explorers and adventurers in the fifteenth century will serve to accelerate the move toward equality. A major step in that direction occurred in September 2004, when the National Indian Museum, supported by Congress and organized by tribal consultants, historians and anthropologists, was opened.

This newest part of the Smithsonian Institution welcomed thousands of representatives of tribes from their homes on reservations, in small towns and big cities. They poured into the capital to take part in opening ceremonies and associated festivities. Many proudly wore the symbols of their cultures and their tribes. Perhaps as important in terms of serving as a stimulant to change was the interest other Americans seemed to take in this extraordinary event. One hopes that the curiosity of the onlookers and the euphoria of the participants widely felt on several fall days in Washington are auguries of better days for the native peoples of the United States.

Conquerors and Colonists

For many years historians debated the question of who first "discovered" America. Some claimed Vikings, led by Leif Ericson, first set foot on these shores around

A.D. 1000. Most long favored the view that it was Christopher Columbus, the Genoese sea captain whose several voyages to the Americas were financed by King Ferdinand and Queen Isabella of Spain. To some observers the whole matter is not much more than a game of ethnic one-upmanship. (Rumor has it that one prominent Italian American jurist once sought to raise money to hire his own historian to discredit "Norsephiles" at Yale University who claimed to have discovered an old Viking chart of the eastern coast, the "Vinland Map.") The debate is also purely academic, for, whichever Europeans—or Africans, for some contend that trans-Atlantic voyages brought people from Africa to North America long before they were forced to come—first set foot in America, they were clearly not the original "discoverers." Yet, it must be said that the shaping of what is today known as "American culture" began with the landings of Columbus. The contact he and other explorers had with the native population was crucial to the shaping of the destiny of the entire Western Hemisphere.

In an article published in the *American Journal of Sociology* in 1921, Arthur Meier Schlesinger, Sr., argued that "The ratio between man and land became changed for the whole civilized world, and there opened up before humanity unsuspected opportunities for development and progress. . . . The event itself stands forth as one of the tremendous facts of history. So far as the human mind can foresee, nothing of a similar nature can ever happen again."[15]

Recent discussions about Columbus's "discovery," now more correctly called "the encounter," have appropriately begun to focus less on who came and more on what happened, on the nature of the interaction between the newcomers and the natives and the legacy that was left by those who overpowered and overran the "New World," establishing new orders and laying foundations for not one but a chain of nations of immigrants from what would become Canada to Tierra del Fuego.

Columbus was followed by many more explorers and conquerors, then by colonists and settlers. The latter groups not only established control but imposed a culture, a way of life.

The first outsiders to lay claim to substantial portions of American soil were the Spanish conquistadores who penetrated the southwestern sector of what was to become part of the United States and established settlements on the Florida peninsula. Unlike the British who were to follow, the Spaniards, many of whom were single men, mingled extensively with the native populations. Their cadres—and their priests—left an indelible impression upon the art and building design (especially that known as "mission style") of the southwestern and Floridian culture. Many of their direct descendants, the Hispanics of mixed Spanish and Indian ancestry, are still to be found in the Southwest, especially in New Mexico. But, most noteworthy of all, are those who would later cross into the United States from what was once the Spanish land of Mexico, now constituting one of the largest ethnic groups in the United States.

Had the Catholic Spaniards remained in power, intergroup problems, attitudes toward minority populations, and patterns of discriminations would undoubtedly have assumed characteristics different from those that now exist. But this was not their destiny.

After the defeat of the Spanish Armada in 1588, rival nations began to establish and develop territories in the Western Hemisphere. Under the auspices of the West India Company, the Dutch established trading posts throughout much of the eastern part of the Western Hemisphere—South and North America—on the coast of Brazil, on the islands of Aruba, Bonaire, and Curacao in the Antilles, and at the estuary of the Hudson River (New York was originally called Nieuw Amsterdam) and northward along its banks. Holland's control over these territories was short-lived, but the Dutch legacy lingers on, especially in the folklore and architecture of many parts of New York State and in the names of many famous families—Roosevelt, Van der Heuvel, Rensselaer, and Vliet. The Dutch also left the English with a nickname, "Yankees," an anglicized version of "Jan Kees," the label given in Holland to the sort of person we might call a bumpkin. According to some historians, it was said to be used in mocking reference to the unsophisticated English farmers the wealthy Dutch met in and around Nieuw Amsterdam and in the Hudson Valley. But, in fact, the English would have the last word on this. Although over the next two centuries small groups of Dutch immigrants would make their way to North America, with the exception of a number of words that enriched the vocabulary of English speakers—particularly those interested in seafaring—such as "schooner," "sloop," and "spinnaker," Dutch influence waned considerably by the middle of the seventeenth century.[16]

In 1654, Holland lost her foothold in Brazil and, only a decade later, New Netherlands and Delaware, a Swedish territory that had been surrendered to the Dutch in 1655, became British possessions.

France, too, had colonial ambitions in America and sent explorers and missionaries to stake out new lands. Eastern Canada and the huge Louisiana Territory came under French domination. Bitter warfare brought an end to French rule over Canada; the Louisiana Purchase during the administration of Thomas Jefferson (1803) ended French control over the Mississippi Valley and the Northwest Territories. Yet, French nationalism persists in the Canadian province of Quebec, where the majority of citizens are Roman Catholic, speak the French language, retain many French customs, and continue to debate the issue of secession and the establishment of a separate French-speaking nation.

In the United States today, thousands of French Canadians reside in New England, especially in Maine, Massachusetts, and New Hampshire, and many of their transplanted relatives, variously called Acadians or Cajuns, still live in Louisiana. There the imprint of France is seen in architecture and festivals such as the famed carnival, Mardi Gras. Moreover, the contribution of French intellectuals, including descendants of the Huguenots, is still apparent.

But it was England, "Perfidious Albion," that became the supreme colonial power in North America. And, both symbolically and literally, it was Albion's offspring that gave birth to the new nation.[17] From the early seventeenth century, for the first time large numbers of common folk crossed the Atlantic to settle here. Unlike the earlier explorers from Spain and France, the English came in family groups, often with others from their hometowns. In not a few cases entire communities moved from the British Isles to America.

The British colonists consisted of soldiers and sailors, tradesmen and fortune seek-ers, civil administrators, political refugees, religious dissenters, rugged individualists and dedicated communitarians. The English settlers had their own ways of living: their own norms and values, their own culture—and subcultures, too. They shared a history, a language, a legal tradition, and a general sense of what it meant to be Brit-ish, but they also differed from each other, sometimes in quite profound ways. The pious Puritans who sought "the city on the hill," a new Jerusalem on New England's rocky shores, were not the same as Virginia's far more cosmopolitan cavaliers, nor were they very much like Pennsylvania's Quakers or those who settled in the hills of Appalachia. Despite their differences of class background, religious belief, and political orientation, what they shared gave them unique opportunities, near exclusive power, and a common identity. The combination of their British heritage and grow-ing "Americanness" created the first new North American "ethnic group." Though in recent decades the term seems to have become almost synonymous with "minor-ity," there is little question but that they qualify for such a sobriquet. Indeed, in the seventeenth and eighteenth centuries and well into the 19th, this country might have been described, only half facetiously, as "a nation of Yankees and other ethnics.[18]

The establishment of British America was a struggle from its inception. The death toll—from the hardships endured en route, from diseases that plagued the settlers after arrival, from conflicts with the native population—was exceedingly high. And for those who survived these hazards there were other problems. Religious prejudices were transplanted from the mother country to New England and the mid-Atlantic colonies. Colonists often were set against one another in their desire to maintain their particular brand of Christianity. Fighting the invisible ogres of blasphemy, heresy, and sin, colonists perpetrated persecutions as acts of faith, the victims often being members of minority sects—Quakers, Unitarians, Roman Catholics, and others.[19]

In addition to the former residents of England who constituted the largest por-tion of settlers, there were the Presbyterians from North Ireland, the Scotch Irish, and German refugees from the ravages of the Thirty Years' War. Small groups of Frenchmen, Welshmen, Irish Catholics, and Jews of Spanish and Portuguese descent, known as Sephardim, were also numbered among the early colonists. Together, they laid the cornerstone of modern American society. Although not all of identical cultural backgrounds, they did share many ideas and practices and in their Declaration of Independence and subsequent struggles to establish a new, independent nation, they became the white, predominantly Anglo-Saxon, and predominantly Protestant majority. It would be almost two centuries before they would acquire the acronym, "WASPs," but the image it conjures today was well established by the time of the American Revolution.

Americans from Africa

The first people of African descent to come to America arrived in 1619. Brought origi-nally to Virginia and later to other colonies they were, like many whites, indentured servants. Servitude was not uncommon in the middle colonies and these black-skinned

Table 3.1 Approximate Colonial Population in 1776

Ethnic Group	New England	%	Middle	%	Southern	%	Total	%
English	461,400	70.5	369,700	40.6	382,400	37.4	1,213,500	46.9
Scots	26,100	4.0	60,700	6.7	71,400	7.0	158,200	6.1
Scots-Irish	18,100	2.8	59,200	6.5	39,200	3.8	116,500	4.5
Irish	9,800	1.5	31,100	3.4	30,500	3.0	71,400	2.8
German	2,400	0.4	138,700	15.2	36,100	3.5	177,200	6.8
Dutch	1,600	0.2	57,700	6.3	2,100	0.2	61,400	2.4
French	5,200	0.8	17,000	1.9	11,100	1.1	33,300	1.3
Swedish	—	—	12,100	1.3	2,500	0.2	14,600	0.6
Unassigned	110,700	16.9	24,900	2.7	6,400	0.6	142,000	5.5
African	14,800	2.3	113,200	12.4	401,100	39.2	529,100	20.5
Indigenous[a]	4,000	0.6	26,000	2.9	40,000	3.9	70,000	2.7
Total	654,100	25.3	910,300	35.2	1,022,800	39.5	2,587,200	100.0

[a]Data for indigenous tribes include only those living east of the Mississippi. Some anthropologists and historians give higher estimates.

Source: Figures result from a compilation and extrapolation of data from the U.S. Bureau of the Census, *Colonial and pre-Federal Statistics*, Series Z 1–132 as presented by Parillo *in Sociological Forum*, December 1994, p. 530.

newcomers did not occupy a unique status. Some gained their freedom after serving their masters for a specified period of time; others became free through conversion to Christianity. Most remained as "unfree" men and women, but even they were not considered to be slaves. In fact, neither Virginia nor any of the other colonies of British America had yet recognized the institution of chattel slavery.

By the 1660s the conditions of the involuntary migrants from Africa began to deteriorate. The expansion of agriculture and the growing demand for a large and cheap labor force brought slavery to American shores. More and more Africans, wrenched from their native villages and sold into bondage by Spaniards and Englishmen, by Muslim and Christian outsiders, and, sometimes, by fellow Africans, were taken to coastal ports to be transported under the most brutal conditions imaginable to the islands of the Caribbean and to the port cities of the East Coast of America. Many died of disease, hunger, and melancholia en route; many—some say the lucky ones—by throwing themselves overboard or by inviting execution by proving too intractable. Once in the New World, the survivors were sold at auction. One such slave, Olaudah Equiano, told his own story in a journal published in the 1770s. There he related how he had been captured, put aboard a slave ship, witnessed and experienced brutal treatment, was taken to Barbados, put on the auction block, and sold.

> After a few days we were sold in the usual way, which is this: A signal is given, such as the beating of a drum. Buyers rush into the yard where the slaves are kept. They choose the group they like best. The general noise, and the eagerness of the buyers, increases the fears of the Africans. They regard the buyers as the people who have come to destroy them.
>
> With no feeling at all, people separate relations and friends. Most of them never see each other again. In the ship that brought me over, there were several brothers. In the sale, they were sold to different buyers. They cried when they were parted.[20]

Stories such as Equiano's have become better known in recent years through various popular accountings, repeated showing of a television series based on Alex Haley's *Roots,* an historical novel published in the late 1970s,[21] and a number of much more recent and widely discussed studies of slavery.[22]

By the middle of the eighteenth century the practice of slavery was legalized in every English colony in America. With the emergence of the United States as an independent nation, the issue became the subject of congressional and local debate. The northern states began fairly early to abolish the practice by law, beginning with Pennsylvania where the Assembly, under the prodding of Thomas Paine, passed the first act for the emancipation of Negro slaves on March 1, 1780. Other states followed suit.

In the South, however, the system was maintained intact. The "peculiar institution" had become a mainstay of the economic structure, and what some have called a "slavocracy" characterized a large section dominated by dependence on plantation labor. [23]

There had been a brief period in the second half of the eighteenth century when declining profits in tobacco (the principal cash crop) seemed to portend a change in the social arrangements, but the invention of the cotton gin in 1793 and the rapid development of the British textile industry not only forestalled the anticipated change but made the southern planters even more intransigent.

The conditions under which the slaves lived and worked varied considerably, not only from one region to another (the upper South as compared with the Piedmont or the Mississippi Delta), but also dependent upon the size and character of the plantations themselves. Moreover, even within slave communities there was stratification, a hierarchy of status determined by the masters but affecting relations with everyone, including fellow slaves. Everyday life under slavery was tempered by reactions to harsh circumstances and molded by necessity. This was true of everything from religious practices to relations between family members.[24]

Social activities were narrowly circumscribed. Freedom in all phases of life was highly limited. Yet, as in any local community (even prison camps), a way of life and complex social organization did emerge, which, significantly, included rules of behavior and patterns of adaptation to cope with the oppressive system. Although there were revolts, they were hardly common. It was difficult to attack the system directly. It was simply too dangerous.

For a number of years a debate has been waged over the question of how the slaves actually fared and how they survived. Some argue, for example, that even with the now widely conceded recognition that there was some sort of "slave culture," blacks still internalized the low status in which they were held and came to see themselves as inferior to whites. Others have said they never fully succumbed. That debate continues.[25]

What is undisputed is the fact that by the 1830s slavery was beginning to come under severe attack. Many southerners, in order to justify their continued subjugation of the Africans, invoked the doctrine of racial superiority. Earlier, few had argued that the Negro slaves were biologically inferior and a menace to white society, but they did so now. Moreover, they underscored the idea that, as "property," the slave had no rights that whites were bound to respect. Even the Supreme Court was to support this argument when it upheld the finding of a lower court in the famous *Dred Scott* decision of 1857.

Dred Scott, a slave, having been taken into a territory that prohibited slavery, considered himself a free man under the rules of the Missouri Compromise. The Court claimed that the compromise was unconstitutional since "Congress has no right to enact a law which deprived persons of their property in the territories of the United States." Even so, there was great agitation to rid the nation of the institution of slavery and a powerful movement for abolition emerged in the North led by such white spokesmen as John Brown and such free blacks as Frederick Douglass.

Ultimately the slavery issue was to be resolved in the midst of the bloody Civil War. Although President Lincoln insisted in the beginning that the war had nothing to do with slavery as such (indeed, early in the war Union soldiers returned slaves to their masters under flags of truce), the matter became one of central concern. In terribly oversimplified terms, the South fought to defend its way of life, which depended significantly on the slave system; the North fought to keep the Union whole. In a short time the emancipation of slaves was regarded as necessary, first politically and then morally, to achieve the northern objective.

On January 1, 1863, by Executive Order, the President issued the Emancipation Proclamation. All slaves in the United States (referring to the rebellious Confederacy as well as the rest of the Union) were declared free—though not yet equal. Equality was to come with the Thirteenth Amendment to the Constitution. By the summer of 1863 the Union Army sought Negro recruits to fight for their country, and it is estimated that close to 200,000 eventually donned uniforms, half of them to see action on the battlefield.

At the end of the war Black Codes were proposed. These were laws that would give freed blacks legal rights to marry and bear witness in courts of law but did not extend to such things as the ownership of land or work in particular trades. In the end, little came of these seriously limited but, given the times, progressive measures. The codes were never put into effect. Others were.

During the postwar era known as "Reconstruction" African Americans gained equal status in law and, in many places, they did so in fact. But these gains were repeatedly overturned. Congress passed a civil rights bill in 1866, but it was vetoed by Lincoln's successor, President Andrew Johnson. In 1868, a million blacks were enfranchised. Yet, the surge toward equal rights in the decade after the war began to fade and radical reconstruction policies, maintained in large part by federal forces, proved to be but a temporary interlude between slavery and segregation.

In a repeat of earlier reverses, although the Sumner Act of 1875 secured equal rights in public transportation, in hotels, and in theaters and other places of amusement, it was to be declared unconstitutional by an eight-to-one decision of the Supreme Court in 1883. Soon what many diehard southerners saw as their redemption, the reinstitution of white power over African Americans, was fully under way.

The era of what we know today as "Segregation" had already officially begun with the Hayes-Tilden Compromise of 1876. Hayes, an Ohio Republican, won the Presidency in an Electoral College victory over the popularly elected New York Democrat. This event, and the deal that brought it about, was to be a major turning point. Local autonomy was returned to the states of the South, the Freedmen's Bureaus that had been set up to help freed slaves adjust to the new conditions were closed, and Federal troops were withdrawn. In their wake many northern businessmen called "carpetbaggers" (a reference to the valises they carried) left, too. With "Redemption" came the chipping away of the newly won rights of blacks.

By the 1890s, "Jim Crow" statutes divided southern society into a two-caste system with whites occupying positions of power and blacks reduced to second-class citizenship. Newly imposed segregation laws prohibited the mixing of the races and barred "colored people" from virtually all white institutions.[26]

The states with the heaviest concentration of former slaves ignored or circumvented the Fourteenth Amendment (giving citizenship to former slaves and free Negroes) and the Fifteenth (specifying that the right to vote could not be denied because of race). Most people in the North seemed no longer to be interested in rallying to the cause of freedom. Moreover, the system of segregation, which had emerged after 1876, was legally sanctified in the famous *Plessy v. Ferguson* decision of the U.S. Supreme Court, which, in 1896, proclaimed the principle of "separate but equal" to be the law of the land.

At the time of the Plessy case, nine out of ten African Americans lived in the South, 80 percent in rural areas. Although segregation existed in many states outside the old Confederacy, it was there that they suffered the most.

In the last decade of the nineteenth century, many southern blacks moved north, "north to freedom." There they often found themselves in competition with other newcomers, people who were very different from the white folks they knew back home. (Conflicts with those who came to the eastern seaboard at the turn of the century will be discussed in a succeeding section, but it should be noted that, with the curtailing of European immigration during and after World War I, many blacks accelerated their northward migration.[27]) Between 1910 and 1920 a half million moved to northern cities where they settled in tenement districts forming black islands in a sea dominated by people more foreign and yet, in some ways, less alien and less alienated than they. And they stayed. The city became their new home and, for far too many, the ghetto became their jail.

Although the opportunity to escape southern conditions led to the ever-growing trek northward, blacks experienced residential, social, and economic discrimination wherever they went. Moreover, with World War I veterans returning and with nativist sentiment running at an all-time high, the new migrants frequently found themselves isolated, alone, and under attack whenever they dared to cross the color line. It was during this era that race rioting became a new feature of urban life. Thirty-three major interracial disturbances occurred between 1915 and 1949—eighteen of these between 1915 and 1919. With the exception of the Detroit riot of 1943, the urban "burnings" of the 1960s, and the conflagration that occurred in South Central Los Angeles in the early 1990s, none of the more recent riots have been as fierce as those of the earlier period. The bloodiest of these were in East St. Louis and in Chicago, both cities in the northern state of Illinois.

The competition between whites—WASPs and those who came later—who sought to maintain their superordinate positions and African Americans who were hungry for work, housing, and respect continued. By and large, the blacks made very slow progress. And even this progress—especially stimulated by the emergence of prideful new political and cultural movements in the 1920s (the era of the Harlem Renaissance)—was slowed, then stopped altogether, by the Great Depression of the following decade. And, as might be expected, competition for increasingly scarce jobs served to intensify the prejudices of competitors. By 1940 a two-to-one black-to-white unemployment ratio emerged—and it persists to this very day. Aside from a growing cohort of college-educated African Americans who hold executive, administrative, or managerial jobs in almost the same ratio as whites, for the vast majority of those employed, a significant black/white income gap remains quite noticeable.[28]

During Franklin Roosevelt's "New Deal" some changes began to bring the African Americans closer to full equality before the law. Various groups, within and outside the black community, tried and sometimes succeeded in gaining fairer treatment for America's largest racial minority. World War II accelerated the move.

Northward movement increased again and so now did the trek to the West where the defense industry served as the magnet. President Roosevelt's Executive Order

8802 sought to assure fair employment practices. By 1940 one in four African Americans lived in the North or West and, with the nation on wartime footing, many found employment in factories earning higher wages than they had ever known and at least a million African Americans entered the armed forces. But even during the war they found themselves in segregated units of the army and navy.

The military was not ordered integrated until 1948 (President Truman's Executive Order 9981), three years after the end of World War II. The order was not finally implemented until 1952 when, during the height of the Korean War, President Eisenhower made the changes in traditional policy.

In the early days of the postwar period, African Americans in the North and in the South did gain new status in law, though relatively few advantages in fact. They shared in the economic boom of the era, but although the absolute gains they made were sometimes considerable, the gap between the racial categories "Black" and "White" remained as wide as ever. Many thought that the independence movements in Africa might lead to the final and irrevocable emancipation of black Americans. The African situation did not have that effect, but it served to provide a new reference to people who knew little of their origins or their heritage. Most important of all was the Supreme Court decision handed down a half-century ago, on May 17, 1954, which unanimously struck down the constitutionality of the separate but equal doctrine and opened the door to widespread desegregation. Unfortunately, this decision proved difficult to enforce and prompted a variety of legal subterfuges that sought to reverse or at least to forestall a 1955 directive to move toward desegregation "with all deliberate speed."

The apparent failure of the people to honor the Court's decision, coupled with the seemingly unfulfilled promises in which African Americans had rejoiced, accelerated a movement that had been growing from the turn of the century: the movement for civil rights. That movement and the changes that have taken place during the 1960s and 1970s are the subjects of Chapter Ten. Several points concerning this period should be made here, however, before moving on to the histories of other American minority groups.

First, in the decade between 1954 and 1963 the principal thrust for desegregation and, in many cases, integration came from a coalition of black and white reformers, most of whom tried to persuade their fellow citizens to honor the nation's highest ideals. Many became disillusioned; many lost faith in interracial organizations; many said that cooperation was a mask for white co-optation. Yet most of those who marched and picketed and boycotted and rode the "freedom buses" during those years saw integration as the primary goal.

The integration phase reached its height with the grand march on Washington in August of 1963 when 250,000 black and white Americans joined hands to sing "We Shall Overcome" and Reverend Martin Luther King spoke of his dream of a society in which people would be known and judged by the content of their characters instead of the color of their skins.[29]

Within a year King's dream seemed shattered or, at least, compromised. What happened is a complicated story, better saved for a later chapter. But it is important to note that whatever progress had been made up to that centennial celebration of the Emancipation Proclamation and even in the years immediately following were in many ways much less the results of goodwill than of hard work and political pressure.

By the second half of the 1960s "integration" as a dominating orientation was largely replaced by a new, more strident, and far more racially conscious ideology: Black Power. New and young leaders began to tire of promises of things to come. They felt that the civil rights movement was failing to reach those who needed help most, especially those in the northern ghettos. Although acknowledging certain successes—the Civil Rights Acts of 1964, 1965, 1968, for example—many of these leaders felt that the victories were, in reality, rather hollow. They had been won at too great a cost and the net result, it was often argued, was that white guilt had been assuaged but too few blacks had really been helped.

Whatever the reality, and doubtless there was more than a kernel of truth in their portrayal, the new leaders shifted the focus and concentrated on the issue of "getting it together," that is, the coalescence of community among black people throughout the nation. In many ways the wildest dreams of Stokely Carmichael and H. Rap Brown and other new-breed leaders were to be realized.[30] At least some of them.

Within a few years African Americans began to walk taller and to express publicly the rage boiling up inside. Within a few years "Black Power" had become a household slogan. Within a few years universities and other particularly vulnerable institutions conceded that they had been guilty of racism or, at least, had failed to cast a wide enough net. These institutions began actively to recruit black students who, in turn, demanded and often won special programs in Afro-American Studies. But during those same years the average wages of black unskilled laborers fell further behind their white counterparts, the average reading level of African American children fell further behind that of white children, and the average contribution of white supporters of black liberation movements (no small factor) fell dramatically.

The period of the mid- and late 1970s was one of both consolidation and hesitation. There was consolidation on the part of certain segments of the black community, particularly those in the growing middle class. However, in making considerable progress, as sociologist William Julius Wilson pointed out, they made even more apparent the widening gap in Black America.[31] The hesitation came from various sources: a government rededicated to moving toward desegregation but beset by contradictory directives emanating from its own various agencies; a wary white community, especially in working-class areas, concerned about the consequences of school busing and forced integration; confused African Americans—and other minorities—uncertain as to whether it was better to continue pressing for "class action," that is, categorical treatment via affirmative action programs or to work toward more strictly meritocratic principles. The situation was not helped by vacillations in official policy, cutbacks in support for reform programs and urban rehabilitation, or court rulings regarding such celebrated cases as that of Allen Bakke, the white California medical school applicant who claimed he was reportedly denied admittance to a state institution solely on the basis of "reverse discrimination." Bakke's claim was eventually supported by the Supreme Court, which still urged that some affirmative action measures be employed. That decision, to be discussed in detail later, was symbolic of the confusion that existed at the end of the decade. It was variously interpreted as a victory for egalitarians and as a cop-out for others.

Before leaving the subject of the African American experience, at least leaving it to be examined further in subsequent chapters, it is essential to note an important caveat: not all blacks in this country are (or were) involuntary migrants. As Roy S. Bryce-Laporte puts it "[although] voluntary immigration has been a principal mode of peopling this hemisphere and has become a prominent aspect of its ideology and self-image—and projection to the world ... as a term and concept, it has rarely been associated with people of African descent."[32] Although doubtless due to the "uniqueness, magnitude, and meaning of the African slave trade and American slavery itself," the experience of black people in this country would be incomplete without consideration of a voluntary movement that has been going on for centuries. There were free blacks at the time of the Revolution and in the War of 1812 and throughout the remainder of the nineteenth century. Beginning early in the twentieth, increasing numbers of West Indians began migrating to the U.S., the largest percentage to New York City. By 1930 more than half the West Indians in the country lived in New York and one-fourth of Harlem's population was from the Caribbean. The movement of Caribbean migrants and Latin American migrants with roots in Africa continued well into the postwar years, averaging some 100,000 new entrants per annum.[33] Exemption of those from former British colonies from the restrictions on Western Hemisphere migration specified in the McCarran-Walter Act passed in 1952 and a subsequent cut-off of access of "Commonwealth Immigrants" to Britain in 1962 pulled, then pushed more West Indians to these shores. According to demographer Elizabeth Bogen, the number of Jamaican immigrants in New York City increased almost nine fold between 1960 and 1980, from 11,000 to 93,000. Immigration from Trinidad and Tobago increased sevenfold, from 5,500 to 40,000. An even more dramatic rise in the presence of a Caribbean group occurred in the case of the Dominicans. According to the census, there were 9,000 Dominicans in New York in 1960; by 1980 there were 121,000. Today the latter number has increased fourfold.[34]

Many came and more were to come—and become more visible—through the liberalization of restrictions as set forth in the Immigration Reform Act of 1965.

Red, White, and Black

Although much is made of the "discoverers" of America and the Founding Fathers, the tricolored heading symbolically characterizes the actual mixture of peoples who populated what was to become the new nation, a nation in which the white Europeans established total control and cultural domination. It wasn't until the middle of the Civil War that the African slaves gained their freedom and their citizenship; it wasn't until the decade after the First World War that Native Americans gained theirs. In the years between the emancipation of the slaves and the mid 1920s, the land of the Indians—and

North Europeans and Africans—was to become a haven for millions of others who participated in the Great Atlantic Migration. Their experiences, in many ways, were to be recapitulated by Asian and Latino migrants who came to America in the next large wave of migration, one that began in 1965 and is continuing to this day.

Notes

1. Walt Whitman, "Song of Myself," in *Complete Poetry and Selected Prose* (Boston: Houghton Mifflin, 1959 edition), p. 36.

2. There are many general texts that describe the history of and reaction to America's minorities. Among the most useful are Roger Daniels, *Coming to America* (New York: Harper Collins, 1990); Leonard Dinnerstein and David Reamers, *Ethnic Americans* (New York: Harper & Row, 1975); Lawrence H. Fuchs, *The American Kaleidoscope* (Middletown, CT: Wesleyan University Press, 1990); Oscar Handlin, *The Uprooted* (Boston: Little, Brown, 1951); Marcus Lee Hansen, *The Atlantic Migration 1607–1860* (New York: Harper Torchbook, 1961); Marcus Lee Hansen, *The Immigrant in American History* (Cambridge: Harvard University Press, 1940); John Higham, *Strangers in the Land: Patterns of American Nativism, 1860–1925* (New Brunswick, N.J.: Rutgers University Press, 1955); Desmond King, *The Liberty of Strangers: Making the American Nation* (New York: Oxford University Press, 2005); and Ronald Takaki, *A Different Mirror* (Boston: Little, Brown, 1993). See also David Reimers, *Still the Golden Door: The Third World Comes to America* (New York: Columbia University Press, 1985); Richard A. Schermerhorn, *These Our People: Minorities in American Culture* (Boston: D.C. Heath, 1949); and Maxine Seller, *To Seek America* (Englewood, N.J.: Jerome Ozer, 1977).

3. John Collier, "The United States Indian" in J. B. Gittler (ed.), *Understanding Minority Groups* (New York: Wiley, 1956), pp. 34–36. See also Frank Lorimer, "Observations on the Trends of Indian Populations in the United States," in Oliver La Farge (ed.), *The Changing Indian* (Norman: University of Oklahoma Press, 1942). Lorimer cites estimates of the number in the Western Hemisphere at the time of the first white settlement as 8 and 13 million.

4. See, for example, Ruth Benedict, *Patterns of Culture* (Boston: Houghton Mifflin, 1934); Paul Radin, *The Story of the American Indian* (New York: Liveright, 1944); and Peter Farb, *Man's Rise to Civilization* (New York: Dutton, 1968).

5. John Collier, *Indians of the Americas* (New York: Mentor Books, 1947), pp. 116–117.

6. Marden and Meyer, op. cit., pp. 361–362.

7. Pierre van den Berghe, *Race and Racism* (New York: Wiley, 1967), p. 86.

8. Alden Stevens, "Whither the American Indian?" in Milton L. Barron (ed.), *American Minorities* (New York: Knopf, 1958), p. 148.

9. John Neihardt (ed.), *Black Elk Speaks* (Lincoln: University of Nebraska Press, 1961), p. 258.

10. Marden and Meyer, op. cit., pp. 362–371. See also William and Sophie Brophy, *The Indian: America's Unfinished Business* (Norman: University of Oklahoma Press, 1966) and the much more recent assessment, Stephen Cornell, *The Return of the Native: American Indian Political Resurgence* (New York: Oxford University Press, 1988).

11. For fuller discussion see Joseph Hraba, *American Ethnicity* (Ithaca, Ill.: F. E. Peacock, 1979), esp. pp. 229–236.

12. Patrick Huyghe and David Konigsberg, "Bury My Heart at New York City," *New York* (February 19, 1979), p. 54.

13. *Native American Population,* 1990, Washington, D.C. U.S Bureau of the Census, 1991.

14. U.S. Bureau of the Census, Census Brief, "American Indian and Alaska Native-Owned Businesses: 1997," Washington: U.S. Department of Congress, October 2001, pp. 1–2.

15. Arthur M. Schlesinger, Sr., "The Significance of Immigration in American History," *American Journal of Sociology* (July 1921), p. 71.

16. See Rob Kroes, *The Persistence of Ethnicity: Dutch Calvinists in Amsterdam, Montana* (Champaign: University of Illinois Press, 1992).

17. See David Hackett Fischer, *Albion's Seed* (New York: Oxford University Press, 1989). See also S. Dale McLemore, "The Rise of Anglo-American Society" in *Racial and Ethnic Relations in America,* 4th Edition (Boston: Allyn and Bacon, 1994), pp. 41–64.

18. Peter I. Rose, "The Persistence of (An) Ethnicity: Nativism Revisited," in Kate Delaney and Ruud Janssens (eds.), *Over (T)Here: Transatlantic Essays in Honor of Rob Kroes* (Amsterdam, The Netherlands: VU Press, 2005).

19. See Arnold and Caroline Rose, *America Divided* (New York: Knopf, 1953), pp. 28–31.

20. "The Interesting Narrative of the Life of Olaudah Equiano, or Gustavas Vassa, the African," as cited in Peter I. Rose (ed.), *Many Peoples, One Nation* (New York: Random House, 1973), p. 77.

21. See Alex Haley, *Roots* (New York: Dell, 1979).

22. Among some of the most important recent studies are George M. Fredrickson, *The Arrogance of Race* (Middletown: Wesleyan University Press, 1988); David Brion Davis, *Challenging the Boundaries of Slavery* (Cambridge: Harvard University Press, 2004), and Ira Berlin, *Generations of Captivity: A History of African-American Slaves* (Cambridge: Belknap Press/Harvard University Press, 2004).

23. See Kenneth M. Stampp, *The Peculiar Institution* (New York: Vintage Books, 1956).

24. See, for example, Herbert Gutman, *The Black Family in Slavery and Freedom, 1750–1925* (New York: Random House, 1976).

25. There is considerable controversy over these issues. See Stanley Elkins, *Slavery* (Chicago: University of Chicago, 1959); and Ann J. Lane, *The Debate over Slavery: Stanley Elkins and His Critics* (Urbana: University of Illinois Press, 1971). See also Peter I. Rose (ed.), *Slavery and its Aftermath* (Vol. I of *Americans from Africa*) (New York: Atherton Press, 1970), esp. pp. 103–194.

26. See C. Vann Woodward, *The Strange Career of Jim Crow* (New York: Oxford University Press, 1957), p. 8.

27. See Douglas S. Massey and Nancy A. Denton, *American Apartheid: Segregation and the Making of the Underclass* (Cambridge: Harvard University Press, 1993), especially, Chapter 2, "The Construction of the Ghetto," pp. 2–59 ff.

28. Steven A. Holmes, "Income Gap Persists for Blacks and Whites," *New York Times* (February 23, 1995), A21.

29. Martin Luther King, Jr., "I Have A Dream," SCLC Newsletter, September 12, 1963.

30. See Peter I. Rose (ed.), *Old Memories, New Moods* (Vol. II of *Americans from Africa*) (New York: Atherton Press, 1970), esp. pp. 237–320

31. See William J. Wilson, *The Declining Significance of Race* (Chicago: University of Chicago Press, 1978).

32. See Roy S. Bryce-Laporte, "Voluntary Immigration and Continuing Encounters Between Blacks: The Post-Quincentary Challenge," in Peter I. Rose (ed.), *Interminority Affairs in the U.S.: The Challenge of Pluralism. The Annals of the American Academy of Political and Social Science,* 580 (November 1994), pp. 28–41.

33. See Suzanne Model, "Caribbean Immigrants: A Black Success Story?" *International Migration Review,* 25, pp. 248–276.

34. Elizabeth Bogen, *Immigration in New York* (New York: Praeger, 1987), p. 23.

From Immigrants to Ethnics

Unto Good Land

From its very beginnings the United States, the country Walt Whitman would label a "Nation of nations," was a magnet for the rich and poor of Europe. It was a land that, by the middle of the nineteenth century, had become, in the poet's immortal words, "Stuff'd with the stuff that is coarse and stuff'd with the stuff that is fine."[1]

Colonial America was made up of distinct and distinctive populations—the natives, settlers, and slaves—all mentioned in the last chapter. But with the establishment of the world's first modern democracy and its appeal to many across the sea, the early national period (from the time of the establishment of the new nation until the Civil War) was to see an unpredicted and surely unprecedented rise in the medley of the origins of those who came on ever larger sailing vessels, many designed as transport ships. Many of these newcomers were from northern Europe, including Scandinavia; many were from the British Isles, especially Ireland. In the second half of the nineteenth century and the first part of the twentieth century millions more were to come as steamships plied the North Atlantic laden with human freight, the majority coming from Southern Europe and various Baltic and Slavic states in the east. Decennial censuses clearly reflected these demographic changes.

The first census to include the "nationalities" of Americans was that of 1820 when all those who had entered the United States along the eastern seaboard and the Gulf Coast were listed by country of origin. According to the findings of the early enumerators there were 9,638,000 Americans, 20 percent of whom were "Negroes" and the rest mainly persons of Anglo-Saxon stock. Between 1820 and 2000 over 70 million immigrants had come to the United States. Although in recent decades, an increasing number have come from Asian and Latin American countries, still, even today, the overwhelming majority of Americans have roots in Europe and Canada.

Despite the poetic ring to the expression of Whitman's "Nation of nations" imagery and to the motto "E pluribus Unum" ("Out of many, one"), historians of the various waves of migration have noted that not all or even most of the immigrants were welcomed with equanimity.[2] The reception was very uneven. Once in this country, newcomers found themselves ranked and treated according to a congeries of criteria that determined their collective as well as individual places in the hierarchy of acceptability and acceptance. Time of arrival, region of origin, cultural attributes, religious preferences, and physical appearance were among the factors that determined how they were greeted and how they were treated.[3]

During the pre–Civil War Era over 3,500,000 Europeans arrived in America. Although quite a number came from Scandinavia, the two largest groups of émigrés were from German-speaking countries and from Ireland. Mixed motives prompted different groups of Germans to leave for the New World. For the Irish, migration had one overriding motivation: poverty. Harsh economic, political, and social conditions led many Irish citizens to seek new lives in America. Between 1847 and 1854 approximately 1,200,000 men, women, and children left the "Emerald Isle" for this country. By the end of the Civil War period the Irish constituted seven percent of the white population.

The Irish

As many writers have pointed out, the Irish Catholics were in the vanguard of the new period of immigration. Forced off the land by the combined forces of British exploitation and repeated crop failures caused by devastating potato blights, they were at once pushed by the disasters that befell their homeland and pulled by the promise of new opportunities for a better life in America. Despite the fact that the majority came from the rural counties of the country, most settled in the growing cities along the eastern seaboard. As the late President Kennedy described them, "in speech and dress they seemed foreign; they were poor and unskilled; and they were arriving in overwhelming numbers. The Irish are perhaps the only people in our history with the distinction of having a political party, the Know-Nothings, formed against them in 1849."[4]

The Know-Nothings, whose main objective was to put an end to Irish immigration, were extremists. Yet, they reflected the thoughts of many Protestants in the cities to which the Irish were coming, especially Puritan Boston. Many of the Bostonians saw the newcomers as disgruntled paupers and superstitious Papists, dirty, ignorant, heavy drinkers whose real allegiance would always be to the hierarchy of their church and to the Pope in Rome. They doubted the Irish had the capacity for functioning in, or contributing to the democratic state. But even among those most hostile to their presence, some did see them as an exploitable labor force. The Irish may have been the first group of many for whom the sarcastic expression "we can't live with them and we can't live without them" was all too apt.

In addition to that dubious distinction, they were unique in another respect: a disproportionate number of early Irish Catholic immigrants were unattached females.[5] It was one of the few cases where single women emigrated in large numbers. By contrast, later history is filled with stories of large influxes of male workers who came from China, Russia, Italy, Mexico, and the Caribbean to find jobs either as migrant workers or latter-day settlers hoping to establish themselves in the United States and then bring their families to join them.

From desperately poor homes in a society in which marriage was frequently postponed until the men were well established, many young women set off from Ireland on their own. Domestic service was, for them, a source of protection and employment. It "provided them with a roof over their head and a degree of personal security until they were able to forge a more desirable set of circumstances."[6] Working in the homes of middle- and upper-class Americans had a latent function of providing the Irish maids with models of "proper decorum," a fact that was to make them valuable agents of acculturation within the growing Irish enclaves.

Of course, women were not the only migrants from Ireland. Millions of men came too. Without the "cap-and-apron" niche the women were ready, willing, and able to fill, the Irish males suffered severe discrimination in the new land and often could find employment only in the lowest-paying and most physically demanding jobs: as ditch diggers, longshoremen, or workers in the canal beds and on the railroads.

It was the Irish "tarriers" working on the railroad that provided the imagery for the folk ballad that began

> Every mornin' at seven o'clock
> There's twenty tarriers, a drillin' on the rock.
> The boss comes along and says keep still,
> And bear down heavy on the cast iron drill,
> And drill ye tarriers, drill.

Yet, despite their own heritage of exploitation by English heavy-handed land owners back home, and the fact that they were subjected to discrimination based upon certain presumptions about their Catholicism and their alleged "racial" proclivities for drinking and fighting, once in this country, few Irish immigrants saw a connection between their plight as a put upon "under class" and that of American blacks. In fact, many Irish newcomers opposed abolitionist activities and, because they often competed with free blacks for jobs on the railroads, frequently sided with some of the most reactionary forces in the North during the Civil War period.[7] Some argue that the Irish proletariat feared the potential competition of blacks—and also Chinese railroad workers—as other European immigrants would in the not-too-distant future. Others claim antiblack sentiment was more a form of displaced aggression, blaming blacks for what they could not blame on white Protestant bosses and landlords.[8]

In time, the Irish adapted to American ways, and other immigrant groups became even more visible targets for the animus of the nativists. In 1891, United States senator and scion of an old Boston family, Henry Cabot Lodge, called the Irish immigrants "undesirable . . . hard drinking, idle, quarrelsome and disorderly."[9] But as Martin F. Nolan has recently noted, even in Boston, where upper-class old family members or "Brahmins" like the Cabots and Lodges had held sway for more than a century, the Irish soon began to challenge their authority. Sixty years after Lodge's nasty remarks, the grandson of one of the first Irish politicians to gain power in Massachusetts, a man widely known as "Honey Fitz," John Fitzgerald Kennedy, defeated Lodge's grandson for the U.S. senate. In 1962, with his brother elected President of the United States, Edward Kennedy beat Lodge's great grandson, George Cabot Lodge for the same seat.

Although these are particularly dramatic examples, there is little question but that what Nolan called "populist" politics among the Irish served to create a sea of change on the local as well as the national stage, signaling one of the best examples of the rising power of ethnic-based politicization.[10] Many Irish would enter politics, establishing effective "machines" largely based on ethnic affinity to press their own causes and promote their own candidates. Many more would find their niche in public service, especially in the police forces of New York, which used to be *the* Irish city, and in Boston, which became and for a century remained the political stronghold of the Irish clans so sharply portrayed in the novels of Edwin O'Connor.

The Irish also were to dominate the hierarchy of the Catholic Church in America. Even today, when Catholic dioceses are undergoing considerable scrutiny from within, the percentage of Irish American compared to Italian or German American or Hispanic bishops and archbishops (to say nothing of parish priests) far exceeds their proportion in the Catholic segment of the population. For decades, for many Irish Americans, parish and precinct were frequently one and the same, and priests frequently spoke out on nonecclesiastical but politically charged subjects. A remnant of this is still seen in attempts to influence fellow Catholics regarding birth control, abortion, attempts to relax rules regarding the role of women in the Church, same sex marriages, and other matters anathema to Catholic dogma.

The Germans

Many German-speaking people came to America, too. They came from southern German lands and from northern ones. They also came from parts of the Austro-Hungarian Empire. Most came for economic reasons, though some came, in the late 1840s and the late 1930s, seeking refuge. Far more apt to have come in family groups than the Irish, many Germans who migrated before the Civil War quickly moved out from the port cities of the East, dispersing themselves widely across the land and entering a myriad of occupations. Many became homesteaders in the Middle West and others settled in such cities as Baltimore, Buffalo, St. Louis, Minneapolis, and Milwaukee. In these cities German Americans began various businesses, including such to-be-famous breweries as Anheuser-Busch, the makers of Budweiser, and Schlitz, "The beer that made Milwaukee famous."

Large numbers of Germans—Protestants as well as Catholics—came to this country early in the nineteenth century, in its middle years (especially as political refugees after the failures of reform in 1848), and well into the early twentieth century. In the nineteenth century they were to become the largest immigrant group to come to America, followed by those of Irish, English, and African descent. That rank order still held in 2000, although those of Mexican background were threatening to break the long established mold. Yet, unlike those of Irish or African—or Mexican—background, few people today think of Americans from German lands as members of a distinct or particularly distinctive ethnic group. Why not?

For one thing, the Germans did not arrive in a single wave that lasted but a decade or two like so many others. For another, they shared many of the values and cultural traits of the older American groups and Scandinavians among whom they often settled. Although they retained some of their own cultural baggage, they also shared it (the Sunday picnic, the kindergarten, New Year's parties, and the frankfurter or "hot dog"). Moreover, adaptation seemed relatively easy for them, perhaps because they were themselves a rather heterogeneous cohort. This made stereotyping and pigeonholing far more difficult. The Milwaukee brewers were a far cry from the St. Louis intellectuals such as the illustrious Carl Schurz, the "Forty-Eighter," historian, and newspaper publisher, who became an advisor to presidents (beginning with Lincoln), ambassador to Spain, U.S. senator, and secretary of the interior. And both were quite different from the stalwart and religious farmers known as the "Pennsylvania Dutch" (the word a corruption of "Deutsch").

During World War I, German Americans did undergo a difficult period when their original "Fatherland" became their new country's enemy. Some suffered from discrimination by fellow Americans encouraged by people in strategic private and public sectors. Even President Woodrow Wilson, who had long advocated the avoidance of involvement in foreign wars, changed his policy early in his second term. He not only urged Congress to declare war on Germany after threats by that country against American interests and shipping, but also soon became a leading advocate to squelch any opposition to his new policies and to strike out against possible subversion by immigrants and those of German extraction.

To avoid identification and ostracism, some Germans anglicized their names: Schmidt became Smith; Eisenhauer, Eisenhower. And, at the same time, other Americans, distaining anything that sounded German made some changes of their own as when "sauerkraut" became "liberty cabbage."

A similar attitude did not emerge during the years after Adolf Hitler took power and some German Americans, sympathetic to the aims of Nazism, joined pro-Hitler organizations known as Bunds.[11] Only a few were singled out and incarcerated as threats to American security. Unlike their Japanese American counterparts (to be discussed in the following chapter), there were never any large-scale round ups from any centers of population or internment of whole communities of German Americans in special camps.

The overwhelming majority of Americans of German origin supported and defended the United States and applauded its victory over the forces of the Third Reich in 1945. (In recent years, although there has been a resurgence of Nazi-like activity, complete with Nazi regalia, paraphernalia, and symbols, including the swastika and iron cross, there is little evidence that German Americans have been particularly prominent in such programs or supportive of them.)

The Great Atlantic Migrations

In 1855 the Castle Garden immigration depot was opened in New York. The depot was put to the test in the years following the Civil War (a war in which many immigrants fought side by side with citizens). After the war immigration began to flow more freely; the flow became a stream, and the stream, a torrent. By the middle of the 1880s hundreds of ships were steaming toward the eastern seaboard carrying human cargo. They epitomized what historians would refer to as the third significant wave of immigration. The first was that of the colonists and settlers that occurred before the Revolution; the second wave took place during the first half of the nineteenth century. (Note: After a hiatus of four decades, between 1924 and 1965, a fourth wave would bring millions more to the United States, mostly from Asia and Latin America. This will be discussed in Chapter 5.)

Between 1880 and 1914 about 7,500,000 Southern, Eastern, and Central Europeans—Italians, Hungarians, Bohemians, Slovaks, Czechs, Russians, and Poles—immigrated to the United States. Here they established or joined specific "nationality" communities and helped to create and maintain what some saw as spiritual and cultural homes away from home. Some such enclaves were named by outsiders: "Little Italy" or "Russian Town" or "The Ghetto";[12] others were known by their locales, "The Lower East Side [of Manhattan]," "Hester Street," "Greenwich Village." For many of the immigrants, it was sometimes the case that their new enclaves were not so much places on the map as places in the mind. "Polonia," for example, the name given by Polish immigrants to their "place" in America, was one such borderless land.[13]

During the period of what came to be known as "The Great Migration," 4 million Italians, mainly from "Il Mezzogiorno" (literally "midday" but popularly meaning the regions of southern Italy) and from Sicily, came to this country. The Italians, like many of those from Eastern Europe, came from farming areas but they did not see themselves as farmers in the conventional sense of the term. They were farm laborers called *contadini*. According to various estimates well over 90 percent of the Italian immigrants settled in cities where they engaged in occupations ranging from pick-and-shovel work in the building trades to shoemaking and barbering.[14]

Unlike so many European immigrants who came with their family members or with the intention of settling down in this country, many of the Italian "bread-winners" ventured to America seeking work to earn money to send home and to support themselves and their families when they returned to Italy. Many came and went back, then came again. In the end, many of these so-called "birds of passage" decided to stay and brought their families to this country.

In the overcrowded tenements of already worn-out slums, they bedded down, sought work, dreamed of success—or of home—and there they rubbed elbows with others who were equally poor, bewildered, and bedraggled. The novelist Pietro DiDonato describes the conditions in a vivid passage from his classic work, *Christ in Concrete.*

Table 4.1 Total Number of Immigrants, by Country of Birth, 1820–1992.

Five periods of immigration, showing the shift of immigrants from their country (or geographical region) of birth, in descending order of numbers (figures in thousands)

1820–1960[a]		1961–1970[b]		1971–1980[c]		1981–1990		1991–2000	
Germany	6,726.3	Mexico	443.3	Mexico	637.2	Mexico	1653.3	Mexico	2251.4
Italy	4,962.4	Canada	286.7	Philippines	360.2	Philippines	495.3	Philippines	505.6
Ireland	4,646.4	Cuba	256.8	Cuba	276.8	Vietnam	401.4	China & Taiwan	424.6
Austria-Hungary	4,275.8	Great Britain	230.8	Korea	272.0	China & Taiwan	388.8	Vietnam	421.1
Great Britain	3,784.6	Italy	206.7	China & Taiwan	202.5	Korea	378.8	India	383.3
Canada	3,555.4	Germany	200.0	Vietnam	179.7	India	261.9	Dominican Rep.	340.9
Russia/USSR	3,344.5	Philippines	1015	India	176.8	Dominican Rep.	251.8	Russia	231.9
Sweden	1,249.8	China & Taiwan	96.7	Dominican Rep.	148.0	El Salvador	214.6	El Salvador	217.4
Mexico	1,158.7	Dominican Rep.	94.1	Jamaica	142.0	Jamaica	213.8	Haiti	181.8
Norway	837.9	Greece	90.2	Italy	130.1	USSR	84.0	Cuba	180.9
France	684.9	Portugal	793	Great Britain	123.5	AFRICA	192.3	Jamaica	173.5
WEST INDIES	619.8	Poland	733	Canada	114.8	Cuba	159.2	Poland	169.6
Greece	487.2	Jamaica	71.0	Portugal	104.5	Iran	154.8	Poland	169.6
Poland	432.3	Colombia	703	Greece	93.7	Laos	145.6	Ukraine	141.3
China	408.5	Yugoslavia	46.2	AFRICA	91.5	United Kingdom	142.1	Canada	137.6
Turkey	365.5	Ireland	42.2	Colombia	77.6	Haiti	140.2	United Kingdom	135.8
Denmark	351.4	Argentina	42.1	Germany	66.0	Colombia	124.4	Colombia	131.0
Japan	325.4	AFRICA	39.3	Trinidad & Tobago	61.8	Canada	119.2	Pakistan	113.6
Switzerland	323.9	Japan	38.5	Haiti	58.7	Cambodia	116.6	Iran	112.6
The Netherlands	320.9	Haiti	375	Ecuador	50.2	Poland	97.4	Peru	105.7
Portugal	283.8	Ecuador	37.0	Japan	47.9	Guyana	95.4	Nicaragua	97.7
SOUTH AMERICA	234.8	Korea	35.8	Hong Kong	47.5	Germany	70.1	Ecuador	76.4
Belgium	189.0	France	343	Guyana	47.5	Thailand	64.4	Hong Kong	74.0
Spain	180.9	India	31.2	Iran	46.2	Peru	64.4	Guyana	73.9
Rumania	159.0	Spain	305	Thailand	44.1	Pakistan	61.3	Germany	67.7
Czechoslovakia	129.3	The Netherlands	27.8	Poland	43.6	Hong Kong	63.0	Thailand	48.4

(continued)

Table 4.1 (*continued*)

	1820–1960[a]	1961–1970[b]		1971–1980[c]		1981–1990		1991–2000	
CENTRAL AMERICA	115.6	Hong Kong	25.6	USSR	43.2	Ecuador	56.0	Honduras	66.8
AUSTRALASIA	79.8	Trinidad & Tobago	24.6	Yugoslavia	42.1	Honduras	49.5	Japan	61.5
AFRICA	475	Czechoslovakia	21.4	El Salvador	34.4	Nicaragua	44.1	Ireland	59.0

[a]*Statistical Abstract of the United States, 1961*, 82nd ed. Washington, D.C., U.S. Department of Commerce, Bureau of the Census. p. 93, Table 113.
[b]*Statistical Abstract of the United States, 1988*, 108th ed. Washington, D.C., U.S. Department of Commerce. Bureau of the Census, p. 10, Table 8.
[c]*Statistical Abstract of the United States, 2005*, 125th, ed. Washington, D.C., U.S. Department of Commerce, Bureau of the Census, p. 11, Table 8.
[d]*Statistical Abstract of the United States, 2005*, 125th ed. Washington, D.C., U.S. Department of Commerce, Bureau of the Census, p. 11, Table 8.

The tenement was a twelve-family house. There were two families on each floor with the flats running in boxcar fashion from front to rear and with one toilet between them. Each flat had its distinctive powerful odor. There was the particular individual bouquet that aroused a repulsion followed by sympathetic human kinship; the great organ of Tenement fuguing forth its rhapsody with pounding identification to each sense.... Missus Donovan, an honest Catholic woman, was old, cataplasmic, and sat for hours in the closet-small hallway toilet breathing in private heavy content, or at the front-room window munching her toothless gums.... The large Farabutti family in one of the upper flats had an oily pleasing aroma—the Maestro carrying with him a mixture of barbershop and strong di Nobili tobacco—and the children savoring of the big potato-fried-egg sandwiches which they chewed while shouting at cat-stick. The Hoopers had a colorless moldy emanation that hung and clung anemically but drily definite. The gaunt woman on the top floor who wore the gaudy old-fashioned dresses and brought men home with her talcumed herself stark flat white and left an insistent trail of old bathrooms littered with cheap perfumes. The top floor right—Lobans'—gave off a pasty freshness as though the bowels were excreting through the pores. Their breaths were revolting, and everyone in the family had snarling lips ready to let go profanities.[15]

Along with the Italians, many other immigrants from the south, as well as Central and Eastern Europe arrived and settled. Together they represented some of the most impoverished peoples on the continent of Europe. Many also had come as labor migrants to work in the expanding industries of this country, intending to return to their homelands. Some of them, like many of the southern Italians and Sicilians, were also known as "birds of passage," a reference to their own movement back and forth across the Atlantic. (Today in Europe such economic sojourners who move from one country to another initially intending to return home are known as "guest workers.")

During this same period, many others came to American shores with no intention of returning to the lands in which they had felt stifled by social systems that thwarted any thoughts of, or opportunities for mobility or where they had been oppressed and persecuted. It was such voluntary émigrés and involuntary exiles about whom Emma Lazarus wrote in her famous poem about the symbolism exuded by the Statue of Liberty (which Lazarus herself called the "Mother of Exile.")

Give me your tired, your poor,
Your huddled masses yearning to breathe free,
The wretched refuse of your teeming shore,
Send these, the homeless, tempest-tost, to me:
I lift my lamp beside the golden door.[16]

The new arrivals, who had often traveled "steerage class" in the bowels of the ships, were put ashore at nearby Ellis Island, the reception facility that replaced Castle Garden in 1892 as the principal portal of entry. None of these immigrants were the adventurers, explorers, traders, or conquerors of an earlier era. Yet they, too, were pioneers. As Max Lerner once put it, "the experience of the immigrants recapitulated the early American pioneer hardships, in many ways on harder terms, since the difficulties they encountered were those of a jungle society rather than a jungle wilderness."[17] Oscar Handlin called them "the uprooted."[18]

Because of their limited resources, few ventured far beyond the ports of debarkation or the inland cities along the main railroad lines. The members of each immigrant group tended to gather together and ethnic islands became a natural feature of the urban topography. Somewhat like the local communities of medieval Jews, these modern "ghettos" emerged in the older sections of the cities. Within their enclaves many tried their hand as entrepreneurs, selling dry goods and foodstuffs from pushcarts and tiny shops. Many more found employment as laborers outside the neighborhoods, working in heavy industry, in the building trades, or as piece-rate workers in the expanding garment trades. Jobs were obtained through labor contractors, old country family and village connections, employment agencies, or through newly found friends and neighbors.

The tasks the men and women performed were arduous, the hours long, the conditions frequently intolerable, and the paychecks often inadequate to provide for growing families. For the first generation there was little time for recreation. What little leisure they had was spent within the confines of neighborhoods where attempts often were made to keep Old World traditions alive. Such practices had both positive and negative consequences. On the one hand they provided a familiarity and some security, lifeboats in a stormy uncharted sea. On the other, they were also viewed as overly protective environments, especially for young people eager to adapt to more "modern" ways and to move out into the bigger world.

It was in the neighborhoods where sex role differentiation and conflict over it was most marked. Although many immigrant women worked—some, like the Irish, as domestics, many more in mills and factories—their home and community lives were often circumscribed by traditional attitudes that continued to define males as the heads of households, principal breadwinners, and decision makers, and exposure to the wider culture and the necessity of earning money to contribute to family coffers led to many problems, especially generational ones. Among the greatest challenges that women faced were those related to socializing, schooling, and the choice of careers. (Even the thought of women having a vocation aside from homemaking and, perhaps, doing piecework to augment income or working in a family enterprise such as a restaurant or shop was anathema to many.) The more patriarchal the environment, the greater the conflicts.[19]

Conflicts were many—and, of course, not all were related to those of gender; but, for many of those who came to America as poor peasants or farm laborers, opportunities were still greater than what most had known at home and, overcoming barriers of language and hostility, many took advantage of them. As individuals improved their economic and social positions, they often moved "uptown," leaving their older neighborhoods to later arrivers. In the metropolitan centers of the North, the pattern, often called "urban succession," was often repeated. The areas of original settlement became the new communities of the latest arrivers: the Irish might be replaced by Germans, then by Jews, Italians, or Slavs, blacks from the South, and Puerto Ricans—and, more recently, Asians and Latinos. A simple exercise in urban ethnography would demonstrate this quite graphically. One can easily note the changes as, for example, finding old churches that became synagogues and later became churches once again or, of late, mosques.

In the process, as the European immigrants and their children began to move from the margins of society toward and, sometimes, into its mainstream, they increasingly began to identify themselves as part of the white majority. This phenomenon is the subject of a fascinating study by Mathew Frye Jacobson called *Whiteness of a Different Color.* [20]

Jacobson points out that it was often the case that their new reference group—white, Anglo-Saxon, and Protestant (WASP)—was not all that welcoming to Italians and Jews and others who were most involved in the process of being "whitened." Indeed, the fact that they were still often thought of as strangers and dangerous threats to American culture would lead to a resurgence of efforts to restrict their conationalists and coreligionists from continuing unrestricted entry into the United States.

The Move Toward Restriction

Many of the children of European immigrants who were born abroad but were to come of age in America found themselves torn between the customs of their parents and the world into which they sought admission. The sociologist Ruben G. Rumbaut aptly labeled these newcomers members not of the "first generation" (that was the proper label for their parents) or the "second" of their American-born siblings, but the "one and a half generation."[21] It was they who were often the most torn between the Old World and the New. They were the ones who experienced the results of the interaction of different sets of rules, roles, and defined relationships—a generation often challenged by conflicting value systems. As they learned the norms of American life and tried to adhere to them, and as their American-born brothers and sisters worked hard to eschew traces of their "immigrant origins" in an effort to be included as full participants in *their* society, they frequently evoked the antagonism, even the wrath, not only of the WASP but of the members of other groups who had already "arrived"—sometimes but a few years before.

It was an old story. Fear of the stranger had greeted their parents; now hostility toward those eager to compete added fuel to the smoldering embers of antiforeign prejudice. In many places restrictive practices became commonplace, and increasing numbers of jobs, schools, fraternities, restaurants, and social clubs became forbidden territory. The signposts were clear: "No Irish Need Apply." "Restricted Clientele." "No Jews Allowed." "Americans Only." The last expression refers not to all Americans, but to those who fancy themselves as the only *real* Americans, usually those who claim that special status by virtue of claiming they, or their ancestors, had gotten here first. Many were legatees of those who opposed the arrival of the Irish in the decades just before the Civil War and the movement of the Chinese in the same period. Their growing animus began to refocus on those who were part of the Great Atlantic Migration, those later called "white ethnics."

The first restrictive legislation directed against European immigrants was passed in 1891. The language of the Immigration Act seemed indiscriminately to link the mentally incompetent with the indigent. An excerpt clearly illustrates the point:

... all idiots, insane persons, paupers or persons likely to become a public charge, persons suffering from a loathsome or a dangerous contagious disease, persons who have been convicted of a felony or other infamous crime or misdemeanor involving moral turpitude, polygamists, and also any person whose ticket or passage is paid for with the money of another or who is assisted by others to come, unless it is affirmatively and satisfactorily shown on special inquiry that such person does not belong to one of the foregoing excluded classes, or to the class of contract laborers excluded by the act of February twenty-sixth, eighteen hundred and eighty-five, but this section shall not be held to exclude persons living in the United States from sending for a relative or a friend who is not of the excluded classes under such regulations as the Secretary of the Treasury may prescribe.... [22]

In 1894 the Immigration Restriction League began. It was to be the strongest force against unrestricted acceptance of immigrants for the next quarter of a century and was largely responsible for congressional action in 1917 that added further limits to earlier legislation by stating that every immigrant had to demonstrate an ability to read. As Joseph Hraba and others have pointed out, such a literacy test was clearly an attempt to cut down the flow of Slavic and Italian immigrants.[23]

Following World War I, mounting isolationism and antiforeign feelings reached their zenith. In 1921 and, again, in 1924 further restrictive legislation was passed, sharply curtailing the immigration of "undesirable" national groups and setting forth rigid quotas favoring North Europeans and all but excluding others. In 1921 the Immigration Quota Act, signed by President Harding, provided that the annual number of aliens permitted to enter the United States from any nation was not to exceed three percent of the total number of foreign-born members of that particular nationality residing in this country in 1910. The Johnson Act of 1924 (sometimes known as the National Origins Act) limited immigration even more severely. The formula provided for the admission of 150,000 persons each year, with national quotas fixed at two percent of the total of foreign-born members of any given nationality group residing in the United States in 1890. These enactments served to close the "Golden Door."[24]

The Immigration and Nationality Act of 1952 (also known as the McCarran-Walter Act) recodified the national immigration laws, slightly improved the opportunities for some, such as those from Asian countries, but, in general, reduced the flow and increased the categories of restriction. Reflecting concerns about "communist subversives" at the height of the Cold War, the bill required very careful screening of "security risks."

The following year President Truman, over whose veto the McCarran-Walter Act had been passed, was able to enact the Refugee Relief Act of 1953, admitting slightly more than 200,000 refugees over the quota limits in a three-year period. Most of the newcomers were expellees and escapees from communist-controlled Eastern Europe. Not long after, 32,000 Hungarian refugees were permitted to enter the U.S. as "parolees." (Parolees were those given temporary visas but who were later able to apply for permanent residence. In succeeding years parolee status was used to give asylum to other refugees, especially Cubans, Soviet Jews, and various people from Southeast Asia after the fall of Saigon in 1975.)

When still a United States senator, John F. Kennedy initiated new legislation that was to significantly alter general immigration policies in the United States. He did not live to see it pass, but in 1965 his successor in the presidency, Lyndon Johnson, signed a bill that allowed people to apply for immigration to the United States not on the basis of strict national ratios but on hemispheric quotas. The government said it would now accept up to 170,000 people from Europe and an equal number from Asia up to a maximum of 20,000 individuals from any single country (regardless of how many had come from that place in the past) and as many as 120,000 from this hemisphere without any national limitation. There was one caveat in all instances: preferences were to be given to relatives of citizens, resident aliens, and those with special skills and talents. Moreover, special provisions were included to continue to consider the admission of certain people seeking political refuge in the United States. (A decade later the Indochina Immigration and Resettlement Act of 1975 was passed to further assist "sponsored" refugees. In many ways, the 1975 Act was a forerunner of the Refugee Act of 1980, the most comprehensive piece of refugee legislation in U.S. history. It finally brought U.S. refugee policy in line with United Nations' protocol addressing the needs of those seeking asylum who had "a well-founded fear of persecution.)[25]

A policy as flexible as this one might have saved thousands upon thousands of victims of Nazism in the years before and during World War II, but, for a variety of reasons, few exceptions were then permitted. Until the postwar period, the general sentiment that prompted the restrictive legislation of the 1920s remained reflected in the laws of the land. Certain peoples were favored; certain others were considered undesirable and severely limited in their opportunities to enter the country.

The Jews

Although some 200,000 Jewish, mostly German and Austrian refugees, including a number of scientists, professionals, artists, and intellectuals, managed to acquire visas to enter the United States, the vast majority of ordinary European Jews in flight from Germany and Nazi-occupied lands in the 1930s and 1940s were barred from entry by restrictive immigration laws. The Administration and, in particular, its State Department, was reluctant to change the rules even during that period of racial oppression in the Third Reich. (Here one finds an excellent example of what was referred to in Chapter One as race being a socially defined concept. The Nazis defined Jews, an ethnoreligious group, as a race, "an inferior race.")

There is considerable evidence that many attempts to relax the quotas by issuing more visas to allow Jewish refugees were met with firm resistance.[26] To many of those who have studied the era, one indirect result of the policies of the Roosevelt administration of "abandoning the Jews" was that hundreds of thousands of those trapped in Europe and who might have been saved would perish in the Holocaust.

Those few who did make it would join the ranks of what was already a well-established Jewish community whose members had come to America prior to the imposition of the "quota acts" discussed above, some many years before it was even proposed. The largest cohort had come from Eastern Europe after 1880. But these were hardly the first Jews to enter the country.

As early as 1654, 23 Jewish refugees from Brazil settled in Nieuw Amsterdam, the Dutch settlement later to be known as New York. By the time of the Revolution almost three thousand Jews—mainly of Spanish and Portuguese descent (called Sephardim)—were living in the seaboard colonies.

The first Jewish settlers, generally traders and merchants, found little opposition to their presence in most of the cities and towns where they worked and lived. There were scattered instances of discrimination in the areas of Dutch control and some Jews suffered religious persecutions in certain English colonies, where they were sometimes forbidden to hold public office or to bear arms. More often, these barriers were absent, ignored, or offset by the fact that many Protestants looked with favor upon the "Israelites" in their midst.

By 1700, freedom of worship was widely recognized and in 1740, when the Jews of British America were granted full citizenship, they achieved a degree of freedom probably unmatched anywhere in the world.

The Sephardim were joined by Ashkenasic Jews (whose origins were in German-speaking lands and Eastern Europe). Throughout the nineteenth century the number of Jews emigrating from Germany rose steadily. It is estimated that the American Jewish population was 15,000 in 1840, 50,000 in 1850, 150,000 in 1860, and 250,000 in 1880. By 1925 it was to exceed 3 million.

Many of the German Jews left the seaboard cities soon after their arrival and moved to smaller communities to the south and west. In many instances they went as peddlers and stayed to build many of the large retail emporia now found scattered in towns and cities across the nation. Although the Jews often had to live down the "curse of Shylock"—the images and portraits of Jewish peddlers and merchants as being dishonest, blatant discrimination was rarely found. Like their more cosmopolitan countrymen from the upper strata of German Jewish society, most had little difficulty in establishing themselves economically, in forming religious congregations, and in adapting themselves to local patterns. It was not until the 1880s, when waves of East European immigrants began moving toward the United States, that anti-Jewish discrimination gained a significant foothold in this country.

At the time Jews in Poland, Russia, Romania, and other East European lands, squeezed between a growing middle class and recently emancipated serfs, found themselves increasingly threatened by forces beyond their control. Their villages became vulnerable to pogroms (anti-Jewish attacks often sanctioned by local authorities) and many decided to leave. For most, America was the city of hope, "the guldene Medina" [the golden city].

Many who came in the large wave of European Jewish immigrants were economically impoverished and traditional in their religious beliefs. Most settled in the largest cities, where they could find work (especially in the expanding garment industry) and where they could continue their religious practices. Like other ethnically distinct groups, they, too, began to develop their own communities.

The conspicuousness of their dress, uniqueness of their customs, strangeness of their everyday language (Yiddish), and religious practices all combined to reinforce the images of Jews as a clannish and mysterious people. Yet, because the Jewish immigrants possessed several cultural traits that enhanced their adjustment and rapid mobility in American society they belied some assumptions and reinforced others. Years of relegation to marginal occupational roles, traditions that placed high value on education and the learned professions, and emphasis on familial responsibility all served to aid many Jews in their struggle to find acceptance and, in time, prosperity in competitive America. But the very fact that a substantial number of Jews began to surpass others in the rapidity of their ascent increased animosity and fanned the embers of anti-Semitism (an old phenomenon distinct from general antiforeign attitudes).

Because some Jews were extremely successful financially, they were referred to as "crass capitalists" (combining traditional ideas about "money changers" with more modern images). Because some Jews were deeply engaged in radical politics and labor organizations, others tried to paint them "red." And some, like the members of the Ku Klux Klan and even as notable and powerful a figure as Henry Ford, ignoring the ridiculous contradictions in their allegations, called the Jews *both* "parvenu" and "pinko."

The search for scapegoats during the Great Depression often found the Jews, including such advisors to President Roosevelt as Bernard Baruch, targets for the bitter frustrations felt by many Americans. (As mentioned previously, the rise of Nazism evoked some sympathy here as well, and several new "hate" organizations sprang up to defame the Jews.)

Postwar revelations of the horrors practiced by the Nazi regime greatly served to reduce anti-Jewish sentiments. In the two decades following World War II virulent anti-Semitism showed a marked decline, although restricted neighborhoods and social discrimination continued to exist in many of our cities and suburbs. Still, an epidemic of swastika daubing in 1960, temple bombings in 1962, the rise of George Lincoln Rockwell's American Nazi party (later called the American National White Workers' Socialist party) and other neo-Nazi organizations, the emergence of certain reactionary patriotic movements of the radical right in the early 1960s, and the occurrence of "black anti-Semitism" and Third World anti-Zionism on the part of the radical left in the late 1960s indicated the continued existence of anti-Semitic feelings in certain segments of the population. Some thought it a portent of more serious difficulties. Yet, by the late 1960s, it seemed reasonable to say:

> American Jews, delighted at Israeli victory in the Six-Day War, have evinced much less enthusiasm for their own country's protracted conflict in Southeast Asia and its stalemated war against poverty at home. Other groups in American life share the sense of frustration. In the search for scapegoats that may soon ensue, Jews may find themselves most vulnerable to attack from right, left, and below. By seeking reform and compromise on most issues instead of radical change they may come increasingly to appear too white for the black militants, too red for the white conservatives, and too yellow for their own children.
>
> Jews are not unaware of such possibilities. They know that latent anti-Semitism can be revived in America as it has been in the past. But they do not seem worried. They feel they can ride out the coming storms. Like their forebears who came to

settle on the Lower East Side, the majority of Jews still believe in America and in the American people.[27]

The predictions were, in fact, quite accurate. Certain black leaders did begin to separate themselves from too strong identification with Jews. Some Jews, with memories of how "numerus clausus" or quotas had been used to deprive them of admission to universities and limited access to certain professions still fresh in their minds, feared that "targets and goals" set to percentages in the population, regardless of the good intentions of the advocates of equal opportunity, would greatly reduce hard won opportunities for achievement based on merit. Objecting to this particular aspect of policies to insure entry of African Americans did not mean that Jews who held such views had rejected the abiding objective of the civil rights campaigns. They still remained, in the aggregate, the most liberal of all minorities in support of blacks. They remain so today.

At the same time that African Americans were raising doubts about the steadfastness of Jewish support, others echoed their own concerns about Jewish liberals. And some Jewish children (like many non-Jewish youngsters) did seek to distance themselves—physically and socially—from parents they thought were too bourgeois.

The Yom Kippur War of 1973 exacerbated the situation as increasing numbers of non-Jews blamed Israelis and, indirectly, all Jews, for the oil crisis that occurred in conjunction with it. In the following seven-year period popular support for Israel among non-Jewish Americans waned considerably as sympathy for the Palestinian refugees and their cause gained favor in various circles, including a number of church groups once publicly pro-Israel.

By 1980, many Jews and blacks seemed to recognize the need to re-form old coalitions, many white conservatives began to have second (or third) thoughts about Israel (seeing it once again as a bastion of democracy and military power in a turbulent Middle East), and many young Jews were found in the vanguard of new religious movements, some of which also involved resurging ethnic pride. Still, tensions continued. Some of these were all too familiar reminders of earlier periods. Jewish institutions—synagogues, community centers, even graveyards—once again became targets for anti-Semites; attacks on identifiable Jews, especially those who were Orthodox and dressed in the traditional manner, increased; and on many campuses, rallies on behalf of supporters of Palestinians sometimes turned their anger on Jewish counterdemonstrators. Ironically, the plight of the Palestinians also led to significant soul searching—and action—within the general American Jewish community.

For years, the majority of American Jews had given unqualified support to Israeli policies. Although most applauded the accord with Egypt engineered by President Jimmy Carter, they remained wary of the intentions of those in other Arab states and of the Palestinian Liberation Organization, which had vowed to recapture what was claimed as Arab land. Yet the hard measures used to suppress the uprising of the Palestinians living within the occupied West Bank and in the Gaza Strip in the late 1980s raised troubling questions for increasing numbers of

American Jews about both the morality and efficacy of Israeli actions. By the end of the decade many broke ranks with those who continued to support the Israeli hardliners, favoring a policy that would give genuine autonomy to the Palestinians. A breakthrough of sorts came in the early years of the presidency of Bill Clinton when his high office was used to forge the first of several agreements between the Israeli government of Yitzhak Rabin and the Palestine Liberation Organization, led by the late Yassar Arafat. Rabin's involvement in fostering a detente with the Palestinians led to his assassination in November 1995 by a Jewish fanatic seeking to torpedo the peace process.

The succeeding ten years were marked with increasingly violent conflict and repeated failure as moderate Israelis and Palestinians and their erstwhile allies in the United States, Britain, and continental Europe all tried to bring about some resolution to the vexing problems of trying to insure national integrity and security for both peoples. That struggle continues and Americans—Jewish, Christian, and, increasingly, those of the Muslim faith—have been drawn into debates over the future of the Holy Land.

The Muslims

Although there has been an American presence of the followers of the Koran for many decades, native-born Americans of the Muslim faith, as well as immigrants, have gained considerable attention in recent years, The Israeli-Palestinian conflict in the Middle East was, perhaps, the catalyst for Muslims to become objects of curiosity and concern, especially when ideas of the Palestinian side were well articulated by such prominent spokespersons as Edward Said. But it was not the most significant. Rather, public consciousness of a large Muslim presence in the United States began with the first Iraq War during the administration of the first President Bush in the 1990s and reached a fever pitch in the aftermath of the attacks on the twin trade towers in New York City in 2001.

What Americans who were willing to listen would learn was that, as there are Jews of varied backgrounds, occupations, and political persuasions, so, too, there are Muslims who are of different origins, engaged in a wide array of professions, and holding both political and religious beliefs that range from very liberal to very conservative.

Although most, like the majority of Palestinians, are Arabs, the followers of Muhammad are found in many parts of the world. They are the dominant group in such non-Arab states as Bosnia, Turkey, Iran, Pakistan, Malaysia, and Indonesia and a prominent minority in India. Followers of the Islamic faith are a major presence in many parts of Africa.

In this country, some, mostly African Americans, are fairly recent converts to the Temple of Islam. Most others are immigrants. And yet, despite significant differences, a spirit of shared religious identity that crosses bounds of political ideology, race, and ethnicity unites them. Their unity was long reflected in the words of the Syrian American poet, Kahlil Gibran.

Light of day and peace of the night ...
Remember, my brother,
That the coin which you drop into
The withered hand stretching toward
You is the only golden chain that
Binds your rich heart to the
Loving heart of God.[28]

Gibran, who was raised in a Maronite Catholic family, was among the first to give voice to people like himself—and his Muslim grandparents. They came from Syria or from the Syrian province of the Ottoman Empire known as Lebanon. Between 1920 and World War II, approximately 100,000 Syrian migrants had come to the United States. Most were Christians, with only a small number (between five and ten percent) being Muslim.[29] Few were Arab nationalists, an attitude far more apt to characterize the large numbers of Muslim Arabs who migrated to the United States more recently. By the mid-1980s the number of all who identified themselves as Muslims had reached 4 million.[30] This figure included people from the Middle East and North Africa (who comprised over half of those in the cohort) and from Asia (slightly more than a third). Others came from sub-Saharan Africa and Eastern Europe. The overall figure also includes African American converts.

Yvonne Yazbeck Haddad, a specialist on the study of Muslims in America, attributes the enormous growth in the percentages of foreign-born Muslims to changes in American society, changes in immigration laws, and the changing demands of the labor market. They are concentrated in three states: California, News York, and Illinois. Haddad and Adair T. Lummis argue that although most have been integrated economically, and frequently become citizens, they have remained a targeted minority, not least because of the stereotypes many hold of Arabs as well as of Muslims.[31] They attribute these to distorted media images of Islam, the lack of substantial political influence, and a general prejudice against Arabs too often seen as "lustful, greedy bungling polygamists."[32] One result, it is argued, is that Muslims in America have to rely on the goodwill of others for their survival.

Summarizing the writings of several commentators, Stephanie Van Buren has suggested that the color-coded racism that pervades American society has helped Muslim Americans transcend differences in national identity, forming interdependent bonds through common faith on the one hand and defense against categorical discrimination, in this country and elsewhere, on the other. Following the views of Haddad and Lummis, she notes that "it may [be] only incidental that the majority of Muslims in the world are located in 'Third World' nations that have been victimized by western imperialism, ... [which] may serve to form a common bond, or brotherhood, among yellow and brown people."[33]

Now, in the wake of the terrorist attacks on New York City and the Pentagon, and more recently, in Madrid and London, and with the ongoing strife in and around Iraq, more and more American Muslims feel beleaguered. They are especially fearful that new rules relating to the screening of migrants, surveillance of communal institutions, and general distrust of those who share their faith may portend both a rise in hostility against them and a hardening of ideological battle lines and fundamentalist beliefs within their ranks. The concerns are hardly groundless. Several thousand Muslim migrants have been deported since September 11, 2001, and many others continue to worry that they are under an increasing threat of expulsion in attempts "to protect the homeland."

In the wake of serious setbacks in America's actions in Iraq in the preemptive war launched in 2003, increasing numbers of Muslims began to feel they and those with whom they are identified were becoming the latest victims of many Americans in need of targets for their frustrations over failures to win their own seemingly crusade-like campaigns for the minds and souls of non-Christian people in such places as Afghanistan and Iraq, an equivalent of the Cold War demons, the "atheistic communists."

Notes

1. Walt Whiteman, "Song of Myself" in James E. Miller (ed.), *Complete Poetry and Selected Prose* (Boston: Houghton Mifflin, 1959).

2. See Ellis Cose, *A Nation of Immigrants: Prejudice, Politics and the Populating of America* (New York: Morrow, 1992); Roger Daniel, *Coming to America* (New York: Harper, 1990); Lawrence H. Fuchs, *The American Kaleidoscope: Race, Ethnicity and the Civic Culture* (Middletown, CT: Wesleyan University Press, 1990); and Walter Nugent, *Crossings: The Great TransAtlantic Migrations, 1870–1941* (Bloomington: Indiana University Press, 1992).

3. See Ronald Takaki, *Iron Cages: Race and Culture in Nineteenth Century America* (New York: Knopf, 1979).

4. John F. Kennedy, *A Nation of Immigrants,* rev. ed. (New York: Harper & Row, 1964), p. 18.

5. See, for example, Hasia R. Diner, *Erin's Daughters in America* (Baltimore: Johns Hopkins University Press, 1983) and Kathryn Kish Sklar and Thomas Dublin, *Women and Power in American History* (Englewood Cliffs, N.J.: Prentice Hall, 1991).

6. Stephen Steinberg, *The Ethnic Myth: Race, Ethnicity and Class in America,* rev. ed. (New York: Beacon Press, 1989), p. 160.

7. See, for example, John B. Duff, *The Irish in the United States* (Belmont, Calif.: Wadsworth, 1971), pp. 31–36; also see Oscar Handlin, *Boston's Immigrants 1790–1880* (Cambridge: The Belknap Press of Harvard University Press, 1987 edition).

8. See Tyler Anbinder, *Nativism and Slavery: The Northern Know Nothings and the Politics of the 1850s* (New York: Oxford University Press, 1992).

9. As quoted in Martin F. Nolan, "In Politics, the Populists vs. the Elitists," *New York Times* (July 25, 2004), DR 5.

10. Nolan, loc. cit.

11. For a recent novel that discusses the appeal for some German Americans and others of the Nazi movement, see Philip Roth, *The Plot Against America* (New York: Houghton Mifflin, 2004).

12. See, for example, Hutchins Hapgood, *The Spirit of the Ghetto: Studies of the Jewish Quarter of New York* (New York: Funk and Wagnalls Company, 1902).

13. Helen Znaniecki Lopata, *Polish Americans* (Englewood Cliffs, N.J.: Prentice Hall, 1976), pp. 12–32.

14. Joseph Lopreato, *Italian Americans* (New York: Random House, 1970), pp. 36–44.

15. Pietro DiDonato, *Christ in Concrete* (Indianapolis: Bobbs-Merrill, 1937), pp. 137–138.

16. Emma Lazarus, "The New Colossus," *Poems* (Boston: Houghton Mifflin, 1889), pp. 202–203.

17. Max Lerner, *America as a Civilization* (New York: Simon and Schuster, 1958), p. 88.

18. Handlin, op. cit.

19. For a comprehensive overview of these issues, see Donna Gabaccia, *From the Other Side: Women, Gender and Immigrant Life in the U.S.: 1820–1990* (Bloomington: Indiana University Press, 1994).

20. See, for example, Mathew Frye Jacobson, *Whiteness of a Different Color: European Immigrants and the Alchemy of Race* (Cambridge: Harvard University Press, 1998).

21. Rumbaut discusses this in many of his writings, most recently in Ruben D. Rumbaut and Ruben G. Rumbaut, "Self and Circumstance," in Peter I. Rose (ed.), *The Dispossessed: An Anatomy of Exile* (Amherst: University of Massachusetts Press, 2005), p. 332.

22. As cited in Hraba, op. cit., pp. 16–17.

23. Ibid. p. 17.

24. See, for example, William S. Bernard, *American Immigration Policy—A Reappraisal* (New York: Harper &Row, 1950), pp. 23–24. Also see Benjamin M. Ziegler (ed.), *Immigration: An American Dilemma* (Boston: D.C. Heath, 1953).

25. Gail Paradise Kelly, *From Vietnam to America* (Boulder, Colo.: Westview Press, 1979). See also Norman and Naomi Zucker, *The Guarded Gate* (New York: Harcourt Brace Jovanovich, 1987).

26. See Richard Breitman and Alan M. Kraut, *American Refugee Policy and European Jewry, 1933–1945* (Bloomington and Indianapolis: University of Indiana Press, 1987); David S. Wyman, *Paper Walls: America and the Refugee Crisis, 1938–1941* (1968), and David S. Wyman, *The Abandonment of the Jews: America and the Holocaust, 1941–1945* (New York: Pantheon, 1984.)

27. Peter I. Rose, "The Ghetto and Beyond," in Peter I. Rose (ed.), *The Ghetto and Beyond* (New York: Random House, 1969), p. 17.

28. Gregory Ofralea and Sharif Elumusa (eds.), *Grape Leaves: A Century of Arab American Poetry* (Salt Lake City: University of Utah Press, 1988), pp. 31–34.

29. Alexia Naff, *Becoming American: The Early Arab Immigrant Experience* (Carbondale, IL: Southern Illinois University Press, 1985), pp. 2–3.

30. See Carol Stone, "Estimate of Muslims Living in America" in Yvonne Y. Haddad (ed.), *The Muslims of America* (New York: Oxford University Press, 1991), pp. 25–36.

31. Yvonne Haddad, *The Muslims of America,* op. cit, p. 4.

32. Yvonne Haddad and Adair Lummis, *Islamic Values in the United States: A Comparative Study* (New York: Oxford University Press, 1987), p. 165.

33. Stephanie Van Buren, "American Muslims: Islamic 'Ethnics' as Models for Pluralism," unpublished report, Smith College, Northampton, MA, May 1995, p. 12.

From Other Shores

Across the Pacific, Across the Rio Grande

It is obvious today that not all Americans are of European or African or Middle Eastern "stock." In the last third of the twentieth century and the first years of the present one, this country became more of a "nation of nations" than even the prescient poet Walt Whitman could have imagined. Our "nonwhite" and "nonblack" citizens represent a diversity of background and appearance, culture and character that has greatly enriched the United States. But this very diversity has also played into the long-held views of those wary of people who are quite unlike themselves, who, in Ronald Takaki's graphic phrase, have come to America "from different shores."[1] Although the majority of those who crossed the Pacific and the Rio Grande are relative newcomers, many of those with whom they are most identified have been in the country a very long time.

Pacific Migrations

The Lower East Side of New York, where Russian Jewish immigrants first congregated, was sometimes referred to as an "Oriental Enclave," for, to some people, the Jews were not Europeans but "Orientals" or, compounding the pejorative tag, "swarthy Orientals." They were also called "Street Arabs." In the years to come many observers would notice that members of each cohort—Jews, Arabs, and Americans from Asia—appeared to have certain common traits, not least rather similar attitudes toward family, work, and education. But the true Orientals (or Asians, as they much prefer to be called) who came to America in the nineteenth

72

century also were very different from the Jews and other trans-Atlantic immigrants. They had physical characteristics that set them apart and made them special targets for those who feared "the Yellow Peril."

The Chinese

The first Chinese came to America during Gold Rush days. In the years following the Civil War their migration increased sharply and by 1880 there were about 320,000 Chinese people living in America, mainly on the West Coast. Most had come from a single province in Southeast China where economic conditions forced many men to leave home as contract laborers or "coolies" to work in this country as miners or track layers on the railroads during the early days of westward expansion. Many intended to return to China to attain new status based on the wages of their toil. As a result of this hope and because of strong allegiance to their emperor and strong filial ties, few made much effort to adapt to Western institutions. Some did return, but most stayed in the United States, to be increasingly perceived as an alien element. Many Chinese suffered from ostracism, exploitation, and extreme violence. There were outright murders in Los Angeles in 1871 and a massacre of 29 persons took place in Rock Springs, Wyoming, in 1885.[2]

When the railroads were finished and the mines were shut down, many Chinese moved back to the West Coast cities where, desperate for ways of earning a living, they were forced into occupations that had nothing especially "oriental" about them—running hand laundries, cigar stores, curio shops, and restaurants—and a few remained in outdoor labor. Moreover, since "merchants" had higher status in the eyes of immigration officials than "workers," many called themselves merchants, thus giving an exaggerated statistical sense of the size of a growing Chinese American middle class.

Immigration officials were an important factor in the lives of the Chinese. California, the state with the largest Chinese population, had long looked with disfavor upon these (and, it turned out, other) people from Asia. They repeatedly passed discriminatory legislation to curtail the activities of Chinese residents.

In 1882 the Chinese had the dubious distinction of becoming the first nationality group singled out by the federal government for separate treatment, when the Chinese Exclusion Act was passed. It was renewed in 1892, and in 1902 all Chinese immigration was made illegal. The ban was not lifted until 1943 when China was our military ally and then only a crack: 105 persons were to be admitted each year. The Immigration Reform Act of 1965, explained in Chapter 4, changed things considerably and hundreds of thousands of Chinese (and other East Asians) were able to come to America.

The restriction against immigration did not reduce anti-Chinese sentiments. "Chinatowns," inhabited mainly by single men, were considered by many Americans to be centers of licentiousness, narcotic addiction, corruption, and mystery. Traditional ties and loyalties, clan connections and "company" allegiances, gave these areas local community control years before that phrase was to become a part of everyday rhetoric. Ever-present suspicions and blatant discrimination increased the pressure for in-group solidarity in Chinese neighborhoods. But, as in the case of so many immigrant groups who had come to America, on their turf and in their own way, economic and welfare and educational institutions were established in Chinatowns in a number of cities, as were places of recreation and amusement. Today, many new Chinese immigrants from the mainland, from Taiwan, and from places where they were already a minority population, such as Vietnam and Laos, still find solace in their own communities and many, especially those who are for-eign-born, want to maintain—and are maintaining—many traditions.

But the "one-and-a-half-generation" and even more American-born Chinese (or "ABCs" as they are popularly called) are more oriented to mainstream American life and culture. It is noteworthy that many third-generation Chinese Americans (the grandchildren of the original immigrants) seem to give support to a much-debated hypothesis that sociologists and historians have long called "Hansen's Law." The idea, first expressed by Marcus Lee Hansen in 1938 (in regard to Swedes) is simply stated: "What the son wishes to forget, the grandson wishes to remember."[3]

These days Chinese Americans suffer much less discrimination than in earlier years; still, Chinatowns remain—especially in San Francisco, Los Angeles, Chicago, and New York—and so do many problems. Most of these have to do with internal conflicts in the communities, as between citizens and recent immigrants from Hong Kong, or between shop owners and those who work in the ubiquitous sweatshops, between the Chinatown-based "downtown Chinese" and the "uptown Chinese" who have moved out of the ghetto, and between the generations. Also, as might be expected, for a time, the shift of American foreign policy toward Beijing and ultimate recogni-tion of the People's Republic of China as the sole legitimate government after almost a quarter of a century of support for Nationalistic China and the Chiang Kai-shek regime confused and angered many Chinese Americans who felt a sense of kinship with the old nationalists who had relocated in Taiwan after the communist revolution of the late 1940s. That change—and the recent changes in the People's Republic itself, especially its rapid economic growth—has also delighted many Chinese Americans who see China the place, not the political entity, as their rich cultural homeland.

Whatever the sentiments of the Chinese Americans held regarding this country's detente with Beijing, the opening of the People's Republic in the 1980s served to interest millions of other Americans in Chinese culture and society. If anything, America entered the 1990s in a positive mood toward China, a sentiment that con-tinues well into the following decade. Now, in the early years of the twenty-first century, the biggest fear is not of an ideological sweep by communism emanating from the PRC but economic domination of much of Asia and, eventually, many other parts of the world.

The Japanese

The Japanese were a half step behind the Chinese at each phase of their early settle-ment on the U.S. mainland. The first Japanese settlers came to Pacific shores in 1869, twenty-one years after the first Chinese landed on the American mainland. The large migration took place a decade after the Chinese Exclusion Act had been invoked. The latter point is important, for it shows that although the two groups were frequently lumped together, significant distinctions were also made between them.

Save for the few members of the Wakamatsu Colony of pioneers who came here in the late 1860s under very special circumstances, no Japanese migrated to this country until 1885; until then almost no one could leave Japan. With a shift in the policy of the new regime of Emperor Meiji, however, many departed their native land to find work in the territory of Hawaii and in the United States itself. When they arrived here some sought work in the cities, but it was hard to obtain and so they turned to mining and logging and, particularly, farm labor. The latter proved to be advantageous to employers and newcomers alike—for a large number of immigrants had worked the soil before and took pride in what they could do with it. But they proved too good for some Californians to tolerate.

As they saved and began to buy land for their own farms or, as in the case of quite a few members of the second generation, left their jobs as laborers or domestics and sought to enter competitive vocations, prejudices began to mount. They also came to feel the brunt of racism used as "a mask for privilege," to use Carey McWilliam's graphic phrase. The Japanese and Korean Exclusion League was formed to protest against "unfair competition."

Immigration was greatly reduced in 1907 as a result of President Theodore Roosevelt's "Gentlemen's Agreement" with the Japanese Government, designed to stop the issuance of passports to potential farm workers. Others, including some merchants and many students, continued to come, as did the storied "picture brides," women selected for marriage on the basis of photographs sent by marriage brokers from Japan. But this was not enough to satisfy the Californian nativists. They sought, and their legislature passed their own Alien Land Law in 1913; it prevented the Japanese—"aliens ineligible for citizenship"—from purchasing their own farms.

Owing to World War I and the need for produce, the threat of denial—and/or removal—was stayed. In fact, immigration restrictions themselves were lifted and about 75,000 Japanese entered the country as farm workers. Harry Kitano, a student of the period, noted "farm income reached a peak in 1920 when the Japanese in California produced land crops valued at 67 million dollars."[4] He also pointed out that "after the war, the release of war workers from city factories, the return of soldiers, and the 'increasing danger' from a rising nationalistic Japan reignited agitation against the Japanese. Although they had developed much of the marginal land of California, they were accused of having secured the richest and most desirable farmland."[5] The land law was soon amended and ultimately served to curtail sharply Japanese agricultural activities—though it did not stop them entirely.

The Japanese reaction to discrimination against them was quite different from that of many other ethnic groups, including the Chinese. Although they often tended to live in enclaves and helped one another in every way possible, for the most part they fought the idea of "ghetto existence." Although feeling pressure from the *Issei* (first generation), the *Nisei* (second generation) were more inclined to live and work beyond the confines of the "Little Tokyos" or "Japan towns" of Seattle, San Francisco, and Los Angeles.

The attack on Pearl Harbor on December 7, 1941, changed everything. Almost the entire Japanese American population—citizens and aliens alike—was removed by military decree from the cities of the West Coast and placed in "security" camps in the desert, the Rocky Mountains, and as far way as Arkansas. Japanese Americans living in other parts of the country were carefully watched, but were not interned. This unprecedented action of the Roosevelt administration was prompted by fear of disloyalty from the Japanese American minority at a time of considerable tension over the actions of the armed forces of Imperial Japan and a fear of subversion by those still loyal to the emperor. But there is considerable evidence that the hysteria played on seeds of suspicion long sown by those for whom the Japanese were perceived as a significant economic threat.

Eventually the order was rescinded, and a year after the evacuation, the 110,000 Japanese internees began to resettle. Many established new homes in the Midwest, some in the mountain states and in the East, and others finally returned to the West Coast.

It is estimated that the Japanese Americans suffered a financial loss of over 350 million dollars through the forced evacuation. Although Congress appropriated some money for restitution to these displaced persons, few were able to recoup their losses, many could not offer sufficient proof of their claims, and no government, of course, could compensate them for the disruption of their lives.[6]

More often than not, Japanese Americans had to begin again in different occupations from those they had engaged in prior to the war. Without sufficient funds only a small number could return to their prewar activities. Nonetheless, in the main, the status of Japanese Americans improved dramatically after 1945.

Being more widely dispersed throughout the country, by the 1960s they began to occupy a minority group position somewhat analogous to that of the highly mobile American Jews.[7] It is noteworthy that it was, however, not the Jews whom sociologist William Petersen singled out as America's "model minority" in his 1971 book, *Japanese Americans: Oppression and Success.*[8] His label became a controversial sobriquet for all Americans from Asia—and many resented the "outsider's" seemingly congratulatory definer. Even while admitting it has more than a kernel of truth, especially when applied to Japanese Americans (as originally intended), "model minority" remains a phrase that evokes considerable controversy.

The Koreans

A rapidly growing community under the rubric of Asian Americans is Korean. The major force of their resettlement in the United States has occurred since 1965.

Long subjected to the same restrictions as the Japanese (whose government controlled Korea throughout most of the first half of the twentieth century), the small numbers of Koreans who came in the early years of the last century were, like the Japanese, mostly farm laborers. A second wave appeared in the mid- to late-1950s, the vast majority Korean wives of American servicemen who had fought in the Korean War. Since passage of the Immigration Reform Act of 1965, a third and much larger influx of Koreans, many of them practitioners of one of the Protestant denominations, have come to the United States as regular immigrants. (The 1970 Census indicated that there were over 200,000 Koreans in this country; by 1980 there were nearly twice that number; by 1990 it had quadrupled, and the trend, although no longer exponential, continues to show rapid increases.)

Often highly educated and armed with bachelor and even higher degrees, but having difficulty with the language and other cultural barriers, many members of the first generation of immigrants reluctantly eschewed professions for which they had been trained and carved their own economic enterprises in this society. Most prominent are the groceries that abound in many of our major cities. In many ways the preponderance of Koreans in this single industry recapitulated an old immigrant pattern of establishing small businesses and providing work for family members and other compatriots. One thinks of Jews in the needle trades; Italian barbers, cobblers, and construction workers; Chinese hand launderers; Greek restaurateurs; and Japanese gardeners.

Like other enterprising immigrant entrepreneurs, those who see them as chauvinistic and clannish have sometimes resented Korean greengrocers. They have also been seen as threats to established shopkeepers and, particularly, as many of the Koreans' customers are blacks and Latinos, as exploiters of other minorities. One dramatic recreation of the latter tension is masterfully portrayed in director Spike Lee's 1989 film, *Do the Right Thing.* The setting is Brooklyn, New York, but it could as easily have been Los Angeles.

Because of their strong commitment to family and education, over a decade ago it had been predicted that few children of Korean grocers would remain in the produce business. The assumption is corroborated by the high and climbing rates of enrollments of Korean American youngsters in American colleges and universities and by the numbers already becoming well established in white-collar jobs, especially in new industries, such as computers, as well as in the more traditional professions.

Other Asians

Aside from the Chinese, Japanese, and Koreans who, in large measure, share common racial origins, certain values relating to familial ties and responsibilities, and the fundamentals of a common written language based on Chinese pictograms, there are two other major immigrant groups in the United States who are also called "Asian" and are so designated in many census statistics. The first are those from one nation, the Philippines, a large, multi-islanded country whose people share a common nationality but are of quite diverse racial, cultural, and religious backgrounds.[9] The second, known in the aggregate as South Asians, are an equally diverse aggregate of Hindu, Muslim, and Buddhist people from the Indian subcontinent and the countries of India, Pakistan, Bangladesh, and Sri Lanka.

The two large cohorts—South Asian and Filipino—have very little in common save for the fact that a disproportionate number of foreign doctors and nurses working in American hospitals come from India and from the Philippines.

South Asians

The Filipinos have a long history of residence in the United States, dating back almost 250 years, to 1763 in New Orleans. The South Asians are, by contrast, recent arrivals. Until 1980, the Census Bureau did not account for the latter group at all, although there have been small numbers of Indians in this country since early in the twentieth century. Most of those in that early group came from the Punjab region to California, where they worked as farm laborers. Despite their long period of residence and their contributions to the local economy, it wasn't until 1946 that they were allowed to own land, become citizens, or request permission to bring in their relatives. And, even then, although their numbers increased considerably, opportunities for immigration from South Asia didn't really open up until the Immigration Reform Bill of 1965 was passed. After that, large numbers applied for and received permission to enter the United States as resident aliens and to work toward citizenship.

Many of those who are of Indian origin in the country today came (or their parents came) directly from the subcontinent. Others migrated from East Africa, the West Indies, especially Trinidad and Tobago, Guyana, and the United Kingdom, where their families had lived, sometimes for several years, often for several generations. Their ranks included both Hindus and Muslims.

Although they represent a wide spectrum of ethnic, religious, and linguistic groups, the most recently arrived South Asians constitute a uniquely high-status group of immigrants. According to several reliable sources, more than 90 percent are either "professional/technical workers" or the "spouses and children of professional/technical workers" when they arrive. Those who are less well trained or have difficulty finding professional jobs have been quite enterprising. Like the Koreans, they have established their own economic niches and become quite successful entrepreneurs, especially in the newsstands, gas stations, and convenience shops they have purchased and operate in large cities and small towns across the country.

One of the most interesting sociological aspects of the South Asians' odyssey in American society is the way they have seen themselves in relation to other minorities, immigrant and native-born.

For many years, prominent Indian and other South Asian spokespersons claimed that their official racial designation should be "Caucasian." The federal judiciary —and the Census Bureau—thought otherwise and repeatedly denied their claim to "whiteness." Maxine Fisher, one of the few scholars who has studied Indians in the United States, reported that, even though they were finally permitted to be classified as they had long wished, some members of the same communities soon desired to change back to a non-Caucasian designation. She cited "the economic benefits to be derived from being considered nonwhite" as a possible reason for this.[10] Despite the objections of many, there have been continuing efforts to use the category "Asian American" to lump such diverse parties as those of Indian and Filipino background and others from countries in Southeast Asia, as well as "Pacific Islanders" (with roots in Polynesia, Micronesia, Melanesia), along with those of Chinese, Japanese, and Korean origins under one broad rubric, "Asian." This, it was claimed, was not only for statistical purposes but in order to achieve the benefits of newly established affirmative action programs. Those Indians and others who feel they benefit from this hardly cultural but strictly geographic designation may owe a debt of gratitude to a little-known Filipino writer, Lemuel Ignacio.

The Filipinos

In his book, *Asian Americans and Pacific Islanders: Is There Such an Ethnic Group?*, first published in 1976, Ignacio argued for a common label that simultaneously would counteract and emulate the successful movement of Black Power brokers. He wanted his people to get their fair share of government funding. Because the Filipinos are, like the South Asians, a highly diverse, multilingual, multiethnic community, he argued they ought to come together, allying themselves with others who shared their fate if not their history.[11] Shortly after the publication of Ignacio's treatise, Maxine Fisher noted that it was clearly evident that "Asian American ethnicity—and even Filipino ethnicity to a lesser extent—are artifacts which he has helped to create."[12]

Ignacio sought to create a powerful third bloc, "Asians," that could make its own claims for special consideration for "group rights" in competition with African Americans and those with roots in Central and South America. In many ways, he was to prove successful. The ostensible rationale for linking these seemingly odd bedfellows was that all had originally come to the United States from the East; all had suffered from some form of racial discrimination; and, the sentiments of some East Indians notwithstanding, were neither white nor black. (The latter contention again offers another cryptic commentary on the meaning of "color" in American society, especially when it is readily noted that many South Asians are far darker in skin tone than many called African Americans.)

That such a move should originate with a spokesman from the Filipino American community is not surprising. For of all the large, trans-Pacific groups that have come here, the Filipinos, or "Pinoys," as they often call themselves,[13] are at once the most marginal and the most "American" of all "Asian" subgroups.

The Philippine archipelago, situated in a strategic area of the South Pacific, was long a colony of Spain from whose King Philip it derived its Western sounding name. Spanish conquerors, administrators, priests, and business men left a profound imprint on the culture, religion, and character of the predominantly Malayan population by the time they were finally expelled at the end of the nineteenth century, at the end of the Spanish-American War. In 1902, after but several years of independence, American forces overthrew the nationalists, took possession of the islands, and reorganized the society, its laws, and, in many ways, its mores. After several hundred years of Spanish rule and then several decades of American influence, the people of the Philippines were subjected to yet another takeover when the Japanese conquered the country in the early days of World War II.

In 1944 American forces, who had been forced to leave the embattled country, were eventually to avenge their defeat at Bataan and return. Two years later, the Philippines became one of the many oxymoronically named "independent dependencies" of the victorious allies.

To some, the modern Philippines is a case study in cultural amalgamation. To others, it is a highly volatile, fragmented, and schizophrenic society that, like Puerto Rico, isn't quite sure what it is or what it wants to be. No better example of its own confusion is to be found than in the practice of many Filipino patriots who, citing the absence of an "F" sound in the principal native language, Tagalog, disdain its use in the spelling of their official name. They say they are "Pilipino" not "Filipino." Ironically, the same local boosters still render gender distinctions in the traditional Spanish manner ("Pilipino" for male, "Pilipina" for female) while requiring everyone in the nation to learn English! To confound matters further, once they get to the United States, they are sometimes classified as "Hispanics" owing to the preponderance of Spanish surnames.

The fact is that, since the first "Manila men" jumped shipped in Louisiana in the eighteenth century, Filipinos have been difficult to pigeonhole. They have never quite fit in to standard schemes and have frequently followed their own paths toward integration. They are from the East but, except for the many people of Chinese background who live as minorities in the Philippines, they may be "Asians" but are surely not "Orientals." They often have Spanish names and some Filipinos of the old, partially European elite can still speak Spanish. Nonetheless, the Filipinos are not "Hispanics" or "Latinos" (at least in terms of the current usage of those terms).

With regard to their migration to this country, it is to be noted that by 1930 there were over 45,000 Filipinos on American soil, many of them agricultural laborers working in the then-territory of Hawaii. After the war increasing numbers came to the United States. Among their ranks were veterans who had fought in American uniforms or served as mess stewards aboard U.S. ships and the Filipino brides of American servicemen. Two decades later, this postwar group would be followed by large numbers of countrymen and women who benefited from the changes in immigration legislation.

Many of the newcomers were far better educated than their predecessors. The immigrants included many nurses, physicians, lawyers, engineers, and teachers who came to benefit from job opportunities. Most recent immigrants come knowing English, already trained in needed skills, and sharing many of the same attitudes about making it in the United States that other trans-Pacific migrants possess. Far from all who wish to come to the United States have been able to do so for even the relaxed immigration laws have set limits to annual flows. And one of the biggest backlogs of petitioners consists of lists of those seeking entry from the Philippines.

The Indochinese

The war in Vietnam and its complicated aftermath brought a new lot of Southeast Asian people to America. Although some were from Thailand, mostly the spouses of American soldiers who spent time in their country on leave from the battlefronts, most were from Vietnam, Laos, or Cambodia, the three countries of what, for a time, was French Indochina.

The first of the Indochinese refugees to come were government officials and military leaders who were airlifted out of Vietnam after the fall of Saigon in April

1975. Aided by public and private agencies, they were moved to Pacific island bases, then to camps in various parts of the United States, and then helped to resettle in many communities where they often began to form new ethnic enclaves.

In late 1970s the world was alarmed by reports of "boat people" who had escaped from Vietnam but were having difficulty finding places of asylum on the shores of neighboring countries. An international agreement set up an elaborate system by which the new refugees could find temporary havens in camps established under the authority of the United Nations High Commissioner for Refugees (UNHCR) in Thailand, Malaysia, Singapore, Indonesia, Hong Kong, Macao, and the Philippines. There, in what were called the "countries of first asylum" they were cared for and interviewed by American immigration authorities and their counterparts from other Western nations for possible movement to their homelands. Acceptance guaranteed what was called "third country resettlement." The vast majority of Vietnamese and Laotians who applied to come to the United States were eventually accepted and brought to this country.

Cambodians were not as fortunate. Victims not only of the international war but also of the terrible reign of Pol Pot and his Khmer Rouge, which took power in 1975, many had escaped into Thailand. There, additional border camps, operated by the UNHCR, were also set up. However, unlike most of the other camps, these were essentially holding centers. In general, only those who had fought with the Lon Nol forces allied with the United States and South Vietnam during the war, a relatively small percentage of those seeking resettlement in the United States, were considered and found eligible.

Under new regulations, the Vietnamese and other Indochinese refugees—and refugees from other lands at the time, including Cubans and Soviet Jews and Pentacostalists—entered the country with refugee status but the right to stay and apply for citizenship at the end of the prescribed period. In the process, their official status shifted from "refugee" to "immigrant," and, as they became acculturated, like other newcomers who often started their new lives in America within the confines of "nationality-based" enclaves, they quickly moved to the next stage, from immigrants to ethnics.

Today there are nearly 1 million Vietnamese and Laotian Americans and around 150,000 former Cambodians in the United States.

In the earliest days of their resettlement, not a few Americans had resented the presence of the refugees. Among those concerned were some African Americans and other nonwhites who argued that the public seemed more concerned with the refugees' plight than with their own continuing needs.[14] Yet, in the aggregate most Vietnamese, Laotians, and Cambodians found acceptance in American communities and made their marks, excelling in a variety of spheres. (These issues are discussed more fully in Chapter Ten.)

Among those who entered the United States from the three countries of Indochina were several groups who were minorities in the lands from which they fled. The most prominent of these are the so-called "ethnic Chinese." Others include tribal people from the highlands of Laos, especially the Hmong. Rejected and exploited in their own society, the Hmong were active allies of U.S. forces during the war.

Statistics gathered by the U.S. Immigration and Naturalization Service and the Bureau of the Census indicate that, in the past two decades, there has been a reverse migration of a small but steadily rising number of individuals who have decided to return to their native lands across the Pacific.[15] Most prominent are highly trained specialists in computers and other high-tech fields who are going back to participate in the economic booms in China and in the "minidragon" states—Taiwan, Singapore, Hong Kong, and Korea. In addition, a number of Vietnamese, Laotian, and Cambodian former refugees have returned home to help rebuild their former homelands.

Latinos

Long before they were to be listed under the rubric "Asian," Filipinos who came to this country were often classified with others having Spanish surnames, as "Hispanics." In fact, among those who share that personal characteristic, directly related to their colonial past, Filipinos comprise a small segment of a very large aggregate. In this country Hispanics, also called "Latinos" (the term many prefer), are in fact a multigroup cohort. In 2003 they became the nation's largest minority, outnumbering African Americans.

Those now grouped under the rubrics "Hispanic" or "Latino" include descendants of very early settlers living in areas taken over from Mexico after the Treaty of Guadalupe Hidalgo at the end of the Mexican American War, recent immigrants from Mexico and other Latin American countries, Cubans (who constitute the largest ethnic group in Miami), Dominicans (the fastest-growing foreign-born population in New York City[16]), and Puerto Ricans, who have been citizens since 1917.

Before being included as a separate census category, most people from any of the backgrounds just listed were more or less forced to identify themselves to enumerators as "White," or " Black," "Asian," "Native American, "or "Some Other Race;" although 48 percent chose to place themselves under the first rubric, 42 percent checked the last one. As Carlos Chardon, chairman of the Census Bureau's Hispanic advisory committee explained in a *New York Times* interview in October of 2004, "We don't fit into the categories that the Anglos want us to fit in."[17] Many opted for a new category: "Latino."

Associate director for the decennial census Preston Jay Waite countered that "if somebody writes down that their race is Latino, that doesn't give us any information about which of the race categories they're in. We're making up the race for 15 million people. We would prefer not to do it. It doesn't seem wise to me that we would put at risk the racial statistics of the nation in order to answer an interesting sociological question."[18] Waite seemed to fail to understand that the "interesting sociological question" about such a blatant example of addressing race as a social construction is at the very core of the concern of those who prefer not to call themselves by one of the fixed categories. As noted previously, many Puerto Ricans, Dominicans, and Cubans are of mixed African, Indian, and Spanish heritage, and most Mexicans are of Indian and Spanish background. Moreover, if asked, many will explain that they come from societies that are "racially continuous" rather than "racially dichotomous" like the United States.

The Mexicans

Perhaps second only to the native "Indian" peoples of what became the United States as the oldest Americans, the Mexicans are hardly migrants, at least in the modern sense. Of mixed racial parentage—Spanish and Indian—whose history dates back to the days of the Spanish conquest, they are often called *Hispanos.* The Southwest has been their traditional home for over four centuries. They became Americans by default when New Mexico, California, and other southwestern territories were ceded to the United States. Prior to their annexation, the social patterns of Mexican society prevailed in these territories, and the life ways of some of the descendants of those who lived there still mirror those of their countrymen south of the Rio Grande.

Shortly after the turn of the twentieth century, increasing numbers of laborers from Mexico crossed the border to work in the United States. Restrictions on overseas immigration during World War I gave impetus to this migration and almost a million Mexicans entered the country between 1910 and 1930. Most found employment doing "stoop labor" on huge farms and ranches in the southwestern states—Texas, Arizona, and California; some became migratory workers moving northward and eastward with the seasons. Over half of these newcomers took up residence in the United States, with increasing numbers gravitating to urban areas; eager to improve their lot and to earn enough money to send remittances back home, they seemed to recapitulate patterns of earlier immigrants from predominantly Catholic, peasant-like societies such as Ireland, Italy, Poland, and French Canada.

In time, especially in the years following World War II, many Mexican Americans would achieve middle-class status, a success story that is largely ignored by those more comfortable with traditional images of Mexican Americans.[19] Still, many Mexican Americans found their paths to mobility blocked by a variety of social barriers reinforced by a particular but convenient (at least for growers) form of racism that contended that Mexicans were only suited for farm labor. This widespread attitude served to keep many influential people in the Southwest from making the necessary changes in the educational system and in social welfare to assist the Mexican Americans in the *barrios* (or Mexican American enclaves) of El Paso and San Antonio, in Trinidad, Colorado, in Tucson, Arizona, and in Los Angeles and San Diego, as well as farm workers in the labor camps and the rural settlements that still pock the fertile valleys of California.

In such places (and similar ones throughout the Southwest) in the past, in addition to legally admitted immigrants, there were two other widely recognized types of migrants from Mexico: "wetbacks," so named for having crossed the Rio Grande illegally in search of employment; and *braceros,* those with permits to work as contract laborers under strict restriction. At its height in 1960, 427,000 entered as "guest workers." Few were admitted under the special provisions of the Mexican Laborer Acts after 1965 and none by 1970.

Although the bracero program was sharply curtailed, then phased out a number of years ago, many Mexicans continue to try to enter the United States to find work. Despite much greater surveillance of the border areas than ever before, undocumented Mexicans have continued to pour into the country. Their crossing is often facilitated by the assistance of "coyotes," men and women who make their living as smugglers of human beings. Even when captured and deported, it is not uncommon for those desperate to get to this country to try again.

Because they were often willing to work for lower wages or contracted in large groups for agricultural and industrial employment—the reason growers found them so attractive—American low-wage workers saw them as an economic threat. Some "Anglos" (as white people in the area are known), steeped in anti-Mexican sentiment, tried to exploit this resentment. To counteract this, several prominent farm worker leaders sought to join with them to fight for union representation and collective bargaining in the vineyards, lettuce fields, and orange groves where they toil. And not only did a growing sense of cohesiveness begin to assert itself among the disparate members of *La Raza,* but a demand for both political power and recognition of cultural pride began to be voiced by an increasing segment of this minority of as many as 8 million people.

"Chicano" (meaning "Little Mexicano") used to be a term of derogation, but for many so labeled in the 1960s it became a term of pride and solidarity. As one well-known Mexican American has said, "Call us whatever you like, we know what we are and are proud of it."[20]

Increasingly, the voices of Mexican Americans—Cesar Chavez in California, Corky Gonzalez in Colorado, Reyes Tijerina in New Mexico, and a variety of new leaders in Texas—were raised, and many, Anglos and Mexican Americans, started to listen closely. They saw changes that altered both the public stereotypes ("Frito Bandito") and the substance of life for Mexican Americans. In the late 1970s one factor, perhaps more than any other, boosted the self-esteem of Mexican Americans, as well as their brothers, sisters, and cousins south of the border. This was the discovery of enormous reserves of fossil fuel in Mexico, a deposit reportedly as large as that in Saudi Arabia. For the first time, the giant to the north was put on the defensive, and Mexicans possessed an important bargaining chip as they negotiated various matters of significance to them, not least immigration policies.[21]

Like other people so often categorized as "nonwhite" minorities, Mexican Americans are seeking a legitimate and equal place in a pluralistic America. The overwhelming majority is determined to be recognized for something far more important than the ubiquitous taco stands that dot the byways of the Southwest.

Today, Mexican Americans are the fastest growing "nationality" group in the United States and this fact has raised concerns in many quarters, not least in the ranks of those who still cling to the notion that, because they are the descendants of the early Anglo-Americans, they have certain entitlements that others are determined to take away from them. There was a time when it was the "unassimilable" Irish, then the Chinese of the "Yellow Peril," then the Jews who were seen as the principal subversives. Today, to some, it is the "brown wave of Mexicans" coming across the border that is said to be poised, not only to undercut the farm labor market but to destroy American civilization itself.

In a chapter in his recent book, *Who Are We?*, political scientist Samuel Hunting-ton minces few words in creating, or contributing to the creation of, a self-fulfilling prophecy. He writes that "The most powerful stimulus to white nativism is likely to be the threat to language, culture, and power that whites see coming from the expanding demographic, social, economic, and political roles of Hispanics [mean-ing, in this instance, Mexicans] in American society."[22] We will return to this argu-ment in Chapter Nine. For now, it is sufficient to indicate that of all the immigrant groups still trying to establish themselves in the United States, the Mexicans have become the most prominent lightning rod.

Before temporarily leaving the latest background in the immigration war, men-tion need be made of the tens of thousands of Central and South Americans other than Mexicans who cross the Rio Grande to enter the United States. Many of them, like a number of Mexican border-crossers, have no papers. Illegal aliens, they, too, are often known as "the undocumented." Although most today are traditional economic migrants eager for employment and opportunities for a better life, for many years some entered this country illegally hoping to find a safe haven from political persecution.

Unlike the refugees from Indochina, Cuba, and the Soviet Union, the agents of the Naturalization and Immigration Service (INS) frequently viewed the Central American asylum-seekers with suspicion. There are many explanations for this. One of the most plausible is that, despite changes in American immigration laws that no longer defined refugees as "individuals fleeing communism" (as they did from 1952–1980), the fact remains that government officials continued to favor those fleeing left-wing regimes (like those in Vietnam or Cuba) over those leaving countries the United States supports (such as El Salvador).

The Puerto Ricans

Often grouped with Mexican Americans and others called "Latinos," including those from South America and such island nations in the Caribbean as the Dominican Republic, are the Puerto Ricans. Although they too are of mixed racial origins and are Spanish-speaking, they are a distinct—and distinctive—people. They are neither refugees nor immigrants.

Puerto Rico has been an American possession since the end of the Spanish-American War. By their own choice the inhabitants of the island became United States citizens in 1917. (Until recently, few Americans knew this, nor much else about these fellow citizens. In fact, until the mid-1950s many mapmakers misspelled the name of their home island, calling it "Porto Rico.")

Migration from the island to the mainland began early in the twentieth century and continues today. Although movement back and forth has fluctuated with economic conditions in the states, since World War II, Puerto Rican migration, with a prime objective of staying in the United States has risen sharply, in large part because of increasing job opportunities, the appeal of the popular culture of large cities, and dramatically improved transportation facilities, which have dramatically closed the distance.

As in earlier days, New York is still the principal gateway for new arrivals, and as in the past, many who first arrive in New York remain there. Puerto Ricans—like their predecessors from Southern and Eastern Europe and southern blacks whose migration to New York has paralleled their own—have found employment in the garment industry and as service workers in the great commercial and tourist center.

Although Puerto Ricans are to be found in all parts of the country—including Alaska and Hawaii—over three-fourths of their total number live in New York, and many others in nearby areas.[23] Like other newcomers to the city, when they first came, the Puerto Ricans found themselves relegated to the worst and most overpriced neighborhoods. Their children attended crowded schools; they often held the lowest-status jobs; they frequently suffered "winter temperatures and more chilling social contacts."[24] Unfortunately, despite the fact that in many ways they have come better prepared for life in the United States than many other ethnic minorities, they are still having difficulty climbing the ladder.[25]

Census Bureau data provides graphic evidence of the difficulties Puerto Ricans have in succeeding, despite the fact that they are far more likely to have come from urban areas and have a much higher proportion of skilled and semiskilled workers than the native population. Furthermore, in contradiction to the assertion that "primarily Puerto Rico's unemployed come to New York," it has been found that the migrants were more regularly employed than the rest of the population back home and received a slightly higher income than the Puerto Rican average. They continue to come not to seek work, but to seek better work. Finding it for many is still a problem and nearly a third of Puerto Rican families continue to live below the poverty level.[26]

There is little question that Puerto Ricans have faced considerable racial discrimination in the United States. Some specialists feel it has been especially hard for members of this particular cohort to cope with the "racially dichotomous" (white versus nonwhite) character of mainland thinking, a rather sharp contrast to the "racially continuous" (from white to black) situation on their home island. In fact, Puerto Ricans were the first major group to migrate to the urban centers of the United States that brought with them a tradition of widespread racial mixing. Although it is true that lighter-skinned Puerto Ricans generally have higher status in San Juan than New York, there are many exceptions. Indeed, it is said "on the mainland, the color of a person determines what class he will belong to; in Puerto Rico, the class a person belongs to determines his color." Another popular expression for the same phenomenon is that "money whitens!"

The Cubans

The Spanish-American War began in February 1898 with the sinking of the American ship known as the *Maine* in Havana harbor. The war ended less than a year later with the signing of the Treaty of Paris. As a result, Spain lost its far-flung empire that stretched from the Philippines and Guam in the Pacific to the nearby Caribbean islands of Puerto Rico and Cuba.

Until the Cuban Revolution in 1959, in addition to those historical facts, most Americans knew Cuba only as a series of snapshot images: Teddy Roosevelt and his Rough Riders charging up San Juan Hill; stories by Ernest Hemingway and Graham Greene; glossy pictures of bars and beaches in Old Havana, and as the locale of a one-night fling by Sky Masterson and his Salvation Army girlfriend in the 1955 musical *Guys and Dolls*.

At that time there were relatively few Cubans in the United States. Of those who were here, mostly in southern Florida, some were in business, some were students, and most were laborers. With the fall of the dictator Fulgencio Batista, and the coming to power of Fidel Castro, hundreds of thousands of Cubans sought and gained admittance to this country as exiles from the new, communist regime.

Between 1959 and 1970 some 700,000 refugees entered the United States, most arriving and staying in the Miami area.[27] Although some were exceedingly wealthy, the majority was of modest means and had to start their lives anew. That these "refugees from communism" were successful accounted for the favorable press they began to receive across the country and the reception extended by a government that often seemed blind to the suffering of others, such as thousands of Haitians, who took great risks to cross open water to get into the country.

In south Florida, however, things were different. Other asylum seekers envied the Cubans—and their tight knit community organization—and they were frequently resented even more by the old minorities, especially African Americans, who claimed the Cubans were elbowing their ways into the system and taking jobs away from members of their community. As the Cubans began to move into the political arena, the tensions rose even higher.

In 1980, a second large wave (approximately 150,000) of Cuban exiles made the 90–mile trip to the Florida coast. These "boat people" were quite different from those in the "first wave." They were generally poorer and less well educated. And many more were black.

Among the boat people were a large subgroup who, unlike those who fled from Cuba, had been given permission by Fidel Castro to go. They sailed from the port of Mariel. It was rumored that Castro saw his chance to rid the country of numbers of criminals and mentally retarded persons and, indeed, some such people were among the Marielitos. Wary of this ploy, American officials allowed them to be "saved at sea" and brought to the beach but they were not given the same refugee status as their countrymen. They were subject to deportation or detention whenever they violated a law, no matter how petty. It took twenty-five years to regularize their status and to remove the blot on the reputation of the vast majority of those who came from Mariel. In January 2005, the Supreme Court handed down the ruling that the open-ended detention policy was illegal and, as writer Mirta Ojita reported, "The highest court in the land they have chosen as their own has validated the status not only of those convicted of crimes but of all Cubans who in 1980 set sail for the United States.[28]

In the late 1980s, thousands of political refugees from Guatemala, El Salvador, and Nicaragua entered the country illegally, mainly from Mexico. Although the authorities were highly selective in their willingness to consider such undocumented aliens as refugees—being somewhat more kindly disposed to those fleeing Nicaragua, a Marxist state, than El Salvador, an ally of the United States and heavily supported by American aid—they finally did allow large numbers to stay in the country, at least temporarily. In January 1989, a large contingent of Nicaraguans moved from the border areas in Texas to Miami and Dade County, Florida, where they were assisted by various social service and employment agencies, many of them run by sympathetic Cuban Americans. The presence of these Central American anticommunists, the political allies of the Cuban expatriates, greatly exacerbated an already strained relationship between the city's black and Hispanic populations and resulted in several days of violent confrontation.

In recent decades, Cuban and other refugees and immigrants from Latin America have succeeded in making Miami one of the principal bilingual, bicultural cities in the United States, often, it is argued, especially by African Americans, at their expense. That reality, coupled with fears expressed by so-called Anglos about the "Mexican invasion" in the Southwest and, especially, in California, is already the subject of much debate about the future of American society, the rights of groups and individuals, and the long dominant "majority culture." These disputes have been occurring simultaneously with the growing chasm between two cultural camps, overly simplified in the election season of 2004 as "red" (mainly conservative, fundamentalist, and Republican) and "blue" (liberal, permissive, and Democratic), each vying for support from certain new American groups. A principal prize for both sides was seen—and will be seen—as the support of Hispanic Americans.

Summing Up

The pie chart (figure 5.1) graphically illustrates the finding of the United States Census Bureau: In 2002 52.2 percent of the foreign-born came from Latin American countries (including those of Central America and the Caribbean); 25.5 percent from Asia, and only 14.0 percent from Europe.

Between 2002 and 2005, while the percentage of immigrants from Asian countries remained relatively constant (around 23 percent), the percentage of Latinos continued to climb, hovering at 60 percent. At present, over two-thirds of Asian immigrants have been entering the United States with college degrees, and only a very small percent (mostly refugees from Cambodia and Laos) lack much formal schooling.

Statistics on the latest migration from Mexico and other Latin American countries show this pattern in reverse, with far fewer (13 percent) holding bachelor's degrees and many more falling under the rubric "Unskilled." The jury is still out as to whether these newcomers will overcome their handicaps and recapitulate the successful mobility of earlier groups, including those severely impoverished, but there are many signs that, eager to fulfill their own American dreams, they, too, will make it in this country.

Many of those who voluntarily migrated to America in the nineteenth and twentieth centuries left their countries of origin seeking freedom and a new life in the New World. Some came to make their fortunes; some came to escape religious persecution or political tyranny; the majority came for economic reasons. For most, immigration was the beginning of a new and exciting adventure, but

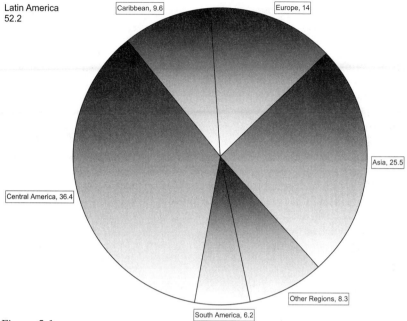

Figure 5.1
Foreign Born by Region of Birth: 2002 (in percent).
Source: Chart prepared by U.S. Census Bureau.

for others the journey to America was a bitter and harrowing experience as it still remains for some.

In the brief sketches of America's principal immigrant groups presented in this chapter and the previous one the reception of newcomers by those already in the United States is only occasionally touched upon. But in Chapter Six a discussion of various proposals for coping with "strangers" in the land, an interpretation of these, an examination of the patterns of ethnic separation that emerged, and a statistical breakdown of America's racial, religious, and ethnic composition are considered.

Notes

1. See Ronald Takaki (ed.), *From Different Shores* (New York: Oxford University Press, 1987).
2. See, for example, Rose Hum Lee, *The Chinese in the United States of America* (New York: Oxford University Press, 1960); Francis L. K. Hsu, *Challenge of the American Dream: The Chinese in the U.S.* (Belmont, Calif.: Wadsworth, 1971); and Stanford M. Lyman, *Chinese-Americans* (New York: Random House, 1973).
3. Marcus Lee Hansen, *The Problem of the Third Generation Immigrant* (Rock Island, Il: The Augustana Historical Society, 1938). Many studies have suggested that the hypothesis is hardly generalizable to all or even most immigrant populations. See, for example, Peter Kivisto and Dag Blanck (eds.), *American Immigrants and Their Generations* (Urbana: University of Illinois Press, 1990.)

4. Harry H. L. Kitano, *Japanese Americans* (Englewood Cliffs, N.J.: Prentice-Hall, 1969), p. 17.

5. Ibid. See also William Petersen, *Japanese Americans: Oppression and Success* (New York: Random House, 1971).

6. Leonard Bloom and Ruth Riemer, *Removal and Return* (Berkeley: University of California Press, 1949), pp. 202–204. See also Maisie and Richard Conrad, *Executive Order 9066: The Internment of 110,000 Japanese-Americans* (Sacramento: California Historical Society, 1976).

7. Stanford M. Lyman, "Japanese-American Generation Gap," *Society* 10 (January–February 1973), p. 55–63.

8. See Petersen, *Japanese Americans.*

9. The discussion of South Asians and Filipinos that follows is an updated and amended section—"The Other Asians"—of a longer essay by the author. See Peter I. Rose, "Asian Americans: From Pariahs to Paragons," in Nathan Glazer (ed.), *Clamor at the Gates* (San Francisco: Institute for Contemporary Studies, 1989), pp. 196–203

10. Maxine Fisher, *The Indians of New York City: A Study of Immigrants from India* (Columbia, MO: South Asia Books, 1980).

11. Lemuel Ignacio, *Asian Americans and Pacific Islanders: Is There Such an Ethnic Group?* (San Jose: Philipino Development Associates, Inc., 1976).

12. Fisher, op. cit., pp. 136–137.

13. See Antonio J. A. Pido, *The Pilipinos in America* (New York: Center for Migration Studies, 1985), p. 87.

14. See Jeremy Hein, *From Vietnam, Laos, and Cambodia: A Refugee Experience in the United States* (New York: Twayne, 1995).

15. For a brief summary, see Ashley Dunn, "Skilled Asians Leaving U.S. for High-Tech Jobs at Home," *New York Times* (February 21, 1995), 1, B5.

16. "Record Immigration Is Changing the Face of New York's Neighborhoods," *New York Times* (January 24, 2005), A16.

17. Rachel L. Swarns, "Hispanics Debate Census Plan to Change Racial Grouping," *New York Times* (October 24, 2004), 1, 16.

18. Ibid., p. 16.

19. See Lionel Sosa, *The Americano Dream* (New York: Plume, 1998).

20. See Ilan Stavans, *The Hispanic Condition: Reflections on Culture and Identity in America* (New York: Harper Collins, 1995).

21. See John H. Burma (ed.), *Mexican-Americans in the United States* (New York: Schenkman, 1970); Ellwyn Stoddard, *Mexican-Americans* (New York: Random House, 1973); and Joan Moore, *Mexican Americans,* 2d ed. (Englewood Cliffs, N.J.: Prentice-Hall, 1976) and such recent studies as Peter Skerry, *Mexican Americans: The Ambivalent Minority* (Cambridge: Harvard University Press, 1993) and Marcelo M. Suarez-Orozco (ed.), *Crossings: Mexican Immigration in Interdisciplinary Perspectives* (Cambridge: Harvard University Press, 1998).

22. As quoted in Peter I. Rose, "Damned Yankees?" *Congress Monthly* (September/October 2004), 13.

23. Joseph P. Fitzpatrick, *The Puerto Rican New Yorkers* (Englewood Cliffs, N.J.: Prentice Hall, 2nd edition, 1987), p. 15.

24. Clarence Senior, *Strangers—Then Neighbors* (New York: Freedom Books, 1961), p.

25. See also Elena Padilla, *Up from Puerto Rico* (New York: Columbia University Press, 1958); Christopher Rand, *The Puerto-Ricans* (New York: Oxford University Press, 1958); and Patricia Cayo Sexton, *Spanish Harlem* (New York: Harper, 1965).

26. See report by Edward C. Burks, "Affluence Eludes Blacks, Puerto-Ricans," *New York Times* (August 17, 1972), 33.

27. Vincent N. Parrillo, *Strangers to These Shores* (Boston: Houghton Mifflin, 1980), p. 417.

28. See Alejandro Portes and Robert L. Bach, *Latin Journey: Cuban and Mexican Immigrants in the United States* (Berkeley: University of California Press, 1985).

29. Mirta Ojita, "The Long Voyage from Mariel Ends," *The New York Times' News of the Week in Review* (January 16, 2005), 3.

Chapter 6

The Dilemmas of Diversity

Coming Full Circle

Sometime in the spring of 1970 a significant part of the "American saga" seemed to come full circle. An attempt was made by a dozen Mohawks to establish a beachhead on Ellis Island, the place where thousands upon thousands of European immigrants had first touched American shores. The motorboat failed and the plot to seize the island on the East Coast as others had seized the island of Alcatraz in San Francisco Bay was foiled.

When someone suggested, "the Indians were stupid for attempting the occupation of the island," a member of the raiding party retorted, "We're stupid? It was your ancestors who landed on these shores, thought they were somewhere else, and called *us* Indians. Indians live on the other side of the world!"

That bit of repartee is more profound than it seems on the surface. In a few words it expresses the frustration of many American minority group members who know that they are seen as ignorant, sneaky, sullen, argumentative, or aggressive and the descendants of the white Europeans seem to fancy themselves as paragons of virtue and intelligence as they have since the earliest days of nationhood.

Ko Lum Bo

But suppose, as George Stewart once suggested, that the English and other North Europeans had not settled our eastern shores first. Suppose that the approach had been from the west and that Asians, rather than Europeans, had landed and established political and cultural hegemony over the new territories. Stewart put it this way:

... during one of the vigorous and expansive periods of the Chinese Empire, one of their navigators (who might have been named Ko Lum Bo) conceived the idea of sailing eastward from China and thus arriving at Ireland, which was known to be the farthest outpost of Europe. The Chinese wished to reach Ireland it may be believed, because they had heard tales that those barbarous islanders made a certain drink called Wis Ki.

Ko Lum Bo made his voyage, and discovered a country that he supposed to be part of Ireland, although he was disappointed in not finding any Wis Ki being manufactured by the natives.

During the course of the next two centuries the Chinese colonized this country, eventually discovering it to be not Ireland, but a wholly new continent. Nevertheless they continued to call the natives Irish, or sometimes Red Irish.

The Chinese colonists introduced their own well-established ways of life. They continued to speak Chinese, and to practice their own religion. Being accustomed to eat rice, they still ate it, as far as possible. Vast areas of the country were terraced and irrigated as rice paddies. The colonists continued to use their comfortable flowing garments, and pagodas dotted the landscape. In short, the civilization was Asiatic and not European.[1]

Dropping Stewart's delightful and pointed bit of social science fiction, we hardly have to remind ourselves that it was Christopher Columbus and other European explorers who first laid claim to the New World, bringing with them their ideas and values and rules from Spain and France and, especially, England to this continent. The English and other North Europeans who had the greatest impact on what were to become the original states of the union came on their wooden barks carrying along much of their own cultural baggage, which, from the start, they thought superior to that of the natives. Manners of speaking and dressing, organizing communities, regulating commerce, teaching and preaching were transplanted across the Atlantic. Of course, the New World (and, especially, the hinterlands of North America) was of a scale that was hard to comprehend.

As the new society developed, adjustments were constantly necessary. Innovations were commonplace. Even so, many aspects of the colonists' cultures were retained. And so, like the Chinese who never came (at least not in the manner imagined), the English and others who did developed modified versions of their old societies. And all who were here (meaning the diverse tribes of indigenous Americans) or were to come (including thousands of slaves and millions of immigrants), discussed in the preceding two chapters, were to be affected by the laws and life ways of the Anglo-American Establishment.

In Search of a Dream

For four centuries America served as a magnet—first for the rich and venturesome and later for the "tired and poor and tempest-tost."[2] The majority of immigrants—English, Irish, German, Scandinavian, Italian, Jewish, and Slav and, more recently, Latino and Asian—came of their own free will, ready and willing to share in the wealth and bounty of America. Many were disillusioned; many suffered from discrimination by those who had so recently been newcomers themselves; many found it difficult to reconcile their Old World ways with those of the new.

Some expressed their frustration by profaning "The Discoverer" himself. In 1892, when the majority was enthusiastically celebrating 400 years since Columbus's "discovery," there were those who saw him and his exploits in very different terms—and said so. "A curse on Columbus," they said in Yiddish and Russian and Polish. Even in the language of his putative *paisani* it was sometimes said: "*Maladitu lamerica e chi la spirminta*"—"Curses on America . . . and the man who thought it up."[3]

Those who recited such maledictions were hardly, like the critics of today, damning Columbus for his "hegemonistic Eurocentricity." They were not disdaining his treatment of the native population or pointing to the rape of resources. They swore at the Genoese mercenary for less lofty reasons. In mock sorrow they deplored the fact that he ever found the place that was, to them, no shining medina where the streets were paved with gold but, instead, cities that were urban jungles and, beyond, a rugged, untamed, uncivilized wilderness. Their sarcastic epithets were spewed out in frustration rather than as true critiques.

In spite of the difficulties and disappointments—and there were many—and despite the divisions and conflicts between the various waves of newcomers and their "hosts," for those *who were white,* almost all things were to prove possible. The early dreams did become realities. As Raymond Aron, the French sociologist, accurately observed:

> As far as I am concerned, the greatest achievement of American society is to have drawn millions of people from the lower classes of Europe and made them into good American citizens. That is an extraordinary performance, an unprecedented marvel of acculturation.
>
> But you didn't do it without paying a heavy price. Poverty in America is aggravated by ethnic heterogeneity, by the unfinished acculturation of certain fragments of the American population. You have a permanently unintegrated fringe, consisting chiefly of Blacks and Puerto Ricans. You did very well in assimilating national minorities, but not nearly as well with racial minorities.[4]

There are various explanations of these facts of American life. One that is the simplest is quite persuasive. Those who proposed programs for the best way of integrating disparate peoples into a single nation did so generally without regard to color and yet rarely were "colored people" ever seriously considered on a par with white immigrants. The theorists and policy makers dealt with those they saw as "national" minorities, not racial ones—at least not until recently.

Eurocentric Ideas of the Integration Process

The nature of adjustment of increasing numbers of immigrants to life in America has been of concern to both scholars and politicians since the early days of the colonial period. In the deliberations and debates over the problem of integrating ethnically heterogeneous peoples into a unified, English-speaking national group, various courses of action with explicit goals in mind have been promulgated. Three of the most discussed theories of adjustment have been popularly referred to as "Anglo conformity" (a term coined by George Stewart and Mildred Cole), "the melting pot," and "cultural pluralism."[5] In sociological terms, these social processes are *assimilation, amalgamation,* and *accommodation,* respectively.

Assimilation

During the eighteenth century the majority of those who had come to America— white, Anglo-Saxon, Protestant—participated in the establishment of what some have described as "the first new nation." The United States itself was conceived in the spirit of liberty and dedicated to the belief "that all men are created equal ... endowed by their Creator with certain inalienable Rights." However, the authors of these phrases shared the belief of many others that American social norms and values of the future lay within the framework of traditionally British social, religious, and cultural institutions; and, although America was sometimes envisaged as an asylum for Europe's refugees, some of the leading figures of the day had strong reservations about what the effects of unrestricted immigration might be. In *The Federalist Papers,* John Jay argued that the Americans were "a united people, a people descended from the same ancestors, speaking the same language, professing the same religion, attached to the same principles of government, very similar in their manners and customs."[6] As for those who didn't quite fit the profile, George Washington expressed the following view: "My opinion, with respect to immigration, is that except of useful mechanics and some particular descriptions of men or professions, there is no need of encouragement, while the policy or advantage of its taking place in a body (I mean the settling of them in a body) may be much questioned; for, by so doing, they retain the language, habits and principles (good or bad) which they bring with them."[7]

Most of those who thought an open-door policy should prevail emphatically maintained that the immigrants "should discard their foreign mantles" (an expression referring to European attitudes and mannerisms) and quickly adapt themselves to *American* ways. John Adams made this position quite clear when he wrote: "They come to a life of independence, but to a life of labor—and, if they cannot accommodate themselves to the character, moral, political, and physical, of this country with all its compensating balances of good and evil, the Atlantic is always open to them to return to the land of their nativity and their fathers. . . . They must cast off the European skin, never to resume it."[8]

If the Founding Fathers had their ideas about the best course of national integration, so, too, did many of the newcomers.[9] The immigrants often envisioned America as a vast land affording unlimited economic and social opportunities in an atmosphere free from harassment and interference. By the mid-nineteenth century many came to this country with clear intentions of maintaining their separate cultural identities. The Germans, for example, who settled in Wisconsin, Missouri, and Texas, succeeded in establishing a number of settlements where the German language was the vernacular and where German nationalism persisted, even though they had to modify many behavior patterns to adjust to the new frontier they faced.

According to historian Frederick Jackson Turner, assimilation itself was enhanced by the opportunities that abounded on the frontier. Writing especially about the settlement and acculturation of German immigrants, Turner stated:

> Our early history is the study of European germs developing in an American environment. Too exclusive attention has been paid by institutional students to the Germanic origins, too little to the American factors. The frontier is the line of most rapid and effective Americanization. The wilderness masters the colonist. It finds him a European in dress, industries, tools, modes of travel, and thought. It takes him from the railroad car and puts him in the birch canoe. It strips off the garments of civilization and arrays him in the hunting shirt and the moccasin. It puts him in the log cabin of the Cherokee and Iroquois and runs an Indian palisade around him. Before long he has gone to planting Indian corn and plowing with a sharp stick; he shouts the war cry and takes the scalp in orthodox fashion. In short, at the frontier the environment is at first too strong for the man. He must accept the conditions which it furnishes, or perish, and so he fits himself into the Indian clearings and follows the Indian trails. Little by little he transforms the wilderness but the outcome is not the old Europe, not simply the development of Germanic germs, any more than the first phenomenon was a case of reversion to the Germanic mark. The fact is that here is a new product that is American.[10]

Turner continued, making a second point: the farther west people traveled, the greater the influence of the frontier and the less the counterpulls of the Old Country. "Thus," he wrote, "the advance of the frontier has meant a steady movement away from the influence of Europe, a steady growth of independence on American lines."[11]

For many years westerners, especially Californians, made a corroborating point, claiming what is now popularly called "ethnicity" is much more an "Eastern" phenomenon than a "Western" one. Referring mainly to those of European origins, they would say that if you ask a New Yorker or Philadelphian or even a Chicagoan where he or she comes from, the answer would likely be "Ireland," "Russia," "Italy," "Poland," or perhaps, "England." But if you ask a person from Los Angeles or San Jose the same question, the reply is more apt to be "Kansas," "Oklahoma," or "back East." In recent decades, there has been a notable inversion of this tendency. Many second and third generation Americans with roots in Asia whose parents or grandparents first settled in Hawaii or on the West Coast and then moved east, identify themselves as being Hawaiian or Californian though many whites persist in seeing them as foreigners.[12]

Still, it is the fact that on either coast and in many cities in between, even casual probing reveals the existence and persistence of ethnic ties and the maintenance of many ethnic communities and neighborhoods. Such enclaves, as noted in Chapter 3, have long existed. They were evident even on the frontier itself. One thinks of those of the Scandinavians, rugged farmers and fishers idealized in Willa Cather's *O Pioneers,* Ole Rolvaag's *Giants in the Earth,* and in Vilhelm Moberg's trilogy, *The*

Emigrants, Unto a Good Land, and *The Last Letter Home.* Although some settled in the Delaware Basin, most did not dally long on the East Coast but moved on to the prairies and woodlands of the northern Midwest, areas that became strongholds of Swedish and Norwegian culture and religion.[13] Their trek to the wilderness, first by wagon train, later by rail, was a lesson in adaptation but also a study in resistance to change as well. They attacked the frontier and shaped it; perhaps, some might say, more than it shaped them—reversing the variables in the Turner hypothesis. Isolation from the dominant drift of American social patterns permitted the widespread and long-lived retention of their "foreign" life ways, many of which continue to this day.

As indicated in Chapter 4, the Irish—and most of the other immigrants who came later—tended to concentrate in urban areas where it was more difficult to maintain a separate existence. Yet, the presence of these new immigrants in the same communities as the older Americans brought about a reevaluation of sentiments about assimilation. The newcomers, whose backgrounds differed even more radically than those of the Germans or Scandinavians from those of the early settlers, were often viewed as constituting a substantial threat to the established majority. Time and again, that "Establishment" asked, "Could *these* aliens ever become real Americans?"

Labor unrest and agitation attributed largely to the "foreign elements" in the population, the specter of Catholicism in Protestant America, and the growth of overcrowded urban slums inhabited by groups of oddly dressed people who seemed to speak in various forms of gibberish revived and reinforced antiforeign attitudes. As a result of those developments, new movements arose to keep the United States "American."

First there was the anti-Irish Know-Nothing party of the pre–Civil War period. In the 1890s the American Protective Association was created to "save the country from the papacy." Later, anti-Semitic organizations arose, including the Ku Klux Klan (which was also violently anti-Negro) and other hate groups mirroring earlier nativist sentiment and the pronouncements of such prominent Americans as the novelist Kenneth Roberts, the industrialist Henry Ford, the aviator Charles Lindbergh, and the "radio priest" Father Charles Coughlin.[14]

We are reminded that it was in 1882 the first restrictive legislation was passed to limit the flow of immigrants (in this case, Chinese laborers) to the United States. In the years that followed, increasing numbers of European nationals established ethnic communities where many Old World customs were perpetuated, and resentment grew against them as well. New organizations, such as the Immigration Restriction League, were established to "reform" immigration policies. Such groups and their growing cadres of allies were eventually successful in realizing their goals of sharply curtailing the influx of outsiders. But in the four decades between the beginning of "The Great Migration" and the closing of the gates for all but a tiny number of would-be Americans by further restrictive legislation—the "Quote Acts" of 1921 and 1924—many felt something had to be done to come to address the more immediate problem of dealing with immigrants who were arriving at the rate of a million a year and whose political strength alone was very great. A new kind of assimilationist policy emerged to enforce more directly the adoption of American ways. This was the Americanization Movement, which, through propaganda and education, sought to break down the immigrants' ties to the past.

Here is how Henry Pratt Fairchild described the situation in 1926:

> It was perhaps in keeping with the interest and faith in education, which has been called the outstanding feature of the American nationality, that the task of Americanization should have presented itself to the pioneers in the movement primarily as an educational matter. Recognizing that the process of assimilation consists in the elimination of unlikeness, it was natural that in considering the unlikeness of the foreigner they should have been impressed with the difference in what he knew. It was perfectly clear that one of the great barriers that separated the native from the foreigner was the fact that the native knew certain things that the foreigner did not know. Prominent among these were the English language and United States civics and history. The first and most obvious step in Americanization, therefore, seemed to be to teach these things to the foreigner.
>
> Thereupon there was launched upon the country one of the most remarkable campaigns of intensive specialized education that the world has ever known. Every conceivable educational device was utilized. The land was flooded with lessons, lectures, and literature. Night schools and shop classes were organized. Rallies, pageants, and conferences were held. A special magazine was established and issued for a few numbers. An elaborate training course for workers among immigrants was planned and offered for adoption among colleges and universities. As the movement grew, and the needs of the immigrant woman as well as the immigrant man were recognized, classes were set up in millinery, dressmaking, diet, and the American care of babies. To these enterprises time, money, and personal service were contributed by men and women, professionals and volunteers, with a devotion and enthusiasm which could be enlisted only by loyalty to the nation in a time of stress and danger. Coming at any other time, when we were not accustomed to displays of self-sacrifice and public spirit, the Americanization movement would have been a striking exhibition of the operation of altruistic sentiments.[15]

Fairchild went on to describe the failure of the movement, which, in his eyes, was never clearly understood for it confused means with ends and its advocates never really appreciated the difficulties of altering character along with language instruction and history lessons. There was more to divesting oneself of "alien" ways than the protagonists, many of them vehemently xenophobic, could understand or effectively deal with.

To be sure, many advocates of Americanization were not antiforeign but were troubled by what they saw as the slowness of assimilation and the growing potential for conflicts, especially during the World War I period. They felt the need for a device to unite the people. Yet, whether antiforeign or assimilationist, there was often the common view that every effort should be made to get newcomers to rid themselves of their old ways. The sentiment was summarized by one American who expressed the views of many nativists. "I am sure foreign people make a mistake in keeping customs of their own land alive and featured in this country. If this country meets their expectations they should forget the folklore of Europe, St. Patrick's

Day Parades, German Days, and get behind American things. If they can't do this they should be returned to the land they love. This country is supposed to be the world's melting pot. If they won't melt, they should not belong."[16]

This is, to be sure, a rather odd rendering of the melting pot expression, which, as shall be explained, referred to combining with, rather than accepting the ways of others. But it is typical of the sentiment of those who saw their country being threatened and changed by outsiders. Similar expressions have been heard in recent years.[17]

Amalgamation

Although the idea of assimilation—or "Anglo conformity"—was most prevalent through much of our history, there have been other views about the best way to achieve "*E pluribus Unum*," an integrated society. Some hoped to develop a society where the "best" traditions of the various nations would be blended into a dynamic unity. This conception of amalgamation was already established in the years immediately following the American Revolution and is clearly illustrated in comments of the French-born, naturalized American J. Hector St. John de Crévecoeur. In his 1782 *Letters from an American Farmer,* he described the new American as he saw him:

> He is either a European or the descendant of a European; hence, that strange mixture of blood, which you will find in no other country. . . . He is an American, who, leaving behind him all his ancient prejudices and manners, receives new ones from the new mode of life he has embraced, the new government he obeys, and the new rank he holds. . . . Here individuals of all nations are melted into a new race of men, whose labours and posterity will one day cause great changes in the world. Americans are the western pilgrims, who are carrying along with them the great mass of arts, sciences, vigor, and industry, which began long since in the east. They will finish the circle.[18]

The English writer Israel Zangwill expanded on Crévecoeur's idea to include persons from every corner of the globe. In a preface to his play, "The Melting Pot," dedicated to President Theodore Roosevelt, a vehement opponent of hyphenation, Zangwill wrote: "In respectful recognition of his strenuous struggle against the forces that threaten to shipwreck the great republic which carries mankind and its fortunes ... ," and then portrayed America as "God's Crucible:" "There she lies, the great melting pot—listen! Can't you hear the roaring and the bubbling? There gapes her mouth—the harbour where a thousand mammoth feeders come from the ends of the world to pour in their human freight. Ah, what a stirring and a seething—Celt and Latin, Slav and Teuton, Greek and Syrian, Black and yellow— ... Jew and Gentile. . . ."[19] The politician William Jennings Bryan echoed the sentiments of Zangwill. "Great has been the Greek, the Latin, the Slav, the Celt, the Teuton, and the Saxon; but greater than any of these is the American, who combines the virtues of them all."[20]

Summarizing the views of various writers, sociologists Donald Light and Suzanne Keller indicate that both assimilation and amalgamation are more likely to be possible when "(1) the immigrants' appearance and customs resemble those of the dominant group, (2) they arrive in small numbers, (3) they are too far from their homeland to return for visits, and (4) they possess skills that the dominant group admire and need."[21]

The problem of immigrant adjustment often has been presented as an either/or proposition. The assimilationists argue that newcomers must become apostates from their old and established ways, "get behind American things," and reconcile themselves to the new and strange way of life of the host society. Those supporting the melting pot view feel that people should merge themselves through cultural fusion.

The first position presumes that by forcibly assimilating immigrants to a single, already established pattern, in time they would benefit from a way of life superior to that which they brought to America. But many newcomers, however eager they were to become Americans, were understandably reluctant to abandon their familiar ways, and many resisted the more draconic aspects of the Americanization campaign.

The melting pot philosophy, although far more democratic in intent, came to be seen by many keen observers as unrealistic. People were not about to simply mix together in the great crucible to form one new American type, the result of a blend of the cultural ingredients of Europe, Africa, and Asia. Recognition of these facts of social life encouraged the emergence of the idea of cultural pluralism.

Accommodation

As the sociologist Milton Gordon once suggested, "Cultural pluralism was a fact in American society before it became a theory—a theory with explicit relevance for the nation as a whole.[22] This theory developed into an image of the United States as a country enhanced by its diversity. Against the ideas of both absorption and fusion, advocates of pluralism saw America as "a multiplicity in a unity."[23] Jane Addams, John Dewey, and Randolph Bourne were among those who spoke out against the policy of "Americanization" and the destruction of traditional cultural values of immigrants. But no one more eloquently presented the case for cultural pluralism than the philosopher Horace Kallen. He likened the new society to a symphony orchestra:

> As in an orchestra, every type of instrument has its special timbre and tonality, found in its substances and form; as every type has its appropriate theme and melody in the whole symphony, so in society each ethnic group is the natural instrument, its spirit and culture are its theme and melody, and the harmony and dissonances and discords of them all make the symphony of civilization, with this difference: a musical symphony is written before it is played; in the symphony of civilization the playing is the writing, so that there is nothing so fixed and inevitable about its progressions as in music, so that within the limits set by nature they may vary at will, and the range and variety of the harmonies may become wider and richer and more beautiful.[24]

Advocates of cultural pluralism based their case on the assumption that there is strength in variety, that the nation as a whole benefits from the contributions of different groups. Cultural pluralism involves giving and taking and, most importantly, the sharing of and mutual respect for other ideas, customs, and values. In such terms America could be seen as a mosaic of ethnic groups (that Whitmanesque "nation of nations"), each retaining its unique qualities while contributing to the overall pattern. Some were later to want to replace the metaphor of a melting pot with that of a "salad bowl," where the various ingredients were still quite distinctive.

Kallen's pluralism was especially appealing to the immigrants from Eastern and Southern Europe. At the time, others, including those in the small Asian communities and the growing Latino ones, seem to have paid it little mind. The same was true of the far larger black community. For good reason. It was heavily biased, "encapsulated," as historian John Higham put it, "in white ethnocentrism."[25]

Although generally sympathetic and frequently in league with supporters of better treatment to those still called Negroes, few of the pluralists had had much to say about the contribution of those from Africa, or, for that matter, from Asia or Latin America, to the society they liked to characterize as "The New America." As Bob Suzuki and Nicholas Appleton pointed out, when first proposed, "Pluralism in the United States was concerned with liberty and equality [of European immigrants] and not with promoting the historic identities of non-English subcultures."[26] The latter was not to come until the last decades of the twentieth century, when "multiculturalism" became an alternate shibboleth, a slogan most enthusiastically endorsed by nonwhite Americans and looked upon with considerable suspicion by many others.

We now know that the acculturation and acceptance of the "national minorities" to which Raymond Aron referred did occur, but not overnight. It was a slow and uneven process, taking place mainly in the four decades between the mid-1920s and the mid-1960s, a time when immigration from outside was almost at a standstill and debates shifted from the rights of foreigners to the rights of Americans; a time when the society underwent a series of dramatic political and economic reversals as well: boom, bust, war, peace, prosperity, and the wrenching conflicts in Vietnam and the streets of America. Affecting the speed of the integration were a number of cultural, social, and situational factors, many related to these ups and downs.

Despite periodic resurgences of old prejudices and the implementation of new ways of blocking entry to neighborhoods, jobs, and social institutions, and a number of serious interethnic conflicts,[27] the majority of white ethnics did begin to move from the margins into the mainstream. Especially after World War II, often abetted by such entitlements for schooling and housing as the G.I. Bill for armed service veterans, the *arrivistes* faced a world of expanding opportunities and took advantage of them. Although some were left behind, increasing numbers moved to new homes in new neighborhoods where they were to enjoy life as proud, patriotic Americans, often defining themselves more in class terms rather than strictly ethnic ones.

One result of their "making it" was the loosening of many bonds to old communities. But, in most cases, the ties were rarely severed completely. Even in what some saw as a twilight of [white] ethnicity,"[28] there was almost always a glow of nostalgia and the retention of symbolic ties.[29] Perhaps a new, more accurate metaphor would be that of a "lumpy stew," which, like the salad idea, still has clearly distinctive parts—in this instance, some sort of anthropomorphized chunks of meat, potatoes, carrots, and so forth—but also is held together by an ever thickening glutinous binder of common values and beliefs.

In the early part of the century, most of those who spoke for cultural plural-ism emphasized the fact that ethnic groups ("nationalities," as they were called) should have the right to remain separated, and Kallen, in an oft-quoted sentence, suggested that individuals who were born into such groups were inextricably bound to them. He said that "Men may change their clothes, their politics, their wives, their religions, their philosophies, to a greater or lesser extent, [but] they cannot change their grandfathers."[30]

Despite a considerable degree of adaptation to dominant patterns of life and the invention of new forms based on the fusion of ideas and practices, America remains in many ways what it has always been, a structurally pluralistic country, a nation of ethnic blocs whose members are joined by the labels they inherited, by the tribal ties of kinship, social organization, and economic interest, and by the prides and prejudices of others. (Other variables—religion, class, region and politics—are important too and, as we shall see, need to be factored in along with ethnicity.)

Those minority individuals who tend to be found enjoying the highest degrees of social integration are likely to be members of the academic community, or art-ists, writers, journalists, and entertainers and many of those in the professions and, increasingly, in business organizations. But although these are no longer strictly exceptional cases, what Milton Gordon observed some forty years ago, those contexts in which persons from different ethnic backgrounds interact in primary group relations with considerable frequency and with relative comfort and ease, although more common today, are still fairly rare.[31] For many Americans, perhaps the majority, closest social relations occur within what Gordon called the *ethclass,* defined as "that subsociety created by the interaction of the vertical stratification of ethnicity with the horizontal stratification of social class."[32] In simple terms this means, for example, that, by and large, upper-class white, Anglo-Saxon, Protestants ("WASPs") associate at an intimate level with those who share their ethnicity and their social class position; and middle-class Jews, middle-class Italian Americans, working-class Polish Americans, or poor white southerners tend to socialize most often with people like themselves.[33]

White Ethnics and Nonwhite Minorities

In the many discussions and debates about assimilation, amalgamation, and, es-pecially, pluralism in American life, all sorts of racial, religious, and nationality groups are included in both the explanations of what has happened and in blue-prints for the future. Yet proponents of each view often have tended to deny or to overlook fundamental differences among and between "voluntary" immigrants, those who belong to Indian nations whose lands were overrun, and, especially, the Africans who were forced to come and who now comprise close to 15 percent of the population.[34]

Many have argued—and, perhaps, wanted to believe—that blacks would take their place, all other factors being equal, in the manner of the other "newcomers." Although it is patently naïve to refer to people whose ancestors came when only indigenous people and Pilgrims and other early European settlers populated the land as "newcomers," it is true that their urban experience is relatively recent and that the northward trek, made by so many African American men and women over the past hundred years, does represent an important migration.[35] There are many parallels. But even in such terms the analogy does not hold completely.

During the late nineteenth and early twentieth centuries, hope, a belief in the American Dream, and definite opportunities were important incentives for poor people from many lands. Overcoming various obstacles, many Irish, Italians, Polish Catholics, and East European Jews managed to make it, and in time found successful accommodation in the new environment. These "national minorities," as Aron had referred to them, did succeed in becoming "ordinary Americans," and, whatever others thought, saw themselves as such. "Wherever our parents came from, whatever language we spoke at home, we reached for a common, overriding identity. Those born abroad, or to immigrants, understood that in part it was an identity given to us by the country. We took it with pleasure. When we sang "land where our fathers died" we knew it was not our fathers we were singing of but it was sure our country. Our teachers knew that. Everybody knew that."[36]

Well, not everybody. The descendants of the involuntary migrants from Africa who, in many ways, had long been quite ordinary Americans in manners and mores and religious practices were not so lucky. They remained marginalized. This reality has continued to affect not only relationships between black and white people—including the white ethnics—but also those many African Americans have had with other newcomers, including those who, although frequently categorized as racial minorities themselves, like Japanese, Chinese, Pilipino, Indians, Vietnamese, Cubans, Mexicans, and many others, were and remain nationality groups, too.

The fact of the matter is that opportunities for Europe's immigrants—even the desperately poor—were always far greater than those afforded nonwhite people and, especially, African Americans. Economist John Kenneth Galbraith is reported once to have quipped: "If you have to be poor, at least have the good sense to be born at a time when everybody is poor."[37] It should be noted that not only did black people enter the urban economy at the wrong time early in the century according to the Galbraith dictum but that, unlike the members of most other American minority groups, they did not have the same choices to inspire them nor did they have the same sorts of communal resources to fall back upon (as had many of the European immigrants). They were different.

Recognition of this fact opens a Pandora's box, packed with practical, political, emotional, and theoretical implications. The argument that African Americans could resolve their dilemma in the manner of other cases of "immigrant adjustment" assumed that their dilemma was the same. It isn't—and, in many ways, it never was.

Sociologist Robert Blauner, one of the early opponents of the "Negro-as-Immigrant" school, has written that

... the entrance of the European into the American order involved a degree of choice and self-direction that was for the most part denied people of color. Voluntary immigration made it more likely that individual Europeans and entire ethnic groups would identify with America and see the host culture as a positive opportunity rather than an alien and dominating value system. It is my assessment that this element of choice, though it can be overestimated and romanticized, must have been crucial in influencing the different careers and perspectives of immigrants [the] colonized in America, because choice is a necessary condition for commitment to any group, from social club to national society.

Sociologists interpreting race relations in the United States have rarely faced the full implications of these differences. The *immigrant model* became the main focus of analysis, and the experiences of all groups were viewed through its lens. It suited the cultural mythology to see everyone in America as an original immigrant, a later immigrant, a quasi-immigrant or a potential immigrant. Though the Black situation long posed problems for this framework, recent developments have made it possible for scholars and ordinary citizens alike to force Afro-African realities into this comfortable schema. Migration from rural South to urban North became an analog of European immigration, Blacks became the latest newcomers to the cities, facing parallel problems of assimilation. In the no-nonsense language of Irving Kristol, "The Negro Today Is Like the Immigrant of Yesterday."[38]

Unique Americans

Black peoples' experience in America is unique—it has no real parallel. Paradoxically, they may well be at once the most alienated and least foreign of all our citizens: most alienated because of their special history, which began in subjugation, continued in segregation, and persists to this day under the legacy of both; least foreign because, ironically, having been cut off from their native roots, they had few guides but those of the master and his agents.

This is not to say that no "Africanisms" survived. Of course they did. And with each passing year we are learning more and more of the linkages in "art, act, and artifact" as anthropologists and folklorists and historians make inroads into recapturing the murky, often suppressed, past. Still, despite the revelations of rich cultural legacies deeply rooted in story and song and other expressions, the principal socialization experiences of most Africans whose ancestors were brought to America, for good or ill, included indoctrination into accepting the importance of many of the same norms, values, goals, and aspirations as those of the dominant group and the region where they found themselves. Many of what are often referred to as cultural traits were similar too.

Putting aside the somewhat different backgrounds and experiences of the many immigrants from Africa, the West Indies, and Latin America who were to enter the United States during the middle and late years of the last century, what most of those who were to become known as African Americans said and what they ate, what they believed, and, in some ways, the way they worshiped, were heavily "American," much of it southern in shape and form and expression. And so with their names. In these names one finds the true paradox of being both a part of and apart from this society.

Names are labels by which others know you. Most black people's names in the United States are those of whites, frequently those of those who held their ancestors in bondage. Because of this it is little wonder that one of the symbolic gestures in the search to assert both selfhood and peoplehood by young African Americans in the turbulent 1960s and 1970s was to cast off their "slave names" and to adopt African ones and, for some who converted to Islam, Islamic ones, or simply to call themselves "X."

For most of our history, African Americans, named Smith and Jones and Brown and Washington, quested after the American Dream and sought to take their place with whites. In the terminology of integration processes: they were mainly assimilationists. Yet, for many, the venture proved quixotic. Some succeeded, however, and became African American equivalents of the white *nouveaux riches,* with all the material trappings to indicate having arrived. Other successful African Americans shunned such lifestyles but sought other benefits in the dominant society, especially through higher education and work in the professions. But even these "mainstreamers" often found that barriers remained; their rejection often heightened smoldering bitterness and exacerbated doubts about the rightness of seeking to integrate in the first place.[39]

The bourgeois blacks sometimes proved more akin to the Arabs in French Algeria than the Italians or Jews or Irish Americans with whom they were so often compared. As Raymond Aron points out: "The French never established an integrated society in Algeria. Ironically, the young Algerians who came closest to being French, by education and training, were usually the most hostile. But this is understandable, because they were the most sensitive to their rejection by the French ruling class."[40]

Persistent relegation to inferior status and the internalization of values regarded as most typically American (such as the idea of individual achievement through hard work) also led to a different sort of response on the part of many blacks compared to members of most other American ethnic groups. Some began to argue that the more they learned about the wider society and its members' unwillingness to honor its own lofty ideals, the less they should encourage their "brothers" and "sisters" to accept its basic tenets. Since whites appeared eager to maintain their position of dominance, some African Americans began saying that integration (again, read: assimilation) was, in fact, highly dysfunctional for them—just as it was for the indigenous people of Algeria.

These observations are not to suggest that all social scientists or policy makers who saw African Americans as the latest immigrants were or are white supremacists. But they may have been quite naïve in thinking that merely by desegregating schools, opening neighborhoods, and saying, in effect, "You're as good as I am" would solve the problem. Assimilation may have been the goal at one time but it has been severely challenged (see Chapter 10).

Many observers simply failed to comprehend the uniqueness of the African Americans' experiences and offered what in an earlier reference to immigrants was called an either/or response. In the context of the 1960s the argument often went like this: If black people are not to be segregated, they must be integrated. But "integration," as used in such a context, turned out to be little more than a liberalized and modernized version of "Anglo conformity." Ironically, the cultural pluralism that many wanted for others (and sometimes for themselves) was rarely even considered as a model for blacks, the people who by all counts would benefit most by accepting their uniqueness.

Until recently many liberal integrationists in the universities, in the government, and even in the civil rights movement itself saw but one side of the problem. They recognized but failed to understand the subculture that had grown out of reactions to barriers erected by whites during and after slavery. To those who wanted a fairer deal at the hands of the society, they were invariably told, "Throw off your unacceptable ways and become like me." James Farmer, the founder of the Congress of Racial Equality (CORE), once put this point of view in very clear perspective. Writing on this type of integration, he said:

> ... We [blacks] learned that America simply couldn't be color-blind, it would have to become color-blind and it would only become color-blind when we gave up our color. The white man, who presumably has no color, would have to give up only his prejudices. We would have to give up our identities. Thus, we would usher in the Great Day with an act of complete self-denial and self-abasement. We would achieve equality by conceding racism's charge: that our skins were afflicted; that our history is one long humiliation; that we are empty of distinctive traditions and any legitimate source of pride.... .[41]

This interpretation was very difficult for many white Americans to accept for they saw little advantage in encouraging blacks to retain behavior patterns that they frequently defined as unproductive or dysfunctional deviations from those considered "standards." Robert Blauner was one of the first to call this stance a part of the "dogma of liberal social science," which reflects in large measure general liberal sentiments.

The argument—or "dogma"—is evident in many places and sources. It is clearly articulated in the monumental study *An American Dilemma,* in which Gunnar Myrdal and his colleagues asserted that "the Negro is an exaggerated American" and that his principal values are "pathological elaborations" of those commonly shared.[42] Historian Kenneth Stampp referred to those who were "white men with black skins."[43] Nathan Glazer and Daniel Patrick Moynihan, in the first edition of *Beyond the Melting Pot,* a study of New York City's ethnic groups, asserted, "the Negro is only an American and nothing else. He has no values and culture to guard and protect.[44] (Glazer and Moynihan were to modify this position in a later edition.)[45]

These ideas were put forth by others, too, many of them relying in no small measure on the work of the late E. Franklin Frazier, one of American's best-known black sociologists. For example, here is what Frazier wrote in his 1957 revision of *The Negro in the United States*:

> Although the Negro is distinguished from other minorities by his physical characteristics, unlike other racial or cultural minorities the Negro is not distinguished by

culture from the dominant group. Having completely lost his ancestral culture, he speaks the same language, practices the same religion, and accepts the same values and political ideals as the dominant group. Consequently, when one speaks of Negro culture in the United States, one can only refer to the folk culture of the rural southern Negro or the traditional forms of behavior and values which have grown out of the Negro's social and mental isolation.... [46]

Frazier went on to say, "Since the institutions, the social stratification, and the culture of the Negro minority are essentially the same as those of the larger community, it is not strange that the Negro minority belongs among assimilationist rather than the pluralist, secessionist, or militant minorities."[47] Yet, even at the time he was writing, others within the black community and outside it were already raising questions about his analysis. Within a few decades, African Americans would prove to be as vigorous in the support of pluralism as any members of white ethnic groups, including white southerners, the latter often described by sociologist Lewis M. Killian as an ethnic group and quasi-minority themselves.[48]

Frazier, along with many commentators on "The Black Experience," assumed that to have a culture, a unique culture, one must possess a distinctive language, a unique religion, and a national homeland. In his critique, Robert Blauner suggested that, although such a view may be appropriate for what anthropologists would call a holistic culture, complete with the institutions of an integrated social system, African Americans did not possess this kind of culture. But they developed their own ways of life and sensitivities, often combinations of African remnants and southern Protestant characteristics developed through encounters with racist America.

African American writers such as Zora Neale Hurston, Countee Cullen, Langston Hughes, Richard Wright, LeRoi Jones, and Ralph Ellison—and, more recently, Cornel West, bell hooks, Ellis Cose, Toni Morrison, Shelby Steele, Henry Louis Gates, Jr., and Derek Bell—in quite different ways have each portrayed the extent to which African Americans have had to respond to the "either/or" interpretation. For example, in his brilliant novel *Invisible Man,* Ellison wrote:

I am an invisible man. No, I am not a spook like those who haunted Edgar Allan Poe; nor am I one of your Hollywood ectoplasms. I am a man of substance, of flesh and bone, fiber and liquids, and I might even be said to possess a mind. I am invisible, understand, simply because people refuse to see me. Like the bodiless heads you see sometimes in circus sideshows, it is as though I have been surrounded by mirrors of hard distorting glass. When they approach me they see only my surroundings, themselves, or figments of their imagination—indeed, everything and anything except me. Nor is my invisibility exactly a matter of biochemical accident to my epidermis. That invisibility to which I refer occurs because of a peculiar disposition of the eyes of those with whom I come into contact. A matter of construction of their inner eyes, those eyes with which they look through their physical eyes upon reality.[49]

In contrast to most whites, most African Americans have long found themselves in a perpetual state of cultural schizophrenia. They have had to deal with what W. E. B. Du Bois called a sense of "twoness." "One ever feels his twoness, "he wrote, "an American, a Negro; two souls, two thoughts, two unreconciled strivings; two warring ideals in one dark body."[50]

Vernon Dixon once argued "the application of the 'either/or' conceptual approach to race relations produces racial harmony [only] when the Blacks and whites embody total sameness."[51] And this is an impossibility. Therefore, Dixon proposed a new and different approach, called by the rather cumbersome term "di-unitalism," in which one simultaneously recognizes the similarities and differences between blacks and whites. Above all, the analyst (and, presumably, the policy maker) would have to learn to understand the ambiguity that marks the social position and often helps shape the personalities of African Americans.[52]

The Motif of Diversity

Increasing numbers of African Americans claimed that they ought not to be defined simply by their color but that they too were members of an ethnic group. Such an assertion had an interesting side effect. It strengthened the general ideology of pluralism and fed the politics of identity.

Responding to the demands of Black Power advocates, many white and Asian and Latino "ethnics" seemed to rediscover their own roots. Although this phenomenon is further discussed in Chapter 10, for now it is to be noted that, in principle at least, the doctrine of cultural pluralism—and several variations on it—once again has come to pervade the conventional wisdom concerning intergroup relations in the United States.

In the 1970s and 1980s, the "nation of nations" idea was extolled by public officials, educators, and religious leaders. School children were told that every group member has the right voluntarily—not by will of the majority—to retain (or to give up) his or her separate identity, and that although people should be judged as individuals, one must recognize the significance of membership in an ethnic, racial, or religious group. Some went further, asserting that groups—at least "minorities"—themselves have rights.

The phrase "affirmative action" was one of the first new expressions that signaled the official recognition of such group-based policy. From its inception as a means of addressing certain grievances such recognition stirred considerable debate among many thoughtful and troubled Americans, especially at the end of the twentieth century. It continues to be a source of controversy.

Behavioral Assimilation and Social Separation

In the United States the dominant group has sometimes adopted the traits of minorities.[53] Well-known examples include such linguistic adaptations as "moccasin," "faux pas," "kibbitz," and "Gesundheit," and such ethnic dishes as pizza, bagels, "Danish" pastry (known in Denmark as *Wiener Brot* or Vienna bread), and "sacramental" wine, as well as such social activities as Latin

American dances, "soul" music, the games of mah jongg and chess, the sports of judo, lacrosse, soccer, and jai alai.

Generally, however, the cultural patterns of the dominant groups have been impressed upon and adopted by members of racial and ethnic minorities. They have accepted as their own, patterns of living, dress, and speech—much in the way that Washington, Jay, and John Adams had hoped would be the case. Constantly exposed to the dominating modes of life of the majority group, it is not surprising that minority group members accommodate themselves to expected behavior patterns. Milton Gordon calls this "behavioral assimilation."

Yet, it must be stressed that taking over dominant group behavior patterns does not necessarily lead to a substantial amount of social interaction on a close, personal basis between members of the established majority and minority group members. Instead, behavioral assimilation is limited to such general norms as a common respect for law and order, acceptance of modes of employer-employee relationships, conformity to styles and fashion touted by the mass media, and widespread use of the symbols of success as nurtured by advertisers. It is less apt to be found in intimate personal relations.

The more personal the nature of a potential situation for social interaction, the greater are the barriers to primary and intimate intergroup participation. Here, once again, Gordon's notion of the *ethclass* is important. Since, as he points out, most close social interaction takes place where social class and ethnicity intersect, it is not surprising that movement in either direction—vertically (up and down the social ladder) and horizontally (from one ethnic category to another)—may present difficulties. Some of the problems are related to normative patterns of what is appropriate behavior with whom; some are related to manners of dress, speech, and other attributes that are class-bound and, often, culturally specific. Of course it is always possible to change one's apparel, learn new ways of speaking, and take on the characteristics of the trendsetters or upper classes. Such adaptation is not unlike the "Anglo-conformity" referred to earlier as a form of behavioral assimilation. But it is not the whole story.

Being able to dress, talk, and act like those in the dominant group does not necessarily carry over into social interaction. Social distances are frequently maintained even as cultural barriers fall. Despite the outward manifestations of acceptance and a high degree of behavioral assimilation, various minorities have been—and are—excluded from social cliques, informal groups, and even such communal activities as religious services and leisure time pursuits. In the not so distant past, Jewish-Gentile relations in a number of American cities were quite clearly circumscribed. There was very limited informal social mixing between Jews and Christians.[54] Even among Christians themselves for a long time there were similar patterns of separation between Protestants and Catholics.[55] Although neither situation characterizes most relations between Jews and Christians (at least white Christians) or Protestants and Catholics (at least white ones) today, such "interpersonal distancing" is still evident in terms of white and nonwhite interaction, particularly at the most intimate of levels.

It is evident that the structural definitions of social situations as formal or informal, secondary or primary, are relevant cues to the levels at which behavioral assimilation breaks down and social separation is required and maintained. It should be noted, once again, that the actual levels of acceptance or tolerance vary markedly; that the behavior of those in "dominant groups" is far from uniform; and that within all minorities differential modes of reaction to rejection and discrimination prevail.

Of course, not all members of minority groups wish to have close relationships with others who differ from them culturally. The desire to maintain social distance is most clearly evident among members of certain religious groups—such as Mennonites, Islamic fundamentalists, and Hasidic Jews—who, in order to retain their systems of belief intact without threat of exposure to, or enticement from the members of other faiths, avoid almost all intergroup activities. Similarly, certain cultural traditions may be thought to be threatened by the overpowering influence of a cordial host society. Solomon Poll's description of the Hasidim of Williamsburg, Brooklyn, provides an illustration of social separation: "Resistance to Americanization is such that although there is no physical wall to isolate them, a strong "sociological wall" separates this group from activities that might encroach on its cultural stability. All the institutions, including the economic activities of the group, are such that they are conducive to a Hasidic 'way of life.'"[56] Yet, such intensive resistance to general Americanization and to opportunities to develop and maintain relationships on the basis of personal considerations rather than ethnic status is not the prevailing mode. In fact, most members of minority groups welcome opportunities for greater acceptance in the wider society. Those holding such views still include many African Americans, despite the growing pride in self and community referred to previously. Many would be pleased not to always be judged as ambassadors or exemplars of whatever group they happened to belong to.

Studies of social distance long have shown that such individual recognition is more possible in certain realms of social life than in others. Even within these spheres, minority groups and their members are ranked according to various criteria of acceptability. As suggested earlier, notable cases include those in the academic world, the arts, entertainment, sports, the "demi-world," and the underworld.

Nevertheless, away from the academy, the ballpark, the arena, or the theater, where people are patrons or spectators or engage in a certain amount of risk-taking, many are unable to be exempted and unable to bridge the status gap. They turn instead to traditional occupations, select friends from within their own groups, withdraw into the minority community, and resign themselves to lives in which their status as members of minority groups becomes of utmost importance, whether they wish it or not. And where the gap between the dominant and minority group is great, social inbreeding within the minority community heightens group cohesion and simultaneously reinforces the image of clannishness. There are variations, but the general and pervasive pattern is one of behavioral assimilation and social separation, or what Milton Gordon calls "structural pluralism."

America's People Today

The United States remains a nation of identifiable and often separable racial, religious, and ethnic groupings. Information regarding the racial and religious composition and national origin of the population is readily available in the periodic reports of the U.S. Bureau of the Census and other sources. This kind of information, however, should be understood in the context of the methods used for data-gathering; the meanings of "race" (consider the changing demands of South Asians and the reactions of Hispanics to the assignment of "racial" categories), "creed," and "ethnicity" each present different problems for both data gatherers and analysts.

Racial designation, for example, has long been assessed on the basis of information that "cannot be hidden from the enumerator, about which [he] can make assumptions without serious error, and about which people will be willing to furnish information."[57] Until 1960 this meant that the census-taker was the ultimate judge of a given respondent's "race" and, as a result, statistics often reflect their biases rather than the preferred identities of respondents. (Since 1960 self-classification has been the method of defining both race and ethnic affiliation, probably resulting in greater accuracy than in earlier censuses.)

"Racial" Groups in the United States

The extent to which the social definition of "race" (referred to in Chapter 2) has long affected the ultimate percentages given for the population is indicated in the description of the category of "Negroes" or "Blacks." For many decades the U.S. Bureau of the Census claimed that besides persons of mixed Negro and white descent, the category includes those of mixed American Indian and Negro descent, "unless the Indian ancestry very definitely predominates or unless the individual is regarded as an Indian in the community."[58] To the present day, although "White" and "Black" (however loosely the terms may be defined) are set aside as separate and distinct groupings, others are categorized by a combination of color and place of ancestral origin. In the 2000 Census, included among the "Other Races" were American Indians, Japanese, Chinese, and Filipinos; under the heading "All Others" were grouped Aleut, Asian Indian, Eskimo or Inuit, Hawaiian, Korean, Indonesian, Polynesian, and "other races not shown separately." New data in 2003 indicated that approximately 235 million or 80 percent of the American population calls itself white—and this included some 36 million people of "Hispanic origins." Roughly the same number, 36 million, said they were "black," meaning of African descent. Of the remainder, close to 3 million checked "American Indian or Native Alaskan," almost 500,000 said they were "Native Hawaiian and Other Pacific Islander," although 4 million said they were of two or more races. [59]

Census Bureau studies show that, compared with the last decennial enumeration, there has been a sharp increase in the proportional representation of "racial" groups in the United States among those who identified themselves as Hispanics, and projections to the years 2005 and 2010 indicate an even steeper climb in the statistics of this multigroup cohort.[60] Moreover, five of every ten African Americans in the country were still residing in the South. (In recent years, the number moving back surpassed the number of blacks moving out of the South). Even more dramatic has been the increase of African Americans in the overall percentage of city residents. An increase in the percentage of whites moving from these same inner city areas to the suburbs has also been noted, thereby increasing the ratio of blacks rather markedly, especially in certain centers. In addition to Washington, a city that was 71 percent black by 1970,[61] Newark, Gary, Atlanta, Cleveland, and Detroit all had African American majorities by the end of that decade and the trend has continued into the new century.

In contrast to the situation of blacks, members of other nonwhite groups are most heavily concentrated west of the Mississippi; seven of every ten members of this category live in the West, eight of ten in the coastal area. The only states with a substantial proportion of residents who are neither black nor white are Alaska (20 percent—mainly Aleuts, Eskimos, and Indians) and Hawaii (67 percent—mainly Japanese and Chinese).

Religious Groups in the United States

In American society the freedom to worship in one's own way is a fundamental guarantee of the Bill of Rights. There is a proliferation of religious organizations, ranging in structure from the highly bureaucratized Roman Catholic Church to transitory and loosely organized storefront Protestant churches. Some religious groups are basically fundamentalist; others are more liberal in their interpretations of sacred writings and theology.

Despite this diversity in organization and religious perspective (and despite the proclivity of Americans to search for new avenues to express religious feelings, as in the appeal of Hare Krishna, Zen Buddhism, and Scientology, which do not follow orthodox Western religious traditions), Americans have long been a church-going people and still score higher on measures of "religiosity" than any other industrialized nation in the world.

Long ago, sociologists of religion suggested that, although the old "melting pot" idea was not ever going to accurately characterize American society, the notion of a "triple melting pot" might. They meant that Americans could increasingly be seen and, presumably see themselves, as Protestants or Catholic or Jewish, rather than as members of particular nationality groups, such as Irish Catholic.[62] Many accepted the idea, observing a tendency of third- and fourth-generation "ethnics" to act more and more like members of the social classes in which they find themselves or toward which they aspire although still retaining nominal affiliations with the churches in which they were raised. However, the trend suggested by Ruby Jo Kennedy and Herberg might have been prematurely predicted. First of all, as Gerhard Lenski pointed out in *The Religious Factor,* a report on a study of Detroit conducted as far back as the 1950s, there were at least four groups: Catholics, Jews, white Protestants, and black Protestants.[63] Lenski's work was followed by a series of studies by Andrew Greeley, which suggested that Catholics were not so ready to slough off their ethnic identities and cease being Irish Catholics, Polish Catholics, or Italian Catholics,[64] though many began to do so with increasing frequency in the next two decades, a period in which "intermarriage" of partners from different religious traditions became more and more common.

To complicate matters, the commitment of many Americans to the basic tenets of their faiths became more and more vague in the 1960s, a period of considerable upheaval in this country and abroad. In the early 1960s religious principles underscored many of the activities of activists who challenged the status quo, especially in the area of civil rights. Most of the leaders came from clerical backgrounds, and many of their organizations were explicitly identified with religious bodies such as the Southern Christian Leadership Conference. Yet, the rising tide of Black Consciousness led simultaneously to a sense of failure on the part of many traditional religious liberals and a resurgence of ideas of separatism. The "roots phenomenon," as we shall see, slowed the trend toward integration in certain circles while bringing about a revival of ethnic pride, including a pride in older traditions and beliefs.

Late in that same decade a second disillusionment, this one over the failure to effect marked changes in the general social system, resulted in a new quest, a quest for meaning. Many young people left the radical political movement for new religious organizations, including the "Campus Crusade for Christ," the Unified Christian Church ("Moonies"), "Jews for Jesus," and similar bodies. Within the traditional churches a new spiritualism was also evident, and new practices involving much more active participation of congregants (as in "charismatic Christianity") attracted many who came to observe and stayed on to enjoy the warmth that they felt now pervaded the sanctuaries.

The next two decades were marked by a steady increase in church participation as well as membership and, by the millennium; more Americans belonged to

Table 6.1 Self-Described Religious Identification of Adult Population (2001)

	Membership, in thousands	% of total
Protestants*	79,096	55.34
Roman Catholics	52,655	36.84
Jews+	5,835	4.08
Eastern Churches	4,026	2.82
Old Catholic	1,024	0.72
Polish National Catholic, and Armenian Churches		
Buddhist Churches of America	100	0.07
Miscellaneous++	191	0.13
Totals	142,926	100.00

*Includes non-Protestant bodies such as Latter Day Saints and Jehovah's Witnesses.
+Estimates of the Jewish community, including those identified with Orthodox, Conservative and Reform synagogues or temples.
++Includes non-Christian bodies such as spiritualists, Ethical Culture Movement members and Unitarian-Universalists.
Source: Statistical Abstract of the United States, 1988, 108th ed. (Washington, D.C.: U.S. Department of Commerce, Bureau of the Census, 1988), p. 52, Table 76.

religious organizations than ever before. But, to many observers, it was the attack on the United States by Islamic terrorists in September 2001 that opened a new chapter in an age old "we vs. they" struggle between the forces of good and the forces of evil, a twenty-first century crusade with each side calling the other infidel. The vast majority of Americans backed the president in his military campaign against the Taliban in Afghanistan and, at least in the beginning, also supported his preemptive strike against Iraq. Although, in the latter case, the rationale was to rid the country of weapons of mass destruction, it soon turned into what many saw as a Holy War.

During that same period, it became more and more common to hear open discussion of faith, particularly of Christian faith, in public forums across the country. Members of groups that collectively became known as the "religious right" fired up renewed debates over teaching creationism or "intelligent design" as a counter to evolutionary theory, urged a return to prayers in school, advocated the promotion of faith-based initiatives and government grants to religious institutions, opposed moves to remove the words "under God"—introduced during the Eisenhower administration—from the Pledge of Allegiance, supported the public display of clearly religious objects like the Ten Commandments, and moved with increasing boldness into the political arena itself.

Candidates for local and state offices wore their religious preferences on their sleeves, urging fellow believers to join them in battling the sinners who opposed them. This was most dramatically evident in the second campaign of the "born again" presidential candidate George W. Bush. Many pundits argued that "value issues," often couched in religious terms, were a determining factor in his second victory.

At the same time as this sort of evangelical fervor was sweeping the country, particularly in those states that were solidly Republican, a growing sex scandal was challenging the power of priests and bishops in the Roman Catholic Church. Although some left the church for other denominations, many more stayed the course though not without embarrassment or self-criticism.

Will Herberg once suggested that ours is a nation ever caught in a paradox of "pervasive secularism and mounting religiosity."[65] This had become has more evident in recent years as greater and greater expressions of profanity, unabashed sexuality, and violent action were expressed in theaters and on television. Many Americans were shocked and many fundamentalists saw these trends as the work of the devil incarnate, often conflated into a single boogie man—liberal, free-thinking, cosmopolitan, atheist—who was seeking to corrupt God-fearing, law-abiding Americans.

In fact, although those who rejected the rigidity of the religiously conservative and so-called "true believers" were often liberal, freethinking, and cosmopolitan, only a few of them were atheists. Most Americans continued to belong to religious organizations and to proclaim some sort of faith.

According to surveys conducted by sociologists at the Graduate Center of the City University of New York in 2001, nearly 210,000,000 American adults claimed identification with some religious body. The largest single group was then and remains Roman Catholic, with nearly 160,000,000 members. Next is a broad array of people in various Protestant denominations, beginning with 50 million Baptists,

14 million Methodists, and an equal number who simply called themselves "Christians." In addition there are nearly 10 million Lutherans, 5,500,000 Presbyterians, and 4,500,000 "Protestants," who also didn't specify a denomination but, given shifts in self-identification, may be more liberal members of that group that now say they are "Christians." There are some four million Pentecostalists, 3,500,000 Episcopalians, and nearly three million Mormons. And these are just the largest groups. The table below includes each of these and many other Christian groupings, as well as the far smaller number of minority religions and sects, Jews, Muslims, Buddhists, Hindus, even Spiritualists, Wiccans, and Druids. It also notes some significant changes that have occurred over the decade between 1990 and 2000.[66]

Ethnic Groups in the United States

The distinctions between the major religious denominations in America are fairly well defined, and membership statistics are not difficult to obtain. Racial breakdowns, although open to many questions about what are the precise definitions of particular racial aggregates, are likewise available, but accurate data on ethnic group membership and identification are far more elusive. As noted in Chapter One, ethnic divisions include various kinds of groupings: people with common national backgrounds, those whose racial designation places them in a special category with which they identify and are so identified by others, and those whose group identity may transcend both racial and national boundaries. The complexity of the problem of ethnic classification is illustrated by such facts as the following: Jews are both a religious and cultural minority; the descendants of Irish, Italian, and Polish immigrants are predominantly Roman Catholic, but they also are members of particular nationality groups—and they are white; Puerto Ricans, mainly Catholic, sometimes considered to be black, bring distinctive cultural and linguistic patterns from Puerto Rico to the mainland; southern-born African Americans, at least to some degree, are culturally as well as racially identifiable, when compared with other black people, such as West Indians or Africans, who may share their appearances but not necessarily their worldviews.

Overlappings of these kinds prevent the clear-cut enumeration of ethnic group membership. Moreover, there are few reliable statistics on the national origins of the native-born. Estimates are most frequently based on projections of statistics on immigration to the United States, on race, and on religion. Although census enumerators continue to request information about country of birth from both the respondent and his or her parents, such data do not provide a valid basis for ascertaining the true size or constituency of nationality groupings in America today.

Although there has been a significant rise in immigration over the past forty years, most people now living in this country were born here, as were most of their parents, and projections of immigration statistics alone do not, and cannot, indicate the degree to which individuals have retained their identity with the land or cultural traditions of their forebears.

The problem of estimating the size of ethnic groups is further complicated by the increasing incidence of intermarriage between individuals of different national and religious backgrounds. (Despite sharp rises, members of racial categories have remained relatively endogamous.) Several recent studies indicate that class affiliation and residential propinquity remain, in large measure, the main determinants of marital choice for those of differing national, but similar religious backgrounds, especially among Roman Catholics.

Even the growing trend toward more intermarriage does not mean that enclaves of ethnic groups no longer exist. The most prominent today are those of recent arrivals from Puerto Rico and the Dominican Republic, China and Korea, Cuba and Haiti, Vietnam and Cambodia, India and Pakistan, Somalia and Ethiopia, and especially from Mexico, a pattern that recapitulates what existed a century ago when the newcomers were mostly from Europe. And even for those of European background, many third- and fourth-generation Americans continue to retain a strong sense of identification with the country from which grandparents or great grandparents migrated. Survey researchers still find that residents often make a single selection when asked to indicate with which of the larger known ethnic groups in the community they identify themselves.

Thus, although in some instances the traditional barriers between certain ethnic divisions are becoming increasingly blurred, ethnic distinctions, as well as those based upon racial or religious factors, persist in the United States.

The Continuing Dilemmas of Diversity

Almost all of America's immigrants and many of their descendants at one time or another have been the targets of discrimination, and many have been its perpetrators: categorical discrimination is not confined to the majority. One might expect that this historical experience, especially within the context of an open (or semi-open) society with a strong democratic ethos, would work to eliminate group barriers and intergroup tensions. In the long run, this may indeed be the case, but, as we know, group antipathy and friction continue. Why do these patterns persist?

This question cannot easily be answered. One clue is offered, however, by the fact that each new group, in seeking its place among those already in the United States, sought to integrate but was often thwarted by others engaged in the same struggle for acceptance. As Max Lerner explained,

> From the beginning there were stereotypes imposed upon the more marginal immigrants. As was perhaps natural, the members of each new wave of immigration were assigned the lowliest tasks, the longest hours of work, the poorest and dirtiest living quarters. The basic pattern was, however, for the immigrants of each new influx to be in time absorbed by the rest, yielding the role of strangeness in turn to the still later corners. Most of them moved up the hierarchical ladder while those who followed grasped eagerly to the lowly places that had been relinquished.[67]

This pattern of group mobility, which shows a rough correlation between time of arrival and social status (with the notable exceptions of Native Americans on the one hand and Jews and some East Asians on the other), may help to account for the fact that there has rarely been any real alliance of minority groups to withstand the prejudice and discrimination from the majority.[68] The rationale for this bold statement will be developed in succeeding chapters on the nature of prejudice and discrimination and the reactions of minority groups to their status.

Notes

1. George Stewart, *American Ways of Life* (Garden City, N.Y.: Doubleday, 1954), pp. 11–12.
2. From the poem, "The New Colossus," by Emma Lazarus, inscribed at the base of the Statue of Liberty, 1892.
3. As quoted in Jerre Mangione and Ben Morreale, *La Storia: Five Centuries of the Italian American Experience* (New York: Harper Collins, 1992), p. xiii.
4. As quoted in Milton Vorst, "Talk with A Reasonable Man," *New York Times Magazine* (April 19, 1970), p. 96. See also Candace Nelson and Marta Tienda, "The Structuring of the Hispanic Ethnicity," in Richard D. Alba (ed.), *Ethnicity and Race in the USA* (New York: Routledge, 1988), pp. 49–74.
5. See, for example, Milton M. Gordon, "Assimilation in America: Theory and Reality," *Daedalus* 90 (Spring 1961), 263–285.
6. As quoted in Richard Shenkman, *Legends, Lies and Cherished Myths of American History* (New York: Harper and Row, 1989), p. 108.
7. W. C. Ford (collector and ed.), *The Writings of George Washington* (New York: Putnam 1889), vol. XII, p. 489. This quotation is discussed in greater detail by Milton M. Gordon, op. cit., pp. 266–67.
8. This letter was published in *Nile's Weekly Register,* 18 (1820), 157–158. See the discussion in Marcus L. Hansen, *The Atlantic Migration, 1607–1860* (Cambridge: Harvard University Press, 1940), pp. 96–97.
9. See Nathan Glazer, "Ethnic Groups in America: From National Culture to Ideology," in M. Berger, T. Abel, and C.H. Page (eds.), *Freedom and Control in Modern Society* (Princeton, N.J.: Van Nostrand, 1954), p. 163.
10. Frederick Jackson Turner, *The Frontier in American History* (New York: Henry Holt, 1920), pp. 3–4.
11. Idem.
12. See Ronald Takaki, *Strangers from a Different Shore* (Boston: Little, Brown, 1989), p. 3.
13. See Dorothy Burton Skordal, *The Divided Heart: Scandinavian Experience Through Literary Sources* (Oslo: Universitetsforlaget, 1974).
14. For a detailed discussion of nativism, see S. M. Lipset and Earl Raab, *The Politics of Unreason* (New York: Harper and Row, 1970).
15. Henry Pratt Fairchild, *The Melting Pot Mistake* (Boston: Little, Brown, 1926), pp.158–159.
16. This is the comment of a lifelong resident of a small town in upstate New York. See Peter I. Rose, "Small-Town Jews and Their Neighbours in the United States," *Jewish Journal of Sociology* (England), 3 (December 1961), 187.
17. See Peter Brimelow, *Alien Nation: Common Sense about American Immigration* (New York: Random House, 1995). See also, Samuel P. Huntington, *Who Are We? The Challenges to America's National Identity* (New York: Simon and Schuster, 2004).
18. J. Hector St. John de Crévecoeur, *Letters from an American Farmer* (New York: Albert and Charles Boni, 1925), pp. 54–55; originally published in London, 1782. For a critical

commentary, see Marcus Cunliffe, "Crévecoeur Revisited," *Journal of American Studies* 9 (August 1975), 129–144.

19. Israel Zangwill, *The Melting Pot* (New York: The Jewish Publication Society of America, 1909), pp. 198–199.

20. As quoted in Robert E. Park and Ernest W. Burgess, *Introduction to the Science of Sociology* (Chicago: University of Chicago Press, 1924), p. 734.

21. Donald Light, Jr., and Suzanne Keller, *Sociology* (New York: Knopf, 1975), p. 241. See also W. Lloyd Warner and Leo Srole, *The Social Systems of American Ethnic Groups* (New Haven: Yale University Press, 1945); and Ronald J. Silver, "Structure and Values in the Explanation of Acculturation Rates," *British Journal of Sociology* 126 (March 1965), 68–79.

22. Gordon, op. cit., pp. 274–275.

23. Horace M. Kallen, "Democracy versus the Melting-Pot," *The Nation* 100 (February 18, 1915), 190–194, and (February 25, 1915), 217–220; see also Horace M. Kallen, *Cultural Pluralism and the American Idea* (Philadelphia: University of Pennsylvania Press, 1956).

24. Kallen, "Democracy versus the Melting-Pot," (February 25, 1915), op. cit., p. 220.

25. John Higham, *Send These to Me* (New York: Atheneum, 1975), p. 208.

26. Nicholas Appleton, *Cultural Pluralism in Education* (New York: Longman, 1993), p.3.

27. See, for example, Ronald H. Bayor, *Neighbors in Conflict: The Irish, Germans, Jews, and Italians of New York City, 1929–1941* (Baltimore, MD: Johns Hopkins University Press, 1978).

28. See Richard D. Alba, *Italian Americans: Into the Twilight of Ethnicity* (Englewood Cliffs, N.J.: Prentice-Hall, 1985).

29. Herbert M. Gans, "Symbolic Ethnicity: The Future of Ethnic Groups and Cultures in America," *Ethnic and Racial Studies* 2:1 (Jan. 1979). See also Stephen Steinberg, *The Ethnic Myth,* rev. ed. (Boston: Beacon Press, 1989), esp. pp. 44–74 passim.

30. Ibid.

31. Gordon, op. cit., pp. 279–285. See also Gordon, "Social Structure and Group Relations," *Freedom and Control in Modern Society,* op. cit., pp. 141–157.

32. Milton M. Gordon, *Assimilation in American Life* (New York: Oxford University Press, 1964), pp. 51 ff.

33. For a novelist's view of the "ethclass" phenomenon, see Tom Wolfe, *Bonfire of the Vanities* (New York: Farrar, Straus and Giroux, 1988). Also see the author's review of *Bonfire of the Vanities,* Peter I. Rose "The Real McCoy?," *Congress Monthly,* 55:4 (May/June 1988), 20–22.

34. See L. Paul Metzger, "American Sociology and Black Assimilation: Connecting Perspectives," *American Journal of Sociology,* 76 (1971), 627–647. See also Harry H. Bash, *Sociology, Race, and Ethnicity* (New York: Gordon and Breach, 1979); and Stanford M. Lyman, *The Black American in Sociological Thought* (New York: Capricorn Books, 1972).

35. See the latest in a series of studies of the migration, Nicholas Lemann, *The Promised Land: The Great Black Migration and How It Changed America* (New York: Knopf, 1991).

36. A. M. Rosenthal, "The Lucky Americans," *New York Times* (December 8, 1992).

37. As quoted in Charles Silberman, *Crisis in Black and White* (New York: Random House, 1964), p. 41. See also James Weldon Johnson, *Black Manhattan* (New York: Knopf, 1930); Claude McKay, *Harlem: Negro Metropolis* (New York: Dutton, 1940); and Oscar Handlin, *The Newcomers* (Cambridge: Harvard University Press, 1959).

38. Robert Blauner, *Racial Oppression in America* (New York: Harper & Row, 1972), pp. 56–57. Irving Kristol's article (referred to by Blauner) and several others dealing with the question of "The Negro as Immigrant" appear in Peter I. Rose, ed., *Nation of Nations* (New York: Random House, 1972), pp. 197–279 passim.

39. See Ellis Cose, *The Rage of A Privileged Class* (New York: Harper Collin, 1993).

40. As quoted in Milton Vorst, op. cit., pp. 96–97.

41. James Farmer, *Freedom—When?* (New York: Random House, 1965), p. 87.

42. Gunnar Myrdal, et al., *An American Dilemma* (New York: Harper & Row, 1944).

43. Kenneth Stampp, *The Peculiar Institution* (New York: Vintage Books, 1956).

44. Nathan Glazer and Daniel Patrick Moynihan, *Beyond the Melting Pot* (Cambridge: M.I.T. Press, 1963), p. 53.

45. See 1971 edition.

46. E. Franklin Frazier, *The Negro in the United States* (New York: Macmillan, 1957), p. 680.

47. Ibid, p. 16.

48. See Lewis M. Killian, *White Southerners* (New York: Random House, 1970).

49. Ralph Ellison, *Invisible Man* (New York: Random House, 1947), p. 3.

50. W. E. B. Du Bois, *The Souls of Black Folk,* 1903 (As published in New York: Fawcett Publications, Premier Americana Editions, 1961), pp. 15–16.

51. See Vernon J. Dixon, "Two Approaches to Black-White Relations," in Vernon J. Dixon and Badi Foster (eds.), *Beyond Black or White* (Boston: Little, Brown, 1971), pp. 22–66ff.

52. The sort of position articulated by Dixon, is much more fully developed in Cornel West, *Race Matters* (New York: Beacon Press, 1993).

53. Gordon, op. cit., pp. 279–285. See also Gordon, "Social Structure in Group Relations," Freedom and Control in Modern Society, op. cit., pp. 141–157.

54. John P. Dean, "Patterns of Socialization and Association Between Jews and Non-Jews," *Jewish Social Studies* 17 (July 1955), 249–251. Dean's hypothesis was substantiated in the author's study of isolated Jews. The majority of Jews interviewed indicated that they enjoyed a degree of close interfaith socializing in their very small city which was unparalleled in the urban community; see Rose, op. cit., p. 182.

55. Andrew Greeley, *Why Can't They Be Like Us?* (New York: Dutton, 1971).

56. Solomon Poll, *The Hasidic Community of Williamsburg* (New York: Free Press, 1962), p. 3.

57. Donald Bogue, *The Population of the United States* (New York: Free Press, 1959), p. 122.

58. U.S. Bureau of the Census, *1960 Census of Population Supplementary Reports,* PC (S1)-10, Washington, D.C., p. 2

59. U.S. Bureau of the Census, "Resident Population by Race, Hispanic Origin, and Single Years of Age," *Statistical Abstract of the United States,* 2003, Table 14, p. 16

60. U.S. Bureau of the Census, "Resident Population by Race, Hispanic Origin Status, and Age—Projections: 2005 and 2010," *Statistical Abstract of the United States,* 2003, Table 16, p. 19.

61. U.S. Bureau of the Census, "Resident Population by Region, Race, and Hispanic Origin 2000, *Statistical Abstract of the United States,* 2003, Table 23, p. 27.

62. Ibid, Chaps. 2 and 3; see also Ruby Jo Kennedy, "Single or Triple Melting Pot? Inter-marriage Trends in New Haven, 1870–1940," *American Journal of Sociology,* 58 (January 1952), pp. 56–59.

63. Gerhard Lenski, *The Religious Factor* (New York: Doubleday, 1961); see also Gerhard Lenski, "The Religious Factor in Detroit, Revisited," *American Sociological Review* (February 1971), p. 50.

64. Andrew Greeley, ed., *Ethnicity in the United States: A Preliminary Reconnaissance* (New York: Wiley, 1974).

65. Will Herberg, *Protestant-Catholic-Jew* (New York: Doubleday, 1955), p. 14.

66. See Barry A. Kosmin and Seymour P. Lachman, *One Nation Under God: Religion in Contemporary American Society* (New York: the Graduate Center of the City University of New York, 1993); and Barry A. Kosmin, Egon Mayer and Ariela Keysar, *American Religious Identification Survey,* (New York: the Graduate Center of the City University of New York, 2001). Summary from U.S. Bureau of the Census, Statistical Abstract of the United States, 2003, Table 79, p. 67.

67. Max Lerner, *American as a Civilization* (New York: Simon and Schuster, 1957), p. 503.

68. This statement is a slightly emended version of what Arnold and Caroline Rose wrote fifty years ago. See Arnold and Caroline Rose, *America Divided* (New York: Knopf, 1953), p. 65.

PART III

ATTITUDES, ACTIONS, AND MINORITY REACTIONS

The Nature of Prejudice

On Being Culture Bound

> All good people agree,
> And all good people say,
> All nice people like Us, are We
> And everyone else is They.[1]

In a few short lines, Rudyard Kipling captured the essence of what sociologists and anthropologists call *ethnocentric* thinking.

Members of all societies tend to believe that "All nice people like Us, are We ... " They find comfort in the familiar and often denigrate or distrust others. Of course, with training and experience in other climes, they may learn to transcend their provincialism, placing themselves in others' shoes. Or, as Kipling put it,

> ... If you cross over the sea,
> Instead of over the way,
> You may end by (think of it!) looking on We
> As only a sort of They.[2]

In a real sense, a main lesson of the sociology of racial and ethnic relations is to begin to "cross over the sea," to learn to understand why other people think and act as they do and to be able to empathize with their perspectives even if one still does not accept them. But this is no easy task. Many barriers—political, economic, social, and personal—stand in the way of such international (and intergroup) understanding. According to William Graham Sumner (who coined the word), ethnocentrism" leads a people to exaggerate and intensify everything in their own folkways which is peculiar and which differentiates them from others."[3] Intensive indoctrination to particular points of view and notions of what is right and wrong and good and bad has a long-lasting effect.

Sometimes the teaching is very explicit regarding the superior quality of one's own culture; sometimes it is subtler. Consider the following poem written by Robert Louis Stevenson and, for years, taught to many English and American children.

Little Indian, Sioux or Crow,
Little frosty Eskimo,
Little Turk or Japanee,
O! Don't you wish that you were me?

You have seen the scarlet trees
And the lions over seas;
You have eaten ostrich eggs,
And turned the turtles off their legs.

Such a life is very fine,
But it's not so nice as mine:
You must often, as you trod,
Have wearied, not to be abroad.

You have curious things to eat,
I am fed on proper meat;
You must dwell beyond the foam
But I am safe to live at home.

Little Indian, Sioux or Crow,
Little frosty Eskimo,
Little Turk or Japanee,
O! Don't you wish that you were me?[4]

Raised on such literary fare, it should not be surprising that children develop negative ideas about the ways of others. Despite greater sensitivity to such explicitly racist language, many young people in this society still make clear distinctions between those like themselves and others. Even the curious often find it hard to understand how those in other lands can worship ancestors, engage in polygamy, or practice infanticide; or why many Moslem women wear the *chador* (the veil to cover their faces), Balinese women go bare-breasted, and some people wear no clothes at all. They may be surprised to learn that many nations emerging from colonial status favored communism or some other form of one-party rule over our political system.

Sometimes ethnocentrism appears in unlikely places, such as in writings by those long viewed as experts on the comparative study of culture. Consider the following remarks of the famous anthropologist Margaret Mead. In a book on American character published in 1942, during the darkest days of World War II, Mead wrote: "If I were writing about the way in which the Germans or the Japanese, the Burmese or the Javanese would have to act if they were to win the war, I would not need to use so many moral terms. For none of these peoples think of life in as habitually moral terms as do Americans."[5]

American ethnocentricity, although manifest in general attitudes toward others is, of course, tempered somewhat by the very heterogeneity of the population that we have been examining. Thus, although there are broad standards expressed in the ways most Americans set goals for their children, organize their political lives, and think about this society in contrast to others, living in our racial and ethnic mosaic makes us more inclined to think in terms of layers or circles of familiarity. Blacks from Chicago feel and think very "American" when they are in Lagos or Nairobi, as do ethnic Chinese from Houston when visiting relatives in Shanghai or Beijing. But when they get home, they may quickly revert to feeling *African* American or *Chinese* American, respectively.

Ethnocentrism is found in political as well as in ethnic contexts. Much of the discussion of patriotism and loyalty is couched in language that reflects rather narrow, culture-bound thinking. At various periods in our history this phenomenon has been particularly marked. The nativistic movements of the pre–Civil War period, the antiforeign organizations during the time of greatest immigration, and the McCarthyism of the early 1950s are three dramatic examples. During the McCarthy era there was a widespread attempt to impose the notion that, in addition to card-carrying Communists, anyone who had ever joined a Marxist study group, supported the Loyalists in the Spanish Civil War, or belonged to any one of a number of liberal organizations was "un-American."

It is clear that not only those "over the sea" are viewed (and view others) ethnocentrically. These distinctions between "they" and "we" exist within societies as well. In modern industrial societies most individuals belong to a wide array of social groups that differentiate them from others—familial, religious, occupational, recreational, and by gender, too. Individuals are frequently caught in a web of conflicting allegiances. A hierarchical ranking of groups as referents for behavior often surmounts this situation. In most societies, including our own, the family is the primary reference group. As we have seen in the United States, ethnic or racial identity and religious affiliation are also relevant referents. Members of other ethnic, racial, and religious groups are often judged on the basis of how closely they conform to the standards of the group passing judgment.

For years sociological surveys indicated that in American society many whites holding Christian beliefs and constituting both the statistical majority and the dominant group rank minorities along a continuum of social acceptability. They rate members of minority groups in descending order in terms of how closely the latter approximate their image of "real Americans." Although, over the years, most Americans generally have considered those of English or Canadian ancestry to be acceptable citizens, good neighbors, social equals, and desirable marriage partners, relatively few feel the same way about those who rank low in scales of social distance.

There is an interesting correlate to this finding. Investigators consistently have found that minority group members themselves frequently accept the dominant group's ranking system—with one exception: each tends to put his or her own group at the top of the scale.[6]

Ranking is one characteristic of ethnocentric thinking; generalizing is another. The more another group differs from one's own, the more one is likely to generalize about its social characteristics and to hold oversimplified attitudes toward its members. When asked to describe our close friends, we are able to cite their idiosyncratic traits: we may distinguish among subtle differences of physiognomy, demeanor, intelligence, and interests. It becomes increasingly difficult to make the same careful evaluation of casual neighbors; it is almost impossible when we think of people we do not know at firsthand. The general tendency is to assign strangers to available group categories, which often include gross personality or cultural traits. "Passionate" Latinos, "melancholy" Irish, "penny-pinching" Scots, "clannish" Chinese are some examples. These are *stereotypes,* a term with origins in ancient Greece, later used to describe a metal printing plate.

In a thoughtful essay, Judith Andre considers the conceptual and normative aspects of stereotyping, and stresses that the practice is more often applied to those thought to deviate from the characteristics of the dominant group.[7] Thus, she writes, "there are relatively few stereotypes about white men; white men are, in this culture, unreflectively taken to be the standard human being from whom women and other races deviate." Andre goes on to suggest, "What stereotypes there are concern not men as such, but men in relation to women."[8] Jeanne Bloch, a psychologist, has reported that sex differences among girls and boys are often related to the pressures and expectations of those most responsible for their socialization, parents and teachers—and, of late, advertising and television. Specific areas she noted based on a study that lasted more than ten years were the boys tend to be more aggressive, engage in more outdoor activities, tend to be risk takers, and have higher opinions of themselves than do girls, although girls are more fearful and anxious, more obedient to authority, and have greater concern for others' welfare.[9] She also indicates "males tend to set higher goals and be more confident, blaming failure on external factors, whereas females blame themselves."[10] Such behavior is largely a reflection of the paths people are encouraged, allowed, or permitted to follow; and those they are prohibited from taking.

If, as noted in Chapter 2, "self-fulfilling prophecies" are predictions made to come true, "self-fulfilling stereotypes" are assumptions that become reified by the actions of those who seek or are forced to live up to (or down to) the expectations of others. Numerous studies of race and gender give ample evidence that minorities such as African Americans and women internalize the views others have of them, including lower esteem, and low rank, and often act accordingly.[11]

Ranking others according to one's own standards and categorizing them into generalized stereotypes together serve to widen the gap between "they" and "we." Sigmund Freud once wrote "in the undisguised antipathies and aversions which people feel toward strangers with whom they have to do we may recognize the expression of self-love—of narcissism."[12] In sociological terms, a function of ethnocentric thinking is the enhancement of group cohesion. There is a close relationship between a high degree of ethnocentrism on the part of one group and an increase of antipathy toward others. This relationship tends to hold for ethnocentrism of both dominant and minority groups.[13]

Many writers see such antipathetic attitudes as bases for *group prejudice*. For example: "It is this very group consciousness, or ethnocentrism, which lays the foundation of group prejudice. If there were no strong feelings for one's own group, there would not be strong consciousness of other groups. Awareness of one's own group as an in-group and of the others as out-groups is fundamental in-group relationships."[14]

Defining Prejudice

Prejudice may be defined as "a system of negative beliefs, feelings, and action-orientations regarding a group of people."[15] This definition characteristically emphasizes the negative side of prejudice. Literally, of course, "prejudice" refers to positive as well as negative attitudes. Yet, because of the detrimental psychic and social consequences that often result from hostile attitudes, sociologists usually concern themselves with and accentuate the "negative."

The definition of group prejudice stated above incorporates the three major dimensions of all attitude systems: the *cognitive* (beliefs), the *affective* (feelings), and the *conative* (predispositions to act in particular ways, or policy orientations).[16]

The cognitive component pertains to the "intellectual" side of prejudice, for it involves knowledge, however faulty. This is expressed in stereotypical conceptions and misconceptions of various social groups by others, for example: whites who think that African Americans are shiftless, lazy, and untrustworthy, but wonderfully musical; Gentiles who imagine that Jews are avaricious, brash, and smart, but "too intelligent for their own good"; Englishmen who think of the Irish as argumentative, heavy drinkers; Irishmen who imagine Englishmen to be stuffy bores; and men of all ethnic backgrounds who think women are "the weaker sex." Cognition refers to "cranial" reactions, that is, pictures in the mind's eye. Although the ethnocentric individual frequently generalizes about groups he knows little or nothing about, the prejudiced person generalizes about groups he thinks he knows well.

The second dimension, called "affective," refers to the way one feels about what is perceived. The emotions evoked are "visceral" in that they are often manifested in gut feelings of revulsion, fear, hate, or indignation, as illustrated by the following expressions:

"It makes me mad just thinking about my kid going to school with all those workaholic Asian immigrants. He'll never be able to keep up."

"Don't you just hate the way Arabs are moving in? I simply can't stand them."

"I know it's wrong, but I really shiver at the thought of rooming with an Iranian student next year."

Often emotions aroused in the prejudiced person are based upon the stereotypes he or she holds of certain people. If one thinks that Greeks are underhanded or sharp businessmen, this tends to elicit apprehension in dealing with them. Similarly, if one believes that Mexicans typically carry knives, one may well feel frightened when confronted by a member of this group. Many Americans of "Middle Eastern background," viewed by some as radical fundamentalists, were considered with such suspicion in the immediate aftermaths of the first terrorist attacks on the World Trade Center in New York City in 1993 and on the Alfred P. Murray Federal Building in Oklahoma City in 1995. They became an even more targeted group after September 11, 2001.

Group prejudices involve both thoughts and feelings about people. "However false as to fact, prejudice has a certain logic, a logic not of reason but of the emotions.... Prejudice is more than false belief; it is a structure of false belief *with a purpose,* however unconscious."[17] This is why prejudice as an attitude represents a predisposition to act (the conative dimension) in a particular way toward a social group. It is a state of readiness for action but not in itself overt behavior or discrimination.

Prejudice and Discrimination

Discrimination may be defined as the differential treatment of individuals belonging to particular groups or social categories.[18] Although frequently they are opposite sides of the same coin, prejudice and discrimination, as both analytical and concrete concepts, should not be confused. The difference between prejudice as an attitude and discrimination as overt behavior was summed up by an English judge in his comments to nine youths convicted of race rioting in the Notting Hill section of London: "Everyone, irrespective of the color of his skin, is entitled to walk through our streets in peace with their heads held erect and free from fear.... These courts will uphold (these rights) ... *think what you like.... But once you translate your dark thoughts into savage acts, the law will punish you, and protect your victim.*"[19]

American civil rights workers have long recognized the significance of the distinction. The late Dr. Martin Luther King, Jr., in his first address to the Atlanta, Georgia, "Jaycees" put it bluntly: "The law may not make a man love me, but it can restrain him from lynching me, and I think that's pretty important."[20]

The prejudiced person may not actually behave outwardly the way he or she thinks or says he or she will act. Attitudes do not always lead to hostile or aggressive actions. Furthermore, many individuals discriminate against others without harboring negative feelings toward the groups to which they belong. In one of several books on intergroup relations published in the mid-1950s, Dean and Rosen reported, "conformity with the practices of segregation and discrimination is often quite unrelated to the intensity of prejudice in the individuals who conform."[21] Others have continued to corroborate the generalization, adding the following corollary: social contact itself and the conventions characteristic of the particular circumstances in which contact takes place often help to determine how an individual will act at a given time. Sometimes people may even behave toward others in direct opposition to their own predispositions. The situation itself frequently provides the cues for "appropriate" behavior. For example, for years many liberals conformed to practices of segregation when vacationing in the South; and southerners who held moderate views about the desegregation issue often remained silent on the matter in their home communities.

Merton's Typology

Nearly 50 years ago, comparing the presence or absence of prejudicial attitudes on the part of individuals with their willingness or reluctance to engage in discriminatory activity, Robert K. Merton described the relationship between prejudice and discrimination. The paradigm that he devised is still useful. It includes four types of persons and their characteristic response patterns.[22]

The Unprejudiced Nondiscriminators

These "all-weather liberals," as Merton called them, sincerely believe in the American creed of freedom and equality for all, and practice it to the fullest extent. They are the vigorous champions of the underdog, take the Golden Rule literally, and cherish American egalitarian values. It would appear that liberal individuals such as these would be most able to influence others in the realm of intergroup hostility and discrimination. Yet, as Merton indicates, their effectiveness is limited by certain "fallacies."

First there is the "fallacy of group soliloquies." Liberals tend to expend their energies in seeking out one another and talking chiefly to others who share their point of view. The feeling of agreement that logically ensues by interacting mainly with those who agree leads to the second fallacy, that of "unanimity." Through discussions with like-minded individuals the liberal may feel that many more people agree with his attitudes regarding ethnic relations than do in fact. [N.B. These two fallacies might well be construed as further examples of ethnocentric thinking and acting.] Finally, there is the "fallacy of privatized solutions," depicted by Merton as follows: "The ethnic liberal, precisely because he is at one with the American creed, may rest content with his own individual behavior and thus see no need to do anything about the problem at large. Since his own spiritual house is in order, he is not motivated by guilt or shame to work on a collective problem."[23] The problem of the unprejudiced nondiscriminator is not one of ambivalence between attitude and action—as in the case of the two types described below—but rather it is a lack of awareness of the enormity of the problem and a clear-cut approach to those who are not so liberally inclined.

Unprejudiced Discriminators

The many homeowners throughout the urban North and Midwest denied having any personal feelings against black people steadfastly tried to keep them out of their neighborhoods for fear of what others would say and do illustrate the case of the unprejudiced discriminator, who is, at best, a "fair-weather liberal." More pragmatic than "all-weather liberals," they discriminate when such behavior is called for, seems to be appropriate, or is in their own self-interest. Expediency is the motto; "Don't rock the boat," the guiding principle.[24] Merton suggests that the "fair-weather liberal" is frequently the victim of guilt because of the discrepancy between conduct and personal beliefs and is thus especially vulnerable to the persuasion of those more willing to press for civil and human rights and more amenable to making changes when authorities impose them.

Prejudiced Nondiscriminators

This third type might be called "timid bigots." Like so many of those who have half-facetiously been called "the gentle people of prejudice," they are not activists. They feel definite hostility toward or dislike many groups and subscribe to conventional stereotypes of their negative attributes. Yet, like the "fair-weather liberals," they too react to circumstances. If the situation—as defined by law or custom—precludes open discrimination, they conform. They serve African American and other minority group customers, sit next to them on buses or trains, and send their children to school with them. Feeling they are forced to "grin and bear it," they often take the position that they are merely cogs in a big machine. "What can I do," they say, "fight the system, fight city hall?"

Although both the "fair-weather liberal" and the "fair-weather illiberal" share the theme of expedience, Merton states:

> Superficial similarity in behavior of the two in the same situation should not be permitted to cloak a basic difference in the meaning of this outwardly similar behavior, a difference which is as important for social policy as it is for social science. Whereas the timid bigot is under strain when he conforms to the creed, the timid liberal is under strain when he deviates.... He does not accept the moral legitimacy of the creed; he conforms because he must, and will cease to conform when the pressure is removed.[25]

Prejudiced Discriminators

These are the people who embody the commonly held assumption that prejudice and discrimination are mutually dependent. Such "active bigots" neither believe in the American creed nor act in accordance with its precepts. Like the "all-weather liberal," the prejudiced discriminator conforms to a set of standards; but in this case "his ideals proclaim the right, even the duty, of discrimination."[26] He or she does not hesitate to express the basic attitude—"all whites are superior to colored people"—or to convert it into overt behavior. He or she is willing to defy law, if necessary, to protect beliefs and vested interests.

In recent years in this country we have witnessed a resurgence of organized "resistance" movements, some taking the form of citizen's militias, made up of those who would readily fit under Merton's rubric "Prejudiced Discriminators."

Each of these categories is, of course, an ideal type, a model against which reality is to be measured. Although it is rare that one finds a single individual who is all saint or all sinner, "fair weather liberals" and "timid bigots" do exist. Several caveats should be borne in mind: although many people prejudiced against one minority, say Italians, often tend to dislike others, such as Jews and blacks,[27] prejudice toward one minority does not necessarily mean prejudice toward all. Those who are antiblack are not, *ipso facto,* anti-Semites—or vice versa.[28]

Nor do dominant groups have a monopoly on prejudice. Many minority group members subscribe to images of other minorities that coincide with those held by members of the dominant groups. Examples include the anti-Semitism manifested by some blacks, as well as antiblack sentiments expressed by some Jews, both of which came to light during the crisis over the community control of schools in New York City in 1968–1969;[29] a decade later, over the resignation of Andrew Young, an African American minister and former Congressman, who was U.S. representative to the United Nations from 1976 to 1979; in the presidential primaries of 1988 when Jesse Jackson was a Democrat contender; and more recently, especially on college campuses.[30] Furthermore, for many racial, religious, and ethnic minorities the dominant group represents "the enemy camp."[31] Brewton Berry and Henry L. Tischler indicate that such hostility is often a direct product of socialization. They cite a story told by the late editor of the *Carolina Israelite,* Harry Golden, to illustrate the point—focusing on how prejudice is learned.

> My first impression of Christianity came in the home, of course. My parents brought with them the burden of the Middle Ages from the blood-soaked continent of Europe. They had come from the villages of Eastern Europe where Christians were feared with legitimate reason.
>
> When occasionally a Jewish drunk was seen in our neighborhood, our parents would say, "He's behaving like a Gentile."
>
> For in truth, our parents had often witnessed the Polish, Romanian, Hungarian, and Russian peasants gather around a barrel of whiskey on Saturday night, drink themselves into oblivion, "and beat their wives." Once in a while the rumor would spread through the tenements that a fellow had struck his wife, and on all sides we heard the inevitable, "Just like a Gentile."
>
> Oddly enough, too, our parents had us convinced that the Gentiles were noisy, boisterous, and loud—unlike the Jews.... . If we raised our voices, we were told, "Jewish boys don't shout." And this admonition covered every activity in and out of the home: "Jewish boys don't fight." "Jewish boys don't get dirty." "Jewish boys study hard."[32]

What Causes Prejudice?

There are many explanations for the causes of prejudice and the sources of discrimination.[33] Until the first quarter of the twentieth century, most theories focused primarily on physical traits and group differences. Some writers attempted to prove that certain groups are innately superior to others; others speculated that there is an instinctive aversion of people to the unfamiliar that accounts for antipathy toward aliens and strangers.

Biology and Behavior

In spite of the influence of Voltaire, Rousseau, and others who argued that there is a universal oneness in human nature, the eighteenth and nineteenth centuries saw the birth of a doctrinaire theory of group prejudice. Taxonomical classifications of human "races" paved the way for elaborate schemes that "proved" that some varieties of humankind were superior to others and that, inevitably, sought to justify the maltreatment of nonwhite people by Europeans.[34]

For example, the eighteenth-century scientist Carl von Linne (also known as Carolus Linnaeus) divided *Homo sapiens* into four racial groupings, each of which was purported to instill a distinctive "mentality" in its members. The African (*Afer niger*) was said to be slow and negligent, cunning and capricious. The American Indian (*Americanus rufus*) was described as tenacious, free, and easily contented. The Asiatic (*Asiaticus luridus*) was viewed as a haughty, stern, and opinionated fellow. The European (*Europaeus albus*) was envisaged as possessing the traits of liveliness and creativity and was considered to be superior to the other racial types. Whereas Linnaeus based his typology on color—black, red, yellow, white—and region, others (such as J. F. Blumenbach, Anders Retzius, Samuel G. Morton, and Josiah C. Nott) divided human beings into categories according to other physical attributes, and each series of measurements led to a different kind of classification of "races."

These classifications, devised by Europeans or white Americans, for the most part seemed to come to the same conclusion: "Nonwhites are innately inferior." The equation of somatic differences with culture traits gave birth to the theory of racial superiority or racism. Throughout the Western world it was asserted that colored people were degenerate, simple-minded, untamed, uncivilized. Such racist thinking was used by several writers to justify the slave system in the United States and to sanction exploitation by American, British, and other colonialists, many of whom viewed conquest and subjugation as the "white man's burden." Darwin's theory of evolution and the possibility of "separate creation" gave added legitimacy to the doctrine. The superordinate status of whites was taken to be evidence that the fittest survive and that the aggressive, not the meek, inherit the earth.

Since its inception, the dogma of racism has persisted in various forms. Nietzsche, Gobineau, H. S. Chamberlain, and Adolf Hitler, among others, argued that certain "racial" groups possess the traits of leadership, greatness, and nobility, and others are born to follow, to serve, or to be exterminated as useless parasites.

Early in the twentieth century many social scientists rejected the doctrine of racial superiority and the supposition that racial origins determine culture patterns. Yet, some held to the view that people instinctively dislike the strange and different. They saw *xenophobia* (the dislike of foreigners) as an inborn trait passed from one generation to the next. This was an element in the social thought of the early American sociologist F. H. Giddings, who argued that people identified with the members of their own social groups and excluded outsiders, owing to a "consciousness of kind." It was "natural" he claimed, for people to like what they know and to fear the unknown. Sociologists E.B. Reuter and G.W. Hart, in one of the early introductory textbooks in sociology, stated that prejudice was to be attributed to "the universal fear of things new and strange."[35] For a time even Robert E. Park, the scholar who was to become one of the major guiding forces behind the empirical study of intergroup relations, subscribed to the view. In 1924 Park wrote, "It is evident that there is in race prejudice as distinguished from class and caste prejudice, an *instinctive* factor based on the fear of the unfamiliar and uncomprehended."[36]

The I.Q. Controversy

Those who assume biological superiority (and inferiority) and innate or natural group aversion imply that there is something inherent in racial and ethnic bodies largely determining the thoughts, abilities, and group-focused loves and hates of their members. To most modern social scientists such a view is unacceptable. Looks may be transmitted through the genes, but not outlooks. The perspectives people have are thought to be the result of nurture, not nature. Even within similarly socialized groups, idiosyncratic differences are very great. Some people are strong and others weak, some are intelligent and some are feeble-minded. But the strong and the intelligent are to be found in all racial and cultural groups. The manner in which given individuals are able to optimize whatever innate potentialities they may possess is dependent, in part at least, upon the opportunities afforded in the social milieu into which they are born and in which they are raised. Indeed, according to the members of the American Anthropological Association, "all races possess the ability needed to participate fully in the democratic way of life and in modern technological civilization."[37]

With the development of systematic methods of investigation and a scientific orientation toward social life itself, the ideas that certain groups are born to lead and others to follow, that xenophobia is rooted in the genes, have been found to be theoretically and empirically untenable. However, this conclusion does not mean that research on the relationship between racial background and behavior has ceased. On the contrary, it has taken new forms—often variations on old themes that seek by use of such culturally biased instruments as intelligence tests to demonstrate persisting differences between blacks and whites.

Intelligence testing began in the 1890s and was used extensively in the early decades of this century. The most famous measures were the Stanford-Binet and the Yerkes Alpha and Beta tests used to assess American soldiers in World War I. Other psychologists, including Carl C. Brigham, who already assumed blacks to be inferior in intelligence, took data from Army tests claiming that native-born, white Americans "proved" more intelligent than new immigrants. Brigham was one of several behavioral scientists whose contentions about the deleterious effects of allowing newcomers to enter the United States lent considerable academic legitimacy to the restrictive immigration legislation of the 1920s discussed in Chapter 4.

Although later research clearly contradicted Brigham's claim regarding the differential scores of "natives" and immigrants (and their children), the black-white dichotomy still remained evident. Perhaps the best examples of such reasoning were to be found in the work of Audrey Sheuey, a Columbia University–trained psychologist and author of *The Testing of Negro Intelligence,* published in the late 1950s,[38] and in the debates over the work of Harvard University psychologist Arthur Jensen, published a decade later.[39] After an extensive review of the literature in which I.Q. test scores of white and African American subjects were compared, Sheuey concluded that the data clearly belie the claim that there are no native differences. The biggest problem was the leap she made between the finding that blacks scored proportionately lower and the argument that this was attributable to innate intellectual inferiority.

In perhaps the most pointed gibe at Sheuey's work (and the work of others who made similar claims), Adrian Dove, a social worker from the Watts section of Los Angeles, clearly illustrated that, at the time she did her research, the vast majority of white people would flunk his black-oriented "Dove Counterbalance Intelligence Test," but most African Americans would do quite well. The test consisted of 30 multiple choice questions, including the following:

Which word is out of place here? (a) splib, (b) blood, (c) gray, (d) spook, (e) Black.
A "handkerchief head" is a(n) (a) cool cat, (b) porter, (c) "Uncle Tom," (d) hoddi, (e) preacher.
"Hully Gully" came from (a) "East Oakland," (b) Fillmore, (c) Watts, (d) Harlem, (e) Motor City.[40]

Not all critics of the Sheuey argument used humor to counter it. Systematic research indicated the persisting cultural biases of the traditional tests.[41] Sometime after the debates over Sheuey's book had simmered down, psychologist Arthur Jensen gained widespread attention for an article, "How Much Can We Boost I.Q. and Scholastic Achievement?" published in the *Harvard Educational Review* in the winter of 1969 in which, on the basis of his research, he stated that it is "a not unreasonable hypothesis that genetic factors are strongly implicated in averaged Negro-white intelligence difference." This hypothesis was based on findings that alleged to show that (1) compensatory education programs designed to improve intellectual performance of those euphemistically called "culturally disadvantaged" failed to raise I.Q. scores; (2) children with low I.Q.'s tend to be handicapped genetically as well as culturally (or environmentally); (3) the genetic proclivity for certain types of performances is an important factor not merely in determining potential differences in intelligence ratings from the same group but also differences between groups; and (4) one should recognize and compensate for the fact that rote learning seems easier for some than abstract learning.[42] Aware that he might raise, once again, the specter of "scientific racism," Jensen nevertheless felt that a number of important questions about the relationship between nature and nurture needed consideration, especially by people who were concerned with the attainment of improved education for all children.

Reactions, especially to the shakiness of some of Jensen's assertions, as expected, were harsh—in some cases quite extreme. "Jensenism" became a word that was linked to "imperialism" and "fascism" and "genocide" by militant critics. Even those who attended the annual business meetings of the American Anthropological Association found themselves asked to vote on the censure of the *Harvard Educational Review* for publishing Jensen—and they proceeded to do so without protest. (The protest came later, and it was not only from reactionary quarters.)[43]

As Christopher Jencks, an authority on educational research, noted in a lengthy review of Jensen and his critics:

> Were there a dispassionate observer, who could look at these arguments without political or personal bias, I think he would conclude that neither Jensen nor his critics have offered a persuasive explanation of IQ differences between African Americans and whites. He would probably also conclude that neither geneticists nor social scientists know enough about the determinants of IQ scores to design a study which would fully resolve our present confusion. Nonetheless, Jensen's decision to reopen this ancient controversy without first gathering more evidence strikes me as a serious political blunder.[44]

An even more thorough assessment of Jensen's work was made by political scientist Philip Green, who, in three lengthy articles published in *Dissent,* challenged what he called "the fallacy of heritability."[45] In a few pointed paragraphs, Green suggested two ways of defining heritability. First he offered the "standard" definition: "The heritability of a trait refers to the extent to which variations in measurement from the average value of the trait may be traceable to genetic variation in the measured population."[46] Noting that the key word is "population," Green pointed out that this has generally meant "specific breeding and rearing populations"—at least according to most geneticists—but he suggests, "the heritability of a trait can equally be conceived of as nothing more than a function of the extent to which salient features of the environments the observed population lives in are themselves alike or unlike."[47] In his three essays, Green proceeded to elaborate on this contention that, after a review of the literature, he found "not a single aspect of the history of inherited deficiency is ascribable to genetics: it is all a product of social conditions and thus potentially susceptible to social amelioration."[48]

In the late 1980s and the early 1990s, a number of articles and new books reopened and reexamined the issue of cognitive stratification. Some, like Mark Snyderman and Stanley Rothman's *The I.Q. Controversy,* focused mainly on the media reactions to a matter that was linked to all sorts of other public policy issues, not least to growing disenchantment with social programs that favored certain groups and the ominous threat of polarization in American society.[49] Some were attempts to review the literature and offer sober assessments, which recognized the difficulties of sorting out truly independent variables. But, according to the biologist Stephen Jay Gould, the books that received the most attention, having zeroed in, once again, on the genetic, "race-based" character of intelligence held "no new arguments or compelling data but cash[ed] in on the depressing temper of our time—a historical moment of unprecedented ungenerosity, when a mood for slashing social programs can be powerfully abetted by an argument that beneficiaries cannot be helped, owing to inborn cognitive limits expressed as low I.Q. scores."[50] By far the most comprehensive and controversial was *The Bell Curve,* by Richard J. Herrnstein and Charles Murray.[51]

In their book, Herrnstein and Murray offer a contemporary argument for what has been called "social Darwinism," the idea that the smartest survive, coupled with a categorical imperative, that the reason that whites and Asians do better than blacks is that there is a "racial" basis to intelligence. This is not the only one they make. In fact, Murray now claims it is not even the central issue, but there is no doubt about the message and the ammunition it provides for those wont to believe that I.Q. tests are fair measures, that they are (or can be made) culture-free and unbiased, and that, given the fact that those belonging to certain cohorts score lower in the aggregate than others, they must be less intelligent, requiring different means of assistance (or treatment) than that now provided. Despite the dubiousness of the tests used to determine intelligence, the failure to address social structural inequities, limits placed on those who are stigmatized, or other mitigating circumstances, *The Bell Curve*'s "scientific approach" has been used as a weapon in recent battles about race and social policy. Although Charles Murray repeatedly denies that this was their intention, no such disclaimer has come from Seymour Itzkoff, author of *The Decline of Intelligence in America,*[52] a volume even more blatant in its acceptance of Social Darwinism, which spells out policy positions akin to those of early eugenicists (such as curtailing immigration), than that of Herrnstein and Murray.

Whatever else, the renewed debates—known by some as "The Bell Curve Wars[53]—forced the examination of a number of important assumptions, not the least being those related to the persistent blurring of the study of race per se (and of race differences) and the study of prejudice and discrimination and their effects. The significance of the distinction becomes clearly apparent when one moves away from the emotionally charged realm of "intelligence" and "performance" to that of health and illness.

It has long been asserted by some that racial purity is a virtue and that, by sticking to one's own race, many problems can be avoided. Perhaps, as some African Americans now argue (and as many whites have long contended) there is a psychological truth embedded in the assumption but not necessarily a physiological one. Recent medical research has shown several important negative results of endogamy (marriage to a member of one's own group, especially an ethnic or racial one) in the so-called race-based diseases, such as Sickle-cell anemia, Thalassemia, and Tay-Sachs disease, which are prevalent among African Americans, Mediterranean peoples, and Ashkenazic Jews, respectively.

The suggestion here is that, as the famous geneticist Theodore Dobzhansky has noted, "Faced with a revival of 'scientific' racism, one is tempted to treat the matter with the silent scorn it so richly deserves ... [Yet] it may perhaps be useful to add a warning against exaggerations which some writers bent on combating racism are unwittingly making."[54] In one sense, making official statements such as the unanimous declaration of the American Anthropological Association cited above, denies to the discreditors the notion that those categorized as members of a given racial group (such as the far-from-"pure"-American African Americans) are innately inferior, but in another sense it begs several questions that remain scientifically legitimate.[55] The study of race and the ideology of racism must be dealt with as separate phenomena.

Social Structure and Individual Personality

Concern about racism is clearly at the center of most current discussions of prejudice in American society. But various students of the subject tend to concentrate their attention on one or another aspect of the overall problem. Some focus on the social system and its various parts (organizations, classes, and institutions), its rules or norms, and its purported values. Society itself is often the principal unit of analysis. Others eschew so grand a scope of study, preferring to concentrate on individual behavior and personality. George A. Kourvetaris has called these polar approaches "macroscopic" and "microscopic."[56] As a number of social scientists have indicated, there are "levels" in between. In their well known, multiedition text, *Racial and Cultural Minorities,* George Simpson and J. Milton Yinger make the point that "to say simply that there is an 'instinct' or natural tendency toward prejudice, or that there is an inevitable 'dislike of the unlike,' or that so-called prejudice against minority groups is a natural reaction to their factual inferiority—explanations that abound in the literature—is to fail to bring the study of prejudice into the framework of contemporary theory of human behavior."[57] They suggest posing a set of questions:

> Do groups differ in the direction and amount of prejudice that they exhibit? If so, why?
>
> Is there change, through time and space in the groups, and kinds of groups toward which prejudice is directed?
>
> What is the process by which an individual acquires prejudice?
>
> What forces, in the lives of individuals and of groups, operate to sustain, and to reduce prejudice?[58]

Simpson and Yinger then attempt to answer the questions they pose by looking from the micro- (or the individual) level, focusing on personal needs, to the macro level, examining the structure of society—power arrangements and economic, political, religious, and other structural variables. In between they look at culture and cultural values and norms and the way in which these are transmitted.[59] This latter category is concerned with socialization, a most significant factor in the writing of the late Gordon W. Allport, author of *The Nature of Prejudice.*[60]

Allport, too, described levels in discussing his diagram reproduced in figure 7.1.[61] The approaches mentioned by Allport include examining the rationalized self-interests of upper classes in various societies; studying traditions that lead to conflict, upward mobility, and the challenge of certain elements in society; and looking at population density and various types of contact, all of which

Figure 7.1 Theoretical and Methodological Approaches to the Study of the Causes of Prejudice

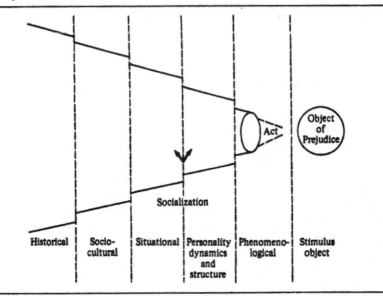

Source: G. W. Allport, "Prejudice: A Problem in Psychological and Social Causation," Journal of Social Issues, Supplement Series, No. 4 (1950).

occur when social change is intensive, as in the case of rapid urbanization. But, said Allport, in addition to these approaches, comprehensive analysis must consider social climates, the settings of social interaction where rules are interpreted and acted upon. Moreover, Allport recognized the importance of the characteristics placed upon groups who are often the very objects of discrimination itself. (For example, in medieval Europe, many Jews, denied the right to own land or to work in any occupations other than those involving high risk such as petty finance, became moneylenders and tax collectors, thereby fulfilling the prophecy that Jews are money brokers.) In the last instance we almost come full circle for, according to Allport, the minority group member is the stimulus object, the object of prejudice, and the target of discrimination. (Here is the classic case of scapegoating to rationalize the self-interest mentioned above.)[62]

In the sections to follow, we look at some of these areas of concern with special attention to economic and class factors, culture and personality, and the socialization process itself.

Economic Causes

Followers of Marx and a good many other social scientists view prejudice as primarily the result of the strained relationship between the exploited and the exploiter. Carey McWilliams, for example, argued that anti-Semitism has traditionally been "a mask for privilege" and is based on the efforts of those in economically advantageous positions to exclude rising groups.[63] Long ago Oliver Cox and others hypothesized that the whole system of race relations and segregated patterns, especially in the United States, is directly related to the maintenance of a cheap labor supply.[64] In not very different terms many contemporary analysts of American racial patterns argue that they are a form of domestic colonialism based on a continuing policy of exploitation of poor people, especially those who belong to such "Third World groups" as African Americans, Puerto Ricans, Mexican Americans, Asian Americans, and Native Americans.[65]

The "Colonial Model," at least when applied to the situation of Third World Americans, according to William J. Wilson, involves four fundamental components: (1) The racial group's entry into the dominant society is forced and involuntary. (2) The members of the dominant group administer the affairs of the suppressed or colonized group. (3) The culture and social organization of the suppressed group are destroyed. (4) Racism exists—that is, "a principle of social domination by which a group seen as inferior or different in terms of alleged biological characteristics is exploited, controlled and oppressed socially and psychically by a superordinate group."[66]

Although all social scientists do not agree that economic interests play the most important role in bringing about and maintaining prejudice and discrimination, many have found that the intergroup conflict continues in large part because of the gains—both material and psychological—that are realized by assuming an attitude of superiority and enforcing social distance between one's own group and others. Early studies of "social distance" suggested that the principal basis for differential ranking of ethnic groups is the desire to maintain or enhance one's social position by associating with groups considered to be of high status and by disassociating from those low in the prestige hierarchy.[67] Since the 1940s investigators have consistently found anti-Semitism and antiblack sentiments to be most common among people dissatisfied with their own economic position or among those whose status has declined.[68] And, as has been recently shown, the rhetoric of resentment over difficulties in breaking out of desperate situations have led to some to blame other, more successful minorities, Jews, Asians, etc., for their continued failure to move out of poverty and into the mainstream of society.[69] Of course, such blame-placing for being stifled economically is psychologically significant as well. It functions as a means of displacement.

Psychological Interpretations

In 1945 Bruno Bettelheim and Morris Janowitz documented the relationship between downward mobility and increased antipathy toward Jews and African Americans.[70] In *Social Change and Prejudice,* a volume published years after the initial study, they summarized the findings of various national sample surveys conducted to reexamine the relationship.[71] In their original investigation Bettelheim and Janowitz suggested that from among the 150 young veterans they interviewed in Chicago, those enjoying moderate upward mobility were more tolerant than those who had experienced no change in status, those who were rising very rapidly, or, especially, those experiencing downward mobility. In explaining these differences the authors said that "one can argue that, given American values which legitimate social mobility ... the moderately upwardly mobile person is likely to have relatively effective personal controls." This theme of effective controls was crucial to the revised theoretical orientation of the investigators. In their more recent work they place heavy stress on new developments in ego psychology in which the person is viewed as part of, not apart from, his wider social milieu. In these terms prejudice is no longer seen as a reflection of an inherently weak ego straining against unacceptable inner strivings (as many psychologists have long contended); rather the emphasis is on the protective shield prejudice affords to those whose identity is threatened, as in the case of those experiencing sudden changes of status.

In societies such as our own, where prejudice is a "normal" rather than an "abnormal" fact of social life, Bettelheim and Janowitz once asserted that it must be understood in functional terms. In popular parlance, prejudice helps to pump up the egos of those who feel deprived or threatened; it reduces anxiety about one's own status; it adds in the assertion of superiority. "Unless other means of ego support are found for the person seeking identity and fearing its loss, prejudice can be expected to exist in one form or other."

The notion that prejudice may prove advantageous to certain individuals is something that bigoted demagogues and militant minority leaders have long known. This idea also has long been explored by social scientists. In the 1930s in his classic study of race relations, *Caste and Class in a Southern Town,* John Dollard examined the functions of prejudice. Dollard was particularly impressed with the level of "social inertia," the reluctance to change traditional patterns mainly because of the gains accruing to those middle-class whites who maintained the institutions of segregation.[72] Among the advantages he saw were those in the spheres of economics, sexual activities, and ego gratification linked to what Dollard called "prestige."

The psychological advantages of prejudice can be demonstrated more clearly in Freudian than in Marxian terms. Some writers have explained prejudice as a means of deflecting aggressions created by personal frustrations.[73] The thesis develops as follows: One goes through life seeking gratification for felt needs and, although many such needs have their origin in the organic structure of the individual, there are others that are culturally determined. These are learned early in life and are channeled and directed toward certain goals. When goal-directed behavior is blocked, hostile impulses are frequently created in the individual who, unable to determine the real source of his frustration but in an attempt to overcome it, manifests "free-floating aggression."[74] Such undirected aggression finds a "legitimate" point on which to focus that becomes a substitute for the actual frustrating agent. Usually the target is weak and unable to strike back. This process is well known: The boss berates his employee, who takes it out on his wife, who in turn berates the children. And so it goes.

Free-floating aggression is often directed toward a minority group or out-group whose status in society puts it in a vulnerable position. One observer has made the point in graphic—though extreme—terms: "The rich take to opium and hashish.

Those who cannot afford them become anti-Semites. Anti-Semitism is the morphine of the small people.... Since they cannot attain the ecstasy of love they seek the ecstasy of hate. The Jew is just convenient.... If there were no Jews the anti-Semites would have to invent them."[75]

When aggression is displaced in this manner the target is a scapegoat. In sociological parlance, scapegoating is the expression used to describe the psychological mechanism of displacing aggression. It refers to placing one's own "iniquities" or "sins" upon others. The scapegoat is therefore a whipping boy for the frustration-invoked hostility of the individuals or groups who use it. And, as Albert Camus has suggested, anyone and anything can become a scapegoat: "We are all exceptional cases. We all want to appeal against something. Each of us insists at all costs that he is innocent even if he has to accuse the whole human race and heaven itself."[76]

The reader who examines these economic and psychological explanations of the basis of prejudice may ask what predisposes certain individuals to attempt to exploit others or to seek scapegoats upon whom they can transfer their own inadequacies. One attempt to answer this question was made by a group of behavioral scientists who hypothesized "that the political, economic, and social convictions of an individual often form a broad and coherent pattern as if bound together by a 'mentality' or 'spirit' and that this pattern is an expression of deep-lying trends in his personality."[77] This statement is taken from a now classic study of *The Authoritarian Personality,* which, 50 years ago, presented a new approach to the investigation of prejudice. The major concern of this large-scale research, conducted in the United States during and after World War II, was to understand the "potentially fascistic individual, one whose structure is such as to render him or her particularly susceptible to antidemocratic propaganda."[78]

Both quantitative and qualitative research techniques were employed in this investigation. Questionnaires administered to groups of college students (and later to others) provided background information about the respondents. Stereotype-laden questions were used as bases for the development of scales of anti-Semitism, ethnocentrism, politicoeconomic conservatism, and fascism. Two types of interviews were administered to the extreme scorers on these scales: one, nondirective, aimed at getting at basic ideology; the other, clinical-genetic, designed to elicit case history material. Analysis of data thus obtained suggested that antipathy toward minorities and ethnocentric thinking—called "social discrimination" by the authors—is part of a generalized ideological system pertaining to groups and group relations. Highly prejudiced individuals were found to possess the following personality characteristics: glorification of power; the tendency to view people as good or bad, and things as black or white; deep concern with status and toughness; repression of sexual feelings; conception of the world as a jungle; cynicism about human nature; the proclivity to blame others rather than themselves for misdeeds and trouble. Out-group hostility was especially prominent among the defense mechanisms of the "authoritarians." Concerning these extreme scorers, the authors wrote: "The basically hierarchical, authoritarian, exploitative parent-child relationship is apt to carry over into a power-oriented, exploitatively dependent attitude toward one's sex partner and one's God and may well culminate in a political philosophy and social outlook which has no room for anything but a desperate clinging to what appears to be strong and disdainful rejection of whatever is relegated to the bottom.[79] Put in other words, the study concluded that many, perhaps most, highly prejudiced persons are mentally disturbed.[80]

This conclusion no doubt holds for many individuals of "rigid personality," including at least some of the leaders of extremist hate movements and, perhaps, quite a few of their followers.[81] But these all-weather bigots are hardly representative of the vast number of Americans who harbor racial and ethnic prejudice and discriminate against minority groups. In fact, follow-up studies of hypotheses presented in *The Authoritarian Personality,* using similar or identical research instruments (especially the "F [for fascism] scale"), report that prejudice and discrimination characterize the attitudes and behavior of many "normal" people.[82] Moreover, careful testing of the hypotheses of the pioneering work suggests that bigotry is by no means confined to politically conservative or reactionary individuals, and that authoritarian personalities are to be found among both the right and the left segments of the nation's citizenry.[83] Given the fact that these patterns are widespread, adequate sociological explanation of prejudice and discrimination cannot be confined to psychological deviation alone. Prejudice and discrimination constitute a major social problem precisely because most of their practitioners *conform to established beliefs and values.*

Socialization and Social Conformity

Rather than conceiving of group prejudice as an inborn tendency or a characteristic rent in one's basic personality, most sociologists today view it as a social habit. This thesis derives from the general proposition that cultural traits are learned. In the process of learning the ways of their groups—the process of socialization—individuals acquire both self-perceptions and images of others. If the teaching is effective, the individual internalizes (in substantial measure, but never fully) the sentiments and customs of his social milieu—including the "appropriate" prejudices. As sociologists MacIver and Page once wrote: "The individual is not born with prejudices any more than he is born with sociological understanding. The way he thinks as a member of a group, especially about other groups, is at bottom the result of social indoctrination, in both its direct and its indirect forms, indoctrination that inculcates beliefs and attitudes, which easily take firm hold in his life through the process of habituation.[84] An old southerner put it this way:

> I grew up just 19 miles from Appomattox. The teaching I received both in school and from my parents was hard-core South, with no chance of insight into the thinking and ways of other peoples. I was taught to look down upon Negroes, tolerate Jews (because we had to do business with them) and ignore Catholics.
>
> We celebrated Jefferson Davis's birthday, but ignored Lincoln's; the name Robert E. Lee was spoken with reverence and Appomattox was a shrine. The Golden Rule only applied to others who were either Methodist or Baptist, white and without a foreign-sounding name.... [85]

The acceptance of various prejudices does not require direct contact between the learner and the members of groups held in low esteem. If the agents of socialization—parents

Conclusion

we have seen, has been attributed to basic economic interests, to
personality structure, to reactions to frustration, to social conformity,
ation. There are, of course, other interpretations; for example: the
on the symbolic significance of the presence of a particular minority
rea;[99] the idea that contact with certain minorities under certain cir-
increases rather than decreases prejudice;[100] and what Allport has called
tation"—the notion that individuals react to ethnic traits that are in fact
d threatening and therefore evoke realistic hostility.[101]

ese interpretations possesses more than a kernel of truth, and each may
in prejudice of a particular sort. Group prejudice is not a one-dimen-
menon. Although we have not exhausted the various explanations for
e, one thing appears certain: Prejudice is learned, not inherited.

Notes

d Kipling, "We and They," in *Debits and Credits* (London: Macmillan, 1926),
By permission of Mrs. George Bambridge, the Macmillan Co. of London &
the Macmillan Co. of Canada, and Doubleday & Co., Inc.

ee also Ronald Takaki, *A Different Mirror: A History of Multicultural America*
e, Brown & Co., 1993).

n Graham Sumner, *Folkways* (Boston: Ginn, 1906), p. 13.

Louis Stevenson, "Foreign Children," In *The Works of Robert Louis Stevenson*
Walter Black, Inc., 1926) (originally published in 1883).

et Mead, *And Keep Your Powder Dry* (New York: William Morris 1965), p. 11.

r example, P. Zeligs and G. Hendrickson, "Racial Attitudes of 200 Sixth-Grade
ociology and Social Research* (September–October 1933), pp. 26–36.

Andre, "Stereotypes: Conceptual and Normative Considerations," in Paula S.
(ed.), *Racism and Sexism* (New York: St. Martin's Press, 1988), pp. 257–262.
. 259.

rted in Vincent Parrillo, *Strangers to These Shores,* 4th ed. (New York: Macmil-
p. 501–502. The findings were discussed on *Nova,* in a program called "The
e Blues," on Public Broadcasting, 1982.

Mark Snyder, "Self-Fulfilling Stereotypes," in *Racism and Sexism,* Paula S.
, ed. (New York: St. Martin's Press, 1988), pp. 263–269.

und Freud, *Group Psychology and the Analysis of the Ego* (New York: Boni
nt, 1950), p. 55.

n and Hong have found that "after social dominance has been taken into account,
ce of ethnocentrism in minorities is a further factor in the development of majority
illiam R. Catton, Jr., and Sung Chick Hong, "The Relation of Apparent Minority
sm to Majority Antipathy," *American Sociological Review,* 27 (April 1962), p. 190.

ph G. Gittler, "Man and His Prejudices," *The Scientific Monthly,* 69 (July 1949),
See also Herbert Blumer, "Race Prejudice as a Sense of Group Position," *Pacific
l Review,* 1 (Spring 1958), pp. 3–7.

or peers, teachers, preachers, or community leaders—are themselves prejudiced
people, they are apt to be effective conveyers of group antipathies whether the
objects of their attitudes are immediate neighbors or distant out-groups.

The lessons learned in this "natural" process of enculturation constitute a serious problem for those educators and other persons who attempt to make more
realizable the values of the American ethos. They are competing with the home,
playground, and, sometimes, the mass media, which for many people represent
the normal and desirable way of life, a way of life that all too often is inconsistent
with and disruptive of ideals of freedom, social equality, and unhampered opportunity. This situation is aggravated by the fact that group antipathy has been found
to exist not only among individuals of high socioeconomic status but also among
those in the rank and file.

Culture and Institutionalized Racism

Many contemporary writers and most militant minority group leaders consider
institutionalized racism to be the principal source of prejudice against nonwhite
peoples (or those treated as a "racial" group, like Jews in Nazi Germany). Their
explanations find expression in many forms—from academic rhetoric to the argot
of the street—but the theme remains more or less the same. The core argument is
that a belief in their own superiority is deeply ingrained in the minds of those in
the dominant sector (in our country this means white people) and in their social
mores. They have internalized the same views as those promulgated by the early
anthropologists and perpetuated by those who, for several centuries, claimed to be
lifting and carrying "the white man's burden." The late Whitney M. Young put it
succinctly when he wrote that "racism ... is the assumption of superiority and the
arrogance that goes with it."[86]

As noted earlier, many southerners found scientific racism a justification for the
exploitation of Africans during the first half of the nineteenth century, a time when
the institution of slavery was being severely challenged. Increasing evidence suggests that others shared their views but, instead of putting down the blacks, they put
them out, out of their minds. Joel Kovel, for example, in his psychohistory *White
Racism* contends that in this country racism is still manifest in efforts to control (or
what he calls the pattern of "dominative racism") or to avoid ("aversive racism").

He explains that: "in general, the dominative type has been marked by heat and
the aversive type by coldness. The former is clearly associated with the American
South, where, of course, domination of blacks became the cornerstone of society;
and the latter with the North, where blacks have so consistently come and found
themselves out of place. The dominative racist, when threatened by the black,
resorts to direct violence; the aversive racist, in the same situation, turns away and
walls himself off."[87]

To pursue the point one step further, it is interesting to note that, like Alexis de
Tocqueville long before him, Kovel asserts that aversive racists have been more
intense in their reaction than their dominative countrymen. As long ago as the 1830s,
Tocqueville had suggested: "The prejudice of race appears to be stronger in the

states that have abolished slavery than in those where it still exists; and nowhere is it so intolerant as in those states where servitude has never been known.... "[88] In the years following the order to end legal segregation in all regions of the United States, the observations of Tocqueville became quite apparent. White northerners who long overlooked what was happening in their midst while condemning southerners for their racial prejudice, began revealing that they were by no means immune to racism themselves.

Institutionalized racism thus pertains to discriminatory practices reflected in customs and laws and practices engaged in, even by those previously called "reluctant discriminators," and the rules surrounding what is required, what is expected, what is forbidden—and with whom. This is the principal subject of the next chapter on discrimination and institutionalized racism. But, before going there it is well to consider the most recent body of thought on the general subject. Much of it falls under the broad rubric "Critical Race Theory."

Critical Race Theory

Based on an assumption that "most people understand that 'race' as it is used in our society is a social construction not a biological truth [the fact remains] that race remains with us as a compelling myth that has real consequences."[89] It is, according to law professor Richard Delgado, the *sine qua non* of "Critical Race Theory."[90] Delgado and other writers on the subject contend that, far more than class or region, "race" has been and remains at the very nexus of inequity in the United States and that discrimination based on assumptions about race (as socially defined) persists not only in custom but, in many places, including the Constitution, in law.

Delgado and his coauthor, Jean Stefancic, summarize the basic tenants of the approach by noting that in our society 1) "racism is ordinary, not aberrational"; 2) "white over color ascendancy serves important purposes, both psychic and material"; and, 3) "race and races are products of social thought and relations."[91]

Much of the writing of those who place themselves (or are placed) in the camp of the Critical Race Theorists frames arguments in language that highlights many of the explanations of prejudice and its effects cited in the preceding sections. For example, Delgado and Stefancic's propositions clearly reflect ideas of some of those we have just discussed: scholars and activists who hold to cultural explanations, claiming that we should worry not only about the bigots but the "gentle people of prejudice," those who are social conformists; we should understand the functions of prejudice according to those who offer both Marxian and Freudian (and other psychological) arguments relating to material advantages and psychic rewards of power over others—and the disadvantages of those whom the exploit and victimize; and be mindful of a *leit motif* that appears again and again throughout this volume, the idea that race, as it is generally used, is a social construction.) But the Critical Race Theorists break new ground in their emphasis on racism itself, particularly, but not exclusively, in its embeddedness within certain influential institutions, most especially the legal and educational systems.[92]

Often the words of the Critical Race The observations about the very real distinction tween professed beliefs and actual conduct, go further, following one of their pioneers, Bell, who suggested that even the creed itse ing document, the U.S. Constitution, favors tendency to maintain the status quo ante. He those (or, perhaps, especially those) who are liberals, rarely support efforts to redress griev minorities unless it is in their own self- or gro to this argument in discussing reactions to th and 1970s in Chapter 10).[93]

Other Critical Race Theorists such as Kimb and Lani Guinier[96] contend that the whole leg to avoid the persisting pitfall of failing to mov the actual structure of a representative democ the expansion of rights in an agenda that empl stead of the traditionally restrictive idea (deepl) an equality of opportunity. A common theme i impossible for those who are handicapped at th Thus, if the law is to be used as a means to figh start by addressing its own inherent weaknesse:

Related to such a critique of the legal syst(nature of research itself. A number of Critical F members of various "minority" groups, argue t the character of prejudice, discrimination, and r pens and computers of those who have never en(class" themselves. Richard Delgado, for examp of the perspectives of victims of oppression to socialization and social conformity in American

In a way, it raises an issue that has long been as a political debate in the social sciences: Who i actions: Outside "observers," or inside "membei paper on the subject in 1978,

> The sociological perspective calls for providing a fr stand what is being studied, what is being read, the which people live and work and play and suffer, the text the variables that relate to human affairs everyv
>
> I now feel very strongly that the work of the socio judge in *Rashomon*, the one who asks various witnes a particular event as seen through their own eyes. I of sociology nor students can be allowed to get off disparate pieces of evidence and then try to figure ou perhaps we will be better able to know the troubles able to understand them.[98]

Prejudice, a
authoritariai
to poor edu
emphasis u
in a certain
cumstances
"earned rep
menacing a

Each of
help to exp
sional phen
its occurrer

1. Rudya
pp. 327–328
Basingstoke
2. Idem.
(Boston: Li
3. Willia
4. Rober
(New York:
5. Marga
6. See, f
Children,"
7. Judith
Rothenberg
8. Ibid.,
9. As re|
lan, 1994),
Pinks and
10. Ide
11. *See*
Rothenberg
12. Sig
and Liveri
13. Cat
the appeara
hostility."
Ethnocentr
14. Jos
pp. 43–47
Sociologi

15. Daniel Wilner et al., "Residential Proximity and Intergroup Relations in Public Housing Projects," *Journal of Social Issues,* 8 (No. 1, 1952), 45. For several classic discussions of the definition of prejudice, see Gordon W. Allport, *The Nature of Prejudice* (Cambridge: Addison-Wesley, 1954), pp. 3–16; Brewton Berry, *Race and Ethnic Relations* (Boston: Houghton Mifflin, 1958), pp. 363–371; John Harding et al., "Prejudice and Ethnic Relations," in Gardner Lindzey (ed.), *Handbook of Social Psychology,* Vol. II (Cambridge: Addison-Wesley, 1954), pp. 1021–1061; George Simpson and J. Milton Yinger, *Racial and Cultural Minorities,* rev. ed. (New York: Harper & Row, 1958), pp. 14–19; and Robin M. Williams, Jr., *The Reduction of Intergroup Tensions* (New York: The Social Science Research Council, Bulletin No. 57, 1947), pp. 36–43.

16. See Bernard M. Kramer, "Dimensions of Prejudice," *Journal of Psychology,* 27 (April 1949), pp. 389–451.

17. Arnold M. Rose, "Anti-Semitism's Root in City Hatred," *Commentary,* 6 (October 1949), p. 374.

18. This is essentially the same definition used by Robin M. Williams, Jr., op. cit., p. 39.

19. As reported in *Time* (September 29, 1958), p. 58. Italics supplied.

20. As reported in *The New York Times* (October 21, 1966), p. 28.

21. John P. Dean and Alex Rosen, *A Manual of Intergroup Relations* (University of Chicago Press, 1955), p. 58.

22. Robert K. Merton, "Discrimination and the American Creed," In R.M. MacIver (ed.), *Discrimination and National Welfare* (New York: Harper & Row, 1949), pp. 99–126. The passages to follow are largely summary statements of Merton's thesis. Only direct quotations will be noted.

23. Ibid, p.105.

24. See, for example, Robert O. Blood, "Discrimination Without Prejudice," *Social Problems,* 3 (October 1955), pp. 114–117.

25. Merton, op. cit., p. 108.

26. Ibid, p. 109.

27. See Allport, op. cit., p. 68.

28. See, for example, E. Terry Prothro and John A. Jenson, "Interrelations of Religious and Ethnic Attitudes in Selected Southern Relations," *The Journal of Social Psychology,* 32 (August 1950), pp. 45–49.

29. See, for example, Herbert J. Gans, "Negro-Jewish Conflict in New York," *Midstream* (March 1969).

30. See Peter I. Rose, "Blaming the Jews," *Society* (November/October, 1994), pp. 35–40

31. See, for example, Gerhard W. Ditz, "Out-group and In-group Prejudice Among Members of Minority Groups," *Alpha Kappa Deltan* (Spring 1959), 26–31; and Catton and Hong, op. cit., pp. 178–191.

32. Harry Golden, *You're Entitled* (Cleveland: World Publishing Company, 1962), p. 259.

33. For a more detailed discussion of various explanations of what have long been viewed as some of the causes of prejudice, see Allport, op. cit., pp. 206–216; Arnold M. Rose, "The Causes of Prejudice," in Francis E. Merrill (ed.), *Social Problems* (New York: Knopf, 1950), pp. 402–424; Arnold M. Rose, "The Roots of Prejudice," in *The Race Question in Modern Science* (a UNESCO publication) (New York: Whiteside, Inc., and William Morrow and Company, 1956), pp. 215–243, and Robin M. Williams, Jr., op. cit., pp. 36–77.

34. See especially Peter I. Rose, *The Subject Is Race* (New York: Oxford University Press, 1968). Also see Oscar Handlin, "The Linnaean Web," in *Race and Nationality in American*

Life (Garden City, N.Y.: Doubleday, 1957), pp. 57–73; and Cyril Bibby, *Race, Prejudice and Education* (New York: Praeger, 1960), pp. 40–62.

35. E. B. Reuter and C. W. Hart, *Introduction to Sociology* (New York: McGraw-Hill, 1963), p. 263.

36. Robert E. Park and Ernest W. Burgess, *Introduction to the Science of Sociology* (University of Chicago Press, 1924), p. 578. Italics supplied. Park later modified his position. For example, in "The Nature of Race Relations," in Edgar T. Thompson (ed.), *Race Relations and the Race Problem* (Durham, N.C.: Duke University Press, 1939), pp. 3–45, he wrote: "Race consciousness, therefore, is to be regarded as a phenomenon, like class or caste consciousness that enforces social distances."

37. This is the closing sentence of a resolution passed by the Fellows of the American Anthropological Association, November 17, 1961. A similar resolution was adopted at the annual meeting of the Society for the Study of Social Problems in 1961.

38. Audrey Sheuey, *The Testing of Negro Intelligence* (Lynchburg, Va.: Randolph-Macon Women's College, 1958).

39. Arthur R. Jensen, "How Much Can We Boost I.Q. and Scholastic Achievement?" *Harvard Educational Review,* 39 (Winter 1969), 1–123. See also *Educability and Group Differences* (New York: Harper & Row, 1973).

40. As reported in *The New Republic* (December 16, 1967), 7. N.B.: The answer is (c) in each case. The full text of the "test" appeared in *The Denver Post* (July 8, 1968), p. 6.

41. See, for example, Melvin M. Tumin (ed.), *Race and Intelligence* (New York. Anti-Defamation League, 1963).

42. Jensen, op. cit. See also Christopher Jencks, "Intelligence and Race," *The New Republic* (September 13, 1969), 25–29.

43. The sharpest barb came from anthropologist Jerry Hyman, who facetiously suggested that the Association had not gone far enough. He suggested "That it is incumbent on all members dedicated to Truth to seek out and destroy any remaining copies of publications that include the views of Herrnstein, Shockley and Jensen so that our libraries and institutions of learning not be used to disseminate such unscientific and potentially damaging material. That special attention be paid to the destruction of *The Atlantic Monthly, Harvard Educational Review,* and *New York Times* in that their complicity in this deception has been more energetic and more constant than other publications. That the method of destruction shall be left to the conscience of the individual follow or voting member but that fire is a particular symbolic and therefore appropriate mechanism." (Quoted from *Newsletter of the American Anthropological Association,* 13 [February 1972], 2–3.)

44. Jencks, op. cit., p. 29. See also H.J. Eysink, *The I.Q. Argument* (New York: Library Press, 1972).

45. Philip Green, "Race and I.Q.: Fallacy of Heritability," *Dissent* (Spring 1976); "The Pseudo Science of Arthur Jensen," *Dissent* (Summer 1976); and, "I.Q. and the Future of Equality," *Dissent* (Fall 1976).

46. Philip Green, "Race and I.Q.," op. cit., p. 183.

47. Ibid., p. 184.

48. Ibid., p. 192. For another useful summary of the controversy see Berry and Tischler, op. cit., Chap. 4, pp. 63–86.

49. Mark Snyderman and Stanley Rothman, *The I Q Controversy: The Media and Public Policy* (New Brunswick, N.J.: Transaction Books, 1988.)

50. Stephen Jay Gould, "Curveball," *The New Yorker,* November 28, 1994, p. 139.

51. Richard J. Herrnstein and Charles Murray, *The Bell Curve* (New York: Free Press, 1994).

52. Seymour Itzkoff, *The Decline of Intelligence in America* (Westport, CT: Praeger, 1994).

53. See Steven Fraser (ed.), *The Bell Curve Wars: Race, Intelligence and the Future of America* (New York: Basic Books, 1995).

54. Theodore Dobzhansky, "Comment," *Current Anthropology,* 2 (October 1961), 31.

55. Rose, *The Subject Is Race,* op. cit., p. 41.

56. George A. Kourvetaris, "Prejudice and Discrimination in American Social Structure," in P. Allan Dionisopoulos (ed.), *Racism in America* (DeKalb: Northern Illinois University Press, 1971), pp. 32–41.

57. George Eaton Simpson and J. Milton Yinger, *Racial and Cultural Minorities,* 4th ed. (New York: Harper & Row, 1972), p. 63.

58. Idem.

59. Simpson and Yinger, op. cit., pp. 63–102 and 139–164.

60. Allport, op. cit.

61. Gordon W. Allport, "Prejudice: A Problem in Psychological and Social Causation," *Journal of Social Issues,* Supplement Series, No. 4, 1950

62. Allport, *The Nature of Prejudice,* pp. 201–212.

63. Carey McWilliams, *A Mask for Privilege: Anti-Semitism in America* (Boston: Little, Brown, 1948).

64. Oliver C. Cox, *Caste, Class and Race: A Study in Social Dynamics* (Garden City, N.Y.: Doubleday, 1948).

65. See, for example, Jack Forbes et al., *The Third World Within* (Belmont, Calif.: Wadsworth, 1972); and Joan W. Moore, "Colonialism: The Case of the Mexican-Americans," *Social Problems,* 17 (Spring 1970), 463–472.

66. William J. Wilson, "Race Relations Models and Explanations of Ghetto Behavior," in Peter I. Rose (ed.), *Nation of Nations* (New York: Random House, 1972), p. 262. The definition of "racism" is from Robert Blauner, "Internal Colonialism and Ghetto Revolt," *Social Problems,* 16 (Spring 1969), 396.

67. See, for example, studies by E.S. Bogardus, including: "Social Distance and Its Origins," *Journal of Applied Sociology,* 9 (1925), 216–226; "Analyzing Changes in Public Opinion," *Journal of Applied Sociology,* 9 (1925), 372–381; "Social Distance; A Measuring Stick," *Survey,* 56 (May 1926), 169–170; and "Race Friendliness and Social Distance," *Journal of Applied Sociology,* 11 (1927), 272–287.

68. See, for example, A.A. Campbell, "Factors Associated with Attitudes Toward Jews," in T.M. Newcomb and E.L. Hartley (eds.), *Readings in Social Psychology* (New York: Holt, Rinehart and Winston, 1947), pp. 518–527.

69. See Peter I. Rose, "Blaming the Jews," op. cit.

70. Bruno Bettelheim and Morris Janowitz, *The Dynamics of Prejudice* (New York: Harper & Row, 1950).

71. Bruno Bettelheim and Morris Janowitz, *Social Change and Prejudice* (New York: Free Press, 1965).

72. John Dollard, *Caste and Class in a Southern Town* (New Haven: Yale University Press, 1937), esp. Chaps. 6 to 8.

73. See John Dollard et al., *Frustration and Aggression* (New Haven: Yale University Press, 1939). "When Marxists have described the dynamic human interrelationships involved in the class struggle ... they have introduced unwittingly a psychological system involving the assumption that aggression is a response to frustration." Ibid., p. 23.

74. See, for example, Clyde M. Kluckhohn, "Group Tensions: Analysis of a Case History," in L. Bryson, L. Finkelstein, and R.M. MacIver (eds.), *Approaches to National Unity* (New York: Harper & Row, 1945), p. 224.

75. Quoted by Allport, op. cit., p. 343.

76. Albert Camus, *The Fall* (Justin O'Brien, tr.) (New York: Vintage Brooks, 1963), p. 81.

77. T. W. Adomo et al., *The Authoritarian Personality* (New York: Harper & Row, 1950), p. 1.

78. Ibid.

79. Ibid., p. 971

80. See Bettelheim and Janowitz, op. cit.; and Selma Hirsch, *The Fears Men Live By* (New York: Harper & Row, 1955).

81. See, for example, Leo Lowenthal and Norbert Guterinan, *Prophets of Deceit* (New York: Harper & Row, 1949).

82. See, for example, Richard Christie, "Authoritarianism Reexamined," in Richard Christie and Marie Jahoda (eds.), *Studies in Scope and Method of "The Authoritarian Personality"* (New York: Free Press, 1954), pp. 123–196. See also Muzafer and Carolyn Sherif, *Groups in Harmony and Tension* (New York: Harper & Row, 1953).

83. See Edward A. Shils, "Authoritarianism: 'Right' and 'Left,'" in Christie and Jahoda, op. cit., pp. 24–49. See also Stanley Rothman and Robert Lichter, *Radical Christians, Radical Jews* (New York: Oxford University Press, 1981).

84. Robert M. MacIver and Charles H. Page, *Society: An Introductory Analysis* (New York: Holt, Rinehart & Winston, 1949), p. 407.

85. Letter to the Editor of *The New York Times* (May 16, 1963). The letter was signed by Tom Wilcher.

86. See Whitney M. Young, Jr., *Beyond Racism: an Open Society* (New York: McGraw-Hill, 1969).

87. Joel Kovel, *White Racism: A Psychohistory* (New York: Pantheon, 1970), pp. 31–32.

88. Alexis de Tocqueville, *Democracy In America* (New York: Vintage Books, 1945), Vol. I, p. 373.

89. From the brochure, *Only Skin Deep: Changing Visions of the American Self,* New York: International School of Photography, 2005. no pagination.

90. For a synoptic view of "Critical Race Theory," see Richard Delgado and Jean Stefancic (eds.), *Critical Race Theory: An Introduction* (New York: New York University Press, 2001).

91. Op. cit. p. 7.

92. See Joe F. Feagin, *Discrimination American Style: Institutional Racism and Sexism* (Englewood Cliffs, N.J.: Prentice-Hall, 1978).

93. Derrick Bell, considered by many a founding father of "Critical Race Theory," has written extensively on this subject. See, for example, *And We are Not Saved: The Elusive Quest for Racial Justice* (New York: Basic Books, 1987). A new collection of Bell's writings has been edited by Richard Delgado and Jean Stefancic, *The Derrick Bell Reader* (New York: New York University Press, 2005). Another useful volume is Kimberlee Crenshaw (ed.), *Critical Race Theory: The Key Writings that Formed a Movement* (New York: The New Press, 1995).

94. Idem.

95. See, for example, Mari J. Matsuda and Charles R. Lawrence III, *We Won't Go Back: Making the Case for Affirmative Action* (Houghton Mifflin, 1997)

96. Lani Guinier has published several books on the subject. The one in which she makes a case proportional representation within electoral districts is *The Tyranny of the Majority: Fundamental Fairness in Representative Democracy,* (Simon and Schuster, 1995).

97. See Peter I. Rose, "Nobody Knows the Trouble I've Seen: Some Reflections on the Insider-Outsider Debate," The Katherine Asher Engel Lecture, Northampton, MA: Smith College, 1978. Another version of this appeared as Chapter 10 "Insiders and Outsiders," in *They and We,* Fourth Edition (New York: McGraw-Hill, 1990), pp. 213–31.

98. Ibid. pp. 230–231.

99. See, for example, Lewis Browne, *How Odd of Jews* (New York: Macmillan, 1943); and Arnold M. Rose, "Anti-Semitism's Roots in City Hatred," op. cit.

100. See Allport, op. cit., Chap. 16.

101. Ibid., p. 217.

Patterns of Discrimination

Insult and Injury

> Eenie, meenie, miney, moe.
> Catch a nigger by the toe.

Not a tiger, a "nigger." Until very recently, the bit of doggerel chanted by children throughout the English-speaking Western world contained that explicit racial epithet. It may have been an "unintended indiscretion" but it was clearly an insult.

Insults are but one in a range of actions we call discriminatory. In this chapter various expressions of behavior that fall under the rubric of *discrimination,* the singling out of people for separate and unequal treatment,[1] are examined. The treatment itself is often institutionalized, an accepted part of everyday life. Examples include pejorative language, the denial of the franchise, selective hiring practices, restrictive neighborhoods, and exclusive social clubs and other forms of segregation. It may involve organized forms of intimidation and physical abuse as well.

Patterns of discrimination may be *de jure,* grounded in law, or *de facto,* that is, part of a tradition or custom. Moreover, as noted in Chapter 7, those who discriminate may do so because they believe they are superior to others or simply because they think "that's the way it is." Too many acceptors of the status quo are reluctant to change what, to them, are economically, psychologically, and socially acceptable or necessary arrangements. It is not surprising to find that many Americans are fair-weather liberals who more often do what is "expected" than what is "right," who often engage in behavior which is in fact racist.

Not so long ago many middle- and upper-class whites in the South regularly employed African American servants whose jobs involved intimate contact with the family, such as cooks, maids, even wet-nurses for the children. Despite such intimate sorts of relationship, these very same people were reluctant to allow blacks to drink from the same water fountain as whites or swim in the same pool, or go to school with their youngsters. Many northern whites, more self-righteous perhaps but equally inconsistent, were less concerned with such "pollution," yet kept African Americans from their neighborhoods, clubs, and churches. The height of northern hypocrisy was most clearly manifest each Sunday morning when loyal parishioners faithfully proclaimed the "Brotherhood of Man" in their very separate churches.

In addition to these seemingly contradictory practices, such patterns demonstrate the compartmentalized character of discrimination and the fact that large numbers of people subscribe to those forms of behavior that are acceptable according to the social and cultural definitions of the situations in which they find themselves. Relatively few are willing to cut the cake of custom, especially when they feel (or are made to feel) that their vested interests are threatened. In this way the fair-weather liberal often ends up being a reluctant discriminator.

Defamation, avoidance, threat, coercion, segregation, colonization, relocation, and annihilation describe points along the continuum of discriminatory practices. Of these practices, the present chapter deals with three distinctive modes: *derogation, denial,* and various forms of aggression.[2]

Derogation

Ethnophaulism is a technical word for a derogatory term used by the members of one ethnic group to describe the members of another. Ethnophaulisms are at the core of the language of prejudice and, when openly expressed, become a form of discrimination known as *antilocution,* a fancy word for name-calling.

The old saying that "sticks and stones may break my bones but names will never hurt me" is misleading, for articulated antagonisms may serve to define and reinforce the images we hold of others and may have serious psychic consequences for those on the receiving end. The repeated reference to the adult black male as "boy" or the married black woman as "miss," to cite examples graphically portrayed by Richard Wright, is like a stain that leaves an indelible imprint on the recipient's personality.[3]

People often fail to know the roots of common expressions they use. Some are quite innocuous. Think of "Cross my heart and hope to die" (a reference to genuflecting) or "Knock on wood" or "Touch wood" (both allusions to swearing on the cross of Jesus). Sometimes people are offended by words that sound like pejorative ones. A case in point is the objection of some African Americans to the use of the expression "niggardly," which has nothing to do with black people but means "stingy" or "tight-fisted."

Frequently, loaded words are used without any intent to disparage but may prove to be pernicious nonetheless. Think of such colloquialisms as "I've been gypped" (which means being cheated as if by Roma people or "Gypsies") and the words "Nigger toes" (a term for Brazil nuts).

Many words and phrases referring to color, religion, and gender are more explicit. Included would be such old-fashioned statements as "Free, white, and twenty-one" (to be a carefree adult) and "Jew him down" (to bargain sharply).

Although far less common than in the past, sometimes, in an attempt to indicate friendliness, a white person may still say to a nonwhite, "You're as good as I am," or a Gentile, speaking to a Jew: "You Jews are a fine race." More common these days is the sort of thing that happens when second- and third-generation Americans with origins in China, Japan, and Korea are confronted with questioners who, assuming they must be foreigners, speak to them very slowly in very simple sentences and are then impressed with their ability to respond in perfect English—and say so!

Exasperated members of the groups in question often receive such testimonials as examples of not very subtle verbal discrimination. Others view them as evidence of narrow-mindedness. Their concerns are compounded when, after correcting a speaker who makes such a blatant faux pas, he or she says, "I didn't mean to offend you; why some of my best friends are ... "[4]

A not uncommon response is a polite acceptance of the apology together with a silent seething by those who are the object of such ignorant and patronizing remarks or of the sort of things that, they know, are being said behind their backs. Such remarks and other indications of prejudice often are paralleled by the comic caricatures of those who put them down. The terms used to describe those others are hardly kinder. And the jokes they tell frequently play up the differences between the cultures, illustrating the superiority of the minority.

Humor is found in all societies, and ethnic humor is particularly prevalent in ours. Most Americans are familiar with racial and ethnic jokes and frequently tell them with abandon—forgetting or failing to consider what they mean to those joked about. In an article pointedly titled "The Sting of Polish Jokes," philosopher and writer Michael Novak discussed the matter in some detail. One of his main points was that "Not all humor is humorous." As he explained:

> Ethnic humor is one of the great resources of this nation. There are forms of laughing at oneself and at others, usually based on the daily absurdities of mutual noncomprehension or double meaning. These are truly amusing, probably the most amusing jokes in the American repertoire. In this humor, all ethnic groups are equal; the barbs are shared by everybody at the same time.
>
> But there is a second genus of ethnic joke. It does not gain its force from that double understanding of the same word or doubly misapprehended event that characterizes multicultural perception. It is based on demeaning the character of one ethnic group, in line with a stereotype, and its function is to make the majority feel superior to the minority. Told in the presence of the minority, these jokes further require those who are their butt to acquiesce in their own humiliation, to laugh obediently, to accept their ascribed inferiority. (Nudging elbow: "No offense, friend. Only a joke.") The tactic is structurally the same as those techniques that force inmates to embrace their own degradation. Rage is not permitted. One must stand there helplessly and acquiesce.
>
> Southern and Eastern Europeans in the United States still seem subject to the last respectable bigotry.[5]

The last turn of phrase, "respectable bigotry," was popularized by Michael Lerner in the late 1960s.[6] It refers to the fact that for many years many liberal white people who "knew better" than to tell jokes about blacks and other nonwhite minorities seemed to have no compunction about telling them about Southern and Eastern Europeans.

Members of minority groups often affect accents and tell jokes that rely on others' stereotypes of what they are supposed to be like. The Irish tell "Pat and Mike" jokes; Italians tell stories about the Mafia—and, of late, the "Sopranos." Among Jews it is not uncommon to hear stories that describe the conflict between the desire for acceptance and the ties to the ethnic community.[7] African Americans frequently joke about their low status, the difficulty of advancement, the special significance of "soul," and the white man's image of their lives.[8] Some stories stress the perverse "advantages" of marginality; others are tinged with the bitterness of self-abasement.

Such "inside" joking is also controversial. Many members of those groups that tell stories about others with whom they are identified are deeply offended. They frequently point to the fact that although self-derogation may relieve tension, the stories also suggest that there is a kernel of truth in stereotypes. This is seen in caricatures of Jews, Italians, Mexicans, Japanese, and especially African Americans offered on stage, screen, and television, to nonmembers.

One of the sharpest critics of such sardonic humor notes that the stories and caricatures may have serious negative consequences for the groups themselves, especially when others become privy to what is being said within the community, and sometimes intentionally as in the commercialization of rap music and the glorification of "bad-ass" behavior of certain black entertainers. In his controversial newest book, *The Artificial White Man,* the African American jazz critic Stanley Crouch claims "Images of black youth seen on MTV, BET, or VH1 are not far removed from those D. W. Griffith used in *Birth of a Nation* [a famous film celebrating the Ku Klux Klan], where Reconstruction Negroes were depicted as bullying, hedonistic buffoons, ever ready to bloody someone."[9]

The criticism is important. Still, there is little question that whatever else it does, for good or, as Crouch and others claim, for ill, in-group humor has subtle social and psychological functions, not least the reinforcement of group identity. The fact remains, however, that to laugh at yourself is very different from listening to an outsider tell stories about you or the members of your group.

Over the past seventy years, in an attempt to deal more forthrightly with racial diversity and ethnic pluralism, a number of radio and television networks introduced comedy programs with "intergroup" themes. First there was "Amos and Andy" (with its minstrelized "Negroes"), "Abie's Irish Rose," "Life with Luigi," "The Goldbergs," and "The Life of Riley," each seeming to outdo the other in stereotype-laden language. Later came the considerably sanitized if not quite yet politically correct television show "Bridget Loves Bernie" (about an Irish Catholic woman married to a Jewish man) and an increasing number of sitcoms starring African Americans, including "Julia," "Sanford and Son," "The Jeffersons," "Good Times," and "The Cosby Show."[10] Then there was the much more sophisticated and controversial "All in the Family."

The show, based on an English program about working class life called "Til Death Do Us Part," pulled few punches. It (purposely) dealt directly with contemporary issues—the role of women, sexual deviance, and, especially, ethnic interaction.

In the 1970s "All in the Family" was one of America's most popular television programs. Millions of people put aside other things to watch Archie Bunker, the bumbling bigot who didn't trust anybody regardless of race, creed, or color; his dutiful wife Edith, who often revealed a crude but nascent feminism; their daughter Gloria, a child/woman caught between parental love, "wifely" responsibility, and cravings for independence; son-in-law Mike, a Polish American graduate student in sociology whom Archie calls "a liberal meathead"; and Archie's neighbors and coworkers.

Archie's language was larded with sexist remarks as well as racist ones. Included in his everyday speech were pejorative words used in direct reference to minorities, words like "spic" and "greaser" (referring to Latinos), "wop" and "dago" (Italians) "jigaboo" and "jungle bunny" (African Americans), "hebe" (referring to Jews), "a-rab" and many others.

Because it was assumed that those so labeled would see such expressions as an extreme form of derogation, many critics argued that "All in the Family" served to legitimize the use of such terms. Moreover, and more important, some argued that Archie Bunker made bigotry somehow respectable.[11] Others disagreed. Those who supported the program contended that it is healthy to make fun of such serious matters; it releases tensions and, perhaps, even creates a climate of understanding.

The few studies that were conducted for the Columbia Broadcasting System (CBS), the network that produced the show, indicated that most of those maligned by Archie Bunker appeared to *like* the program. One reason may be that the minority individuals portrayed usually came out on top (and even Archie Bunker seemed to learn something each time). Some of those who identified themselves with Archie said that he reminded them of what they used to be like.

Other studies of "All in the Family" came to the conclusion that a process of selective perception seems to take place when one is exposed to certain derogatory material or interracial satire. Researchers Neil Vidman and Milton Rokeach explained "nonprejudiced viewers and minority group members may perceive and enjoy [the program] as satire, whereas prejudiced viewers may perceive of, and enjoy the show for 'telling it like it is.'" They further speculated, "By making Archie a 'lovable bigot' the program encourages bigots to excuse and rationalize their own prejudices."[12] Vidman and Rokeach came close to the position taken by Michael Novak.

Archie Bunker remained on the air for many years and is not frequently seen as a rerun along with other classics such as "MASH," a long-running series about a frontline surgical hospital in Korea in the early 1950s. Like "All in the Family," the MASH crew addressed many issues of social importance, including racism and sexism, but did so in a far less "in-your-face" manner. That series was followed by others such as "Hill Street Blues" and, more recently, "NYPD Blue," and many motion pictures that pull few punches in addressing the same persisting problems. The difference is that the more recent shows tend toward realism rather than comedy to get their points across, including those that involve exposing the exploitation of minorities and women. Their stock in trade is the use of strong, direct language.

Direct language is also prevalent among members of the contemporary counter-culture, best represented by numerous rap groups who spice up their song/poems with racist and sexist words with abandon. But they are not the only ones. Many people in the mainstream have taken to using racial epithets more freely.

Erdman Palmore, on the basis of a careful study of ethnophaulisms, concluded that "all racial and ethnic groups use ethnophaulisms. The greater the number of ethnophaulisms used against a group, the greater the prejudice. When the out-group is a different race, most ethnophaulisms express and support the stereotypes of highly visible physical differences. When the out-group is the same general racial type, most ethnophaulisms express and support stereotypes of highly visible cultural differences. The derivations of most ethnophaulisms express some negative stereotypes."[13]

Since ethnophaulisms appear to be essential to the support and spread of ethnocentrism, they provide one indication of the relationship between ideas and action. As noted in Chapter 7, the conative dimension of prejudice is that aspect of the attitude construct concerned with predispositions for behavior. There is little question that referring to people in particularly derogatory ways or portraying them in terms of negative stereotypes or caricatures heightens one's sense of animus and, if supported by "appropriate" norms that allow, even encourages the further acting out of one's predispositions.

In his book *Hate Speech,* published in 1994, Samuel Walker indicated why such derogatory expressions are appropriately labeled "fighting words."[14] They are words so incendiary that they are said to exceed the constitutional protection of free speech.[15]

The use of defamatory language is often intentionally provocative, particularly in the hands of racist demagogues. Throughout history those wishing to find scapegoats and to teach others to use them have used trumped-up charges, distortions of social roles, and guilt by association.

The Roman historian Tacitus explained this practice as well as anyone. Describing the burning of Rome, an act that most historians (and many Romans) attributed to Nero himself, Tacitus wrote: "Heaven could not stifle scandal or dispel the belief that the fire had taken place by order. Therefore, to scotch the rumour, Nero substituted as culprits, and punished with the utmost refinements of cruelty, a class of men, loathed for their vices, whom the crowd styled Christians."[16] It should be noted, however, that Tacitus himself was ambivalent about the Christians, if not about their alleged deed. Thus he further wrote:

> Christus, the founder of the name, had undergone the death penalty in the reign of Tiberius, by sentence of the procurator Pontius Pilatus, and the *pernicious superstition* was checked for a moment, only to break out once more, not merely in Judaea, the home of the disease, but in the capital itself, where all things horrible or shameful in the world collect and find vogue. First, then, the confessed members of the sect were arrested: next, on their disclosures, vast numbers were convicted, not so much on the count of arson as for hatred of the human race.[17]

The practice of demagoguery is very old. In addition to such examples from ancient times, examples are found throughout history. Parallels to such anti-Christian statements are found in references to Muslims during the Crusades, Jews in the Middle Ages, native peoples during periods of colonization. Modern times have hardly been immune to such phenomena. Sometimes the old scapegoats, sometimes new ones have been the targets for vilification and other forms of discrimination.

It was in Germany during the 1930s that verbal abuse of Jews, called anti-Semitic propaganda, was refined to an "art" under the direction of Joseph Goebbels and through the pen of Julius Streicher. Although the Nazis almost succeeded in ridding their country and those it occupied of the entire Jewish population by turning their words about the unworthiness of these *Untermenschen* (subhumans) to live, this kind of "art" (and the characterization of Jews as parasites) did not disappear with the end of the Nazi regime. In the Soviet Union, similar caricatures were presented with one notable difference. Some of the Soviet propaganda, and, more recently, propaganda disseminated in Iran and many Arab countries, portray Jews as Nazis, a curious juxtaposition but one that clearly served the needs of the demagogues who use such imagery.

Our own country has not been immune to anti-Semitic writing or speech. In the early days of World War II several social scientists conducted a study of anti-Semitic demagoguery in the United States. In the volume *Prophets of Deceit* they described the mind and ideology of the hatemonger. The book provides many examples of the sort of message being delivered by such anti-Semites as Gerald L.K. Smith and Father Charles Coughlin. Here are samples:

> When will the plain, ordinary, sincere, sheep like peoples of America awaken to the fact that their common affairs are being arranged and run for them by aliens, Communists, crackpots, refugees, renegades, Socialists, termites, and traitors? These alien enemies of America....
>
> Hitler and Hitlerism are the creatures of Jewry and Judaism. The merciless programs of abuse which certain Jews and their satellites work upon people who are not in full agreement with them create terrible reactions.
>
> We are going to take this government out of the hands of these city slickers and give it back to the people that still believe that 2 and 2 is 4, that God is in his heaven and the Bible is the Word ... [18]

Despite denials by his brother, former President Jimmy Carter, the late Billy Carter seemed to echo some of these sentiments when he claimed that Jews had too much power and influence in America, especially in what he termed "the Jewish media."[19] Others in prominent positions, including such African American leaders as Louis Farrakhan and his erstwhile assistant Khalid Abdul Muhammad, made similar public utterances a few years later, signaling a resurgence of anti-Semitic populism.[20]

In 1969 Seymour Martin Lipset and Earl Raab published a political history of right-wing activities. In *The Politics of Unreason* they describe in detail the activities and mentalities of such movements as the Anti-Masonic League, the American Protective Association of the 1890s, the Ku Klux Klan in its various incarnations, the Coughlinites of the 1930s, the McCarthyites of the 1950s, and the followers of George Wallace and other reactionary leaders in the 1960s.[21] In 2001, Neil Baldwin's book, *Henry Ford and the Jews,* wrote of each of those eras and offered an updated examination of what, in his subtitle, he calls "The Mass Production of Hate."[22]

Summing up their views of those who listened to the demagogues and joined the movements, Lipset and Raab suggest that "the adherents of extremist movements have typically felt deprived—either they have never gained their due share or they are losing their portion of power and status. We might call these two groups the "never-hads" and the "once-hads." These deprived groups are not necessarily extremist, but extremism usually draws its strength from them.[23] When the demagogue speaks, somebody listens.

"Once-hads" feel outraged by the thought of newcomers and outsiders getting what they believe to be legitimately theirs; "never-hads" seem to be particularly incensed by what they see as people demanding privileges that, they claim, they never had. In the early days of the civil rights struggle not a few white ethnics and even more poor whites in the South and many "middle Americans" were attracted by the appeals of those who blamed the blacks not only for wreaking changes throughout society and having the audacity to make demands for equality but calling for compensatory acts to make up for their harsh treatment. Some of their sloganeering harkened back to the turbulent days of the Klan when blatantly racist words were spoken from a stump or written in *The Fiery Cross.* Others linked the demands of African Americans with communist conspiracies. One of the favorite charges of the radical right in the late 1950s and early 1960s was that Daisy Bates, the president of the NAACP in Little Rock, Arkansas, who helped to bring about school integration there, and others like her, were fronting for "commies."[24] Labeling of this sort and the reintroduction of classic stereotypes and more provocative rhetoric fanned the flames of hostility.

Used by demagogues, ethnophaulisms serve well as vehicles for stirring up latent prejudices, fomenting hate, and calling people to take action against their "foes." Name-calling is a widely used and highly effective form of discrimination.

Denial

Discrimination often goes far beyond using ethnic labels, telling humorous anecdotes, engaging in poisonous oratory, and direct defamation. Words are inflammatory and, as the Nazi propagandist Joseph Goebbels diabolically demonstrated, they can have far-reaching effects, stirring masses to political action.

As noted previously, the saying about "sticks and stones" denies the fact that name-calling does hurt. Still, there are more direct means used to break one's bones (and one's spirit). Most discriminatory behavior is more than talk. It usually involves establishing and maintaining some measure of physical and social distance from minorities, either by avoiding contact as much as possible or by "keeping them in their place" or depriving them of access or opportunities others enjoy. *Avoidance* and *segregation* are two effective techniques of institutionalizing discrimination. In many ways, they are related.

Discrimination often involves the practice of avoiding face-to-face relations with members of certain specified groups. Fundamental lessons in avoidance are learned early in life when children learn from parents or playmates about groups with whom they should—or should not—associate. In adulthood these lessons manifest themselves in a variety of devices used to prevent or minimize contact with group members socially defined as being of low repute, unpleasant, or even untouchable. The diversity of avoidance taboos is well known.

One method of avoidance is the economic boycott. In the not so distant past, stores, restaurants, and conveyances known to be owned, operated, or frequented by certain minority group members on an equal basis with those in the dominant group were boycotted as a protest against their integrated policies. Fear of this kind of protest led quite a few department store owners (many of whom were themselves fair-weather liberals) to refrain from desegregating certain facilities such as lunch counters. In turn they often became the targets of civil rights groups seeking a redress of grievances. Two techniques were used in challenge: one was the sit-in, which forced proprietors to bring in police and, ultimately, to seek adjudication in the courts; the other was a counter-boycott to discourage members of the minority from using other facilities in the targeted stores.

Discriminatory boycotts have also been used in public places such as play-grounds, parks, and beaches abandoned by those who used them in protest against new integrated policies. Frequently leading to a self-fulfilling situation, a common pattern is for certain groups to withdraw from participation or utilization of such facilities as others move in. Ultimately what is most feared takes place. The minority takes over and the initial boycotters say, "We told you so!"

In some cases such boycotting is seen as a worthwhile inconvenience ("You can always go farther up the coast to another beach" or "Nobody in his right mind would go there!"). But the beginning of an end of segregated schools created a setting for a somewhat more permanent pattern. In the urban centers of the North and in many parts of the South, white parents responded to the threat of integrated schooling by sending their children to private schools or by establishing such schools where they had not existed previously—sometimes with the tacit support of local and state authorities. The implementation of busing to achieve greater racial balance intensified the use of the boycott. In city after city newspapers noted the *Washington Post*'s headline of December 20, 1972: "8000 Boycott Prince George's Classrooms" (in protest against court-ordered desegregation).[25] That was only the beginning. The pattern continued in many areas throughout the decade. One of the most dramatic examples occurred in Boston, Massachusetts, where many working-class whites felt their sanctuaries were being invaded by court-ordered integration of the schools. Angry mobs and organized groups of local residents tried to disrupt the process and end busing. That failing, many simply refused to go to school, or to send their children.

The most widespread method of avoidance is flight or "white flight," panic-driven movement away from neighborhoods into which minority group members are enter-ing. For more than a century, the ecological history of large American cities was marked by the "invasion" of residential areas by certain ethnic and racial minorities, initial resistance of earlier inhabitants, then attempts to frighten or cajole people to sell out in response to the perceived threat, and then the eventual abandonment of the block or neighborhood and the succession of the newcomers.[26]

In recent decades, once all-white areas in Northern and West Coast cities turned into predominantly black neighborhoods. Not infrequently the exodus of whites was prompted by the panic of those residents who would not accept African American neighbors under any circumstances.

Although the process of changing neighborhoods is far from uniform and the time sequence is highly variable—depending upon such factors as the size of the incoming group, the nature of residential mobility already under way, and the extent of prejudice—many move simply because of the perceived threat of an "invasion"[27] Others may be prompted to go because of the scare tactics of realtors and others who intentionally move in and become "block busters." An example of this which was carefully studied by Hillel Levine and Lawrence Harmon is the transition of a stable Jewish community, in the Dorchester section of Boston, into an African American ghetto in the late 1960s, the root cause of which is attributed to the decision of bankers and blockbusters that Jews would be more receptive to integration than Italian or Irish Americans who occupied nearby neighborhoods.[28]

A theme runs through all the methods employed for maintaining distances by avoidance. It involves *action or movement on the part of the dominant group rather than the minority.* To do something about "them" means, in these cases, doing something to one's self, one's family, or one's group.

Although related, segregation differs from avoidance. In segregation, instead of doing something to one's self or group, action is directed against others. A variety of devices are used to set up and maintain barriers between one's own group and those considered unworthy of normal social interaction. Segregation involves restrictive and exclusionary policies established to keep minorities out of communities or sections of them, or to place and hold them in particular areas such as reservations, barrios, and ghettos. Segregation has sometimes evolved on a voluntary basis, as did the famous ghetto of Cologne, Germany, where the Jews of the thirteenth century sought and obtained permission to set up their own community within the city walls.[29] Most segregation, however, is not voluntary, as suggested by the term itself and by its definition as a "form of isolation which places limits or restrictions upon contact, communication, and social relations."[30] With several notable exceptions—for example, the communities of Hasidim, the Amish, and several other religious sects and cults—most of the segregation practiced in the United States has been of an involuntary nature. The caste-like restrictions that applied to African Americans are the most obvious examples but there are many others. Until quite recently, one of the most common was the virtual exclusion of women from certain male bastions. Even when women began to make progress in achieving access into the inner sanctum of corporate America, a "glass ceiling" served to slow the process of getting to the top.

Involuntary segregation usually involves both spatial and social barriers. Social distance is most easily maintained through physical distance. In the past, Native Americans who survived the bullets and bacilli of the Europeans were forcibly restricted to reservations, a pattern followed much later in South Africa where *apartheid* (the maintaining of a separated society) was institutionalized into an elaborate hierarchy with blacks on the bottom with few civil or even human rights to protect them. Above them was a layer of "coloured" people (the descendants of Europeans and native African tribal peoples, especially the Hottentots), then Malays and Indians, and, at the top, Englishmen and Afrikaners, the latter, descendants of the Dutch settlers, and, for a long while, despite its small size relative to the black African population, the strongest group politically. Restrictions of another sort were much in the news in the mid-1990s, most notably "ethnic cleansing," as Bosnian Serbs referred to their scheme for ridding disputed territory of their opponents, the Bosnian Muslims. In what turned out to be a replay of Nazi tactics of round-ups and mass assassinations, in some areas it began with restrictions on movements, forced marches, and ghettoization in refugee camps. In the first decade of the twenty-first century similar tactics were being used to isolate hundreds of thousands of rural people in the Darfur region of the Sudan.

In this country ghettos have often persisted, not only because of poverty but because there was no easy escape. At various times in American history, working- and middle-class minorities, including African Americans, Asian Americans, Mexicans, and members of various European "nationality" groups, and others have been barred from purchasing homes in certain urban and suburban neighborhoods. Clearly, this physical separation served to limit the interaction with members of other groups.

Residential segregation accounts for many other patterns of separation—even when these are unenforceable by law, as in the case of education where school districts tend to follow neighborhood patterns. Among the various devices used in the past to maintain America's own form of *apartheid*[31] were restrictive covenants and "gentlemen's agreements." The former were often legally binding contractual arrangements where buyers promised not to sell to anyone other than another white, Christian family; the latter were based on a symbolic handshake. Well into the last third of the twentieth century one could still find deeds to property with provisions such as the following:

> ... And, furthermore, no lot shall be sold or leased to, or occupied by, any person excepting of the Caucasian race.
>
> Provided further, that the grantee shall not sell to Negroes or permit use or occupation by them, except as domestic servants.
>
> ... shall not permit occupation by Negroes, Hindus, Syrians, Greeks, or any corporation controlled by same.[32]

Perhaps the most infamous of neighborhood policies was the "point system" maintained as recently as three decades ago for admittance to residence in highly restrictive Grosse Pointe, Michigan. Community leaders required that all prospective residents had to be screened and evaluated on the basis of race, religion, education, occupation, accent, "swarthiness," and other invidious criteria, and then allotted points for each "favorable" attribute. Only high scorers were allowed to purchase property. The Grosse Pointe pattern is an extreme example of an established, though declining practice in many communities in the United States.[33]

Housing is not the only area where restrictive regulations, formal and informal, official and sub rosa, prevent outsiders from entering the circle of the dominant group. City clubs and country clubs, sororities and fraternities, lodges and service organizations have required applicants or initiates to be "members of the Christian faith," or to "believe in Jesus Christ," or to be "white and Caucasian." Not long ago many Greek-letter college fraternities went so far as to exclude Greeks.[34]

Admission to some private schools and colleges has also been limited by quota systems under which only certain percentages of the members of specified groups are considered eligible—irrespective of academic abilities. Since the 1940s, anti-discrimination legislation has prohibited colleges and universities in many states (and those receiving federal support) from requesting photographs, indications of religious preference or affiliation, or information about national origin from applicants. Still, such restrictions were sometimes circumvented through an old device, the implementation of "area quotas." By accepting only a certain percentage of city dwellers or easterners, for example, certain schools, particularly those in the "Ivy League," kept tight rein on the number of Jewish students admitted, irrespective of their academic qualifications. More recently, such area quotas have been used on the West Coast to control the numbers of Asian Americans.

In spite of the increasing recognition of performance standards in the world of work, some business corporations (especially smaller, family-controlled firms), professional organizations, and labor unions still continue to disqualify members of minority groups from employment or membership or limit the heights to which they may rise, severely hampering their opportunities to pursue occupations for which they are trained. The timeworn practice of hiring minorities and women last and firing them first still holds in many industries.

In a hard-hitting essay on "Inequality in America," Edna Bonacich makes the following observation: "The United States is an immensely unequal society in terms of the distribution of material wealth, and consequently, in the distribution of all the benefits and privileges that accrue to wealth—including political power and influence. This inequality is vast irrespective of race. However, people of color tend to cluster at the bottom so that inequality in this society also becomes racial inequality.... it is deeply embedded in this [capitalist] system."[35]

Bonacich is convinced that, professions of "all men being equal" notwithstanding, the entire American political-economic system is bound to racism because capitalism itself depends on an ideology of inequality and the exploitation of certain especially vulnerable groups to assure its hierarchies of power and privilege. Although many may argue with the starkness of the indictment and its concentration on the singularity of capitalism-as-cause, none can gainsay the fact that racial discrimination has served to keep many groups down and dependent.

The following statement from an annual official government document, "The Social and Economic Status of the Black Population in the United States," published in the early 1970s, revealed the effects of segregation and exclusion in this country despite the powerful civil rights movement of the 1960s. "In the 1960s significant advances were made by the Black population in many fields—notably, income, health, education, employment, and voter participation. The current statistics indicate continued progress in some areas of life, although other areas remained unchanged. Overall, however, in 1972, Blacks still lag behind whites in most social and economic areas, although the differentials have narrowed over the years."[36]

That pattern, African Americans behind whites, in almost every sphere—education, voting, and political participation, as well as employment and income—persisted well into the next decade.[37] Indeed, despite gains on some fronts, such as greater access to higher education through the initiation of more far-reaching recruitment schemes to make campuses "more diverse," much of this triggered by the requirements of affirmative action rules, the overall picture, especially in the crucial areas of employment and income, offered little evidence of significant breakthroughs.

The generally sluggish economy and inflationary pressures in the mid- and late-1970s had a dampening effect on the chances of the able-bodied poor in all cohorts, white, African American, Hispanic, or Asian. As for the working class, that is, those already steadily employed, whites in the aggregate made some slight gains, blacks hardly any. In 1977, for example, about 30 percent of African American families in the United States had incomes of $15,000 or more, compared to some 57 percent of white families. Moreover, the median income of African American males in the labor force twenty years ago was $6,290, compared to $10,600 for white males. (The figures for the median income African American and white women in 1977 were $3,460 and $4,000, respectively.)

Many conservative citizens believed that things could be dramatically changed if the "tired old policies of the 1930s" were finally replaced with new, innovative economic strategies (views to be echoed in the 1990s). The opportunity to effect such changes came to pass with the election of Ronald Reagan, whose new administration sought "to get the country moving again," convinced that the trickledown effects of supply-side economics would help all Americans realize the dream of a better life. Yet, even the economic boom of the 1980s had little direct impact on the hard-core sufferers, many of whom were members of minorities. Much of the blame for the failure to reach them has been placed directly at the feet of the government.

In a hard-hitting statement, John Jacob, president of the Urban League in 1986, put it this way:

What columnist David Broder called the "fatal blend of ignorance and arrogance" [regarding such foreign policy blunders as "Irangate"] also describes the administration's civil rights policies. It tried to win tax exemptions for segregated schools, fought extension of civil rights laws, undermined affirmative action, destroyed the U.S. Civil Rights Commission, stacked the judiciary with right-wingers, and refused to budge from its support for South Africa's apartheid government—all the while implementing a public relations policy designed to convince Americans that we are now a color-blind, racially neutral society.

At the same time, it ignored mounting African American poverty. In place of substantive domestic policy, it substituted demonstrably false statements designed to convince the public that unemployment was no longer a problem, that the poor don't want to work, and that social programs simply compound social problems instead of helping to resolve them.[38]

Jacob's remarks were offered in a preface to a lengthy report on "The State of Black America" in 1986. Based on data gathered from a wide variety of sources, the document underscores a widening gap in the society. For example, it pointed to Labor Department statistics showing that at the height of the economic "recovery" nearly 4 million part-time workers wanted to work full time, and almost 1.2 million discouraged workers gave up searching for jobs. It noted a U.S. Census Bureau report specifying that, in 1985, over 33 million people were poor in this country—a rise of 4 million from 1980. At the same time, more than one of every five of all American children were classified as poor; for African Americans, the ratio was one in two.

There was a growing employment gap, a growing income gap, and a growing wealth gap. Again according to the Census Bureau, the typical white family in the mid-1980s had a net worth twelve times as great as the net worth of the typical African American family. And almost one-third of all black families had no assets at all.

Although Jacob did indicate that the gaps between rich and poor cut across racial lines, a point forcefully argued by the sociologist William Julius Wilson in his thoughtful volume, *The Declining Significance of Race,*[39] neither Jacob nor Wilson denied the persistence of discrimination—both blatant and subtle—would continue to hobble nonwhites in their effort to find a securer place in the wider society.

Many social scientists contend that although discrimination is no longer a sufficient explanation for all the problems of ghetto living—street crime, delinquency, drug abuse, unwanted pregnancies, child abuse, and "welfare dependency"—so often discussed in the press, it is surely necessary to take into account the effects of patterns of institutionalized racism so deeply woven into the fabric of this society.

Twenty-five years after the publication of the first of the census reports discussed above, the overall black/white gap remained very wide. In a detailed summary of the 1990 census, journalist Sam Roberts noted that, overall, one in seven Americans was living below the official poverty line, and that "two years later, the ranks of America's poor had swollen to nearly 36 million—the most since 1964 when President Lyndon B. Johnson boldly declared war on poverty."[40] The 1990 census data indicated that the rate of poverty is rising. Although it is true that the majority of the poor in this country are still white, it is also true that the majority of blacks and Hispanics are still poor. Much of their poverty is the legacy of discrimination. As Roberts shows, "even when white social, economic and demographic characteristics were imputed to Black households, blacks came up short,"[41] and, he continued: "The contrasts may have become more visible but, like the poor, they are not new. Nor is the notion of an irredeemable underclass.... . What's novel is the conspiracy of economic, social, political, racial and spatial factors that have fostered and perpetuated dependency."[42]

William Julius Wilson contends that this dependency is aggravated by the concentration of various populations in particular sectors of society and their isolation from the rest of the community, the lack of jobs and job opportunities in traditionally labor-intensive factories and the fragmentation of the urban areas themselves by new roadways built over and often right through old neighborhoods.[43] The result, says Alan Wolfe, is that "The condition of the urban Black poor has deteriorated over the past quarter century to the point where it threatens all the other gains in race relations that were realized during the same period."[44] Indeed, the situation had become so bad that it was not unreasonable to speak of many inner-city ghettos as separate, deteriorating societies, cut off—and even cut loose—from their mainstream moorings.[45]

In spite of a number of positive changes in the behavior and attitudes of increasing numbers of those in the dominant sector who were coming to accept the reality of America as a multiracial, multiethnic society, the categorical disparities manifest in one area of life after another are related to long-institutionalized patterns of discrimination which, to this day, still make it more difficult for blacks (and, in many instances, other nonwhites) to run an equal race. They have known it for years; so, as numerous studies have shown, have policy makers. This last point was made abundantly clear nearly 40 years ago when, in the wake of the urban riots that erupted in city after city during the summers of 1966 and 1967, a Presidential Commission was invited to investigate their causes. Asked to find out why these outbreaks had taken place and what could be done to prevent them in the future, a group of leading citizens headed by then-governor Otto Kerner of Illinois carried out an extensive study of twenty-four disorders in twenty-three different American cities. A year later the report was published. In one version, Tom Wicker, a former columnist for *The New York Times,* wrote a special introduction in which he focused on the central issue that constantly confronted the commissioners and the investigative staff. "In the end," Wicker claimed, "not without dispute and travail and misgiving, in the clash and spark of human conflict and human pride, against the pressures of time and ignorance, they produced not so much a report on the riots as a report on America—one nation divided.[46]

Wicker based his conclusion on his assessment of the report, which included the following summary statements about the explosive mixture that contributed to the potential for upheaval:

> *Pervasive discrimination and segregation* in employment, education and housing, which have resulted in the continuing exclusion of great numbers of Negroes from the benefits of economic progress.
>
> *Black in-migration and white exodus,* which have produced massive and growing concentrations of impoverished Negroes in our major cities, creating a growing crisis of deteriorating facilities and services and unmet human meets.
>
> *The Black ghettos* where segregation and poverty converge on the young to destroy opportunity and enforce failure. Crime, drug addiction, dependency on welfare, and bitterness and resentment against society in general and white society in particular are the result.[47]

In *Two Nations*: *Black and White, Separate, Hostile, and Unequal,* Andrew Hacker corroborated Wicker's earlier assessment. Segregation and poverty, Hacker concluded, had created in the racial ghetto a destructive environment totally unknown to most white Americans.[48]

Pathology for many nonwhites is doubtlessly still related to the patterns of life they are forced to adopt. Upheaval may be construed as a desperate cry for help; it may also be viewed as one of the few healthy alternatives to despair in a sick society. Whichever view one takes (and there is considerable controversy over this fundamental question), there is little question that the barriers erected to keep nonwhites in their place have done more than isolate large numbers of people.

> Segregation and poverty have created in the racial ghetto a destructive environment totally unknown to most white Americans.
>
> What white Americans have never fully understood—but what the Negro can never forget—is that white society is deeply implicated in the ghetto. White institutions created it, white institutions maintain it, and white society condones it.[49]

Practices of segregation, such as those reported by the Kerner Commission, are easier to observe than the more subtle patterns of social separation. Yet these have equal, if not more, sociological significance. In many communities where direct physical contact between whites and nonwhites was far more frequent than in the riot cities, and where spatial separation was not nearly as pronounced, local customs served to insulate the groups from one another. Pre–World War II studies of "Negro–white" relations in the United States provide numerous examples of southern "etiquette" that enhanced the separation of the races.

> In content the serious conversation should be about those business interests which are shared (as when a white employer instructs his Negro employee or when there is a matter to be discussed concerning the welfare of the Negro community) or it should be polite but formal inquiry into personal affairs. There can generally be no serious discussion.
>
> The conversation is even more regimented in *form* than in content. The Negro is expected to address the white person by the title of "Mr." or "Miss.... From his side, the white man addresses the Negro by his first name, no matter if they hardly know each other or by the epithets "boy," "uncle," "elder," "aunty," or the like.[50]

Although few practices such as those discussed by Gunnar Myrdal are still to be found, there are a number of subtler variations on the same themes, particularly in condescending references to inner-city minorities. Here we see a direct linkage between derogation and denial. In the old days, the main function of racial etiquette was to remind African Americans of their place in the social hierarchy, which persistently demeans them. Such institutionalized intimidation, with respect to its psychological consequences, is one of the cruelest forms of discrimination.

Aggression

Intimidation is sometimes subtle. Most of the time it is blatant. ("Just try stepping out of line!") Violence or the threat of violence has long been used to keep racial and ethnic minorities mindful of their subordinate status. Tied to both derogation and denial, there are many forms of aggressive action in which individuals or groups participate, ranging from the jeering at, and threatening of little children to gang fights or organized terror and mob rule. The lexicon of racial conflict is filled with words related to violent aggression: "lynching," "pogrom," "genocide," and hundreds of others—and examples of their use are not hard to find.

Thousands of Indians are exterminated to make the country safe—and profitable for colonists.
Hundreds of Chinese are savagely attacked and many are killed by white mobs.
A Puerto Rican is beaten for trespassing on "white man's turf" ...
A synagogue is symbolically smeared with swastikas and the slogan "Hate Jews."
A black man is lynched for having "stepped out of line."
A mosque is burned to the ground "to teach those people a lesson."

"Violence," Gordon Allport once wrote, "is always an outgrowth of milder states of mind. Although most barking does not lead to biting, yet there is never a bite without previous barking."[51] Led by the demagogue, the ardent segregationist, and the fanatic patriot, solid and respectable citizens have done unspeakable violence to their enemies.

Even in our society of "law and order" the social conditions for mob violence still exist, as does the violence itself. Not long ago many southern blacks lived in terror of the lynch mob. Their anxiety was well justified for, according to the records of the NAACP, there were 5,112 lynchings between 1882 and 1939 (3,657 of the victims were African American).[52]

In the past, lynchings occurred mainly in those areas where the practice of segregation was maintained by the harshest forms of intimidation. Some social scientists have interpreted lynching as a means of venting frustrations against a convenient scapegoat. For example, it has been argued that the falling price of cotton portended an upsurge in the number of lynchings in the South. Whether one can make a causal reference from the correlation, the wide use of lynching indicates a tacit acceptance of such activity as a legitimate way to maintain the caste-like social system. The facts—that lynchings were often not prevented even when known of by the authorities and that when culprits were known and apprehended they were seldom punished to a degree commensurate with the crime—give ample evidence to support the contention that such behavior was condoned by those in official positions of authority.[53]

Although the number of lynchings remained relatively negligible from the end of World War II to the late 1970s, in those same years vigilantes sometimes took the law into their own hands, meting out "cracker barrel justice." The desire to fight against changes in the status quo saw a rebirth of mob aggressiveness in the South. In the 1950s, black parents attempting to send their children to schools desegregated by court decision in Clinton, Little Rock, New Orleans, and more than a score of other southern cities were met with angry crowds of white demonstrators who burned crosses, threatened them, and severely beat them. All too frequently the local authorities failed to provide adequate protection for the African American citizens. In some cities, once law and order were established or reestablished—sometimes with the aid of federal troops—segregation was maintained by whites who withdrew their children from public schools.[54]

Sit-in demonstrators who sought equal service in restaurants, kneel-in demonstrators desiring to attend integrated church services, wade-in demonstrators wishing to swim in areas restricted to whites, read-in demonstrators wanting to take books from segregated libraries, and freedom riders challenging the policy of segregated interstate transportation and separate terminal facilities met with similar outbursts of aggression and violence. In the spring of 1961, for example, a busload of freedom riders was greeted by an angry mob in Anniston, Alabama, who threw rocks, smashed windows, and eventually burned the bus. White men armed with clubs attacked another group that had gone to Birmingham, and several riders were brutally beaten.

In the early fall of 1962 an especially ugly incident in the long fight for desegregation occurred at Oxford, Mississippi, when, aided by several hundred U.S. marshals and 24,000 soldiers, James Meredith was forcibly admitted to the University of Mississippi under a court order restraining the school from denying his admission. His presence on the campus triggered a series of riots that took several hours to quell. By the time order was restored by the imposition of virtual martial law, two adults had been killed and over one hundred people injured.

Only two weeks earlier, four Black churches in rural Georgia were burned to the ground. All but one was being used for registering new voters. On September 17, 1962, the Student Nonviolent Coordinating Committee sent the following telegram to President Kennedy: "Another church burned this morning. Four churches burned in the past month, reminiscent of Nazi burning of synagogues. Imperative you investigate and apprehend arsonists. Halt the outrageous terror of peaceful American citizens. The national shame must be ended."[55] The President's own violent death a little over one year later indicated that terror remained rampant in our society. And we were to see more and more senseless killing—much of it related to racial tensions—in the years to come.

The annals of civil rights martyrdom are filled with names of young black and white civil rights workers gunned down by those who could not tolerate the changes in the status quo that they represented: among them Herbert Lee, Medgar Evers, and the Nobel Prize–winner Reverend Martin Luther King, Jr., the "apostle of nonviolence."

James Chaney, Andrew Goodman, and Michael Schwerner, who were trying to encourage African Americans to vote in the summer of 1964, were brutally murdered in Neshoba County, Mississippi. Their assassins were members of the White Knights of the Ku Klux Klan, many of whom were identified as far back as 1967, but not until 2005 was the former Klansman Edgar Ray Killen convicted of the killings, forty years after the fact.[56]

In addition to these dastardly deeds, hundreds of other acts of violence continued to be perpetrated in big cities and rural towns. Crops were burned, workers were fired, and women and children were threatened. Even policemen, sworn to uphold the law, sometimes ran amuck, venting their wrath on unarmed protesters and innocent bystanders. The whole world reeled at the image of young blacks being attacked by police dogs in Birmingham and elsewhere in the South.

A headline in the December 12, 1972, issue of *The New York Times* stating "City Unit Sees Violence Pattern by Whites Against Minorities" was a stark reminder that vigilantism persisted in a period many have viewed as a time of interracial progress. The article described a study conducted by the City Commission of Human Rights that revealed eleven cases in which homes owned by blacks or Puerto Ricans in New York City had been set afire or vandalized and instances of arson in churches and attacks on school buses. Blaming white gangs, the Commission wrote: "We can no longer maintain the myth that violence and pathology of Southern racism is totally absent in the North. These occurrences, while unconnected, nonetheless suggest an ominous trend that could mean that continued integration in the North will be resisted as forcefully and violently as in the South."[57]

The commentary proved prophetic. In the years that followed, America witnessed further evidence of the persistence of violent resistance along with other forms of reaction against moves toward desegregation. The major arena of confrontation was the northern school district and the basic issue was busing, the movement of black and white children to schools that were sometimes far from home in order to achieve "racial balance."

A debate has continued over the effects of such policies on attitudes and behavior relating to race relations and their effectiveness on the educational process itself. Sociologist James Coleman, an early advocate of desegregation and author of one of the most widely quoted reports on the problems of separate schooling, argued along with others that forced busing was counterproductive, especially since it accelerated "white flight," the movement from city to suburb.[58] Others said the evidence, including evidence from a later study conducted by Coleman himself, belied such claims, that, in fact, whites were leaving the cities whether busing was being imposed or not. And some continued to suggest that, although desegregation would not be accomplished by school integration alone, it still was essential to get people to know one another even if it meant requiring them to leave the neighborhood to do so.

Although the debate over techniques of breaking down what the English call "the color bar" continued in many quarters, there were those who seemed to be little interested in weighing the issues. "Righteous racists," as some called them, sought to maintain closed communities, white bastions, often white, Christian bastions. They opposed "race mixing" in any form. Some such protesters joined the ranks of a revitalized Ku Klux Klan. Others found their ideological home in other right-wing groups.

In the late 1970s both the KKK and the neo-Nazis gained some strength and considerable publicity. Perhaps the most widely discussed case was the proposed pro-Nazi march scheduled to be held in Skokie, Illinois, a suburb of Chicago with many Jewish residents, including a number of concentration camp survivors. The Nazis sought and, through the intercession of the American Civil Liberties Union (ACLU), obtained a permit to demonstrate, speak their piece freely—blatant anti-Semitism and attacks on others they, like those whose banner they carried, deemed inferior and parasitic. The question of whether they should have been given a permit or not evoked a debate of its own and much soul-searching on the part of many civil libertarians. Although the American Civil Liberties Union defended the right to march, a number of ardent supporters of free speech (including several prominent former members of the ACLU) reminded their fellow liberals that, in the words of Chief Justice Holmes, the First Amendment does not give one the right to shout "Fire" in a crowded theater. And, they argued, calls for the expulsion, even the annihilation, of Jews were surely more than expressing opinions.[59] Although the Skokie March was finally called off, it represented a clear case of how our first concern with antilocution is (or may be) linked to the last, genocide, the planned elimination of an entire people.

Lynchings, cross burnings, calls to arms, rallies to whip up attacks on racial, religious, and ethnic minorities in this country are painful reminders of the crimes against humanity perpetrated in Nazi Germany. Genocide was the national policy of a sovereign state less than half a century ago. Over 9 million Jews lived in Europe before World War II. Nazi leaders were determined to eradicate this group and nearly succeeded.

Forced to carry identification papers marked with a "J" and to wear identifying yellow stars with the word "Jew" (*Jude* in German, *Jood* in Dutch, *Juif* in French) across them, driven from their homes, often ghettoized, herded into concentration camps, used as forced labor, experimented upon, violated in countless ways, and ultimately murdered by firing squads or liquidated in gas chambers, the Jews of Europe suffered the most heinous of all fates that can befall a group, genocide, the slaughter of an entire people.

Death camp survivor Primo Levi, an Italian Jew, described his recollection of the steps taken to break the spirit of the healthier camp inmates, those who, it turned out, were to be used for forced labor and then executed, joining the others who had been killed earlier.

> A dozen SS men stood around, legs akimbo, with an indifferent air. At a certain moment they moved among us, and in a subdued tone of voice, with faces of stone, began to interrogate us rapidly, one by one, in bad Italian. They did not interrogate everybody, only a few: "How old? Healthy or ill?" And on the basis of the reply they pointed in two different directions....
>
> In less than two minutes all the fit men had been collected together in a group. What happened to the others, to the women, to the children, to the old men, we could establish neither then nor later: the night swallowed them up, purely and simply. Today, however, we know that in that rapid and summary choice each one of us had been judged capable or not of working usefully for the Reich; we know that of our convoy no more than ninety-six men and twenty-nine women entered the respective camps of Monowitz-Buna and Birkenau, and that of all the others, more than five hundred in number, not one was living two days later.[60]

The initiation rite continued. Heads were shaved, the people were thrown in boiling showers, then immediately forced to run, naked and barefoot, in the icy snow. Finally they were given uniforms to put on.

There is nowhere to look in a mirror, but our appearance stands in front of us, reflected in a hundred livid faces, in a hundred miserable and sordid puppets....

Then for the first time we became aware that our language lacks words to express this offense, the demolition of a man. In a moment, with almost prophetic intuition, the reality was revealed to us; we had reached the bottom. It is not possible to sink lower than this; no human condition is more miserable than this nor could it conceivably be so. Nothing belongs to us anymore; they have taken away our clothes, our shoes, even our hair; if we speak, they will not listen to us, and if they listen they will not understand. They will even take away our name.[61]

And they did take away their names. In many camps, including Auschwitz, where Levi was finally taken, inmates were tattooed on the forearm with prison numbers, their only form of identification. They carried their numbers to the grave.

The word "genocide," itself, emerged during the war trials at Nuremberg, where it was defined as "a denial of the right of existence of entire human groups in the same way as homicide is the denial of the right to live for individual human beings." Although the term is newly coined, the practice itself is very old. It was known in biblical times when Menahem smote Tiphsah,[62] it was practiced by the British when they destroyed the Tasmanians in the "triumph of 'civilization' over 'savagery,'"[63] a version was used in early America when settlers offered bounty for the scalps and sometimes the heads of Indians,[64] and when Lord Jeffrey Amherst distributed smallpox-laden blankets to the indigenous peoples in a concerted effort to eliminate them.

In 2003, Robin M. Williams, Jr., noted that the twentieth century was the bloodiest in history.

The statistics numb the mind. Although estimates vary widely, the tale of death and destruction is monumental: since 1900 some 115 million persons killed in battles—plus perhaps an equal number of civilian fatalities. These were mass killings in organized wars, [but].... The slaughter was not confined to wars between states, for governments have savaged their own people....

Ever since World War II, the basic facts are stark. The vast majority of deaths from collective violence since 1945 have been within national states rather than between states; credible estimates say some 80 percent.[65]

In recent times violence has raged in our society—much of it based on racial hatred and ethnic rivalries, there is no evidence of such terrifying mass killing on our shores or sponsored genocide. But Americans have been witness to such acts. In the past few decades, television scenes have made us eyewitnesses to Pol Pot's murder of millions of his fellow Cambodians, the butchering of hundreds of thousands of Tutsi people by Hutus in Rwanda, the campaigns of "ethnic cleansing" by Serbs in various states of the former Yugoslavia, and the more recent slaughter of those in Darfur by the government-supported killers in the Sudan. Each of these actions falls clearly under the definition set forth at Nuremberg.

Conclusion

These cases of discrimination have been cited not to indicate how inconsiderate and brutal people can be (though such might be purpose enough), but rather to describe briefly the varying degrees of discrimination—*derogation, denial,* and *aggression.* Each, except *mass* murder, is a contemporary example of discrimination in the United States and an expression of both unwitting and willful behavior to which too many Americans, including fair-weather liberals, subscribe.

We have examined some formal and informal policies of those with majority status and some ways in which they seek to maintain it. Little attention has been paid to the reactions of those discriminated against. The following chapter examines the impact of discriminatory treatment and some sociological implications of minority status.

Notes

1. Robin M. Williams, Jr., *The Reduction of Intergroup Tensions* (New York: Social Science Research Council, 1947), p. 39.

2. See, for example, Gordon W. Allport, *The Nature of Prejudice* (Cambridge: Addison-Wesley, 1954), esp. pp. 14–15 and 49–51; and Ernest Works, "Types of Discrimination," *Phylon* (Fall, 1969), pp. 223–233.

3. Richard Wright, *Black Boy* (New York: Harper & Row, 1945), esp. pp. 128–129 and 163–170.

4. A good summary of the language of prejudice is to be found in John P. Dean and Alex Rosen, *A Manual of Intergroup Relations* (University of Chicago Press, 1955), Chap. 2. This chapter was written in collaboration with Robert B. Johnson and the ideas expressed are largely based on Johnson's unpublished Ph.D. dissertation, "The Nature of the Minority Community" (Ithaca, N.Y.: Cornell University, 1954).

5. Michael Novak, "The Sting of Polish Jokes," *Newsweek* (April 12, 1976), p. 13.

6. Michael Lerner, "Respectable Bigotry," *The American Scholar,* 38 (Autumn 1969).

7. Bernard Rosenberg and Gilbert Shapiro, "Marginality and Jewish Humor," *Midstream,* 4 (Spring 1958), pp. 70–80.

8. See, for example, Russell Middleton and John Morland, "Humor in Negro and White Subcultures: A Study of Jokes Among University Students," *American Sociological Review,* 24 (February 1959), pp. 61–69. See also John H. Burma, "Humor as a Technique in Race Conflict," *American Sociological Review,* 11 (December 1946), pp. 710–715; Milton L. Barron, "A Content Analysis of Intergroup Humor," *American Sociological Review,* 15 (February 1950), pp. 88–94.

9. Stanley Crouch, *The Artificial White Man* (New York: Basic Civitas Books, 2005). The quotation is at the center of a critical review of Crouch's book by Emily Eakin, *New York Times Book Review* (January 16, 2005), p. 7.

10. For an excellent analysis of such shows, see Henry Louis Gates, Jr., "T.V.'s Black World Turns But Stays Unreal," *New York Times* (November 12, 1989), Section II, 1, p. 40.

11. Laura Hobson, *New York Times* (September 12, 1971), Section II, 1 and continuation. See also Robert Alter, "Defaming the Jews," *Commentary,* 45 (January 1973), pp. 77–83.

12. Neil Vidman and Milton Rokeach, "Archie Bunker's Bigotry: A Study of Selective Perception and Exposure," *Journal of Communication,* 24 (Winter 1974).

13. Erdman Palmore, "Ethnophaulisms and Ethnocentrism," *American Journal of Sociology,* 67 (January 1962), pp. 442–445. See also William B. Helmreich, *The Things They Say Behind Your Back,* (New Brunswick, N.J.: Transaction Books, 1984).

14. Samuel Walker, *Hate Speech: The History of an American Controversy* (Lincoln: University of Nebraska Press, 1994).

15. The expression "fighting words" first appeared in the 1942 "Chaplinsky Decision" of the Supreme Court relating to the persecution of Jehovah's Witnesses. Walker, loc. cit, pp. 64–65.

16. Clifford H. Moore (trans.), *The Annals of Tacitus* (Cambridge: Harvard University Press, 1937), Vol. IV, Book XV, p. 285.

17. Ibid., pp. 285–287. Italics supplied.

18. These phrases are part of a composite speech made up of actual statements by American demagogues; they serve as introduction to the study by Leo Lowenthal and Norbert Guterman, *Prophets of Deceit* (New York: Harper & Row, 1949), pp. 1–2. Current examples of inflammatory writings are *Common Sense, America's Newspaper Against Communism,* published in Union, N.J., and *The American Nationalist,* published in Inglewood, California. The support given to such publications is analyzed in an article by Hans H. Toch, Steven E. Deutsch, and Donald M. Wilkins, "The Wrath of the Bigot: An Analysis of Protest Mail," *Journalism Quarterly,* 37 (Spring 1960), pp. 173–185, 266.

19. Martin Tolchin, "President Won't Condemn Brother's Remarks on Jews," *New York Times* (February 28, 1979), p. A16.

20. See Peter I. Rose, "Blaming the Jews," *Society,* 31:6 (September–October, 1994), pp. 35–40.

21. See Seymour Martin Lipset and Earl Raab, *The Politics of Unreason* (New York: Harper & Row, 1969).

22. Neil Baldwin, *Henry Ford and the Jews: The Mass Production of Hate* (New York: Public Affairs, 2001).

23. Seymour Martin Lipset, "Prejudice and Politics in America," in Charles Y. Glock and Ellen Siegelman (eds.), *Prejudice U.S.A.* (New York: Praeger, 1969), p. 18. Italics supplied.

24. See, for example, *Common Sense* (September 15, 1958), p. 1.

25. *Washington Post* (December 20, 1972), p. C1.

26. See, for example, Charles Abrams, *Forbidden Neighbors* (New York: Harper & Row, 1955); and Oscar Handlin, *The Newcomers: Negroes and Puerto Ricans in a Changing Metropolis* (Cambridge: Harvard University Press, 1959).

27. Two early and now classic examples of the problems of "race and housing" are Morton Grodzins, *The Metropolitan Area as a Racial Problem* (Pittsburgh: University of Pittsburgh Press, 1958); and Eunice Crier and George Crier, *The Impact of Race on Neighborhoods in the Metropolitan Setting* (Washington, D.C.: Washington Center for Metropolitan Studies, 1961).

28. Hillel Levine and Lawrence Harmon, *The Death of an American Jewish Community* (New York: Free Press, 1992).

29. See, for example, Louis Wirth, *The Ghetto* (Chicago: University of Chicago Press, 1956), pp. 18–19.

30. Brewton Berry, *Race and Ethnic Relations,* 2nd ed. (Boston: Houghton Mifflin, 1958), p. 273.

31. See Douglas S. Massey and Nancy A. Denton, *American Apartheid: Segregation and the Making of the Underclass* (Cambridge: Harvard, 1993).

32. Allport lists these and other examples of restrictive covenants, op. cit., p. 53.

33. See Benjamin R. Epstein and Arnold Forster, *Some of My Best Friends . . .* (New York: Farrar, Straus & Cudahy, 1962), esp. pp. 106–139.

34. This practice has lessened in recent years, largely as a result of college administration action. See Epstein and Forster, ibid., pp. 165–167. See also Alfred McClung Lee, *Fraternities Without Brotherhood* (Boston: Beacon, 1955); and, "A Study of Religious Discrimination by Social Clubs," *Rights,* 4 (January 1962), pp. 83–96.

35. Edna Bonacich, "Inequality in America: The Failure of the American System for People of Color," in Alberto Aguirre, Jr. and David V. Baker (eds.), *Sources: Notable Selections in Race and Ethnicity* (Guilford, CT: Duskin Publishing Group, 1995), pp. 134, 136.

36. *The Social and Economic Status of the Black Population in the United States,* Current Population Reports, Series P-23, No. 42 (Washington, D.C.: Department of Commerce, 1971), p. 1.

37. *The Social and Economic Status of the Black Population in the United States: An Historical Overview 1790–1978,* Current Population Reports, Series P-23, No. 80 (Washington, D.C.: Department of Commerce, 1979), pp. 168–169.

38. John E. Jacob, *The State of Black America* (New York: National Urban League, Inc., 1987), pp. 7–14.

39. William J. Wilson, *The Declining Significance of Race* (Chicago: University of Chicago Press, 1978).

40. Sam Roberts, *Who We Are: A Portrait of America Based on the 1990 Census* (New York: Times Books, 1993), p. 189.

41. Ibid., p. 191.

42. Idem.

43. William Julius Wilson, *The Truly Disadvantaged: The Inner City, the Underclass, and Public Policy* (Chicago: University of Chicago Press, 1987).

44. Roberts, quoting Wolfe, op. cit., p. 192.

45. See Gary Orfield, "Ghettoization and Its Alternatives," in Paul E. Peterson (ed.), *The New Urban Reality* (Washington, D.C.: The Brookings Institution, 1981), p. 103.

46. Tom Wicker, "Introduction," *Report of the National Advisory Commission on Civil Disorders* (New York: Bantam Books, 1968), p. x.

47. *Report of the National Advisory Commission on Civil Disorders* (New York: Bantam Books, 1968), p. 10.

48. Andrew Hacker, *Two Nations: Black and White, Separate, Hostile, Unequal* (New York: Scribner's, 1992). See, especially, Chapter 1.

49. Ibid., p. 2.

50. Gunnar Myrdal, *An American Dilemma* (New York: Harper & Row, 1944), pp. 610–612. See also John Howard Griffin, *Black Like Me* (Boston: Houghton Mifflin, 1961).

51. Allport, op. cit., p. 57.

52. As reported in George E. Simpson and J. Milton Yinger, *Racial and Cultural Minorities,* rev. ed. (New York: Harper & Row, 1958), p. 515.

53. See Allport, op. cit., pp. 61–62.

54. For descriptions of several instances of school desegregation crises, see the following *Field Reports on Desegregation in the South,* written by social scientists and published in New York by the Anti-Defamation League of B'nai B'rith: a report on Beaumont, Texas, "College Desegregation Without Popular Consent," by Warren Breed; on Sturgis, Kentucky, "A Tentative Description and Analysis of the School Desegregation Crisis," by Roscoe Griffin; on Mansfield, Texas, "A Report on the Crisis Situation Resulting from Efforts to Desegregate the School System," by John Howard Griffin and Theodore Freedman; and,

on Clinton, Tennessee, "A Tentative Description and Analysis of the School Desegregation Crisis," by Anna Holden, Bonita Valien, and Preston Valien.

55. Reprinted in *New York Times* (September 18, 1962), p. 27.

56. See "Arrest Made in Notorious '64 Civil Rights Killings," *New York Times* (January 7, 2005), pp. 1, 15.

57. *New York Times* (December 12, 1972), pp. 1, 54.

58. See, for example, James Coleman, "Liberty and Equality in School Desegregation," *Social Policy,* 6 (January 1976), pp. 9–13.

59. See, for example, David Goldberg and others, "Thoughts about Skokie," *Dissent* (Spring 1979), pp. 226–230.

60. Primo Levi, *Survival in Auschwitz,* trans. by Stuart Woolf (New York: Orion Press, 1959), pp. 21–22.

61. Idem.

62. II Kings 15:16.

63. G. P. Murdock, *Our Primitive Contemporaries* (New York: Macmillan, 1934), p. 18.

64. See Berry, op. cit., pp. 187–194. See also Alain Locke and Bernhard Stern, *When Peoples Meet* (New York: Progressive Education Association, 1942), pp. 165–170.

65. Robin M. Williams, Jr., *The Wars Within: People and States in Conflict* (Ithaca: Cornell University Press, 2003), p. xii.

Chapter 9

In the Minority

The View from Outside

Henry James, the American novelist, spent twenty years of his life, from 1883 to 1904, away from his native land. Between his departure and return the country had undergone profound changes, most noticeably in the quality of urban life. When he left, it was English (or Anglo-American) in style and in sound. When he returned to New York the modest city had been transformed into a bustling metropolis, and homogeneity no longer marked the character of the social structure.

The old streets of the city had become warrens of poor immigrants, Little Italies and Little Jerusalems—polyglot enclaves even more strange than the shantytowns of the Irish who had come during James's youth, already signaling the beginning of the end of Protestant preeminence and Anglo conformity.

James was especially moved by the Jews he observed on the Lower East Side of New York City. His firsthand account of impressions gleaned from a visit to "that outpost of Jerusalem" was vivid as well as pointed. He likened the Jews to squirrels and monkeys. He was awed and repulsed by the crowded conditions in which they lived, enchanted and dismayed by their exotic ways and lively manners. He drank deeply of the summer city scene and then departed, as if from a voyage to the moon. (One is tempted to say as if from "abroad" but, more surely than not, he would have found London or Edinburgh or Paris less foreign than the Lower East Side of his own New York.)

If Henry James were to come back to life and visit Rutgers Street today, he might have a haunting sense of déjà vu. To be sure, the "squirrels" and "monkeys" he would now observe scampering up and down the fire escapes of the tenements would be even darker than the "swarthy Orientals" he saw one hundred years ago.

The argot of the street would be marked by a Spanish accent or "Black English" and rap talk rather than the babble of Yiddish. And the kitchen odors would be of paella and plantain or ribs and collard greens rather than the soups and pickled herrings of the "Israelites." Still, it would strike him that, once again, his fair New York was "swarming" (a favorite word) with alien elements.

Pushing this fantasy a bit further, James, if he listened carefully, might hear some outlandish proposals: demands for group rights and recognition, schemes for resisting the untenable choice of either completely conforming to the ways of the dominant society (*his* society) or continuing to be excluded. He might hear rumblings about slumlords that overcharge, politicians who take bribes, teachers who make fun of those who have difficulty with the language. He might even hear of plots to organize against the bosses, plans for greater community control within the ghetto, notions of developing local political organizations or bloc power.

There are many parallels between what was going on in James's New York at the turn of the century and in the New York almost a century later as described in Tom Wolfe's controversial novel *Bonfire of the Vanities*.[1] There are differences, too. To understand these, one must carefully examine the nature of minority status as it affected (and continues to affect) the various groups of white immigrants, who, for whatever reason, chose to come to these shores from Europe; and as it affected other nonwhite peoples like the Native Americans, African Americans, Asians, and many Latin Americans.

Minority Status

For most Europeans, migration to America was followed by successive stages of contact, competition, and some form of accommodation with the Old Settler population. For some (starting with the Protestants from Northern Europe and Scandinavia) accommodation led to gradual assimilation into the dominant society, leaving but a vestige of ethnic difference. For others (including many Africans, Latin Americans, and Asians) the process stopped short of full assimilation. In spite of the fact that there has been increasing intermarriage in recent years, especially between members of various Catholic ethnic groups, between Protestants and Catholics, Jews and non-Jews, and, in the past two decades, between blacks and whites, clearly identifiable ethnic communities continue to exist. The most prominent of these are those sociologists call "minority communities." Such communities have several distinguishing characteristics, not least the fact that members are both differentiated from others and discriminated against in some fashion.

Minority status is sometimes "given;" often it is inherited. It may stem simply from the ascription of a differentiating label to a category of individuals who share certain social and physical traits deemed inferior to those of the dominant group—for example, persons with dark skin, atheists, women, and homosexuals. Statistical aggregates such as these are not social groups in the sociological sense of the term. They do, however, possess the potential for becoming groups or collectivities, especially when their members are categorically singled out for differential treatment.

Minority status is often ascribed to those social groups whose members have a history of patterned interaction, shared or similar beliefs and values, a sense of in-group solidarity, but who are also relegated to subordinate positions in the prestige hierarchy.[2] The two words *subordinate positions* are central, for all sociological minorities, no matter how tightly knit, share the fact that they have only limited control over their destinies. Put differently, minority status is socially defined.[3]

In 1945, sociologist Louis Wirth spelled out the concept of minority group in some detail and, implicitly, noted its relation to the concept of power. Stressing both its internal characteristics and the relation of the subordinate group to the wider society, Wirth wrote:

> ... A minority must be distinguishable from the dominant group by physical or cul-tural marks. In the absence of such identifying characteristics it blends into the rest of the population in the course of time.
>
> Minorities objectively occupy a disadvantageous position in the society. As con-trasted with the dominant group they are debarred from certain opportunities—eco-nomic, social and political.
>
> The members of minority groups are held in lower esteem and may even be the objects of contempt, hatred, ridicule and violence.
>
> They are generally socially isolated and frequently spatially separated.
>
> They suffer from more than the ordinary amount of social and economic insecurity.[4]

Because of these attributes, Wirth felt that "minorities tend to develop a set of attitudes, forms of behavior, and other subjective characteristics which tend further to set them apart."[5]

In an earlier chapter it was noted that while Wirth was greatly concerned about the deleterious effect of the inferior status position of particular ethnic groups, he and others, such as E. K. Francis, stressed the fact that most ethnic groups, includ-ing many "minorities," frequently shared a positive sense of unity or "we-feeling," an ideology (however vague and unreflective it may be) and an interdependence of fate (whether based upon religious or political or cultural or racial characteristics). Moreover, ethnic group ties tend to be maintained as long as individuals feel bound to the community, "a community dependent as much upon the idea of communal-ity as on actual proximity; a community one can 'feel' if not 'touch.'"[6] One of the controversies that persists among students of racial and ethnic relations concerns the extent to which minority status is injurious to the individuals who occupy such a position and the benefits, if any, of prescribed separateness. This debate is most clearly joined in discussions of marginality, the concept that refers to those who appear to be on the edges of the dominant society.

Marginality

More than a few sociologists have suggested that those whose group identity is determined in part by external pressure, who are categorically excluded from op-portunities for equal status, who are barred from assimilation and thus must live on the periphery of the dominant society, are "marginal men ... whom fate has

condemned to live in two societies and in two not merely different from antagonistic cultures."[7]

Perhaps the clearest articulation of this viewpoint was offered by the sociologist W. E. B. Du Bois in 1897 when he spoke of his people, African Americans,
in the following way:

> After the Egyptian and Indian, the Greek and Roman, the Teuton and Mongolian, the
> Negro is a sort of seventh son, born with a veil, and gifted with second sight in this
> American world—a world which yields him not true self-consciousness, but also lets
> him see himself through the revelation of the other world. It is a peculiar sensation,
> this double-consciousness, this sense of always looking at one's self through the eyes
> of others, of measuring one's soul by the tape of a world that looks on in amused
> contempt and pity.... [8]

Max Weber, Werner Sombart, Georg Simmel, and Thorstein Veblen all described
the ambiguous role of the "stranger." Usually referring to European Jews, their
prototypes also seemed both to enjoy and to suffer from the double-consciousness
Du Bois used to describe the paradoxical situation of blacks in the United States.
Simmel, for example, wrote of the "stranger" in the following manner: "His position in the group is determined, essentially by the fact that he has not belonged
to it from the beginning, that he imparts qualities into it which do not and cannot
stem from the group itself."[9]

Robert E. Park gave a new label to this phenomenon. He called it *marginality*.
Park suggested that members of many racial and ethnic groups suffer from the ambivalence of values created by their longing for the old and their desire to participate
in the new. Park and Everett Stonequist, author of *The Marginal Man,* described
such persons as "cultural hybrids."[10] One of the results of their marginality, Park
and Stonequist suggested, was personal maladjustment; another was the tendency
to engage in deviant behavior.

Critics of the Park-Stonequist thesis have argued that "belonging to a minority
group in and of itself does not necessarily predispose one to inner strain, personal
disorientation, psychic difficulties, or various types of deviance such as crime."[11]
Moreover, problems in one era do not necessarily mean groups or their members
are destined to repeat them time and again. As many historians have pointed out, the
well-known term "Paddy Wagon" (for police vans) originated because of the large
number of once-marginal Irish immigrants who got in trouble with the police in the
late nineteenth century. Today it is often said that "Paddy drives the wagon" and
others ride in the back.

This does not mean that minority status is irrelevant; rather that it is often relative
and many sociologists think the main problem is related to status consistency and
inconsistency. Personal stability depends, in large measure, on the sense of security
the individual members feel within the community as well as within the society.[12]
Who one thinks he or she is and where he or she belongs are crucial matters; so, too,
is the support system provided for the person growing up in a minority setting.

Challenging the conventional wisdom, economist Thomas Sowell has suggested
that the differential mobility of various ethnic groups is often unrelated to the

amount of discrimination they suffered. On the basis of his analysis of available statistical data, Sowell asserted that

> Groups may be subject to very similar treatment by society at large and yet differ enormously in their economic achievements and social problems. Japanese Americans and Mexican Americans, for example, came to the United States in large numbers at about the same time (the early 1900's), settled in the same region (the Southwest), and faced discrimination in schools and on the job. Yet today Japanese Americans' incomes are almost double the incomes of Mexican Americans, and their crime rates and broken homes are only a fraction of the figures for Mexican Americans. As for how they were treated by "society," the Japanese suffered more—being legally denied citizenship and land ownership for many years, and being interned with great loss of property during World War II. They were also much easier targets for racism.[13]

Similar findings are reported in comparing other groups who, at one time or other found themselves on the margins of society. For some, minority status has proved functional, or, at the least, a rallying point around which to mobilize. In recent years white women, an often overlooked category of marginal persons (both part of and apart from the dominant group) have found that much of what Betty Friedan once called "the feminine mystique"[14] resulted in their marginalization. Recognizing the effectiveness of using their separate and, often inferior position came to be useful as a rallying point around which to raise their own and their "sisters'" consciousness and to mobilize resources to challenge the status quo ante.

Minority status repeatedly has been found to intensify already existing group identity or to create it where it has not existed prior to discrimination. Forced to live in particular areas and to associate with one another, members of minority groups frequently come to view themselves as a community, to feel a keen sense of responsibility for their fellow members, and to build institutions that contribute to the protection of individuals and to furthering the sense of fellow-feeling.[15] Such a development suggests that the concept of *marginal man* is too narrow; it may even be inappropriate for vast numbers of minority group members.

Thus, in one of the many attempts to reformulate the concept of marginality, Milton M. Goldberg, relying in large measure on the work of the anthropologist Alexander Goldenweiser and his idea of "marginal cultural areas," suggested that:

> If (1) the so-called "marginal" individual is conditioned to his existence on the borders of two cultures from birth, if (2) he shares the existence and conditioning process with a large number of individuals in his primary groups, if (3) his years of early growth, maturation, and even adulthood find him participating in institutional activities manned largely by other "marginal" individuals like himself, and finally, if (4) his marginal position results in no major blockages or frustrations of his learned expectations and desires, then he is not a true "marginal" individual in the defined sense, but is a participant member of a marginal culture, every bit as real and complete to him as is the nonmarginal culture to the nonmarginal man.[16]

Contrary to the views of Park and Stonequist, Goldberg (and those sharing his conception) does not see most minority group members as maladjusted products of cultural ambivalence, but as adjusted participants in a marginal culture, itself a product of accommodation to differential treatment. This interpretation is consistent with the conviction that members of American minority communities manifest certain common characteristics normal to groups with similar marginal experiences, including certain traits that outsiders sometimes define as pathological. Goldberg's view jibes with others' perspectives, especially those who have examined historically marginal groups who, like Jews, Greeks, and Armenians, have often been traders within others' societies, at once needed and kept at arm's length. These "middleman minorities" as Hubert Blalock once styled them,[17] engaged in the professions or in risky businesses exist today. Many are sojourners with roots in East Asia (Chinese and Koreans) and South Asia (especially Indians).

While minority communities may differ from one another in racial and ethnic composition, their levels of socioeconomic status, patterns of social mobility, and local customs—those retained and those newly created—they tend to possess a transmitted remembrance of how the community developed. Everyone, of course, is "ethnocentric" to some degree. Moreover, spokespersons for almost every group engage in "the creative distortion of history" to emphasize their group's historical legacy and to underscore its unique contributions. Thus references are frequently made to the first members of the group to arrive and the conditions under which they came, how they were received and how they fared, the discrimination they encountered and how they coped with it, the grounds on which the community was established in this country, and the deeds of important leaders.

Many minorities have their own territorial bases, sometimes marked by physical boundaries ("the other side of the tracks," "down by the riverside," "in the hollow"), sometimes by psychological or social walls that set them apart from the larger community. In his memoir, *A Walker in the City,* Alfred Kazin explains: "We were the end of the line. We were the children of the immigrants who had camped at the city's back door, New York's rawest, remotest, cheapest ghetto, enclosed on one side by the Carnarsie flats and on the other by the hallowed middle-class districts that showed the way to New York. "New York" was what we put last on our address, but first in thinking of the others around us. *They* were New York, the Gentiles ... ; we were Brownsville—*Brunzvil,* as the old folks said."[18] Today Brownsville is predominantly African American and those who now write of their estrangement often describe Kazin's people, the Jews, as the "they" who represent the "Establishment."[19]

When separated from the dominant society, minorities frequently maintain their own traditional and social institutions. Some of these run counter to the ways of the larger community and are viewed by those who peer into their enclaves as deviant, mysterious, dangerous, as "un-American." One thinks of different ways various people "use" time, worship, and relax, to say nothing of the myriad differences in ways of perceiving themselves, each other, and the society in which they live.

The last point was most poignantly expressed through the research of the late Oscar Lewis. Here is a short excerpt from his famous essay in which his Puerto Rican respondents compare life in New York with that on the home island. The passage begins with Lewis asking, "Have you ever been in New York, Hector?"

"Yes, yes, I've been to New York."

"And what did you think of life there?"

"New York! I want no part of it! Man, do you know what it's like? You got up in a rush, have breakfast in a rush, get to work in a rush, go home in a rush, even shit in a rush. That's life in New York! Not for me! Never again! Not unless I was crazy.

"Look, I'll explain. The ways things are in New York; you'll get nothing there. But nothing! It's different in Puerto Rico. Here, if you're hungry, you come to me and say, 'Man, I'm broke, I've had nothing to eat.' And I'd say, 'Ay, Bendito! Poor thing!' And I'd give you some food. No matter what, you wouldn't have to go to bed hungry. Here in Puerto Rico you can make out. But in New York, if you don't have a nickel, or twenty cents, you're worthless, and that's for sure. You don't count. You get swallowed by a horse."[20]

But even such harshness of urban life is coped with by hundreds of thousands of Puerto Ricans and others who feel the attraction of places like New York where opportunities for work are thought to abound. While often disillusioned by what they find, many stay and attempt to survive. They do so in part by trying to maintain old ways or by engaging in a process that has been called *ethnogenesis,* the establishment of a new sense of ethnicity, often more pronounced in the country to which they move than the one left behind.[21]

Many who rarely think of themselves as Puerto Rican or Italian or Chinese or Mexican back home where everyone is Puerto Rican or Italian or Chinese or Mexican quickly learn that they are labeled as such by those around them and, in response, often create a new hyphenated social form that is manifest in a new identity (such as Chinese American) and in ways of behaving that reflect both acculturation and accommodation.

The street culture of Cuban Miami, the tight-knit social organization of Chinatowns in San Francisco and Seattle, New York and Boston, the ubiquity of storefront churches in poor, Puerto Rican areas, the twang of western music in Chicago neighborhood bars, the array of ethnic newspapers found on the stands of every large city, all indicate that many Americans carry on by retaining or reviving that which they once knew, which become lifelines of sorts, especially for those of the first generation. But they and their children also often create new institutions and organizations such as teenage gangs, athletic clubs, ethnically based patriotic clubs (such as the "Polish-American Veterans"), religious bodies ("African Methodist Episcopal Church"), social agencies (the "Catholic Youth Organization"), after-school schools (such as those offering Armenian, Greek, Chinese, Hebrew, Arabic, Vietnamese, et cetera), and many kinds of businesses—some set up specifically for particular foods and special services.

Many members of minority groups make their living and spend much of their money within the ethnic community itself. Some, including those who have become quite successful, find themselves in what Norbert Wiley once called an "ethnic nobility trap."[22] Having chosen to make his or her way within the confines of the ethnic enclave, the individual may become locked in with a skill or specialty that is difficult to transfer to the wider world.

Wiley began his discussion of this phenomenon by reminding the readers of William Foote Whyte's famous study *Street Corner Society,* a detailed description and analysis of a working-class Italian area in the north side of Boston. There, Whyte noted, two avenues of socialization led to two sorts of "opportunity ceilings." If one was a "corner boy" he could aspire to work in local (ethnic) politics or to a high position in the rackets; if one was a "college boy" he was groomed for professional and managerial positions. Many, frustrated by the seeming remoteness of middle-class jobs, opted to follow the line of least resistance. Some of them even became big men in the local community, but they were nothing on the outside.[23]

Many members of minority groups fall somewhere between the "corner boys" and the "college boys." While some spend their entire lives inside the enclave and some break away completely, a common pattern is to make one's living away from the neighborhood. It is in the workaday world that one tends to have the greatest amount of interaction with members of other groups and with representatives of the wider society. When night falls, as the saying goes, "The WASPs return to their nests—and the others return to their own." Ethnic nests vary, of course, from old law tenements to high-rise apartments to ranch homes in wealthy suburbs that some have called "gilded ghettos."[24]

On-the-job participation is frequently quite formal and segmentalized, with each person playing his appropriate role. Those with whom he has contact often see the minority group member as an "ambassador of his people."[25] Because exposure is frequently limited to outstanding figures (such as athletes, entertainers, professionals), to workers, or to servants, and rarely involves intimate or informal exchanges, individuals in the dominant group tend to have distorted images of minority peoples and of their personal existence. Their views are frequently a combination of hunches (based on limited observation) and prejudices (which they have learned through contact with other prejudiced people).

The pattern is generally asymmetrical, however, for minorities are continually exposed to the values and norms of the dominant group through public schooling, mass media, employment, advertising, and just living. Survival requires the ability to function in two worlds: that of the minority (the "membership group") and of the dominant "reference group."[26]

Although it is not unusual to hear blanket indictments of the entire "Establishment," members of minority groups learn fairly early in life that the dominant group itself is highly differentiated in various ways. They are surprised when they find that so many of those beyond the confines of their communities are unaware that they, too, have their own hierarchies, interest groups, leaders and followers, successful members and ne'er-do-wells, poets and preachers, artisans and laborers, professionals and provocateurs.

Like most communities in complex societies, minority enclaves consist of clusters of subgroupings, varying in socioeconomic status, occupational interest, and political proclivity.[27] Certain ethnic groups, to be sure, put more stress on one activity than on another and certain occupations hold greater prestige than others. One thinks of the role of the priesthood in a French Canadian village, of law and politics—and the priesthood, too—in an Irish community, teaching and the professions for Jews, or of business and science for the parents of Chinatown's children or many from Southeast Asia. While not every French Canadian child aspires to be a priest nor every Irish American wishes to be a "pol," there is no question that many members of their communities get a certain amount of satisfaction from seeing one of their own people become successful, especially in those areas toward which they feel particularly partial for sentimental, ideological, or practical reasons.

Even where there are relatively parallel systems of social stratification, there is no assurance that persons considered to be upper class by members of their own group would be accorded the same status by outsiders; nor does it mean that the respected members of a given minority would be held in the same esteem by those in the dominant group.[28]

Pride

Group identification is revealed in intragroup attitudes and actions; it is reflected in expressions of intergroup behavior and minority reaction to treatment by others.

Pride in one's ethnic or racial identity may be illustrated in the fellow feeling that predisposes many young blacks to identify with "brothers" and "sisters" they have never met. When introduced they may go through an elaborate handshake, signifying to one another that they are together. Members of other groups perform similar rituals to indicate their sense of identification and their group-based pride.

In a study of small-town Jews and their Christian neighbors, the author asked each Jewish participant what first came to mind when he or she read the following newspaper headline: "Mischa Goldberg Lauded for Concert Performance." The most frequent response emphasized a special sort of satisfaction in seeing a fellow Jew receive recognition. Many echoed the sentiment expressed by one of them who said, "I'm glad when it's one of ours who does well, it makes me feel good." When the same individuals were then asked their reactions to a second headline—"Max Cohen Indicted for Fraud"—the characteristic responses were vexation, embarrassment, and anger. "It's bad for us when a Jew gets in trouble."[29] When asked if they knew Mischa Goldberg or Max Cohen (names I had made up), to a person they said, "No." Still, assuming they were Jewish from their names, they had answered in very personal terms.

When the same individuals were asked to respond to another set of fake headlines, this time with Anglo-Saxon names, as for example, "John Smith Wins Race," or "Thomas Jones Suspect in Murder Case," they looked puzzled. One after another would counter, "I don't know what to say, who is John Smith?" Or, "It sounds bad but I really don't know Thomas Jones."

Not surprisingly, many Jews, whatever their political proclivities, take special pride in the prominence of Jewish senators, Supreme Court Justices Ruth Bader Ginsberg and Stephen Breyer, financier Edgar Bronfman, and publisher S.I. Newman, and, whatever their taste in entertainment, identify with the celebrity of Paul Newman, Ed Asner, Beverly Sills, Barbra Streisand, Itzak Perlman. They also share a sense of collective embarrassment over the notoriety of the likes of David Berkowitz, the convicted murderer, or Ivan Boesky, the discredited "inside-trader."

In similar fashion many Hispanic Americans are still pleased to recall the champion of the farm labor, Mexican American Cesar Chavez, and take special

pleasure in cabinet members named Alberto Gonzales and Carlos Gutierrez, U.S. sena-
tors Mel Martinez and Bill Richardson, baseball players named Manny Ramirez, Juan
Gonzales, and Pedro Martinez, and even if they have never swung a club, to boast of
the accomplishments of golfers Lee Trevino and Nancy Lopez. They can't help but
be upset when the accused in a celebrated mass murder case is named Corona. Italian
Americans often display similar feelings of nostalgic chauvinism when they think of
Frank Sinatra, Joe DiMaggio, and John Sirica, and when they see the names of former
New York State governor, Mario Cuomo, or Associate Justice of the Supreme Court
Anthony Scalia—and the pop star Madonna. For Irish Americans names like Jimmy
Walker and Jimmy Cagney, the late Senator Daniel Patrick Moynihan, talk show host
Phil Donahue, commentator Andy Rooney, actress Rosie O'Donnell, Associate Justice
Kennedy—and almost anyone else named Kennedy—have special meaning, even
though they may have never met any of them.

Two factors are operating in these cases: a sense of interdependence of fate
with others with whom one is identified, and a vicarious connection with those in
the limelight. This phenomenon is related to a broader one, referred to by Herbert
Gans as "symbolic ethnicity."[30]

Symbolic ethnicity is manifest not only in feelings of identity but in ethnically
specific activities, including eating of traditional cuisine, participating in folk festivals,
trying to recapture lost languages, that remain important even for those who have found
acceptance and are about to enter what Richard Alba once called "the twilight of ethnicity."[31] Of course, they are highly significant for those still subject to discrimination. Such
groups often encourage participation and instill pride by creating new institutions. The
African American celebration of Kwanzaa, created by Ron Karenga, a black political
scientist and founder of an organization called "Us," is the best recent example.

During the annual festival celebrating freedom and Afro-American cultures,
special foods are prepared, stories are told, and candles are lighted in ceremonies
that remind others of everything from Christmas and Chanukah to Thanksgiving.

Minority group members often see themselves as part of a whole community,
of those they know intimately and those they know only by sight or sign or name.
The group identity is expressed in innumerable ways. Perhaps it is best expressed
through the immediate response to the question many ask themselves about a
stranger being met for the first time: "Is he a 'brother'?" "Is she a 'sister'?" "Is
he a *landsmann*?" "Is he a *compadre*?" "Is she a *paisana*?" All subsequent social
intercourse is apt to be shaped by this definitive beginning.

Self-Hatred

It has been hypothesized that "the greater the pressure of prejudice and discrimination, the greater is likely to be the feeling of interdependence of fate within the
minority community."[32] While this relationship has been found to apply to many
members of minority groups, it does not necessarily hold for all. Some individuals,
objects of severe discrimination, may internalize the negative stereotypes held of
them by others and, as a result, display little in-group solidarity. In fact, rather than
drawing into the ranks of the minority, they may seek to withdraw from it.

As noted above, even those with a positive sense of group identity may feel self-conscious at the thought of "one of theirs" getting into trouble since it puts the whole minority in a bad light. Those who possess a low degree of self-esteem owing to their minority status are sometimes so anxious about their subordinate position that they attempt to disavow membership. To such persons the minority community is not a source of pride but of self-hatred.

In order to combat their inability to adjust to minority status they may change their names, deny their racial or ethnic origins, alter their appearance by changing the shape of their eyes (in the case of Asians) or straightening their hair (as have many African Americans) or having their noses made stubbier (as have many Italians and Jews) or narrower. (It is facetiously said that Michael Jackson "cut off his nose to spite his race.") Some refuse to associate with group members with whom they might be identified. Others attempt to pass as a member of the dominant group.

If they still find themselves rejected, they are caught between two social worlds, suffering the plight of the original marginal man as described by Du Bois and Park and Stonequist.

Reactions to Discrimination

What sorts of individual and collective action can minority group members take to deal with or alter their social position in a society such as our own? What happens when, driven by the same norms and values as those in power, they are barred from full participation or made to feel inferior? Or, putting the point in the words of Langston Hughes, "What happens when a dream is deferred?"

What happens to a dream deferred?

Does it dry up
like a raisin in the sun?
Or fester like a sore—
And then run?
Does it stink like rotten meat?
Or crust and sugar over—
like a syrupy sweet?

Maybe it just sags
like a heavy load.

Or does it explode?[33]

Many attempts have been made by sociologists to describe the responses of minority group members to their social situation. While, to be sure, various minorities suffer greater or lesser discrimination, nonetheless, within most minorities in the United States there are those who "want in" and are willing to do anything to obtain entry, there are those who simply want to be left alone, there are those who want what they feel they are rightly entitled to. Thus, as George Simpson and Milton Yinger suggest, most discussions of minority responses consider at least the following models: those who favor "acceptance," those who seek "accommodation," and those who are "aggressive."[34] (They may be aggressively for reform to get themselves in; they may be aggressively for radicalization to get themselves out or to form something entirely new.)

While taking into consideration these three models it is suggested here that reactions to minority status are most fully understood when two questions are posed. Answers to the questions reveal at least four types of reaction (each paralleling Hughes's metaphors) that, as shall be shown, may be further broken down and, in some ways, represent points on a spectrum through which some individuals may pass at various stages of their lives. The questions are these: (1) Does the minority group member accept or reject the image of subordinate status imposed on him or her by the majority? (2) Is he or she willing to play a humble role as expected by those in positions of power?

Table 9.1 presents the four possible types of reaction suggested here: submission, withdrawal, separation, and integration. (The first two incorporate what Simpson and Yinger call "acceptance"—at least on one axis; the latter two only partially parallel the categories of "accommodation" and "aggression" for, as noted below, both may involve the process of detente and militant action to achieve certain defined goals.)

Before examining these types it should be reiterated that all of these reaction patterns are possible, and a given individual may manifest two or more of them at different times or in different circumstances. Since it is the largest single minority group in the United States at present, illustrations of these types will be drawn from the experiences of African Americans.

Submission

Malcolm X once said, "The worst crime the white man has committed is to teach us to hate ourselves." There is little question that one of the first things many African Americans learn is their "place" and the roles they are expected to play in the white man's world. They learn "to be Negro" (or, in currently popular terms "to be Black"). In 1929 A. L. Holsey wrote,

> At fifteen I was fully conscious of the racial difference, and while I was sullen and resentful in my soul, I was beaten and knew it. I knew then that I could never aspire to be President of the United States, nor governor of my state, nor mayor of my city; I knew that I could only sit in the peanut gallery at our theater and could only ride on the back seat of the electric car and in the Jim Crow car on the train. I had bumped into the color line and knew that so far as white people were concerned, I was just another nigger.[35]

Recognizing one's fate as "just another nigger" among whites has led some African Americans to accept their inferior status and to play the segregated roles

**Table 9.1 Four Types of Reaction to Discrimination
by Members of Minority Groups**

| | Dominant Image of Minority Member's "Inferior Status" | |
Segregated Role:	Accepted	Rejected
Accepted	1. Submission	3. Separation
Rejected	2. Withdrawal	4. Integration

socially assigned to them. American folklore is filled with stories of "Uncle Toms," the defeated persons who knew the score and could play the tune as well. They bow and scrape, crack jokes, and play dumb to please the white folks. Uncle Toms exist in real life too.

Some minority people feel that the best way to live is to accept second-class status and do the bidding of those in the dominant positions. One such individual is described by Richard Wright in his famous autobiography, *Black Boy*. Wright tells of a black elevator operator with whom he worked in a Memphis hotel. One day Shorty needed lunch money and told Wright to watch him get it from the first white man who came along. When such a person eventually got into the elevator, Shorty said to him:

"I'm hungry, Mister White Man. I need a quarter for lunch."

The white man ignored him. Shorty, his hands on the controls of the elevator ...

"I ain't gonna move this damned old elevator till I got a quarter, Mister White Man"

"The hell with you, Shorty," the white man said, ignoring him and chewing on his Black cigar.

"I'm hungry, Mister White Man. I'm dying for a quarter," Shorty sang, drooling, drawling, humming his words.

"If you don't take me to my floor, you will die," the white man said, smiling a little for the first time.

"But this Black sonofabitch sure needs a quarter," Shorty sang, grimacing, clowning, ignoring the white man's threat.

"Come on, you Black bastard, I got to work," the white man said, intrigued by the element of sadism involved, enjoying it.

"It'll cost you twenty-five cents, Mister White Man, just a quarter, just two bits," Shorty moaned.

There was silence. Shorty threw the lever and the elevator went up and stopped about five feet shy of the floor upon which the white man worked.

"Can't go no more, Mister White Man, unless I get my quarter," he said in a tone that sounded like crying.

"What would you do for a quarter?" the white man asked, still gazing off.

"I'll do anything for a quarter," Shorty sang.

"What, for example?" the white man asked.

Shorty giggled, swung around, bent over, and poked out his broad, fleshy ass.

"You can kick me for a quarter," he said, looking impishly at the white man out of the corner of his eyes.

The white man laughed softly, jingled some coins in his pocket, took out one and thumped it to the floor. Shorty stooped to pick it up and the white man bared his teeth and swung his foot into Shorty's rump with all the strength of his body. Shorty let out a howling laugh that echoed up and down the elevator shaft.

"Now, open this door, you goddam black sonofabitch," the white man said, smiling with tight lips.

"Yeess, siiiir," Shorty sang, but first he picked up the quarter and put it into his mouth. "This monkey's got the peanuts," he chortled.

He opened the door and the white man stepped out and looked back at Shorty as he went toward his office.

"You're all right, Shorty, you sonofabitch," he said.

"I know it!" Shorty screamed, and then let his voice trail off in a gale of wild laughter.[36]

There are, of course, two possible interpretations of Shorty's acceptance of his role as buffoon. On the one hand, he was manipulating the white man—he got what he wanted; on the other, his behavior served to demonstrate the depth of his submissiveness, for he played his role according to his image of the white man's expectations.

For many minority group members, acceptance of subordinate status is the only way to eke out a living. The "red cap" with a master's degree and the Puerto Rican waiter with a high school diploma are well-known examples.

In many cases, submission to the inferior status imposed by others is a rational acceptance, a seeming necessity for survival. Brewton Berry, for example, states "it is not uncommon for one to conform externally while rejecting the system mentally and emotionally."[37] Yet, there are significant exceptions to this generalization. "Contemporary sociology and cultural anthropology have shown that people can learn to adjust to, and even accept extremely diverse circumstances that seem strange, painful, or evil to those who have received different training. Standards of value by which the desirability of a given status is judged, as well as the status itself, are a product of the society. A whole group may accept what to others seems to be an inferior role."[38]

For some individuals, acceptance of such inferior roles is simply conformity to the traditions of the community in which they happen to be raised. While whites may learn that they are superior to blacks as part of a more general socialization experience, some blacks similarly may accept the standards of racial inequality. Thus, acceptance of inferior status may be seen as a conditioned reaction in a prejudiced society. Today many of their militant children and grandchildren disparagingly refer to such people as "Nee-groes," rather than using the preferred terms "Blacks" or "African Americans."

Withdrawal

One reaction to discrimination is submission to inferior status; another is the denial of identity. In this case the individual accepts the majority image of his group[39] and—because of self-hatred or expediency—withdraws from it. In rejecting the segregated role that they are supposed to play, some light-skinned "Negroes," Jews who wish to be taken for Gentiles, Puerto Ricans who claim they are Spanish, and others attempt to pass into the dominant group. Not infrequently they hold ambivalent attitudes toward themselves and others, and their conflicting allegiances are apt to induce anxiety, which is further provoked by the constant threat of exposure. Thus a fictional character asks himself: "But what if a lot of people know it already? Or can detect the Negro in me? I hear lots of Southerners claim they can do that. That man goggling at me down the car—can he see I'm part Negro? Has everybody always guessed it?"[40]

In 1945, St. Clair Drake and Horace Cayton estimated that each year at least 25,000 persons permanently left the Negro population to become assimilated into white society.[41] While one suspects that number would not be as high today, still there are innumerable individuals who pass on a part-time or segmental basis, for example, working as whites by day and returning home to the black community. In this way they avoid the strain of breaking contact completely and turning away from lifelong friends and neighbors.

"Passing," a course open to those who possess no identifying racial or ethnic characteristics or those who can mask them, is the only method of assimilation available to persons who wish to enter an environment that would reject them out of hand if their true identity were to be revealed. In some areas of society, racial identity is relatively unimportant, and individuals can withdraw from the minority community while still being associated with it by others. Black athletes who attend big universities or join the armed forces, African American artists who become expatriates or entertainers, others who engage in such illicit activities as gambling and prostitution, frequently find acceptance in the white world because of the special skills or characteristics that they bring to the situation. Many such individuals, while not denying their minority identity, prefer not to be "professional race men;" they wish to be accepted in spite of—rather than because of—their racial or ethnic background. In most instances assimilation for such exceptional members of minority groups is only partial, for when they step out of their specialized roles many Americans consider them as "just another nigger."

Separation

The reaction patterns of both submission and withdrawal used by certain minority group members presume acceptance of the inferior image held of them by the majority. Yet, accepting their plight as members of a group considered by the majority to be of lower status does not necessarily mean total capitulation to the stigma of second-class citizenship. In recent years, the vast majority of African Americans have rejected the idea that they are inferior and have attempted either to avoid contact with those "in the camp of their oppressors" or to integrate and take their place alongside those in the dominant group. Here we consider the first of these two response patterns.

For many years some blacks who attained a moderate amount of security and rose to relatively high status within their own segregated community seemed resentful of those who submitted to the indignities imposed upon them. Long ago, Hortense Powdermaker reported: "Those at the top deplore the others' submission to white assumptions of superiority and their recalcitrance to white standards of behavior. They decry the loose morality and the ignorance by which, they feel, the lower class of Negro lends credence to unfair notions about the race."[42]

Although these attitudes are still prevalent in certain circles, a qualification is in order: In rejecting white assumptions of superiority, many blacks accept pervasive "white" middle-class cultural standards and frequently establish parallel social institutions that mimic the presumed manners and mores of whites, sometimes to the extent of becoming distorted parodies. Such efforts—often exaggerated accounts of the achievements of individuals—have been described as flights of fantasy. The late E. Franklin Frazier, speaking of middle-class urban Negroes, claimed that "their escape into a world of make-believe with its sham 'society' leaves them with a feeling of emptiness and futility which causes them to constantly seek an escape in new delusions."[43]

The extent to which old "Negro" newspapers and magazines (some of which still exist) were imitative of white society was evidenced by the advertisements and articles that appeared in them. *Ebony, Jet, Tan,* and others used to be filled with pages of ads for skin whiteners and hair straighteners. Furthermore, stories of fancy cotillions and exclusive clubs, of expensive homes and problems with the help, were reported. The preeminence of white standards, even among those who by subscribing to such journals supported their own institutions, was manifest.

Discussing the general problem, Maurice Davie once wrote: "Avoidance is thus a protective device, a way of adjusting to ... [segregation] with the least pain and uneasiness. It may be carried to the point of almost complete voluntary segregation."[44]

What might be considered a conventional response to separate treatment, namely, the development of institutions paralleling those of the dominant society, is not uncommon, especially by middle-class members of minorities (the white *nouveaux riches* are little different from the black bourgeoisie). But it is surely not the only reaction pattern of people who reject others' views of their alleged inferiority but see little point in trying to enter their social world.

Some, most often those too poor to emulate middle-class whites or too disgusted to want to, have taken what seem to many to be more drastic measures. They not only seek to maintain separation and a sense of communal integrity, they also foster the rejection of "white" standards. This type of response is frequently an active and sometimes aggressive method of furthering the goals of the group as a group, strengthening its position, and justifying its separate existence. To combat discrimination, exponents of this reaction pattern sometimes adopt a chauvinistic doctrine of their own superiority. Rather than paralleling dominant institutions and values, they challenge them—often acting out certain stereotypes in the process. Jeremy Larner has addressed himself to this last point when he notes the tendency of certain black nationalists and their spokesmen to engage in a self-indulgent (and, to him, self-deluding) game of mirroring, particularly in playing on three common white themes: "the noble savage" (with its emphasis on creativity, spontaneity, and willingness to fight), "the hipster" (a black Negro to replace Norman Mailer's famous "white Negro," portrayed as a sort of nihilistic superman who is the cock of the walk), and "the Black proletarian" (who is part of the vanguard of the revolution to come).[45]

Another key concept marking separation is "soul." In the late 1960s the Swedish anthropologist Ulf Hannerz made a careful study of an African American neighborhood in Washington, D.C. His observations offer one interesting view. He concluded that "soul as solidarity is a reaction to the threat of a split in the community" among those whose lives are circumscribed by the values and norms of mainstream (or wider American) society and those values more specific to ghetto living. Thus Hannerz argues that: "In order to make [the] solidarity encompass even the least privileged, it must be symbolized by those most undiluted forms of Black proletarian experience which everybody can claim as his heritage, and to give it a positive valence weakness must be turned into strength. Thus poverty, oppression, and troubled relationships are interpreted as the foundation of an endurance, which can only be appreciated by those who have passed the same way."[46] Others contend that "soul" is simply a label broadly applied to the shared perspective of all blacks, the basis of their "cultural" character.

As shall be shown in the next chapter, at various stages African Americans have opted for revitalization through separation, through the exaltation of all that is Black and the denigration of all that is white, and, frequently, through making capital of what outsiders (and some high-status insiders) consider to be lower-class cultural traits specific to the black ghetto.

Thus, under the general heading of avoidance one must consider the paths of both parallel participation and ethnic chauvinism.

Integration

Protest is not always manifest in attempts to pull away, to go it alone. As James Baldwin indicated, however, the appeal for such action is very great.

> The brutality with which Negroes are treated in this country simply cannot be overstated, however unwilling white men may be to hear it. In the beginning ... a Negro just cannot believe that white people are treating him as they do; he does not know what he has done to merit it. And when he realizes that the treatment accorded him has nothing to do with anything he has done, that the attempt of white people to destroy him—for that is what it is—is utterly gratuitous, it is not hard for him to think of white people as devils.[47]

Despite such sentiments, and they are still widespread, not all African Americans have attempted to solve the problem of inequality by joining the cause of Black Nationalism and rejecting the possibility of eventual integration. In fact, a very large percentage of African Americans, even today, seek equality without any strings. They do not want to be separate and equal or separate and superior. They want what is constitutionally guaranteed and are willing to fight to get it.

Here, again, such integrationists may try one of two routes. The first is essentially integration-at-a-distance, the kind that most other minorities (namely so-called white ethnics) enjoy; the second is full integration or, better stated, amalgamation.

Most of those we call ethnics in this society do live in two distinct, though not necessarily antagonistic, worlds (as pointed out above). One world is that of their kith, kin, and community; the other is the broader society in which they study and work and sometimes play. The former comes closer to possessing what sociologists call a *gemeinschaftlich* character, a sense of total involvement, of real belonging or "we-ness;" the latter is more *gesellschaftlich,* that is, marked by secondary relationships, impersonal ties, partial involvement, and remoteness. Thus a surprising number of ethnics (white and nonwhite) keep to their own neighborhoods and enjoy their own activities even when the formal barriers are removed. What they want, at least what many want, is the right to do as they please. Once they have that free choice they often opt for life with their own people.

Now there are some members of minority groups who wish to live in a truly color-blind, ethnically neutral society, a society where no one is judged, considered, or even recognized on the basis of skin color or any other potentially invidious criterion. They differ from those in the "withdrawal" category in Table 9.1, for they desire not to leave their own group but to abolish the idea of group difference itself. In terms introduced in Chapter Six, they are the true advocates of amalgamation—the legatees of Crèvecoeur and Zangwill—and wish their children to be the best that the crucible can pour out.

In both instances militancy may mark the road to emancipation. For whether people want the right to decide whether or not to integrate at a distance or to foster fusion, they must often work to convince others that it is their choice to make, not that of others. Since both of these responses are well within the value framework of the American ideal, many of the activities of the civil rights movement were, and are oriented toward these goals and many of the important pieces of legislation—including the Civil Rights Acts of 1964, 1967, and 1968—were testimony to the efficacy of integrationist pressure for many Americans.

Mixed Responses

There are times when those in the minority find that they cannot really go it alone (seeking separation or coexistence), nor can they abide the slowness of change as advocated by those whose perseverance is ever tempered by the call for patience and goodwill, as in the civil rights movement. Feeling stifled by recalcitrant institutions and reluctant officials, hampered by powerful opponents and anxious neighbors, some leaders have pressed their followers to push beyond the tolerance limits and have advocated radical tactics designed to force society to give in to their demands, to play not only on sympathy but also on fear of disruption, to appeal not merely to charity and righteousness but to countervailing power marshaled by those considered powerless. America has long been witness to such movements: the struggle for women's rights, the labor movement, and the Black Power Revolution. It is the last-named that concerns us here.

In the preceding section we looked at four typical ways minority peoples, including African Americans, have reacted to their treatment. We noted variations within each type, such as (1) unconscious as well as intentional (or calculated) submission; (2) partial or complete withdrawal; (3) avoidance, that is, mimicking the majority but avoiding contact, or opting for nationalism and putting emphasis on real, imagined, or created differences; (4) partial integration (or what was earlier called structural pluralism) or full integration (or amalgamation). Discounting those in the first two general categories because they accept dominant group definitions of their group's inferiority, it may be said that the third and fourth responses and their variations are permissible, even expected, within our normative structure. Like them or not, most Americans would acknowledge that people have the right to remain separate as long as they do not make trouble; to seek to integrate as long as they accept the values of others—and it does not cost too much. The trouble appears to begin when the limits are broached. Integrating a park is one thing; a neighborhood is quite another. Of course, as noted in Chapter 1, these limits—and the norms that define them—vary from region to region and from community to community. Still, in general, one can say that when blacks (or Chicanos or Puerto Ricans or Native Americans) become nationalistic, at least some Americans approve (they may even find it quaint or amusing) so long as they do it in their own area, on their own turf. Likewise, when integrationists press to have the country honor its own ideals, to force the door open through the slow, tedious, and expensive process of litigations, well and good. Liberals applaud; conservatives complain—but generally they go along once a decision is made.

In other words, both "Ethnocentric Blackwardness" (sometimes called "Chauvinistic Nationalism") and "Soulless Militancy" are tolerable from the majority viewpoint, even if not warmly welcomed. (Numerous public opinion polls bear testimony to this response.) But when chauvinism is joined with direct action (even nonviolent direct action), when pride and protest are linked together, the critical balance is upset and new responses are devised.

It is instructive to consider what Table 9.1 would look like if one thinks in terms of *radical responses* to minority status. Figure 9.1 represents this view.

Of course, "Black Power" and similar derivative movements are not historical accidents. They grew out of the mounting realization that unidimensional programs—whether chauvinistic or reformist—are usually inadequate to meet the basic challenge, the challenge posed by those who have the power to control the lives of others. And the lack of power, as noted at the beginning of this chapter, is a fundamental attribute of minority status.

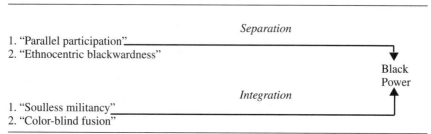

Figure 9.1 Black Power in Relation to Two Typical Reaction Patterns.

Notes

1. See Tom Wolfe, *Bonfire of the Vanities* (New York: Farrar, Strauss and Giroux, 1987).

2. For a more thorough discussion of groups, collectivities, and statistical aggregates, see Ely Chinoy, *Society,* rev. ed. (New York: Random House, 1967), pp. 40–43.

3. See Martin N. Marger, *Race and Ethnic Relations,* 3rd. ed. (Belmost, CA: Wadsworth Publishing Company, 1994), pp. 44–45.

4. Louis Wirth, "The Problem of Minority Groups," in Ralph Linton (ed.), *The Science of Man in the World Crisis* (New York: Columbia University Press, 1945), p. 348.

5. Ibid.

6. Peter I. Rose, *The Subject Is Race* (New York: Oxford University Press, 1968), p. 71.

7. Robert E. Park, "Human Migration and the Marginal Man," *American Journal of Sociology,* 33 (May 1928), p. 891; see also Everett V. Stonequist, *The Marginal Man* (New York: Scribner, 1937), p. 217.

8. From W. E. B. Du Bois, *The Souls of Black Folk* (1903), reprinted in *Three Negro Classics* (New York: Avon, 1965), p. 215.

9. Kurt H. Wolff (trans. and ed.), *The Sociology of Georg Simmel* (Glencoe, Ill.: Free Press, 1950), pp. 402–408.

10. See Robert E. Park, *Race and Culture* (New York: Free Press, 1951), p. 354.

11. For example, Golovensky's study of the Jewish community contradicts many of Park's contentions. See David Golovensky, "The Marginal Man Concept: An Analysis and Critique," *Social Forces,* 30 (October 1951 to May 1952), pp. 333–339.

12. George E. Simpson and J. Milton Yinger, *Racial and Cultural Minorities: An Analysis of Prejudice and Discrimination,* 4th ed. (New York: Harper & Row, 1972), p. 186.

13. Thomas Sowell, "Myths About Minorities," *Commentary,* (August 1979), pp. 34–35.

14. Betty Friedan, *The Feminine Mystique* (New York: Norton, 1963).

15. See Kurt Lewin, *Resolving Social Conflict* (New York: Harper & Row, 1941), esp. pp. 145–216; and a recent critique of Lewin's thesis, Jack Rothman, "Minority Group Status, Mental Health and Intergroup Relations: An Appraisal of Kurt Lewin's Thesis," *The Journal of Intergroup Relations,* 3 (Autumn 1962), pp. 299–310.

16. Milton M. Goldberg, "A Qualification of the Marginal Man Theory," *American Sociological Review,* 6 (February 1941), pp. 52–58.

17. Hubert Blalock, *Toward a Theory of Minority Group Relations* (New York: Wiley, 1967), pp. 79–84. See also Edna Bonacich, "A Theory of Middleman Minorities," *American Sociological Review,* 38 (1973), pp. 583–594.

18. Alfred Kazin, *A Walker in the City* (New York: Grove Press, 1951), p. 12.

19. See, for example, Candice van Ellison, "Introduction," in Allon Schoener (ed.), *Harlem on My Mind* (New York: Random House, 1968). The author's remarks were adapted from Nathan Glazer and Daniel Patrick Moynihan's *Beyond the Melting Pot* (Cambridge: M.I.T. Press, 1963).

20. Oscar Lewis, "In New York You Get Swallowed by a Horse," *Commentary* (November 1964), p. 69.

21. See, for example, L. Singer, "Ethnogenesis and Negro Americans Today," *Social Research,* 29 (Winter 1962), pp. 419–432.

22. Norbert F. Wiley, "The Ethnic Mobility Trap and Stratification Theory," *Social Problems,* 2 (Fall 1967), pp. 147–159.

23. Ibid. Also see William Foote Whyte, *Street Corner Society* (University of Chicago Press, 1943).

24. See Judith R. Kramer and Seymour Leventman, *Children of the Gilded Ghetto* (New Haven: Yale University Press, 1961). See also Part 1, "Jews, Gentiles and the American Dream," in Peter I. Rose (ed.), *The Ghetto and Beyond* (New York: Random House, 1969), pp. 21–97, passim.

25. See, for example, Peter I. Rose, *Strangers in Their Midst: Small-Town Jews and Their Neighbors* (Merrick, N.Y.: Richwood Publishing Company, 1979), especially pp. 76–79. Most of the small-town Jews interviewed by the author were keenly aware of the role they were forced to play as "ambassadors to the gentiles."

26. See Robert K. Merton, *Social Theory and Social Structure* (Glencoe, Ill: Free Press, 1957), pp. 290–291.

27. Edward A. Suchman, John P. Dean, and Robin M. Williams, Jr., *Desegregation: Some Propositions and Research Suggestions* (New York: The Anti-Defamation League of B'nai B'rith, 1958), p. 67.

28. See, for example, E. Digby Baltzell, *The Protestant Establishment* (New York: Random House, 1964), pp. 329–334.

29. See also, Peter I. Rose, "Small-Town Jews and Their Neighbours in the United States," *Jewish Journal of Sociology,* 3 (December 1962), pp. 1–17.

30. Herbert Gans, "Symbolic Ethnicity: The Future of Ethnic Groups and Cultures in America," *Ethnic and Racial Studies,* 2 (January, 1979), pp. 1–20.

31. See Richard D. Alba, *Ethnic Identity: The Transformation of White America* (New Haven, CT: Yale University Press, 1990).

32. Suchman et al., op. cit, p.198. See also Arnold M. Rose, *The Negro's Morale* (Minneapolis: University of Minnesota Press, 1949), pp. 85–95.

33. Langston Hughes, *Selected Poems* (New York: Alfred A. Knopf, 1951).

34. Simpson and Yinger, op. cit., pp. 205–233.

35. A. L. Holsey, "Learning How to Be Black," *The American Mercury,* 16 (April 1929), pp. 421–425.

36. Richard Wright, *Black Boy* (New York: Harper & Row, 1945), pp. 198–200.

37. Brewton Berry, *Race and Ethnic Relations,* 3rd ed. (Boston: Houghton Mifflin, 1965), p. 483.

38. Simpson and Yinger, op. cit., p. 251.

39. "Individuals may belong to membership groups that are different from their reference groups, and thereby manifest positive prejudice toward a social category other than that to which they apparently belong." Robin M. Williams, Jr., "Racial and Cultural Relations," in J. B. Gittler (ed.), *Review of Sociology* (New York: Wiley, 1957), p. 428.

40. Sinclair Lewis, *Kingsblood Royal* (New York: Random House, 1947), p. 69.

41. St. Clair Drake and Horace Cayton, *Black Metropolis* (New York: Harcourt, Brace, 1945), p. 160.

42. Hortense Powdermaker, *After Freedom* (New York: Viking, 1939), p. 357.

43. E. Franklin Frazier, *Black Bourgeoisie* (New York: Free Press, 1957), p. 213.

44. Davie, op. cit., p. 440.

45. Jeremy Larner, "To Speak of Black Violence," *Dissent* (Winter 1973), pp. 76–78.

46. Ulf Hannerz, *Soulside: Inquiries into Ghetto Culture and Community* (New York: Columbia University Press, 1970), p. 157; also pp. 144–158.

47. James Baldwin, *The Fire Next Time* (New York: Dial Press, 1963), pp. 82–83.

PART IV

POWER, POLITICS, AND PLURALISM

Chapter 10

Pride and Protest

Whose History?

History is often written in terms of the images people in power wish to project. American history, for example, was long recounted as if the English, Scotch Irish, and a few Dutchmen were the only ones to have had an impact on the growth and development of the country. Early textbooks and classroom lectures dealt almost exclusively with "The Anglo-American Tradition" or with "Our Christian Heritage." Throughout most of the eighteen and nineteenth centuries, newcomers from northwestern Europe were encouraged to forget about the customs of Germany or Scandinavia and to adapt themselves to eminently superior *American* life ways. Other immigrants were often considered beyond the pale of social acceptance. In story and song, Irish Catholics, Italians, Poles, and Russian Jews—and, those who came from China or Japan—were referred to as "unassimilable aliens." Many politicians expressed serious doubts about whether such immigrants would ever have the makings of "real Americans."

In time, the majority of historians and many teachers adopted a different viewpoint. Pluralism came into vogue and school children and college students were then told that "our differences make us strong," or that "America is a multiplicity in a unity." It became fashionable to teach about the Judeo Christian heritage. And, as if to bear public witness to such a revisionist view, the single Protestant preacher who had always intoned opening prayers at official gatherings was supplanted by a triumvirate: minister, priest, and rabbi, "representatives of our three great religions." (In time some sociologists gave expression to this new conception, a clearly symbolic recognition of the "triple melting pot" phenomenon.)[1]

In the early 1960s yet another persona stepped onto the dais—and another culture was "added" to the heritage. The figure was an African American. By mid-decade bookstores were flooded with hundreds of volumes on the Black Heritage. (By the end of the next decade the representational array of Americans would include Latinos and Asians and Native Americans in an expression of the rainbow-like character of our "multiracial and multicultural society." With the onset of the twenty-first century, especially after the attacks on New York and Washington by Arab terrorists and the clear recognition that Americans knew little about Islam, a new figure, representing those of the Muslim faith, was often also seen on the platform of public meetings.)

But the most dramatic changes occurred in the wake of the Black Power revolt of the 1960s. The textbooks that were prepared in its aftermath began to indicate that there was much more to African American history than the familiar litany: slave blocks; the old plantations; Emancipation; Reconstruction; the Hayes-Tilden Compromise; *Plessy v. Ferguson*; Booker T. Washington; race riots during two world wars; Jackie Robinson, the baseball player; Ralph Bunche, United Nations official; Thurgood Marshall, council for the NAACP and, later, Associate Justice of the Supreme Court; and that same Court's *Brown* decision of 1954. Although the new volumes continued to tell a story of the categorical treatment of those who came from Africa, readers were to learn far more about the people themselves, about *their* perspectives on the challenges created by their circumstances. For perhaps the first time, those who were not African American were exposed to the fact that, besides being victims, those long called Negroes were, like all others, parts of complex, stratified, and far from monolithic systems in which people live and work and play and suffer. They learned that, although having to respond to their particular and unique treatment, African Americans, like everybody else in the society—and in all societies—institutionalize their behavior patterns, set criteria for the conferring or denying of status, indicate the tolerance limits of accepted and expected behavior, and maintain social systems of great intricacy.

There was a surge of interest and writing about the family, occupation, politics, and stratification in various sectors of African American society. There was also a trend toward celebrating "Black History" and its heroes, heroes such as Crispus Attucks, the first "patriot" to be shot in the Revolutionary War; George Washington Carver, "the Peanut Man"; black soldiers who fought in the Union Army; black politicians in the turbulent days of Reconstruction; black troopers who rode with Teddy Roosevelt; black workers who toiled along the rail beds and in the factories and on the farms; those who were field hands; and those described by W. E. B. DuBois, author of *The Souls of Black Folk* and political leader, a part of the "talented tenth," the Afro-American elite. They described the heady days of the Harlem Renaissance and the dark days of the Depression. And they began to concentrate on the postwar migration to the cities of the North and the expansion of the ghetto.

New publications went further, extolling the virtues of blackness and the solidarity of "soul" and exposing what was often characterized as the pallid character of Euro-American culture in contrast to that of those of African descent.

Together the factual and the fanciful, the analytically and politically oriented tracts, treatises, and textbooks, along with the various campaigns for recognition and control, served two important sociological functions: they strengthened communal ties among those celebrated and, simultaneously, taught others that those whose stories were being recounted also had a noble past and are, like themselves, a proud people worthy of respect.

Because these phenomena are so crucial for understanding the significant changes that have occurred in terms of the sociology and politics of intergroup relations in the United States in the last third of the twentieth century, this chapter focuses almost exclusively on "black consciousness" and the politics of identity. Beginning with the rationale for a shift toward greater autonomy, we quickly move back in time, back to the early days of protest and the rise of the Civil Rights Movement.

The Roots of Redress

Feeling that many of the hard-won victories of the 1950s and 1960s had not made that much difference, increasing numbers of African American spokespersons began challenging a number of basic assumptions of the reform-minded civil rights advocates. First, they argued, liberal white leaders (whatever their personal goals) could rarely offer much more than palliatives that, often as not, were viewed as programs to keep their cities from erupting rather than being expressly designed for helping poor blacks. Second, they claimed that traditional black leaders rarely were much better: they were either out of touch with the people for whom they claimed to speak or were too willing to play "the Establishment game." Saying that their people had been deluded by whites who had taken up the "burden" and by "Negroes" (the term being used with more than a tinge of sarcasm) who were trying to lighten it, the new militants wanted to turn them "blackward," wanted them to have an identity that was truly their own.

They began their campaign by excoriating white liberals, "Uncle Toms" (those blacks who kowtowed to white people), and "racist Amerikkka" itself. They carried it forward with appeals to Black Nationalism. Much of this obviously had to do with two issues: identity and community.

In the early 1960s, James Baldwin wrote an essay entitled "Nobody Knows My Name."[2] In a sense, it dealt with only half of the problem. White people did not know what to call him and he did not know either. Baldwin's people—variously called African, Colored, Negro, and Black, and now African American—needed something to look forward to and something to look back upon. This is where the revisionist historians and sociological commentators came in. They showed that there has always been such a thing as African American culture, shared in some measure by every black person in this country. Not surprisingly, like all cultures, they noted that it was made up of many things—memories and moods and myths. What makes it different is that the memories and moods and even the myths remembered are unique: they are linked to slavery and its aftermath, the continued subjugation by those who repeatedly tried to prove that white was always right.

Not a few who focused on "The Black Experience in America," especially—though not exclusively—those collectively known as Afrocentrists, began to contend that, as a result of their unique trials and tribulations, African Americans were left with different conceptions of time and space and property—and life.

Many new studies indicated that the worlds in which black people lived, although dominated by the rules of segregation, were not simply societies of inmates, as some earlier critics would have it. The authors claimed that the hardships they endured were tempered by resilience, richness, hope, and spiritual uplift.[3] They point to the fact that these were not anomic subsocieties marked by chaos but communities with a high degree of social integration and sense of place.[4] The African American world had its own rules of conduct, its lingo, its literature, and its sound. It also had its own complex system of social stratification—and its problems; the most difficult was overcoming the barriers of segregation in the *apartheid*-like society.

Being frozen into the rigidity of a caste-like system and unable to become full partners in the society from which so much of their own customs, beliefs, and values were derived, what black people frequently lacked was the organizational apparatus characteristic of many other minority groups in America—the very groups with which they had long been compared and, perhaps more significantly, with which they had often compared themselves.

Segregation had long kept African Americans down and out of the mainstream. Sometimes their own leaders aided and abetted their oppressors. Early in this century, both black preachers and white segregationists spoke of their children, both tended their flocks. Later on, the rhetoric shifted—as did the analogies—and a parallel began to be drawn between the plight of blacks in this country and those of mental patients. By that time few well-educated white people would argue that all blacks were innately inferior; they knew better—or knew better than to express such sentiments. Yet, the new conventional wisdom sounded strikingly like that of the old planters and ministers of God. Acting as if "only we know what's good for them," many viewed and treated disadvantaged black people as "culturally deprived" victims or patients in need of care and succor. And many blacks, in turn, like the inmates of mental institutions, continued to internalize the roles ascribed to them and acted accordingly. It was in this context that the late Malcolm X wrote that self-hatred was the worst of all the legacies of racist policies.[5]

Resistance and Rebellion

As indicated in earlier chapters, most efforts to redress the grievances of the past were channeled into campaigns for integration. Many African Americans believed (or wanted to believe) that, someday, somehow, color would really be overlooked. And sometimes white liberals, held in contempt today by some of the angriest African American spokespersons,[6] helped to perpetuate this assumption without, for the most part, realizing what they were doing and without having very much personal contact with those they claimed to accept as equals.

The foregoing observations refer to "many" African Americans, but not to all. In there was a large cohort of blacks who had "made it"—some by the same techniques used by members of other minority groups, including the exploitation of those whose identity they shared; some by becoming athletes and jazz musicians and soul singers performing for both their own people and a wider audience; most by sheer determination to overcome the barriers of segregation, often working their way up by entering government service as postmen and clerks, secretaries and soldiers and teachers. Together, these members of what had come to be called the "Black Bourgeoisie," the "Colored Entertainers," and the "Negro Respectables," represented to many white people (especially middle-class whites) living evidence that African Americans could succeed if they tried hard enough and were willing to thicken their skins against whatever abuses the system and its agents meted out.

As has been discussed so often since the success of Colin Powell and Condoleezza Rice gained recognition as the "Exhibit As" of the continuing achievements of those who believe in the American dream, since the late 1960s black people who had grown up in the days of *de jure* segregation have taken pride in the progress of those with whom they are most identified and, for all their difficulties, represent exemplars of middle-class respectability: friendly, hard-working, religious, and community-minded.

Many of the children of such successful blacks who entered college in the mid-1960s had different memories. They remembered more of the failures of the civil rights struggles to achieve true integration than the significant gains from which they, themselves, frequently benefited. They, and not merely the poor residents of Watts or Harlem, felt they really knew what nationalist spokesman Ron Karenga meant when he cried: "There are only three kinds of people in this country: white people, black people, and Negroes. Negroes? They are black people that act like white people."

Black college students, particularly in northern schools and the larger southern ones, knew that part of Karenga's rhetoric was addressed to them and their parents. ("Which side are you on?") Ironically, it was often those who had suffered least from the stigma of color who began to feel the strain the most. Many reacted by forming Afro-American organizations on campus or by going "home" to Harlem or Hough or Hattiesburg (often places they had never been) to work and teach and organize.

Some, to resolve their race/class schizophrenia, joined ranks of the most militant members of the black community. Stressing both poverty and race, those who lived in the urban ghettos became their cause. With the poor, they argued, they could put to use some of the direct and fringe benefits of a college education. And for them they could try to uplift their spirits and offer a new and different view of the Americans who came from Africa.

The new orientation had a long prehistory. Like most social movements, it was the culmination of years of struggle and crisis during which an oppressed people was trying to come to grips with its situation and the constantly thwarted attempts by those who sought to become full-fledged Americans. In one context after another, political, social, and religious leaders claimed they wanted nothing more but nothing less. Among the various techniques of protest they had used in the past, and that were finally to be joined, two were most prevalent from the time of Emancipation to its centennial. One centered on black people themselves and was concerned with "uplift"—the learning of useful skills, the instilling of pride in self and neighbor, and emphasizing such puritan virtues as thrift and practicality. The other focused on integration and the gaining of civil rights. In the first instance, the underlying notion was that African Americans would show others that they were responsible, upright, and talented citizens and that, in time, they would be ready to take their place beside anyone. In the latter case the argument was that the problem was not the blacks' at all but the whites' and the system they controlled: both should be made to change.

Uplift

The first sustained challenge to Jim Crow laws and the entire system of segregation was to come from highly educated and remarkably well-integrated northern blacks. Men like Monroe Trotter and W. E. B. Du Bois challenged what they saw as the tendency of southern blacks and their leaders to acquiesce and accept their second-class status. A prime target was Booker T. Washington, who, before the turn of the present century, had sought to come to terms with the problem of black alienation. Washington, himself born a slave, saw the hope of his people—at least in a southland of deeply rooted segregation—in the development of pride and self-esteem, and in the learning of skills of the honest tradesman. A speech of his, delivered at the Atlanta Exposition in 1895, has been branded as a classic in acquiescent thinking.[7] The implication was clear: black people were not ready to take their place beside whites.

What Washington and others saw, however, was not simply the "Uncle Tomism" his critics such as Trotter and Du Bois claimed. Rather, it was, to some at least, a sort of live-and-let-live pluralism. As Washington himself put it: "In all things that are purely social we can be as separate as the fingers, yet as one in hand in all things essential to mutual progress."[8] He also said, in the same speech, that "the wisest among my race understand that agitation of questions of social equality is the extremist folly, and the progress in the enjoyment of all the privileges that will come to us must be the result of severe and constant struggle rather than of artificial forcing."[9] It was Washington's unwillingness to advocate direct action that won for him contempt in the minds of several generations of radical leaders. Yet, there is little question that Washington did begin to come to terms with two of the most serious problems plaguing African Americans, self-reliance and the question of communal solidarity, especially in the economic arena.

At the Tuskegee Institute, which he established, Washington sought, and in many ways succeeded in implementing his plan. For a time he became the idol of millions of blacks and to this day he remains a symbol for some blacks and many whites (especially older school teachers) of the "responsible and reasonable Negro." Today, few young African Americans share these sentiments, although a growing number have reverted to the argument of self-help and, in some instances, even to the fingers-of-the-hand policy Washington promulgated.

Washington's famous theme of seemingly subservient accommodation turned toward one of more intentional separatism for some lower-class African Americans, especially those in the urban centers. They joined the ranks of Marcus Garvey's "Back-to-Africa" movement in the 1920s, followed Daddy Grace and other charismatic evangelists in the 1930s, and joined the Temple of Islam (the Black Muslims) more recently. All such actions were, in their own way and time, challenges to the status quo ante. In their expression, often stridently self-assured and sometimes confrontational, especially taking on other members of the black community, activists were very different from those who first followed Washington. Yet the members of each group, including the Muslims, were—and are still—participating in uplift organizations, in bodies that give a sense of identity to downtrodden followers, a measure of importance, lessons in proper decorum and, above all, a purpose for living.

In a very real sense, what the astute observers August Meier and Elliott Rudwick said in the beginning of the days of the dramatic sea change in attitudes and actions still obtains: "Washington's separatist ideology functioned both as a mechanism of accommodation to American racism and as a device for overcoming it."[10] Yet, until very recently, the latter point was not at all apparent or, at least, acknowledged by Washington's critics who saw accommodation and separatism as blind alleys that merely gave support to segregationist sentiment.

The Burden of Responsibility

Washington's most vocal early adversary was W. E. B. Du Bois, Harvard graduate, professor of sociology at Atlanta University, and cofounder of the then quite radical Niagara Movement, an all-black organization that he and sympathetic colleagues tried to set up explicitly to oppose Washington and his program. Taking an entirely different tack, the radicals argued that the burden of redressing grievances was "not the Negroes' problem but the whites' and *they* should be made to change." (Although at odds about approaches, on certain issues Du Bois and Washington did agree. Both believed firmly in the idea of racial solidarity. Indeed, Du Bois, whom many saw as the quintessential integrationist, went considerably further than Washington in proposing a pan-African movement to unite black people everywhere.)

Washington and his followers were able to stop the Niagara Movement of 1905 from getting started. They were unable to do the same with its successor, the National Association for the Advancement of Colored People (NAACP), founded in 1909, with the announced goal of "fighting for the Black man's constitutional rights and the undeclared aim of curbing Booker T. Washington's power."[11] The NAACP, like the Urban League, established a year later, was an organization of black and white progressives who sought to fight the battle for justice and civil rights through education, politics, and, later, and most significantly, litigation. Closely associated with the organization was its Legal Defense and Education Fund (LDEF), the result of the efforts of what was known as "The Committee of 100," established in 1943 and initially chaired by a former NAACP board member, the Edinburgh-born William Allan Neilson, former president of Smith College in Northampton, Massachusetts.[12] The LDEF, supported by the general membership, brought numerous suits against various parties accused of violating the Constitution through adherence to state and local statutes upholding segregation.

The lawyers were skilled and persistent and, in time, one barrier after another was to fall as the Supreme Court ruled in favor of the complainants. The culmination of the legal movement came in 1954 when, in a unanimous decision, the high court overturned the old Plessy ruling and proclaimed that separate could never be equal. Many black and many white integrationists believed that the critical point had been passed and that rapid compliance with the court's mandate for "desegregation with all deliberate speed" would toll the death knell of segregation in the United States. They were wrong.

As far back as the 1920s a number of black intellectuals had begun to question the advisability of following the slow and deliberate course of taking cases up through the courts while, as they saw it, African American people were suffering without relief. Some, even then, questioned any piecemeal approach of attacking one institution—for example, the educational system—instead of trying to alter the entire social order. A resolute few, such as A. Philip Randolph, president of the Brotherhood of Sleeping Car Porters, and several outspoken socialists, branded popular leaders like Du Bois—who, as noted, was in his day considered a radical—as " handkerchief heads," "hat-in-hand Negroes." In *The Messenger,* which Randolph edited, the NAACP was attacked as a bourgeois organization and an alternative, workingman's movement, was advocated.

With capitalism defined as the enemy of all poor people, Randolph sought to rally blacks and whites to the cause of socialism. He did not succeed. His ideological rhetoric was too much for many blacks to accept; his integrationist appeal was too much for many white workers to stomach.[13] (There is an ironic twist to all this. In the later years of his life, Du Bois moved increasingly to the left and became a member of the Communist Party in Ghana where he had gone to live, and where he died at the age of 93. Randolph, still alive in the 1970s, found himself branded as a "handkerchief head" by militant young blacks for holding to the notion of a unified—black and white—attack on the system.)

Randolph never reached the urban masses to which he appealed. But Marcus Garvey did. The Jamaican founder—in 1914—of the Universal Negro Improvement Association (UNIA), Garvey claimed that the integrationists were naive for seeking to win concessions from a society that was and would always be racist.

Instead he favored the development of separate institutions in the United States and, in time, a return to Africa, the "Black Zion." He and his followers opposed miscegenation and extolled everything that was black. One sociologist noted the attractiveness of this movement as follows: "The Garvey movement was based on good psychology. It made the downtrodden lower class Negro feel like somebody among white people who said they were nobody. It gave the crowd an opportunity to show off in colors, parades, and self-glorification."[14] For a time the UNIA had great appeal, but neither Garvey nor his followers ever got to Africa. He, himself, was eventually denounced by prominent leaders of the black community, barred from bringing his people to Liberia (which was seen as the African Zion), and finally indicted and sentenced to a prison term for using the mail to defraud in selling shares of stock for his "Black Star Ship Line."

What had once been an important movement of Black Nationalism ended when Garvey was deported in 1927 as an undesirable alien.

But Garvey left a rich legacy. In fact, his banner of red, green, and black was flown anew in the late 1960s and through the next decade, especially by the cultural nationalists who, in addition to Afro hairdos, dashiki shirts, and other symbols of their African roots frequently sported buttons with the three colors—the first represents life's blood; the second, hope, and, some say, the green hills of "home"; and the third, "the color of our skin."

The Civil Rights Movement

In the 1930s new organizations emerged, many of these seeking to find alliances with New Deal agencies that were more favorably inclined to the plight of African American citizens than their predecessors had been. Again criticism of the NAACP arose. Young leaders such as Ralph Bunche, who later became the Deputy Secretary General of the United Nations, felt that the organization was not sufficiently militant to deal with the pressing needs created by the Depression and the persistence of discrimination throughout the country.

During World War II two new movements arose that presaged what was to come in the following decade. The first was A. Philip Randolph's "March on Washington" movement, which pressured President Roosevelt into issuing the famous Executive Order 8802, establishing the first federal Fair Employment Practices Commission. As Meier and Rudwick explained, "even without enforcement powers, the FEPC set a precedent for treating fair employment practice as a civil right. The short-lived March on Washington Movement prefigured future trends in three ways: (1) It was an explicitly all-Black organization; (2) It based its strategy on mass action by the urban slum dwellers; (3) It concentrated on economic problems."[15]

The second significant movement of the era was the Congress of Racial Equality (CORE), the first of several innovative civil rights organizations that gained prominence through their efforts to accelerate desegregation by means of nonviolent direct action. CORE began in 1942. Bayard Rustin and James Farmer, members of the pacifist Fellowship of Reconciliation both heavily influenced by the teachings of Henry David Thoreau,[16] the nineteenth-century poet and pacifist, suggested the founding of an organization devoted to the use of "relentless noncooperation, economic boycotts and civil disobedience," to fight for racial equality. A sit-in at a Chicago restaurant that same year led to the founding of the Chicago Committee on Racial Equality. Out of that organization CORE was born.

In the late 1940s radical-pacifist CORE was sponsoring sit-ins and freedom rides in the North and in Virginia, North Carolina, Kentucky, and Tennessee. And it was CORE that sponsored the integrated bus rides into Alabama in 1961 that ended in the beating of many of the participants. Those trips may have been a turning point, for, in the years to follow, CORE, an organization that had prided itself on its color-blindness, a civil rights group whose membership was for a long time two-thirds white, turned away from the course of integration and toward the building of racial consciousness. In time its founder, Farmer, was succeeded by Floyd McKissick, who, in turn, was followed by the more nationalistic Roy Ennis, who completed the process of purging the membership of whites and, in the process, lost considerable political and financial support. By the end of the twentieth century, CORE was but a shadow of its former self, riven with dissensions and doing little to aid the cause of desegregation or ghetto improvement.

A third new civil rights organization, perhaps the best known, arose from the highly successful bus boycott in Montgomery, Alabama, in 1956 initiated by Rosa Parks on December 1, 1955. Parks, secretary of the Montgomery Chapter of the NAACP and active member of the Women's Political Council, had refused to give up her seat and move to the back of the bus as was the rule. Soon afterward a young minister named Martin Luther King, Jr., founded a support group called the Southern Christian Leadership Conference (SCLC). Within a few years he became the most important leader and spokesperson for nonviolent direct action in the United States. He and his followers, including fellow Protestant ministers Andrew Young, Jesse Jackson, and Ralph David Abernathy (who would become King's successor) took their campaign from community to community. People from many parts of the country joined in marches on the bastions of segregation, marches designed to prove African Americans could walk with pride even in the face of strident opposition. These committed young men and women followed their leader and turned the other cheek and, all too often, got their skulls cracked open.

In 1960 a fourth organization informally began at a lunch counter in Greensboro, North Carolina, when a group of black students decided to defy the proprietor who refused to serve them. The sit-ins of young people spread from town to town and, with the backing of the Reverend King and the coordination of Ella Baker, the peer-centered collective action movement soon became institutionalized as the Student Nonviolent Coordinating Committee (SNCC). Its early leadership included Stokely Carmichael, coauthor with Charles V. Hamilton of the book *Black Power,* which some saw as a manifesto of the new movement,[17] and James Forman, who would later write *The Making of Black Revolutionaries,* the story of a critical era.[18]

In its early days SNCC led a door-to-door campaign to register voters and helped to organize "freedom schools." Unlike many of the other groups, it relied heavily on the voluntary efforts of women activists. Within a year, however, SNCC severed ties with SCLC, claiming that the parent organization was too cautious. Within five years, some critics cynically would say that the meaning of the letters in the acronym SNCC (pronounced "Snick"), no longer had meaning because so many members had turned away from their previous stances of nonviolence and integration in favor of aggressive separatism. It, too, was a portent.

But, in the late summer of 1963, before the break was complete, the old guard and the new—including A. Philip Randolph, Roy Wilkins of the NAACP, Whitney Young, Jr., of the Urban League, James Farmer of CORE, Martin Luther King, Jr., of SCLC, and some but not all of the SNCC leadership—joined forces to lead a massive march on Washington. To many, it was the culmination of years of struggle. To most of those who were there, it was a time of rededication, a time of hope, a time of dreams fulfilled—or about to be.

From the steps of the Lincoln Memorial, in a powerful and impressive voice, Martin Luther King, Jr., gave his oft-repeated speech:

> I say to you today, my friends, that in spite of the difficulties and frustrations of the moment, I still have a dream. It is a dream deeply rooted in the American dream.
>
> I have a dream that one day this nation will rise up and live out the true meaning of its creed: "We hold these truths to be self-evident; that all men are created equal."
>
> I have a dream that one day on the red hills of Georgia that sons of former slaves and the sons of former slave owners will be able to sit down together at the table of brotherhood.
>
> I have a dream that one day even the state of Mississippi, a desert state sweltering with the heat of injustice and oppression, will be transformed into an oasis of freedom and justice.
>
> I have a dream that my four little children will one day live in a nation where they will not be judged by the color of their skin but the content of their character....

Dr. King concluded his oration with the following words: "When we let freedom ring, when we let it ring from every village and every hamlet, from every state and every city, we will be able to speed up that day when all of God's children, Black men and white men, Jews and Gentiles, Protestants and Catholics, will be able to join hands and sing in the words of that old Negro spiritual, 'Free at last! Free at last! Thank God Almighty, we are free at last!'"[19]

Affirmation

By the time of Emancipation's centennial (and, for some, before), it was becoming increasingly evident to many—outside observers and workers in the movement—that neither chauvinistic nationalism nor a soulless militancy, that is, a militancy devoid of a distinctive "black" content, could, by itself, turn the tide of racism, so deep did it flow.[20] Since there was little likelihood that they could really go it alone and even less that they could (or would) ever turn white, a rising generation of African American leaders argued that their people had to learn (or relearn) to take pride in themselves *and* to become political activists. They had to hark to what Frederick Douglass had prescribed a hundred years before the Student Nonviolent Coordinating Committee was born:

> Those who profess to favor freedom yet deprecate agitation are men who want crops without plowing up the ground; they want rain without thunder and lightning. They want the ocean without the awful roar of its many waters.... Power concedes nothing without demand. It never did and it never will. Find out just what any people will quietly submit to and you have found out the exact measure of injustice and wrong, which will be imposed upon them, and these will continue till they are resisted with either words or blows, or with both. The limits of tyrants are prescribed by the endurance of those whom they oppress.[21]

Black Power did, in fact, begin as a movement of words, impassioned words, exhorting poor sharecroppers to exercise their franchise. But it was not enough.

Intimidation and threats had raised the ire of the civil rights workers and turned many Black pacifists into soldiers and turned away many white allies. The pacifist codes of Henry David Thoreau and Mohandas Gandhi (an idol of Martin Luther King, Jr., and many of his followers) were replaced by the "eye for an eye" law of Hammurabi—much as Frederick Douglass had suggested.

For years, black leaders and their white allies had counseled patience and fortitude. And for years their authority went unchallenged, for it was widely felt that these liberal integrationists were on the right path. The civil rights campaign in the late 1950s and early 1960s, and the bills passed by Congress in their wake, seemed, to some at least, positive proof of the efficacy of their Gandhian tactics. But, as many of the victories proved hollow; as tensions mounted between those, mainly black, civil rights workers who saw radical pacifism as a pragmatic device and those, mainly white, integrationists for whom it was an ideology; as the Vietnam War siphoned off funds that (it was said) would have been earmarked for social programs; and, most of all, as the relative deprivation of African Americans became more apparent, the climate shifted. The movement went sour and the old coalitions began to break apart.

Unquestionably, urban riots in a dozen major cities were also an exacerbating factor. Many whites in the general population who had begun to feel some sense of sympathy with the embattled civil rights workers or who, at least, were talking of "giving Negroes their due," grew increasingly fearful—and hostile—as they saw the flames of Harlem and Rochester and Detroit and Watts in central Los Angeles and the section of Cleveland known as Hough on their television sets or, in some cases, from their upstairs windows. There were charges and countercharges, cries of duplicity on one hand and of corruption on the other, shouts of "Burn, Baby, Burn" and "Get the Honkies" mixed with "Send them back to Africa."

Given the disillusionment, the uncertainty, and the persistence of institutionalized segregation, and, especially, given the fact that little was being done to satisfy those poorest blacks whose expectations had suddenly begun to rise, it is not surprising that "We Shall Overcome" was replaced—literally and figuratively—with the call for "Black Power."

A new mood began to reach out and envelop the unorganized black masses, particularly in the northern ghettos where few meaningful communal institutions existed around which people could rally and where even the oratory of Martin Luther King, Jr., had not been able to stir people into action. Now the focus began to shift away from integration and toward the more basic matter of "getting it together."

Half a century earlier the black sociologist E. Franklin Frazier said that "if the masses of Negroes can save their self-respect and remain free of hate, so much the better. But ... I believe, it would be better for the Negro's soul to be seared with hate than dwarfed by self-abasement.... "[22] Once again it was being argued that there was a psychological need for black people to call the white society to task rather than to accept and internalize second-class status and all that it meant. At the time, William H. Grier and Price Cobbs suggested that, among African Americans, there had long been an almost desperate need to find a sense of both positive self-hood and meaningful people-hood.[23] To accomplish these goals meant that the leadership would have to change. Whites had to be eased or pushed out of positions of dominance to make room for those who could more easily identify with, and be identified with, the Black masses. And in a very few months, they were.

As groups such as the Black Panthers—a name used by several different groups, some of which were engaged in such mainstream activities as voter registration, others involved in highly charged revolutionary politics—gained notoriety, those in the traditional organizations changed too. SNCC had already become more separatist; CORE was turning away from its original stance of integration in favor of black membership and black consciousness and also what many African American women would later criticize: masculinity and male assertiveness. Even the members of the Urban League and the NAACP sounded more revolutionary though they tried to walk the tightrope to maintain the fragmenting ties with white liberals. (The NAACP was later to abandon such a policy in the early 1990s, when its short-lived director stressed the fact that he welcomed all "brothers and sisters" regardless of ideology. By forming an alliance with the outspokenly anti-Semitic Muslim leader, Louis Farrakhan, NAACP President Benjamin Chavis lost much of the remaining white liberal support. In 1994 Chavis was forced out of office, partly for his alliances but mainly because of financial difficulties in the NAACP. Since his departure, his successors—Myrlie Evers-Williams, the widow of the slain civil rights leader Medgar Evers, and former activists and Congressmen, Kweisi Mfume and Julian Bond—each tried to stabilize the situation and win back old allies. In recent years, the NAACP has turned a considerable amount of its energy" to strengthening the African American communities themselves and addressing the crises of poverty and anomie in the inner cities.)

The Southern Christian Leadership Conference continued fighting its battles for jobs and freedom but also began forming coalitions with other organizations, including those representing other embattled minority groups. Despite differences in symbol (the clenched fist or the double bar of equality), in slogan, and in style, pride and protest were joined and, for many, it had become a time to be "Black."

Black Studies, White Responses

The struggle was waged in many parts of the country, in small towns and big cities, North, South, East, and West. But it was almost invariably the university campus that was the seedbed and most frequent scene of some of the most extreme tactics. In response to mounting pressure, college officials, often less liberal than their faculty members, who were often sympathetic and sometimes supportive of the challengers to the status quo ante, tried to hold the line. They called for the establishment of *ad hoc* committees to consider the changes sought through petition. But the protesters, undeterred, steadily increased the pressure—and upped the ante. In the face of mass demonstrations and intimidating actions including the takeover of college buildings or student unions,[24] many administrators not only capitulated, they helped to legitimate and found the funds to support the demands. On campus after campus they agreed to increase the recruitment of minority students and faculty members, underwrote ethnically specific political organizations such as Black Student Alliances, provided facilities for cultural centers and, in some places, separate dormitories, and introduced African American programs and curricular innovations geared to the special needs of black undergraduates and, in time, other students "of color."

From among the welter of proposals and pronouncements requesting or, as often, demanding such programs, one message came across loud and clear: the tactics were working. The protagonists had seized control and, sometimes dressed in revolutionary garb, even with bandoleers of bullets and intimating weapons (as happened at Cornell University),[25] they told their teachers and fellows students, and the rest of the world through the media, whose representatives were follow-ing the events with considerable interest, "We will be *Negroes* no more." There is little doubt that this mood, seized on by increasing numbers of minority students, including many from middle-class and liberal backgrounds, signaled the end of an old era and the beginning of a new phase in racial and ethnic relations in the United States.

One of the most tangible signs of the success of the student uprisings was the establishment of Black Studies programs at many universities across the country, and, soon on their heels, Chicano, Puerto Rican, Native American, and Asian American Studies programs in appropriate geographic areas. Some institutions, particularly those on the West Coast, placed several such programs under a single roof, creating departments of Ethnic Studies or of Comparative American Cultures. Whether separate or united, the newly—and often quickly—created programs and departments were, from the start, staffed by a mixture of highly trained academics who specialized in the study of ethnicity, race relations, history, and literature; activists whose professional skills were frequently far more organizational than analytical; and assorted instructors whose main claim to expertise was their status as members of the group being studied and whose main staying power depended on the support of student claques. Not surprisingly, the arguments over whether or not Black [and other sorts of] Studies had a place in the academy gave way (once it was a *fait accompli*) to debates over what was being taught and by whom.

Several studies were conducted that examined these questions. One of the most comprehensive was that carried out by C. Wilson Record. Record's research and his findings provide a still-useful paradigm for understanding reactions to the even more controversial subject of "multiculturalism" today.

With grants from the Metropolitan Applied Research Center and the American Philosophical Society, Record moved around the country visiting 70 campuses and interviewing 209 black and white sociologists who "at the time or in the previous few years considered race and ethnicity as a teaching or research field."[26] Among this admittedly limited sample, Wilson found that reactors to his questions could be grouped under four rubrics: (1) the *Embracers,* those who welcomed the in-novation of ethnically specific courses and programs (although they were rather sharply divided as to the rationales for doing so); (2) the *Antagonists,* those who openly opposed Black Studies as a separate field and resented the tendency of its supporters to exclude them from participation or dismiss their prior contributions;

(3) the *Accommodators,* those who reluctantly accepted what they saw as inevitable and tried to make the best of a dubious situation; and (4) the *Dropouts,* those who withdrew from the field under the fire of black militants.

Each group had a diverse array of members. The first, the "Embracers," although dominated by critics of the Establishment, also included conservatives who saw Black Studies as a device of both containment and decompression (much in the way that urban police forces had set up "human relations units" in the wake of the riots of the previous decade, and then went about business as usual). And there were those who saw Black Studies courses as a needed challenge to the traditional ways sociologists and others had addressed themselves to studying "The Black Experience."

The "Antagonists" were also a heterogeneous group, but at their core were a number of white integrationists (and some blacks) who saw themselves as part of the solution not the problem. It was this subgroup more than any other that was caught between the rock and the hard place. For years, many had studied race relations and tried to implement policies that would serve to make society more sensitive to discrimination and more tolerant of diversity. Many had been civil rights activists who were also frustrated by the slowness of change and saw the necessity for African Americans and other minorities to become more assertive. What they hadn't expected was that they would become targets and, in many cases, scapegoats for those who saw them as establishment-types themselves.

Some reacted to attacks upon them by pointing to the ideological rigidity of the promoters of the new programs. Said one "antagonist" interviewed by Record, "They read Fanon but not Rustin; Malcolm X but not Kenneth Clark; Angela Davis and LeRoi Jones but not Roy Wilkins; the latter-day Du Bois but not Booker T. Washington; Marcus Garvey but not the mature Frederick Douglass. And a lot of time they don't read anything."[27]

The third category, "Accommodators," seemed better able to ride the tide, many undoubtedly thinking that, in due course, it would ebb. Condescendingly they would say "Of course it isn't academically respectable, but there are a lot of things around here that aren't—physical education, home economics, social work, business administration."[28] In other words, Black Studies was something that had to be tolerated and even legitimated as part of the general offerings of a multiversity.

"Dropouts," roughly 20 percent of the sample, were older and more bitter than most of the others, including the "Antagonists." Unlike the "Antagonists," whose members dug in their heels to fight against the separatist bent of the Black Studies supporters, those in this last category threw in the towel. Like all the others those in the drop-out group included black as well as white sociologists, but particularly individuals who were often accused of being "Uncle Toms," whatever their skills or prior commitments. In fact, most seemed to have dropped out only after having had a series of confrontations with reactionary nationalists or cultural revolutionaries who publicly denounced them or barred them from speaking or blocked access to classrooms and offices. Included in this last group were a disproportionate number of old leftists (many of them Jewish) who were particularly troubled by two aspects of the protest. As Record explained:

> Black assault upon individual merit, traditionally defined, as the single criterion for entry and achievement rattled the age-old Jewish fear of quotas. Furthermore, the separatist thrust of the Black Studies movement offended a heavy Jewish commitment to integrationist ideology.
>
> Perhaps more pointedly, the rhetoric of the Black militants who typically promoted the Black Studies movement was often openly anti-Jew and anti-Israeli.[29]

Of course, demands for, and the establishment of Black Studies programs were not the only manifestations of conflict between conservatives and radicals, integration-ists and separatists, or Jews and African Americans. Campuses also came under increasing pressure to alter traditional standards for admission to facilitate the entry of more minority students. Sometimes the pressure took the form of demands for "affirmative action" on the campus.

Although it became a descriptive term for a process of targeted aid and group-based efforts during the administration of Richard M. Nixon, the idea of reaching out with special programs for minorities had deep roots, going back to the days of Franklin D. Roosevelt. The label itself came into vogue with President John F. Kennedy's Executive Order 10925, urging federal contractors to seek and employ more minority group members. In the period immediately following his assas-sination, there was further recognition of the extent to which, as Jill Quadagno notes, "race ... had moved from the periphery to the center. No longer a regional embarrassment, racial inequality had become a national malady."[30] In the days of FDR and JFK the emphasis was on jobs and job training, not special consideration for entry to colleges.

Such new demands seemed shocking to many who argued that they flew in the face of meritocratic principles despite the fact that advantages had long been given to certain categories of applicants: offspring of alumni, super athletes, and those from distant places, "to provide geographical diversity." Why not do the same to insure racial and ethnic diversity? That was the real question. And those who asked it had become quite skilled in pressing the point.

Designated Minorities and Affirmative Action

Responding to the change of strategy and, in turn, of policy as it was beginning to be reacted to by sympathetic power brokers, vulnerable governmental agencies, frightened managers, school boards, union leaders, politicians, and college admis-sion boards, historian Daniel Boorstin once wrote a facetious essay. Zeroing in on college admission boards, Boorstin suggested that if the trend were to be followed to its logical conclusion, the I.Q. and other such tests would be abandoned as criteria for academic admission and would be replaced by an "E.Q.," an Ethnic Quotient.[31] This would mean that students and eventually teachers and their subject matter would have to be apportioned strictly according to background. There would be so many blacks and so many whites; so many Jews and so many Catholics—these to be further subdivided according to whether they were children or grandchildren of Italians or Irishmen, Slavs or Slovaks. (Fractional men, as Vance Bourjaily once called people of "mixed marriages" like himself," would prove difficult to judge.)[32] What, for example, would one do with an application from a modern-day Fiorello La Guardia, that half-Italian, half-Jewish Protestant mayor of New York? Boorstin offers an answer: give him so many points for each of his traits in proportion to their representativeness in the overall population and make sure, of course, that his curriculum is balanced in similar fashion! What Boorstin lampooned more than thirty years ago was soon to become a very real issue, and one that went far beyond the college and university campuses.

The problems of racial inequality had migrated north and west along with the tens of thousands of blacks who left the South after the Second World War.[33] In the next two decades the dichotomous—white/nonwhite (usually meaning African American) character of southern society began to become a pervasive reality in many cities far removed from the Old South. Although some, such as Michael Harrington, author of *The Other America,*[34] tried to alert the public to the damaging effect of the deepening chasm, most public officials paid little heed until it was thrust upon them by the widely publicized activities of civil rights activists in the South and the angry outbursts of those who lived in the black ghettoes of the North. Much of what became known as the War on Poverty, and, according to a number of scholars, much of the nature of the welfare policies that came in its wake, was directly related to the continuing presence of racial injustice in America.[35]

The Civil Rights Act of 1964, signed by President Lyndon B. Johnson, barred discrimination in the workplace and supported LBJ's contention that casting wider nets for employees, providing training for those who need it, and taking extra steps to insure that opportunities existed for all would enhance his goal of seeking "equality as a result." Johnson went farther. Executive Order 112246 established an Office of Affirmative Action in the Labor Department. And his successor, Richard Nixon, went farther still. His administration's "Philadelphia Plan" (named for building contract arrangements in that city) put in place a system of quotas.[36]

The gradual shift from a plan to insure equal employment opportunities for anyone to favoring those who had belonged to a category of persons who had been discriminated against (often referred to as "group rights") was the basis of a renewed controversy, a controversy less about goals of overcoming the impact of racism and more about the means to achieving a truly just society. It not only pitted traditional libertarians against interventionists but created coalitions of unlikely allies. For example, many of the strongest advocates of "affirmative action"—the phrase now used variously to describe the casting of wider nets for minority applicants, offering compensatory advantages to lower-scoring but still qualified potential students, and establishing targets and goals and, sometimes, actual quotas for minorities—found it increasingly difficult to implement their new policies without triggering resistance from those who felt that such programs were designed only for certain segments of the population, which, for obvious reasons, they were. Even if what some call "benign quotas" were applied across the board, it was argued that certain groups would have to lose. Many critics saw the trend as "racism in reverse."[37] And some brought suit. In the spring of 1973 complaints were filed against several schools and universities.

The most celebrated case at the time was that of Marco DeFunis, a white applicant to the University of Washington Law School who was twice denied admission and brought suit claiming that his constitutional guarantee of equal protection of the laws under the Fourteenth Amendment had been violated. DeFunis charged that the Law School used racial categories to admit less-qualified minority students on a preferential basis. In time his claim was rejected by the highest court in the state but in many ways, the die was cast. A quite similar case, brought by Allan Bakke, a twice-rejected applicant to a University of California Medical School, eventually made it to the Supreme Court where, in an ambiguous decision, the Court ordered Bakke admitted since it appeared that the only grounds for his denial were racial. Yet, it also upheld the use of affirmative action measures in which the race of the applicant was to be one of a number of criteria admission boards might use in recruiting and selecting candidates.[38] Here is what was actually said in the brief filed by the Office of the Attorney General of the United States as *amicus curiae* in October 1977:

> ... the judgment of the Supreme Court of California [which upheld the University's exclusion of Bakke] should be reversed to the extent that it forbids the Medical School to operate any minority-sensitive admissions.
>
> The remaining question is whether respondent is entitled to admission to the Medical School. We have argued that it is constitutional in making admissions decisions to take race into account in order fairly to compare minority and nonminority applicants, but it is not clear from the record whether the Medical School's program, as applied to respondent in 1973 and 1974, operated in this manner.
>
> The trial court found, and the University did not contest, that 16 places in the class were reserved for special admittees. The record did not show, however, how this number was chosen, whether the number was inflexible or was used simply as a measure for assessing the program's operation, and how the number pertains to the objects of the special admission program. . . .
>
> The deficiencies in the evidence and findings—which pertain to both the details of the program and the justifications that support it—may have been caused by the approach both parties, and both courts below, took to this case. They asked only whether it was permissible to make minority-sensitive decisions, but that it is necessary to address, as well, questions concerning how race was used, and for what reasons. The findings with respect to these latter, critical questions are insufficient to allow the Court to address them.
>
> Accordingly, the judgment of the Supreme Court of California should be vacated to the extent that it orders respondent's admission and the case should be remanded for further appropriate proceedings to address the questions that remain open. In all other respects the judgment should be reversed.[39]

In its arguments the majority made the following points, which, to many, served as guidelines for future action: "Minority-sensitive decisions are essential to eliminate the effects of discrimination; both the legislative and executive branches of the federal government have adopted minority-sensitive programs for the purpose of eliminating the effects of past discrimination; Minority-sensitive relief is not limited to correction of discrimination perpetrated by the institution offering admission; and, Discrimination against minority groups has hindered their participation in the medical profession."[40]

Then stating, "The central issue on judicial review of a minority-sensitive program is whether it is tailored to remedy the effects of past discrimination,"[41]citing numerous cases, the Court concluded: "A program is tailored to remedy the effects of past discrimination if it uses race to enhance the fairness of the admissions process; and, There is no adequate alternative to the use of minority-sensitive admissions criteria."[42] All told, knowledge of racial group affiliation could be considered a necessary criterion, but it could not be the only one.

Many followed these cases with considerable interest. Not a few were uneasy about the pressure to right recognized wrongs by accepting a change in the ground rules for "making it" into the university, onto public school faculties, or into public service, or entering a profession. These were not merely philosophical differences. The seeming challenge to the traditional ground rules for both opportunity and advancement meant that some, no matter how hard-working or smart, might be passed over for others less qualified by conventional standards.

The problem, as Allan Sindler pointed out, is partially the differing perspectives (and understandings) of what "affirmative action" or "equal opportunity" actually mean. Sindler summed up the traditional view by asserting that

> The traditional concept of equal opportunity, when applied, say, to jobs, emphasized a fair process of evaluation among the applicants competing to be hired. This involved assessment of applicants on an individual basis by use of nongroup criteria relevant to satisfactory handling of the job in question. The result of such a meritocratic process was the selection of the persons best qualified to do the job, judged in terms of the current performance abilities of the competitors. By definition, a genuinely meritocratic process was fair and, therefore, both guaranteed and defined a fair outcome and equality of opportunity. The elimination of racial discrimination in hiring thus represented a belated purification of the traditional concept, not a challenge to it. Hence both nondiscrimination and government enforcement of nondiscrimination have become comfortably incorporated within the prevailing notion of equal opportunity.[43]

At least one justification that embodied an alternative view of equality was the claim that, in contrast to the traditional concept, it stressed groups and outcomes, not individuals and processes. If all other things were truly equal, asserted this view, a genuinely fair and meritocratic process would result in roughly the same proportion of nonminorities and minorities gaining the school admissions, the jobs, or whatever the competition. Where disparate group proportions were the outcome, that indicated the existence of unfairness and unequal opportunity for the underrepresented groups, for which the selection process had acted simply as a "pass-through" rather than a corrective. The proper measure of fair process and equal opportunity was, then, proportional group results.[44]

Many poor and working-class whites were wont to accept the first view, feeling (as suggested earlier) that being unlucky or not having tried hard enough could explain their failures. Few would accept the second argument, saying no one ever gave them special treatment just because they were poor even though they, too, knew the meaning and effects of discrimination.[45]

In 1980, the very beginning of the Reagan Era, the Burger Court had upheld a congressional plan that required 10 percent of federal work contracts to be set aside for businesses controlled by minorities, a clear attempt to alter the imbalance in opportunities. Although opposed by many conservatives in the new administration, such set-asides were viewed as a victory for civil rights forces that felt that without special consideration it would remain very difficult for Blacks and others long excluded from full participation in all aspects of the economy to break the pattern. The opponents saw the set-asides, and other schemes to increase minority participation, as "affirmative discrimination."[46] Many scholars and lawyers debated the morality and legality of programs that were based not on a specific company's acts but were intended as general ways to redress past grievances. (The arguments echoed those heard surrounding the DeFunis and Bakke cases discussed in the previous section.)

In a landmark 6–3 decision, early in 1989, the Supreme Court (still known to many as "The Reagan Court," owing to the conservative justices appointed by Reagan) ruled that the Richmond (Va.) City Council unconstitutionally discriminated against whites by demanding (presumably in compliance with the earlier ruling) that a contractor with any city building contract must give at least 30 percent of the value of the project to firms that are at least one-half minority-owned. Speaking for the majority, Associate Justice Sandra Day O'Connor claimed that the city had violated the Constitution because it had relied on past societal discrimination to justify the quota. "Since none of the evidence presented by the city points to any identified discrimination in the Richmond construction industry.... the dream of a nation of equal citizens, in a society where race is irrelevant to personal opportunity and achievement, would be lost in a mosaic of shifting preferences based on unmeasurable claims of past wrongs."[47]

The late Associate Justice Thurgood Marshall, one of the three dissenters and the only African American member of the high court at the time, bitterly stated that the new ruling "sounds a full-scale retreat from the Court's longstanding solicitude to race-conscious remedial efforts." He continued by claiming, "[the] decision masks a deliberate and giant step backward in the court's affirmative action jurisprudence."[48] Within several weeks the Supreme Court followed its Richmond decision with two other related reversals of prior policy. In the first, the Court set new limits on measures minorities could use to attempt to prove that they had been relegated to less desirable jobs. In the other, *Martin v. Wilks,* a case involving white firefighters in Birmingham, Alabama, who contended that they were being discriminated against because of affirmative action policies, the Court ruled in their favor. President George Bush, viewed by many as more sensitive to minority concerns than his predecessor, although claiming he believed in fairness and the protection of civil rights, did not challenge the Court's decisions in these critical cases.

Is Affirmative Action a Form of Discrimination?

The issue of identity politics, usually centered on the matter of affirmative action, was to be revisited a number of times in the 1980s and early 1990s as the case was made for it, against it, and "against the case made against it," as Michael Kinsley noted in *The New Yorker* in March, 1995.[49] His essay opened with a thoughtful statement that "Affirmative action is one of those controversies, like abortion, in which opponents have the advantage of moral clarity. They are defending a seemingly absolute principle, although supporters are defending something much more ambiguous."[50] They are often wont to give "on the one hand/on the other hand" responses to their critics, suggesting that, although not everything that falls under the broad umbrella of affirmative action is good, there are approaches with which all reasonable people ought to be able to agree. Among these are: the casting of the widest nets possible to insure broad-based pools of applicants to schools or candidates for jobs; using minority group membership as a tie-breaker in the case of equal qualifications to enhance diversity in the academy or the workplace; and, the most common argument used today—defining "disadvantaged" in nonracial (and nongendered) terms with "class" becoming the favored variable.

The latter argument is a powerful one, but it is not as easy to defend as it seems on the surface. Even if a scheme could be devised to decide who was the most deserving, such favoritism could lead to a once-familiar form of discrimination. In both the Soviet Union and Communist China children of the middle classes were penalized for their advantages. This included those whose parents had struggled to assure better lives for their progeny only to be stifled in their own attempts to attain it.

Affirmative action is a matter that continues to be debated and has recently become the focus of a vigorous campaign to "return to meritocratic principles" and stop "favoring minorities and women." The division of the people was most clearly evident in a California initiative petition, endorsed by the then leading Republican candidates for President, including California governor Pete Wilson, to abolish even the limited use of preference decided by the Warren Court in the case of Bakke.[51] The issue, which was initially the topic of considerable discussion in the universities, remains alive there as well. In fact, at the University of California, a gigantic institution of many campuses came under the severest attack for its policies. Berkeley was almost entirely "white" in 1964; twenty years later whites were still in the majority (around 60 percent). In 1994 slightly less than a third of the students were white (32 percent). Thirty-nine percent were of Asian background, 14 percent Hispanic, and 6 percent Black. In the intervening years, several criteria had been established for admission to the highly competitive university: slightly more than half were to be admitted on the basis of grades and test scores alone, another 46 percent are welcomed under a combination of grades, test scores, essays, and background (meaning, in the instance, racial and ethnic background), and the rest, 3 percent are brought in under "the special decision of the admissions committee."[52]

Despite this attempt to satisfy a number of constituencies, it seemed to have antagonized most. Some whites, many of whom resented the whole system, joined with African Americans and Hispanics in protesting what they saw as undue advantages for Asians (long considered one of the four affirmative action categories) and called for restrictions on their "disproportional representation." The argument sounded strikingly like that used to keep Jews out of Ivy League institutions from the 1920s to the 1940s. The whole matter had become a political football and a part of the politics of resistance that has been mounting, especially among those who feel that they are forced to pay the price for something for which they claim to have had no responsibility, the discrimination of minorities.

Although their rebellion reached full steam in the run-up to the 1996 presidential race with most Republican leaders pressing for the elimination of all affirmative action and "set-aside" programs that seem to hold back opportunities for white males, the issue had been brewing ever since it was first implemented on a wide scale during the days of the Johnson and Nixon administrations.

On July 21, 1995, the University of California's Board of Regents in a 14–10 vote struck down "the use of race, sex, religion, color or national origin as criteria for admission to the university."[53] A parallel measure on hiring and contracting passed 15 to 10. The former measure was to be put into effect on January 1, 1997, the second a year earlier. What happened in Sacramento was a portent of what was to come in other parts of the country.

An Unsteady March

In 1999 Philip A. Klinker and Rogers M. Smith published a retrospective examination of changes in race relations in the life course of American society. They contended that it has been an unsteady march, marked by "two steps forward, one step back."[54] What they wrote was hardly a new idea. As Hosea Williams put it on the occasion of the thirty-fifth anniversary of the dramatic events that occurred in Selma, Alabama, on March 16, 1965: "We're not where we used to be but we're not where we ought to be either." What is significant in Klinker and Smith's study, and extremely relevant for our own understanding, is the explanation the two social scientists offer for the fact that the course has been marked by short bursts of dramatic reform lasting for a decade or two, almost invariably followed by long periods of retreat, retrenchment, and a kind of home-grown nativist revanchism.

On the basis of their analysis of the politics of race, especially as practiced by those in power, the authors challenge conventional schoolroom rhetoric about the triumph of Judeo-Christian principles and the basic decency of people imbued with strong liberal proclivities upon which they are wont to act and often do. Instead, it is argued that significant advances that have been made have rarely occurred as a result of the initiatives of the pure of heart, but reactions of those who realized what they might lose if they failed to react to external and internal threats.

Klinker and Brown cite three principal determinants of such reactions. The first is the response to the outbreak of large-scale wars requiring extensive economic and military mobilization that, time and again, led to the reluctant but necessary recruitment of blacks. (N.B.: It is important to note, once again, that African Americans usually served in segregated units of the U.S. Army. Desegregation was not ordered until 1948 and only implemented during the Korean War in the early 1950s.)

The second condition for change, though also pragmatic, was more reflexively ideological. At certain critical times, such as during the Revolution, the Civil War, World War II, and the Cold War, national leaders found themselves in a situation when the character of the country's enemies prodded them "to justify such wars and their attendant sacrifices by emphasizing the nation's inclusive, egalitarian, and democratic traditions."[55] They were then forced to demonstrate the efficacy of that which they professed. Minorities, including blacks, were the beneficiaries.

The third reaction is related to a different sort of threat, not one that encouraged sacrificing tradition to "nobler ends" but one that meant bowing to the force of domestic political protest movements for civil rights and access such as those described above. (The passage of the Voting Rights Act of 1965 is a good case in point.)

What is especially useful to students of race relations in their analysis is that Klinker and Smith put flesh on the bones of their history. The core chapters, presented in chronological order, offer in-depth ethnographies of the national political, economic, and social climates in eight distinctive eras, beginning with "Slavery, 1619–1860" and ending with "Post–Civil Rights America, 1968–1998." Each is a critical assessment of the behavior of principal actors and their shifting positions, which frequently reflect more calculated compassion than genuine commitment to the ideals of equality and justice. Hundreds of illustrations of such politically motivated concessions and compromises are offered and explained. Among them are such cases as the severe shortage of fighting men that lead to the recruitment of blacks after the disastrous winter at Valley Forge; the melding of racism and opposition to slavery's expansion to enhance recruitment to the new Republican party in the 1850s; and President Eisenhower's decision to call in federal troops to restore order around Central High School in Little Rock, Arkansas on September 24, 1957, in reaction to the mounting risk of domestic discord, a looming constitutional crisis, and international embarrassment.

All told, the researchers see ample evidence to suggest that events and actions, provocations and publicity, rather than goodwill, triggered reactions that proved beneficial to the cause of desegregation and mobility for African Americans, taking them—along with other minorities—"two steps forward." In the next chapter another type of action provoking reaction, that often referred to as "backlash," is examined.

Notes

1. See Will Herberg, *Protestant-Catholic-Jew* (New York: Doubleday, 1955).

2. James Baldwin, *Nobody Knows My Name: More Notes of a Native Son* (New York: Dial Press, 1961).

3. See, for example, James Baldwin, *Go Tell It on the Mountain* (New York: Knopf, 1952).

4. See Henry Louis Gates, *Colored People: A Memoir* (New York: Knopf, 1994).

5. *The Autobiography of Malcolm X* (New York: Grove Press, 1964), pp. 169–190.

6. See, for example, Eldridge Cleaver, *Soul on Ice* (New York: McGraw-Hill, 1968), p. 46.

7. Booker T. Washington, "The Atlantic Exposition Address, September 1895," from *Up from Slavery* (New York: Doubleday, Page and Company, 1901), pp. 218–225.

8. As reprinted in August Meier, Elliott Rudwick, and F. L. Broderick (eds.), *Black Protest Thought in the Twentieth Century,* 2nd ed. (Indianapolis: Bobbs-Merrill, 1971), p. 6.

9. Ibid., p. 7.

10. August Meier and Elliott Rudwick, "Radicals and Conservatives: Black Protest in Twentieth-Century America," in Peter I. Rose (ed.), *Old Memories, New Moods* (New York: Atherton, 1970), p. 124.

11. Ibid., p. 125.

12. See Peter I. Rose, "Making a Difference," in Peter I. Rose (ed.), *The Dispossessed: An Anatomy of Exile* (Amherst: University of Massachusetts Press, 2005), pp. 120–121.

13. Ibid., p. 127.

14. Maurice Davie, *Negroes in American Society* (New York: McGraw-Hill, 1949), p. 440.

15. Meier and Rudwick, op. cit., p. 130.

16. Thoreau himself was influenced by the utopian educator Bronson Alcott. See Geraldine Brooks, "Orpheus at the Plough," *The New Yorker* (January 10, 2005), pp. 62–63.

17. Stokely Carmichael and Charles V. Hamilton, *Black Power: The Politics of Liberation in America* (New York: Vintage, 1967).

18. James Forman, *The Making of Black Revolutionaries* (New York: Macmillan, 1972).

19. Martin Luther King, Jr., "I Have a Dream," *SCLC Newsletter,* 12 (September 1963), pp. 5, 8.

20. See, for example, James Farmer, *Freedom, When?* (New York: Random House, 1965).

21. The quotation is from a West Indian emancipation speech delivered by Douglass in 1857. It appears in Carmichael and Hamilton, op. cit., p. x.

22. Richard Wright also expresses this most poignantly. See his "Foreword," in St. Clair Drake and Horace Clayton, *Black Metropolis* (New York: Harcourt, Brace, 1945).

23. William H. Grier and Price M. Cobbs, *Black Rage* (New York: Basic Books, 1968), esp. pp. 152–167.

24. See Cushing Strout, *Divided We Stand: Reflections on the Crisis at Cornell* (Garden City, N.Y.: Doubleday, 1970).

25. Idem.

26. C. Wilson Record, *"Responses of Sociologists to Black Studies,"* in *Black Sociologists: Historical and Contemporary Perspectives,* James Blackwell and Morris Janowitz (eds.) (Chicago: University of Chicago Press, 1974), pp. 368–401.

27. Ibid., p. 381.

28. Ibid., p. 386.

29. Ibid., p. 398.

30. Jill Quadagno, *The Color of Welfare* (New York: Oxford University Press, 1994), p. 4.

31. Daniel Boorstin, "Ethnic Proportionalism: The 'E.Q.' and Its Uses," in *The Sociology of the Absurd* (New York: Simon and Schuster, 1970), pp. 25–35. See also Martin Mayer, "Higher Education for All? The Case of Open Admissions," *Commentary,* 45 (February

1973), pp. 37–47; and, "An Exchange on Open Admissions," *Commentary,* 45 (May 1973), p. 4–24.

32. Vance Bourjaily, *Confessions of a Spent Youth* (New York: Dial Press, 1952). See, especially, the chapter, "The Fractional Man."

33. See Carol Marks, *Farewell—We're Good and Gone* (Bloomington: University of Indiana Press, 1989.)

34. Michael Harrington, *The Other America* (New York: Macmillan, 1962).

35. See Quadagno, op. cit., pp. 4–5; also pp. 10–15.

36. For an excellent thumbnail summary of the history of, and controversy generated by affirmative action programs, see Nicholas Leman, "What Happened to the Case for Affirmative Action?," *New York Times Magazine* (June 11, 1995), pp. 36–43, 52–62, 66.

37. See, for example, Pierre van den Berghe, "The Benign Quota: Panacea or Pandora's Box?" *The American Sociologist,* (June 6, 1971); Murray N. Rothbart, "The Quota System, in Short, Must Be Repudiated," *Intellectual Digest* (February 1973), pp. 78, 80. See also Earl Raab, "Quotas by Any Other Name," *Commentary* January 1972), pp. 41–45; Bart Barnes, "Reverse Bias Alleged in College Hiring," *The Washington Post* (March 5, 1973). See also Nathan Glazer, *Affirmative Discrimination* (New York: Basic Books, 1978).

38. See Allan P. Sindler, *Bakke, DeFunis and Minority Admissions: The Quest for Equal Opportunity* (New York: Longmans, 1978).

39. *The Regents of the University of California, Petitioner v. Allan Bakke,* Brief for the United States as *Amicus Curiae,* 76–811 October Term, 1977, pp. 28–29.

40. Ibid., pp. 30, 33, 38, 41.

41. Ibid., p. 50.

42. Ibid., p. 55, 63.

43. Sindler, op cit., p. 12.

44. Ibid., pp, 14–15.

45. See Ralph Levine, "Left Behind in Brooklyn," in Peter I. Rose (ed.), *Nation of Nations* (New York: Random House, 1973), pp. 335–346.

46. See Nathan Glazer, *Affirmative Discrimination* (New York: Basic Books, 1975).

47. This quotation appeared in *The New York Times* and in Associated Press releases on January 24, 1989.

48. Idem.

49. Michael Kinsley, "The Spoils of Victimhood," *The New Yorker* (March 27, 1995), pp. 62–69.

50. Ibid., p. 62

51. Leman, op. cit.

52. See Peter Applebome, "Gains in Diversity Face Attack in California," *New York Times* (June 4, 1995), pp. 1, 22.

53. As reported by William H. Honan, *New York Times* (July 23, 1995), p. 7.

54. See Philip A. Klinker, with Rogers M. Smith, *The Unsteady March: The Rise and Decline of Racial Equality in America* (Chicago: University of Chicago Press, 1999).

55. Ibid., p. 3.

Chapter 11

Social Physics

Action and Reaction

One of the basic laws of physics is that every action has an equal and opposite reaction. The laws of society are not that simple. Yet, it is safe to say that in "social physics" (a label Auguste Comte, the "father" of sociology, wanted to use for his new discipline) there are numerous examples of changes provoking reactions. This is certainly the case in the area of racial and ethnic relations. It was evident in the responses of nativists to the increasing flow of immigrants into "their" country. As noted in the last chapter, it was clearly evident in the growing militancy among the ranks of minority groups who had grown restive as they waited for the nation's institutions to uphold its own ideals. It was seen again in the response to *their* demands by many other Americans, particularly those who had come to be called "white ethnics," in the wake of the new policies wrought by the consciousness-raising movements of the 1960s and 1970s. It is evident today in reaction to what some have called the "declarations of independence" by those who continue to feel excluded by institutional racism. The resurgence of militant black nationalists and their less strident but equally determined brothers in the Million Man March on Washington by African American men in the fall of 1995 gave new voices to such old and deep-rooted sentiments. Now, a decade later, those voices are still being heard.

The "Unmeltable Ethnics"

In a book with an intriguing title, *The Rise of the Unmeltable Ethnics,* published in 1971,[1] social philosopher and commentator Michael Novak claimed to speak

for many children and grandchildren of Eastern and Southern Europe whose relatives left the Old Country to seek a better life in the new and often found it. They
also found that they were outsiders and, in many ways, were to remain so despite
the fervor of their patriotism and their willingness to prove it. To many, they were
"peasants"; looked down upon not only by white Protestants who saw them as
socially, religiously, even racially inferior, but also by more than a few intellectuals
of varying backgrounds themselves who depicted them as unwashed, uneducated,
uncouth—in general, culturally inferior.

> [Those] ... who appear most willing to sacrifice time and effort in a "good" cause,
> whatever the cause, prove invariably to be those who can retreat to upper middle class
> sanctuary and rejoin the "establishment" whenever the need arises. Such [individuals]
> seem either unable or unwilling to recognize a simple truth; that people considerably
> lower (although not the lowest) in the class structure, lack a similar sense of mastery
> and freedom, but rather are fighting desperately to achieve the sense of economic and
> social security which these [people] accept as their birthright.[2]

In corner bars and coffee shops working class ethnics remonstrated about "the
squeeze," about the insensitivity of the people uptown. Then, after decades of
public silence, spokespersons for increasing numbers of angry, frustrated, and self-
styled "abandoned" people began to express their feelings more publicly. They did
so by supporting conservative candidates for local and national political offices,
by organizing neighborhood associations, which some observers saw as northern
equivalents of white citizens' councils, by playing on the growing resentment that
others were feeling. Not only did all Americans hear what was being said, they began
to read about their sentiments in a spate of articles and books on ethnic Americans
(an interesting counterpoint to the raft of books on nonwhite minorities that had
also begun to appear at the same time).[3]

Common themes ran through many of these writings: The earlier immigrants
faced great difficulties and obstacles, but they accepted the challenges and internalized the values of the wider society, values that were often quite alien to their
own heritages. They knew camaraderie of kin and countrymen, their own people
who understood them, respected them, and stood by them when others failed to
do so. Indeed many had become more prideful of being Irish or Polish or Italian
or Greek than they had been "back home."[4] They knew what it meant to be helped
by others in similar straits and how to use certain public institutions to advantage,
especially the schools, political machines, and, eventually, the civil service. But
what they also knew, and this is perhaps the most persistent theme, was that one
could not ask for special favors because of background or by pleading "special
conditions." (Most failed to indicate that, whatever the dire circumstances of the
previous lives of their forebears, the vast majority of them—or their parents or
grandparents—had come to America voluntarily, not in the chains of slavery or
under conditions of some form of indenture.)

Given the sentiments of having had to find their own ways, many white ethnics
reacted with astonishment at the seeming capitulation being made to demands by

blacks and other nonwhites for group rights and privileges. "Who do they think they are?" They began to ask, "Why can't they be like us?" A growing resolve to get their own share arose. A sense of righteous indignation at being put down by those above them to satisfy the demands from below them in the pecking order became more and more apparent and more and more annoying. Many argued that they were loyal, decent, hardworking, God-fearing, and patriotic Americans who had had nothing to do with slavery or with segregation but were being forced to pay for the sins of other peoples' fathers. Many were especially upset by the fact that the authorities seemed too willing to buy urban peace at their expense.

Much of the animosity was directed at the members of the more affluent liberal community, those, they said, who seemed to love the poor (often at a distance) and champion the underdog but condemned white ethnics and middle Americans for "their complacency," "their ignorance," "their lack of compassion."[5] They grew equally impatient with the "radical chic" displayed by many celebrities who appeared to kowtow to militants. The comments of a steelworker, Mike Fitzgerald of Cicero, Illinois, interviewed by Studs Terkel, are illustrative:

> Terkel: Does anger get you, bitterness?
> Fitzgerald: No, not really. Somebody has to do it. If my kid ever goes to college, I just want him to realize that when I tell him somebody has to do it, I just want him to have a little bit of respect, to realize that his dad is one of those somebodies. This is why even on (muses)—yes, I guess, sure—on the black thing ... (Sighs heavily) I can't really hate the colored fella that's working with me all day. The black intellectual I got no respect for. The white intellectual I got no use for. I got no use for the black militant who's gonna scream about 300 years of slavery to me while I'm busting my back. You know what I mean? I have one answer for that guy.... Don't bother me. We're in the same cotton field. So just don't bug me....
>
> It's very funny. It's always the rich white people who are screaming about racism. They're pretty well safe from the backlash. You ever notice it's always: go get the Klansman, go get the Hunkies, go get that Polack. But don't touch me, baby.[6]

People like Mike Fitzgerald felt—and expressed—a backlash sentiment most strongly. Although of a variety of backgrounds themselves, many had begun to move up and away from seeing themselves solely in terms of their ethnic identity. Since such people were often the first to be affected by the new policies, a forceful reactive assertion of ethnicity occurred in many communities, even at the expense of class-based allegiances. Nathan Glazer and Daniel Patrick Moynihan noted in 1970 that "ethnic identities have taken over some of the task of self-definition and in definition by others that occupational identities, particularly working-class identities, have generally played. The status of the worker has been downgraded; as a result, apparently, the status of being an ethnic, a member of an ethnic group, has been upgraded.... Today, it may be better to be an Italian than a worker. Twenty years ago, it was the other way around."[7]

The following year, the sociologist Andrew Greeley wrote, "the new consciousness of ethnicity [among white ethnics] is in part based on the fact that the blacks have legitimated cultural pluralism as it has perhaps never been legitimated before."[8]

This new reality significantly altered a number of other aspects of American life. For the last three decades, policies for dealing with recognized—and, sometimes, institutionalized—diversity has been one of the most hotly debated issues in government circles, in the universities, in the journals of opinion, and, in very direct ways, in the streets of America's cities.

Even as the debates were heating up, there were many who, despite certain misgivings, believed that the resurgence of ethnicity among those no longer viewed as minorities was highly functional for our society because, after all, Americans must appreciate that this is a kaleidoscope of separable pieces of a complex if ever-changing social structure.[9] Some went further. They argued that not only would African Americans benefit from their newfound sense of consciousness but so too would other minorities, white as well as nonwhite, who had suffered far too long under the cultural domination of "the WASP Establishment."[10]

Other observers contended that reality was simply catching up with the dreamers who were convinced that ethnicity was rapidly becoming a thing of the past. Irving Levine and Judith Herman, for example, claimed that their data indicated that Glazer and Moynihan were wrong. There had not been as much change as they suggested. What was different was that the strains and divisions that had always existed were now being recognized and validated.

> In most of the cities where the white working class is ethnic—in the Northeast and Midwest particularly—common origin is reflected in distinctive neighborhoods. People tend to live near one another according to ethnic background, even "unto the fourth generation." For some, the choice is a conscious one, influenced by the presence of such institutions as the church. For others, the ethnic neighborhood is a convenience, maintaining some features of the extended family, lost (but yearned for) in more heterogeneous neighborhoods.
>
> Even suburbanization has not diminished the intensity of many ethnic neighborhoods. In many cases, what looks like an economics-based blue collar suburb is in reality a community consisting of several ethnic enclaves. For instance, Long Beach, a Long Island town, has been described as "three worlds," Italian, Black, and Jewish—though to the outsider it may seem a "typical lower income suburban community."[11]

Two disclaimers, each dealing less with the substances of the analyses and more with the sympathy expressed for the tendency to support or even advocate further mobilization or separation along ethnic lines, were offered. The first, a "class" rather than "ethnic" argument, stated that too much attention was being given to ethnic feelings and too little to the sense of alienation of all who are relatively powerless in the context of the larger society. Their contention was that fostering the ethnicity of any group serves mainly to keep the separate entities from uniting into a coalition of opponents to a repressive economic system. Foremost in the ranks of those who took this stand was the late Bayard Rustin, who opposed both "Black nationalism" and white ethnic revivalism. Rustin wanted the people to have power collectively and believed that they would not achieve it by putting their special, separate interests above more basic social and economic needs.[12]

The second critique came from liberal integrationists who had long stood firm against the winds of change, if for somewhat different reasons than those of Bayard Rustin. Most notable among them was Harold Isaacs, who condemned what he saw as a "retribalization."[13] Reviewing Murray Friedman's volume, *Overcoming Middle Class Rage,* which sought to explain backlash politics and ethnic insularity, Isaacs wrote:

> The two themes—on the Middle American as a harassed man and as an ethnic—are presented ... as if they harmonize. They are in fact tunes beaten out by separate drummers who march down quite different roads. In effect, the appeal here to the Middle American is to depolarize on social issues and to repolarize ethnically.[14]

Referring to the older pluralists, particularly Horace Kallen and Randolph Bourne and their imagery of symphonic harmony, Harold Isaacs warned against too high expectations, for modern symphonies often resound with disturbing dissonances. "This [repolarization along ethnic lines] may make beautiful music in the heads of some of these composers, but it has to be played out loud to hear what it actually sounds like."[15]

Isaacs was prophetic. In recent years the orchestra has indeed sounded less and less polyphonous and more and more cacophonous. Some find the raucous "polyrhythms," as the performance artist and playwright Andrea Hairston[16] calls them, quite exciting. Others think they are disruptive—and they mean it in a more than symbolic sense. They contend that the new players are the vanguard of a movement that could disunite the country. The "either-it-is-good-or it-is-bad" dichotomy is what grabs the headlines and the attention of talk show hosts.

However, to characterize all differences of opinion about such matters as so sharply polemical is to minimize the importance of a large center cohort of Americans baffled by what was going on in the post–Civil Rights Era and quite ambivalent about how to react to it. Leaders in the different camps, sensitive to this reality, often exploited it, vying for the support of those not already polarized into extreme positions. One side did so by attacking what they saw as the failures of the civil rights campaigns to right historic wrongs; the other by claiming that the successes of those campaigns led to excesses and to escalating demands.

Not surprisingly, as the American political parties became more like those of Europe, that is, working under far more ideologically consistent guidelines, the question of "One America—or Many?" was raised again and again. It was also answered in a series of policy decisions that altered previous practices quite dramatically. The changes were not only structural. They were "climatic" as well—affecting the social atmosphere and the civic culture in rather profound ways.

During the years of the Carter administration, the president from the Deep South had rekindled the spirit of "welfare-minded" Democrats from the New Deal days of Franklin Delano Roosevelt through the Kennedy-Johnson Era, lent his weight to a variety of programs to assist the poor, especially those in racial minorities, and vigorously advocated human rights at home and abroad. But Carter, an outsider to the Washington establishment, had difficulty in a variety of other spheres.

Not least was his inability to curb mounting inflation (which reached double digit heights before he left office) or to quell the feeling of serious malaise throughout the country, a sentiment that he sometimes expressed himself. By the time of the presidential election of 1980, it seemed to many that America was in deep trouble and needed a change.

Carter's opponent, Ronald Reagan, had campaigned on a "Get-America-Moving-Again" and "Get-the-Government-Out-of-Private-Life" ticket and won handily. Once in control, he moved to keep the promises made during the campaign. Through a variety of economic strategies, including a massive increase in spending for defense, inflation was reduced, as was the percentage of Americans unemployed. In addition to those on the right (both political and religious), many middle Americans—now including numerous white ethnics—felt that at last there was someone in the White House who understood their plight and was not only willing to articulate it but was acting to stop the drift of the "welfare state."

Watershed

Under the first Reagan administration hundreds of programs designed to aid the poor were disbanded, thousands of conservative judges were appointed to federal courts, and millions of dollars were diverted to matters other than human services. The curtailment of the role of the U.S. Civil Rights Commission as both arbiter of interracial conflict and as a dynamic force for the advocacy of fairer practices sent a very clear message across the land: "Activists for group rights: Beware!"

In many ways the representatives of the Reagan administration and their sympathizers were returning to what the sociologist Michael Lewis aptly named the "individual-as-central sensibility."[17] Those who took such a stance argued that responsibility for success and failure is highly personal, not collective. They contended that, in America, one must always be encouraged to strive to be the master of his or her own fate—that too much reliance on others, particularly on the institutions of government, threatens the moral fiber and weakens the whole conception of a true meritocracy.

Although emphasizing the work ethic and praising individual initiative, the proponents of Reagan's policies also stressed the importance of patriotism and the idea that "We are all Americans." Not inconsistently, given the interplay of individualistic and nationalistic themes, many opposed (openly in some cases, more circumspectly in others) affirmative action policies. These, it was argued, were not only unfair but, perhaps, unconstitutional—because they gave special advantage to the "designated minorities," contributing to a fragmentation of the polity.

All told, those in positions of the greatest power seemed determined to move minority demands low down on their list of priorities—and did.

Many civil rights advocates were troubled but not surprised. They had seen the handwriting on the wall. Still, not a few predicted that the anticipated retrenchment would trigger new outbursts of protests from the quarters of those who seemed to be losing the most from new federal action as well as inaction. In fact, the response was not as explosive as many had expected. When it came, very late in the decade, it took rather unexpected forms.

For almost ten years those still concerned about continued discrimination against racial and ethnic minorities watched in sadness but did little to attempt to stem the erosion of the federal commitment to redress legitimate grievances. There is little doubt that the lack of vigorous response was related, at least in part, to the failure of the civil rights movement's aging leadership to replace itself. There were far fewer spokespersons for integration, and those who were there were hardly the charismatic leaders of the earlier era.

As America entered the 1980s, schools, although far from being truly integrated in their student bodies, had curricula that had begun to more accurately reflect the true nature of America's checkered history and the heterogeneous character of its people. Factories, although not yet realizing parity of placement and achievement, were beginning to respond to the pressure of federal requirements first imposed during the Nixon administration and supported by the moral suasion of those in Carter's administration and the more progressive labor leaders. Political parties and local organizations clearly showed the effects of the struggle for enfranchisement, recognition, and a share of the spoils. The gains in the political arena were the result of challenges to the old system, the growing strength of African American and other minority blocs, and anxiety among the once-dominant forces about their own vulnerability. The last factor undoubtedly led to many concessions to stave off disruption.

Black consciousness, black mobilization, and black pressure—and similar developments among those in some other minority communities—appeared to have paid off in two realms: one highly personal, the other, political. Psychologically, those who had been seen, and often saw themselves, as second class, increasingly rejected such imagery and took increasing pride in who they were. That pride undoubtedly gave impetus to the outward expressions of a unified sense of peoplehood. As members of a group, now seen as an ethnic group and not just a social category, more and more African Americans sought to use their collective consciousness to get their piece of the action. In many instances they succeeded. But in other arenas, especially the economic and the social, the record was far more mixed.

On the one hand, many African Americans with sound educational credentials— and some with rather marginal ones, as critics of certain new policies were quick to point out—benefited dramatically from mandated efforts to improve employment opportunities. Not a few came from the already well-established "black segment" of the working class (an often neglected part of the population). But, as William Julius Wilson has shown, many who were "eligible" to make it, were ready and willing and often able to move. And move they did.[18]

By 1978 a far larger percentage of college students, graduate students, foremen (and women), junior managers, and local, state, and federal government officials were from minority groups than ever before. But as the decade ended, the country entered a period of stagflation, a time when recession and inflation simultaneously threatened all Americans, taking a heavy toll on those in the precarious position of having just entered the middle-class technocracy. Moreover, as Department of

Labor statistics revealed, those in the lower class had even less hope of breaking out of their dependency. They remained as unemployed and as unemployable as did so many of their older siblings and parents 10, 20, and 30 years before.[19] That situation still persists in many parts of the society.

In many ways it might have been expected that the presidential campaign of 1988 would have been the context for contending parties to put forth their ideological positions on such issues as the character and direction of intergroup relations in America. Race, class, and gender were thought to be prominent among them. Yet, with the exception of the powerful voice of Democratic candidate Jesse Jackson, this did not prove to be the case. Such matters were among the most significant issues buried under Republican rhetoric about good times brought on by peace and prosperity and Democratic rhetoric about helping the little guy access the system. When race was raised, it was by innuendo—such as the Bush campaign's celebrated exploitation of the decision of Governor Michael Dukakis's administration to furlough the convicted murderer Willie Horton, a black man who then committed violent crimes while on leave. The Democrats' counterattack was weakened by reluctance, until the waning days of the campaign, to take strong, identifiably liberal stands.

Waving the Flag

Both parties used patriotism to rally support, with American flags being more common icons of the 1988 election than bumper stickers or lapel buttons. The Republicans claimed that things had never been better; the Democrats promised (with clear echoes of the campaigns of Adlai Stevenson in the 1950s) greater tomorrows. Although acknowledging that there were still unsolved social problems, neither of the chosen candidates seemed willing or able to specify how he would address the needs of millions of Americans who had not only failed to benefit from the vaunted boom of the Reagan Era but had fallen farther and farther behind. Nor were either specific in speaking to the realities of homelessness, teenage pregnancy, drug trafficking and substance abuse, the ills of the elderly, and continued racial unrest in our cities.

The election itself proved to be a mandate for continuity as the majority of Americans appeared to be more willing to rally to a team that, to them, had brought stability than to the vague promises of the Democrats. And, in the beginning, stability seemed to be what they got.

However, almost immediately upon his inauguration, George H.W. Bush began to send out signals that, in favoring what he called "a kinder, gentler nation," he would be reaching out to those generally ignored, including the members of racial minorities. His words were applauded by many Democrats, including a number who had supported the unsuccessful candidacy of Jesse Jackson in the primaries and who now suggested the possibility of some shifting of party allegiances if Bush began to deliver on his newly proclaimed promises.

Still, most advocates of minority rights remained skeptical of the new administration's ability to do so, particularly with its continued commitment to avoiding the imposition of new taxes or other means of revenue enhancement—as well as its position on those previously mentioned Supreme Court decisions that signaled a continued erosion of hard-won gains relating to improving opportunities for minorities to gain access to the social, political, and economic systems.

The first Bush administration inherited a number of old, unresolved foreign policy problems, some of which had indirect if not direct bearing on ethnicity—and ethnic politics—in this country. Most critical were relations with the Soviet Union and the matter of the opportunities for emigration for Jews, Armenians, Pentacostalists, and ethnic Germans; the then-40–year-old Arab-Israeli conflict and the effects of the Palestinian uprising in the occupied territories on the future of the area, its people, and those who supported them here; the much older civil and religious war in Northern Ireland, fought in the streets of Belfast and Londonderry but also the source of tension in the homes and community centers of Irish Americans; the powerful impact of the Japanese on the American economy and the growing resentment it engendered in many parts of the country, especially in the industrial sector; the continuing conflict with Iran, greatly exacerbated in the winter of 1989 by the violent reaction throughout the Muslim world to the publication of Salman Rushdie's controversial novel *The Satanic Verses* and some prominent Muslim clergymen who ordered the killing of its author for blaspheming against Islam; the Gulf War and persisting conflicts in Central America and the outflow of persons from Nicaragua, Guatemala, and El Salvador who sought asylum as refugees—the same status which was more easily obtained by those fleeing Indochina, Cuba, the U.S.S.R., and (after the violent suppression of the prodemocratic demonstrations in the late spring of 1989 in Beijing) China; and the general matter of immigration from Latin America and from across the Pacific. Many of these issues also became points of contention in the next presidential campaign when, after a series of bruising primary battles in the Democrats' camp, Bill Clinton was nominated to run against George Bush in 1992.

Clinton's victory in November of that year was hardly a mandate. The independent candidacy of the millionaire electronics entrepreneur, Ross Perot, siphoned considerable votes of erstwhile Republicans as well as many conservative Democrats. Clinton won the popular vote with a narrow plurality but succeeded in securing his success in the Electoral College. Although the Democrats did manage to control both houses of Congress, and though a number of liberals were elected (more minorities and females than any time in history), many feared the victory would prove Pyrrhic. In many ways, it did.

Despite a good deal of rhetoric about getting America back on course, solving social problems, controlling spending, and dealing more forcefully with racial issues, only part of the Democratic agenda was realized. Various explanations have been given for the failure. One of the most persuasive is that, for all the talk of commitment to change, for all the involvement of minority representatives, for all the meetings and hype about sweeping reforms of health care and welfare, the Clinton administration did not know how to buck the continuing tide of resentment over what was seen as special treatment for special interests. Actions relating to health and welfare were seen by many as litmus tests of the willingness of the new government to temper its "Big Brother" approach and hew more closely to the campaign-based sloganeering about giving the power back to the people. (A theme that ran through the materials put out by all the candidates, including Clinton.)

George H.W. Bush's four years in office were marked by a failure to keep his promise not to raise taxes and by his putative victory in the Gulf War, a war waged to roll back the invaders from Iraq in Kuwait. Following the advice of the Joint Chiefs of Staff, and, particularly, its head, General Colin Powell, American troops, once securing the country, decided not to level Baghdad nor remove Saddam Hussein from power. Instead it agreed to United Nations sanctions and patrols over much of the country. This did not sit well with many of the more conservative members of the President's own party.

Old Agendas, New Alignments

Toward the end of his own second year in office, Clinton, who, despite significant moves to bring the country together had never firmly established himself as a unifier, became the principal target of the Republicans. In 1994 they swept into office in one of the greatest routs in modern American history.

Led by the new Speaker, Newt Gingrich, and the new majority leader, Dick Armey, the House Republicans tried to implement the very conservative "Contract with America" on which they had campaigned with such obvious success. Not long in office, they threatened—and, in many cases, succeeded in—the dismantling of a raft of social programs that had been hallmarks of Democratic governments and accepted by Republican ones since the days of the New Deal. Among the many that were targeted for extinction or, at the least, drastic curtailment by House committees on Labor, Health and Human Services, and Education were such federally supported activities as job training, assistance to homeless youth, and a variety of educational programs at every level, primary, secondary and tertiary. Also included in the list of what were construed by many as superfluous bodies or those that were anathema to the ideological stances of the majority party and many of its members was the Corporation for Public Broadcasting. It was all part of what Norman Podhoretz, a neoconservative sympathizer with many of the ideas of the new leadership, called a true "counterrevolution."

Although some of the recommended changes were to move specific funding from the federal government to bloc grants for states, where statewide and local authorities who were closer to the scene would determine spending priorities, opponents worried that, with states already burdened with increasing costs of social services, their administrators would divert funds to pet projects. Furthermore, it was argued, when the grants ran out, there would be a natural inclination to close down programs that seemed too expensive. The losers in all such moves would doubtless be the poorest folks, those least able to care for themselves, those already dependent on assistance. This category of often unemployed and, even more often, only marginally employable people would clearly be disproportionately Native American, Puerto Rican, and African American citizens and millions of newcomers, mostly from Asia and Latin America. Here again, the plight of old minorities and new Americans seemed to hang in the balance.

To many observers the Republican sweep seemed to signal the solidification of a party of reactionary, white males (and many white females too), a cohort that numbered in its ranks not only many white Protestants from every part of the country, including the once solidly Democratic South, but also increasing numbers of Catholic conservatives, many of whom had voted for Reagan and retained local loyalties were now shifting allegiances across the board. The Democratic Party seemed to be so crippled as to hardly serve as the bastion of succor and support of the nonwhite minorities it had generally championed. Many surviving members, especially in the House of Representatives and in many state governments, found themselves worried about being seen as too "prominority" and began to echo the sentiments of the Republicans relating to such issues as affirmative action for minorities, the treatment of newcomers, legal as well as illegal, and the sharp rescission of entitlements even for those called "the deserving poor."

In the third year of Clinton's first term, there was increasing talk of disillusion with the major stances of both major parties. Many commentators noted that, although there was a wide chasm between the hard-line conservatives and old-fashioned liberals, the disaffected middle was searching for a home. What was apparent to those who examined the socioeconomic character and the political views of that vast center was that there were at least two very different constituencies. Journalist Michael Lind summed up the differences. He called one the "moderate middle" and the other the "radical center" (a label first used by sociologist Donald Warren).[20]

To Lind, the moderate middle consists of those sometimes known as "Eisenhower" or "Rockefeller Republicans" and others sympathetic to their highly pragmatic and Progressive views. Well educated and well-heeled, living in better urban neighborhoods (many of them in gentrified homes in downtown areas) or in the suburbs, members of the moderate middle are fiscally conservative and critical of many government programs which they feel are based on outdated as much as misguided policies; but take strong libertarian stances on such hot button issues as abortion and gay rights. They are also internationalists, centrists of the left.

Their opposite numbers were more apt to be alienated Democrats, the sort of Populists of the right who abandoned their party before: to vote for George Wallace in the 1960s and Ronald Reagan in the 1980s (and, later, for George W. Bush in 2000 and, again, in 2004). They hated big business and big labor and big government, too. And, although far more apt to wear the flag on their sleeves like other conservatives (who would soon be wearing theirs on their lapels), their attitudes toward foreign policy had more to do with maintaining trade sanctions than keeping the troops at home. As for civil rights and matters of affirmation action, there was a further crossing over of attitudes.

The Progressives, most of whom had come from Republican backgrounds, tended to be more supportive of mainline Democrats; the Populists, most of whom grew up as Democrats, were more likely, like Mike Fitzgerald, quoted earlier, to sound like conservative Republicans: opposed to "special favors."

The election of "Bush II," George W., in 2000, seemed to capitalize on the splits witnessed in the late 1990s. It had been an extremely close race, marked, as had all recent elections, by sharply divided ideologies and an increasing amount of political and personal mudslinging. Clinton's vice president, Albert Gore, who campaigned as a Progressive, won the popular vote but lost in a highly contested struggle over the electoral process in Florida. The Republican's victory was assured only by a decision of the Supreme Court of the United States.

The new president appointed a cabinet that, even more ethnically diverse than that of his predecessor, Bill Clinton, reflected in appearances and in surnames a true composite of "American types." There were whites and blacks, Asians and Latinos, in strategic positions. What they had in common, with the exception of the new Secretary of State, was a commitment to a very conservative agenda, one that, ironically, would hardly serve the most basic needs of many with whom they, at least the nonwhites, were identified. Reflecting more of the rhetoric of his father, George H.W. Bush, George W. spoke of his desire to bring the country back together, but not at government expense. He fostered "compassionate conservatism" and advocated more private initiatives, faith-based charitable activities, and the desire to stay out of foreign entanglements. And he wanted to impose a huge tax cut to bolster a flagging economy through the same sort of "trickle down" economic policies that Ronald Reagan had instituted—and which critics of both administrations argued could not succeed. George W. Bush had entered the White House with a huge surplus and did implement a huge tax cut, one that gave a big boost to millionaires but did little for the middle and working classes and left everyone with a burden that would set the treasury in arrears for years.

The new president, who seemed to have little interest in other lands or peoples prior to his election, was also critical of the interventionist practices of his predecessor, particularly in the Balkans when he tried to stem the tide of "ethnic cleansing." President Bush saw no reason for Americans to be involved in peacekeeping or nation-building abroad. However, many Democrats and a number of journalists and scholars were concerned about the seeming influence of a group of people inside and outside the administration known as "neoconservatives," who were bent on asserting America's power throughout the world, especially in oil-rich countries, and, to some, seeking to complete the first President Bush's battle with the Iraqi dictator, Saddam Hussein. Then, on September 11, 2001, the day suicidal hijackers forced pilots to fly their planes into the World Trade Tower in Manhattan and the Pentagon in Washington, many things began to change.

Within a month, American forces were attacking targets in Afghanistan, then ruled by the militant Islamic regime of the Taliban and said to be the home base of Al Qaeda, the terrorist organization headed by the Saudi expatriate Osama Bin Laden. Claiming that Iraq, too, was a sanctuary for anti-American terrorists with links to Bin Laden, as well as having a large arsenal of weapons of mass destruction (despite claims to the contrary on both charges by numerous United Nations' inspectors and a number of prominent Americans), the president persuaded Congress to back him in a preemptive war against Saddam Hussein. He and his advisers argued that it would be a quick fight and that the masses of Iraqis would welcome our forces and those of our allies (to become known as the "Coalition of the Willing") as liberators. Then, presumably, together American "liberators" would help to rebuild the society, its infrastructure, and its oil business. But, as is well known, it did not work out that way.

The war in Iraq was one of the principal matters in heated debates during the campaign season of 2004. But other issues, some of which echoed those of the previous three campaigns, became flashpoints. Not least were those related to "moral values," including "a woman's right to choose" (to have an abortion) and homosexual marriage. Rarely did the spokespersons for the President, nor did he, speak with conviction about the treatment of prisoners in American prison camps at Guantanamo Bay in Cuba or in those in occupied Iraq by our own forces. Nor was there much said about values of tolerance for those of different faiths and ethnic backgrounds. Indeed, there was an underlying linkage in much of the arguments of those in power that implied in some instances and contended in others that they, along with members of the "Christian Right," were keeping America safe from the scourge of Islamic fundamentalism.

Bush's opponent, Senator John F. Kerry, who had voted for the resolution to go to war and then became one of its biggest critics (though he was unwilling to say that, had he known when he voted what he claimed to know during the campaign, he would have opposed it), seemed to waffle on many cutting-edge value issues. He went down to defeat in November 2004.

As the second inauguration of George W. Bush approached, a new crisis confronted the nation: the gigantic tsunami, or tidal wave, that rolled across the Andaman Sea and the Indian Ocean killing over 150,000 people in Indonesia (the country with the world's largest Muslim population). This time, after a slight delay, the administration pledged 350 million dollars, joined forces with other nations, accepted the titular authority of the United Nations, and, perhaps as important, deployed thousands of American troops to assist in the rescue and reconstruction efforts. Some thought the prime motivator was the opportunity to offer a different face to other countries, such as Indonesia, with its huge Muslim population. Others, less cynical, chose to see this as a true change in orientation, but one that seemed to be in keeping with earlier views of compassionate commitments.

A second matter also raised questions about motivation. The subject was immigration, especially from Mexico, and the growing concern across the country that illegal entrants were overwhelming the United States. A survey conducted in May through August of 2004 with a nationally representative sample of 1888 respondents 18 years of age and older by the NPR/Kaiser/Kennedy School Poll, offered some interesting findings. Among them:

> The public's views on immigration are significantly less negative than they were in the months after the Sept. 11 terrorist attacks. [By October 2004, 41 percent said that they thought immigration to the U.S. should be decreased; a much lower figure than the 59 percent that CBS and the *New York Times* found when they asked the same question in December 2001] ... .Although attitudes are less negative than they have been in years, many negative attitudes toward immigration persist ... The public is divided on whether the large influx of recent immigrants has been good or bad for the country, with 30 percent saying good, 39 percent saying bad ... Americans express ambivalence, if not downright unease, about the cultural impact of immigration.

Many nonimmigrants believe immigrants are changing American culture and values when they ought to be adopting them.... .Generally, native-born Americans with higher levels of contact with immigrants have more positive views of immigrants and immigration than those with less contact.... .The public is concerned about illegal immigration and wants the government to crack down.... .Immigration is not a particularly partisan issue, and the president's proposal to deal with it draws stronger opposition than support.[21]

The report further noted that, although those in the two major political parties do differ in some of their attitudes about immigration, the differences are far less than on other issues. However, there was widespread concern about two proposals, mainly focused on would-be migrants from Mexico: President Bush's suggestion that would allow some illegal immigrants currently in the United States to legally stay in the country for several years as long as they hold jobs that no U.S. citizens want; and the establishment of a renewed *bracero*-like "guest worker program" that would insure a cheap labor supply for growers in the factory farms of the Southwest. Without saying so, many in the administration seemed to believe that if they were to impede the flow of migrant workers to the factory farms of the Southwest and the restaurants and other service industries in big cities across the nation, all dependent on cheap labor, the "food and fiber industry" would collapse.

Whether true or not, the pollsters learned that three out of four of their respondents believe that, once allowed to stay or admitted on short-term contracts, most workers will never go home. Even among supporters of the guest worker initiative, 61 percent doubt that workers would go back.[22]

A third major issue, and one that would most affect those, including many minorities, in the lower third of the nation's hierarchy of income levels, was what to do about Social Security. Here the President was pushing hard for a reform package that would move in the direction of privatization of retirement benefits by allowing individuals to invest a certain portion of their money in hopes of future growth.

At this writing, the jury is still out on the short- and long-term effects of the Tsunami Relief efforts, immigration reform, and changes in Social Security. Each of these has important implications, first for those of varying backgrounds overseas, second for those wanting to come to the United States, and third for citizens.

Persisting Issues

Parallel to the political debates mainly centered on the role of government in addressing and redressing age-old social problems, including health and welfare, employment and social security, and the lingering effects of discrimination taking place at the highest levels of government, others had their own thoughts about these and other matters.

Going back once again to the late 1960s and 1970s, in the ranks of what was left of the old race relations community—which still included the remnants of the civil rights movement, a number of mainstream politicians, and several prominent social scientists—an old issue much discussed in the turbulent 1930s (and again in the 1960s) became the focus of deliberation once again. Some called it the "Race versus Class Debate."

In its earlier manifestations, it tended to be an either/or matter. Some argued that racial oppression was a unique phenomenon, relating to particular attitudes toward those viewed and treated as different from themselves ("the white man's burden"), and was therefore almost immutable. Others contended that racial oppression was hardly unique but was instead a clear example of capitalist exploitation and that "difference" was being used as a mask for privilege.

The more recent debate is more complex. The sociologist William Julius Wilson attempted to put it in perspective. In his 1977 book, *The Declining Significance of Race,* referred to previously,[23] Wilson argued that, as traditional barriers were removed or lowered as a result of the political, social, and economic activities of the civil rights era, they were replaced with a new set of problems, problems that, with what now turns out to have been considerable prescience, "may prove to be even more formidable for certain segments of the Black population."[24] Among the most significant were the lessening need for unskilled workers (the traditional road to stabilization if not instant success), extreme poverty and deprivation of the basic amenities of living, the anomic conditions of home environments and decaying neighborhoods, the lack of middle-class role models, diversion from conventional paths by drugs and other means of escape (most of which give but short-term gratification), and increasing dependence on a welfare system that, many have long argued, undercuts incentives.

Wilson noted that " ... whereas the old barriers bore the pervasive features of racial oppression, the new barriers indicate an important and emerging form of class subordination."[25] Those being left behind are what he and others have come to refer to as "the truly disadvantaged."[26]

Wilson's claim of an expanding gap in "Black America," and, by extension, in other minority communities, was widely acknowledged, but his seeming unwilling-ness to place the principal blame for difficulties faced by African Americans and other nonwhite members in one basket labeled "Racial Discrimination" rankled many critics. Indeed, the Association of Black Sociologists, a group to which Wilson had belonged, attacked him for downplaying what, to them, remained the principal issue: institutional racism.[27] They contended that, despite the changes in law and practice, it remained true that, although most poor people in the United States were (and are) white, a disproportionate percentage of African Americans and Hispanics in the country were (and continue to remain) poor—and that unemployment rates among such cohorts had hardly changed in four decades. Moreover, they pointed to the resegregation of society (usually citing the increasing number of all or mostly black schools in northern cities, a function, in large part, of "white flight" to the suburbs) as evidence of the narrowness of Wilson's arguments.[28]

Furthermore, Wilson's use of the term "ghetto underclass" to describe those inner city dwellers most disadvantaged served to increase criticism of his overall thesis. Although many saw it as an apt descriptor, others saw it as an unfortunate use of language, as something akin to "outcaste." Yet, some went further, asserting that it is a pejorative label, or put-down. More critical than its usage was the persistent implication that the concept "underclass," itself, reified the socioeconomic thesis at the expense of its "racist sources." Stephen Steinberg, for example, offered the following commentary:

> The first thing that needs to be said is that the very existence of a ghetto underclass is evidence of institutionalized racism. That is to say, if the cumulative disadvantages that ensue from past racism leave many blacks without education and skills to complete for the better jobs, we are left with patterns of racial exclusion and inequality even if employers are not personally motivated by racial prejudice. That less than half of black men of working age are part of the labor force speaks for itself. This is a measure of the extent to which American labor markets are perpetuating patterns of racial inequality.[29]

Steinberg went on to note that black workers are being discriminated against to a far greater extent than Wilson allowed. Commenting on Wilson's claim that a large and growing black middle class was relatively immune from racial stereotypes and acts of overt discrimination was not really germane, it only shifted the nature of stereotyping, isolating those who live in the inner city even further.

> Instead of blanket stereotypes that once applied to all blacks, whites have learned to discriminate between those respectable blacks who are reasonably tolerated, and those other blacks who bear the stigma of the ghetto and are still objects of racial stereotyping, fear, and scorn. This elaboration of a once monistic system of beliefs may well be part of a long-term attenuation of racist ideology, with parallels to other ethnic groups (as when lace-curtain Irish were distinguished from shanty Irish, uptown Jews from downtown Jews, and so on).[30]

Peter Kwong made a similar point in distinguishing between the "Downtown Chinese" who live in the crowded and often poorest sectors of Chinatown and the "Uptown Chinese" who are increasingly exempt from the traditional stereotypes and patterns of discrimination which still plague those left behind.[31] In fact, as he and others suggest, the success of some reinforces the image of the failure of others.

The matter of the character and vulnerability of the "underclass" is also the concern of other social scientists.

Taking a position very different from Steinberg, others have long linked the Race/Class Debate to another one, that of "ethnic background and social values." Writers such as Thomas Sowell[32] pointed to the differential success of those whose groups faced severe bigotry—including clearly race-based derogation, denial and even violent acts—but were, nonetheless, able to rise and even flourish in the system, suggesting that the critical variable is culture and adaptability, not discrimination. Citing Jews and several Asian groups, Sowell also singled out fellow blacks, namely, West Indians,[33] as exemplars of what others have called, in a related context, "model minorities." Sowell's argument, and that of others who support the position, stated that those raised with values that emphasize self-control, delayed gratification, respect for education—and the belief that it has a double benefit, one aesthetic, the

other highly instrumental—and norms that support family togetherness, achievement and its rewards, have a better chance in a modern, industrial, and capitalist
society like that of the United States than will those who come from cultures and
subcultures more fatalistic or hedonistic or collectivistic in orientation.

In point of fact, the situation is always more complicated. Considering West Indians,
for example, Suzanne Model has suggested that they may be more successful than other
blacks in the United States because they are a "positively selected population, i.e. those
most prepared for life in a society like the United States are more apt to migrate to it."[34]
Orlando Patterson, in an article about Colin Powell and other Jamaican Americans, cor-
roborates this and notes that "Those left behind tell a different story: Jamaican family
life today is in even greater trouble than is African American."[35]

The debates about culture and character almost inevitable turn to proclivities
for or resistance to dependency on public assistance.

Another issue, that of "welfare dependency" in the United States itself, has been
the basis for considerable criticism and vigorous reassessment. Among the central
issues was a questioning of traditional, and mainly Democratic, approaches to care
for the indigent, the elderly, the infirm, and those single parents with dependent
children. Increasing numbers of those who favored considerable direct government
involvement have begun to rethink the efficacy of programs that seemed to prolong
rather than eliminate dependency, programs their more conservative critics had
always claimed, "paid people more not to work than to get a job." Although such
claims were generally off target, since they failed to allow for the special needs
of many who were not only unemployed but often also unemployable, they did
raise questions about the overall system. More and more people came to espouse
"workfare," a program where the able-bodied poor would be required to do community service in order to earn their allotments.

In actual practice, the workfare programs that were instigated varied widely. Most
effective seemed to be those most sensitive to the conditions under which those in
need came to be dependent. Understanding both the problems and the "culture" of
poverty, the programs altered outmoded and outrageous stipulations that limited
access to certain programs (for example, accepting a family into the program with
the father present even when it was almost necessary to be husbandless to obtain
Aid to Families with Dependent Children [AFDC] benefits) and provided two very
necessary services: childcare and training.

The "Welfare versus Workfare Debate" symbolized in concrete terms the more
widespread reassessment of various long-entrenched social policies and practices,
many of which focused on services for racial and ethnic minorities. It also led to
the realignment of advocates, contributing to—and accelerating in a number of
dramatic ways—a process that had already begun to take shape in the late 1960s and
throughout the 1970s when many liberals, who in the aggregate were consistently
the staunchest supporters of minority causes, became critical of certain trends that
deeply disturbed them.

For example, close connections between the Jewish and African American
leadership began to come unstuck as a result of strains dating back to the end of
the Civil Rights Era when whites, many of whom were Jews, found themselves

rejected by former allies in the struggle. It was exacerbated by disagreements over certain aspects of affirmative action programs and by diverging political attitudes, especially toward the warring factions in the Middle East (most Jews, even those critical of "West Bank" policies, continued to support Israel while increasing numbers of African Americans sided with the Arabs).[36] These were not the only strains in old alliances.

Labor movement leadership, traditionally at the forefront of the struggle for human and civil rights, found itself under increasing pressure from rank-and-file members to resist the kind of categorical imperative required by the advocates of "affirmative action" programs. Those in small businesses also raised questions about the fairness of policies that seemed to be discrimination in reverse.

The Immigration Debate Revisited

By the end of the 1980s, in addition to the debates about class versus race, the re-alignment of confederates in various civil rights struggles, the matter of the legality and significance of "affirmative action" and "set-asides" off the campuses and on them, and the meaning of foreign policy matters for those in various interest groups in the United States, the ever-smoldering immigration debate was fanned afresh by the increasing presence of new "foreign elements" on American soil. Immigrants, legal as well as "undocumented," came to be seen by many as an undue economic and social burden and by some as a cultural and political threat. They also were to become convenient scapegoats for some who needed a new "other" to blame for their own misfortunes.

As the numbers increased to over 750,000 per annum (it is now double that), including refugees, old nativist sentiments began to resurface. There was talk, once again, of the dangerous influx of "foreigners." This time, however, others' views were added to the more traditional opponents of immigration. The new opponents argued that, until American society takes care of its own, it should not allow others to enter. Some of the neorestrictionists, whose most effective lobbying organization was called FAIR, for the Federation of Americans for Immigration Reform, were white ethnics; others were members of American minority groups: African Americans, Puerto Ricans, Native Americans, and some Mexican Americans, too. Sometimes their leaders and spokespersons expressed the view that it is they who would have to pay the highest price for assistance to immigrants and for refugee relief, a contention made by labor economist Vernon Briggs.[37] They claimed that whatever scarce government funds there are they were likely to be diverted to more appealing causes. They also contended that their constituents were at a disadvantage in the job market since "immigrants will do anything" and will often do it for well below minimum wage. Both points sounded strikingly similar to what was said by Anglo-Americans in the mid-nineteenth century about the Irish; what the Irish said about the Italians and Southern and Eastern Europeans; and what those now labeled "white ethnics" have been saying about African Americans and other "preferred" minorities more recently.

To help the newcomers overcome the problems they faced, two matters took center stage: the familiar issue of Americanization and a newer one—bilingualism. The former is, to many civil rights advocates and pluralists, an old code word used by many who believed firmly in the idea that forced assimilation into Anglo-American molds was the only way outsiders could ever be accepted. Critics once again argued that Americanization would be responsible for turning ethnic pride into self-hatred and for leaving many immigrants in the unenviable position of being cast adrift without a firm anchor, the sort that the ethnic group so successfully provides. Supporters of the program, by contrast, expressing the ideas of early assimilationists, voiced the opinion that only when foreigners cast off their alien skins and forget the customs of their "homelands" can they really be absorbed. To be sure, they admitted, the immigrants would have to give up a great deal, make tremendous sacrifices; but, they argued, "Think of what they are getting."

Bilingualism is a more modern concept. In the nineteenth century, many European immigrants retained their native languages. There were areas where German was the *lingua franca,* others where Norwegian, Swedish, and other languages predominated. However, with the increasing influx of Southern and Eastern Europeans toward the end of the century, a campaign was mounted to see that everyone spoke English. It became a part of the Americanization process.

Despite ambivalences and insecurities, most newcomers accepted the idea that learning English was critical in order to move into society. Their children learned it in school "sink-or-swim" style and, highly motivated, many swam. Some of the adults also attended night schools where they studied English, sometimes with those who knew nothing of their culture or native languages, sometimes with those who, in perhaps the first instance of bilingual education, taught them English as a foreign language. In order to prevent their offspring from being totally immersed in the new language and culture, some immigrants set up and maintained private language after-school schools. Some of these still exist.

The migration of large numbers of Spanish-speaking Puerto Rican Americans to the New York area in the late 1940s and early 1950s, prompted by the economic boom of the post–World War II period and the availability of cheap and fast air service, changed the culture and the character of the city, brought about vigorous resistance to assimilation, and more formally introduced the idea of bilingualism. As indicated previously, some sociologists have speculated that clinging to their Latin heritage was one way Puerto Ricans could separate themselves from African Americans with whom they were often being grouped. Others say that easy access to Puerto Rico made acculturation less necessary or desirable.

The latter argument also came to be used to explain the reluctance of some Mexican immigrants to Americanization. The closeness of the motherland meant that one could be in one world (that of the United States) although in a sense living in another (Mexican). Whatever the reason, the result was that many Mexican Americans, like many Puerto Ricans, felt they should be allowed to retain their ways and their language. Some argued that their children should have instruction in Spanish and that their home language should be used as a transitional vehicle for moving along the road to learning to use English in everyday life. (In 1974, in the case of *Lau v. Nichols,* the Supreme Court ruled that being taught in a language they did not understand was discriminating against Chinese-speaking students of San Francisco. Schools were required to find bilingual teachers to work with these students.) Others claimed that even such a strategy was too "assimilationist," that they—and other non-English speakers—ought to be encouraged to maintain their own language, even to the extent of having it as an recognized option to English in all public matters, following the pattern in Francophone Quebec.

Because Hispanics make up the largest linguistic minority in the United States, debates about bilingualism have tended to revolve around the teaching of Spanish and the provisions for bicultural as well as bilingual programs for them. However, Latinos are not alone in this controversy. Other groups began pressing for similar opportunities and many have received them. There were schools in Virginia, near Washington, and in metropolitan parts of New York, and in other states where fifteen or more bilingual programs were running simultaneously. In Massachusetts, for example, the success of such a campaign is evident, and controversial. At the end of 1995, any school with twenty or more children of a particular language background is offered some instruction in their native tongue. In a most extreme case, in Boston young people whose parents came from Cape Verde, where Portuguese, and not the Creole spoken at home, is the official language and the language of instruction, are taught in Creole—from primers with newly constructed grammar.

The reaction against bilingualism, and what were seen as its excesses, increased quite dramatically in the 1980s, culminating in a campaign to establish the rule of "English Only," not only proclaiming but mandating that Americans have a single official language: English. The effort soon led to the passage of laws in fifteen states, and more battles are expected in the years ahead. One ironic twist in the controversy is that some of the most fervent supporters of English Only—the result of whose campaign imposes severe hardships on those who must fill out forms for medical assistance, welfare, further schooling, and employment—also argued that once the singularity of "our" language is established in law, we can then encourage the teaching of other languages to "enhance the understanding of others."

Americanization and bilingualism were not the only issues that occupied policy maker members of the public concerned about the status and impact of new Americans. Others include questions about how assistance is offered and given to newcomers and the extent of control service providers should have on their settlement in this country, especially refugees who receive support from federally funded programs. Should refugees be allowed to cluster, to form and maintain enclaves where they might find security through familiarity, or should they be scattered to encourage their early absorption into the mainstream?

If past history were any indication, it would seem most logical to allow people (indeed, to assist them) to form ethnic communities, thereby easing the transition into the American scene from often totally alien cultural milieus. Although some immigrants and refugees, especially those with higher education and familiarity with the language and customs of this country, have successfully moved into dominant communities with little difficulty, the evidence suggests that, for many, the acculturation process is painful and often prolonged. The support of compatriots who have traveled the difficult road from "foreigner" to "American ethnic" has always been a boon to newcomers.

In recent years and, especially, during the administration of George W. Bush, immigration has again become a most controversial issue. To be sure, some of it has to do with "homeland security" and the desire to do a better job of patrolling the borders to prevent acts of sabotage and terrorism, but most of it has to do with a feeling among many that Americans (mainly white Protestants) are losing their birthright.

As noted, the language of many critics of recent immigration policies is familiar, especially concerns about "unassimilable aliens," a phrase often used in regard to the Irish in the mid-nineteenth century and, later, to the Jews and Poles, Italians, Greeks, and Slavs. It was prejudice against such groups that, in the 1920s, led to the most restrictive legislation against "foreign invasion." In a recent book, *Assimilation American Style*, Peter Salins indicates that those old worries proved unjustified. Over several generations after rocky starts, millions of immigrants (almost exclusively European) were accepted into the mainstream of American society. It wasn't always easy, but a belief in "The Dream," a commitment to full participation in the civic culture, and effective use of their ethnic "bloc power" helped to get them *into* the system. But Salins sees such a movement as more problematic today, not so much because of greater discrimination against recent immigrants (though there is considerable resistance to their presence) but because too many have fallen under the spell of "multiculturalism," a group rights counter to the melting pot ideology, strongly rooted in the Black Nationalism.[38]

Salins rightly argues that "[s]ince the birth of the republic, black Americans have been the great exception to its assimilation paradigm" but he doesn't think "ethnic federalism" is the answer to the persisting racism that has kept those least foreign of all American minorities so alienated; nor does he favor its emulation by other nonwhite minorities, many of them recent immigrants from Asia and Latin America.

Salins is not alone in his concerns. The latest broadside attack on the new immigration, in particular the immigration of those from Latin America, is Samuel P. Huntington's *Who Are We?: The Challenge to America's National Identity*, published in 2004.[39] Although couching his concerns in learned language, Huntington expresses sentiments that are not far from those of old nativists. The message is a familiar one: There are strangers at the gate, and strangers within the gate. And, once again, they are seen as a threat to "real Americans." In yesterday's lingo, in addition to the racial slurs, the outsiders were also called "un-American dissidents," "communists," "anarchists"—and "moochers"; in today's they are "destabilizers," "disuniters," "deconstructionists"—and "welfare queens."

Huntington's book offers a very personal commentary on what he sees as the beginning of the end of *his* tormented tribe. His thesis is, in many ways, an argument claiming that something must be done to reverse course and reinvest power and privilege to those most deserving, that is, his fellow ethnics and coreligionists, those he calls the "Anglo-Protestants." In making his case, Huntington appeals to those who, like himself, see themselves as "victimized minorities in a country that once was theirs," clearly reviving what John Higham once called "the central apotheosis of a tribal spirit."[40]

Huntington begins with the following "observation" about "the low salience of national identity" before September 11, 2001.

> Among some educated and elite Americans, national identity seemed at times to have faded from sight. Globalization, Multiculturalism, cosmopolitanism, immigration, subnationalism, and antinationalism had battered American consciousness. Ethnic, racial and gender identities came to the fore. In contrast to their predecessors, many immigrants were ampersands, maintaining dual loyalties and dual citizenship....
>
> The celebration of diversity replaced emphasis on what Americans had in common. The national unity and sense of national identity created by work and war in the eighteenth and nineteenth centuries and consolidated in the world wars of the twentieth century seemed to be eroding.[41]

His observation ends with a bit of sarcastic hyperbole. "By 2000, America was in many respects, less a nation than it had been for a century. The Stars and Stripes were at half mast and other flags flew higher on the flagpole of American identity."[42] And it gets worse. So harsh are some of his words and judgments that many parts seem as if they were written in 1904, a time when other notable scholars were terribly worried about alien and subversive threats to a very precious way of life, instead of 2004.

In language that might have been written by some of the outspoken xenophobes mentioned in Chapter 4, "Immigrants become citizens," Huntington asserts, "not because they are attracted to America's culture and Creed, but because they are attracted by government welfare and affirmative action programs." [43] It is again being argued that immigrants—legal and illegal—imperil the system with their questionable pedigrees, their foreign ideas and bad habits, their subversive intentions, their willingness to toil for low wages, which undercut those of hardworking Americans, and their dependence on handouts from kindly almoners and public agencies when they can't find work.

Huntington seems to have little empathy for anyone who would disagree with his monoculturalism. Put differently, for Huntington there is only one culture. His.

In a thoughtful *New Yorker* review of *Who Are We?* Louis Menard calls the book "as blunt a work of identity politics as you are likely to find ... [It is] against foreigners and their threat to the very fabric of our society, echoing in its language and reasoning diatribes written a century earlier." Menard suggests that Huntington "is not interested in values per se; he is interested in national security and national power. He thinks that the erosion or diffusion of any cluster of collective ideals, whatever those ideals may be, leads to weakness and vulnerability."[44]

Menard may be correct in his assessment, but it must also be said that, because the members of the Old Establishment feel they have lost considerable influence, economic clout, and social standing over the past three or four decades, Huntington and those of his ilk seem to have reverted to old, simplistic arguments to hang on to the vestiges of their proclaimed entitlements while reverting to the practice of scapegoating on a grand scale. Today, instead of the unacceptable Irish, or the

Chinese of the "Yellow Peril," or the Jews and Italians and Slavs, or the Afrocentrists, it is now a frightening "Brown Wave" of Mexicans coming across the Rio
Grande who are poised to destroy American civilization.

In a critical chapter called "Fault Lines Old and New," Huntington minces few
words in creating, or trying to create, a self-fulfilling prophecy: "The most powerful stimulus to white nativism is likely to be the threat to language, culture, and
power that whites see coming from the expanding demographic, social, economic,
and political roles of Hispanics in American society."[45] One can almost hear the
voice of John Rowland once again: "And the one thing we can do right now is to
lock and bar the gate."[46]

In the arsenal of Huntington's cant are expressions that have recently been
heard in debates across the country: righteous indignation coated with cloying
religiosity, the protective posturing, and the assertion of how different and right
and better are "real Americans" in contrast to those with the audacity to challenge
them. Like George W. Bush, Huntington encourages a return to nationalism and
patriotism with fighting words about defending the *culture* (and "the homeland")
and protecting *the people*. Not surprisingly, he highlights the Arab-Islamic threat
post–September 11, 2001.

Although it may well be argued that there is a need for better screening of
outsiders and for greater surveillance of those in suspect populations, even worry
about organized terrorists entering through the porous southern border does not
explain the near paranoiac concerns Huntington and his sympathizers have about
our neighbors to—and from—the south, the Mexicans. In what is perhaps the most
substantive—and telling—chapter, "Mexican Immigration and Hispanization,"
Huntington offers his view on what he sees as an increasingly bifurcated society.
These pages are filled with statistics and charts that show rising numbers of immigrants, rising costs, and rising concerns about the political clout of the Mexicans.
Like Sam Roberts, the author of *Who Are We Now?*[47] Huntington points to the huge
growth of population in the United States in the 1990s and the fact that much of it
is attributable to increasing rates of immigration, especially from Mexico.

Samuel Huntington does raise a number of legitimate points about the character
of that flow and the failures of the Amnesty Bill of 1986 to stem it. He highlights
some important differences between Mexicans and other large groups of immigrants in the past, not least the fact that, save for the indigenous Americans,
Mexicans are the only people whose lands had been forcefully incorporated into
the United States—in the 1830s and 1840s. He notes the continued proximity of,
and easy access to Mexico today, which provides a constant cultural counterpull
to assimilationist entreaties. He notes that in the not-too-distant future (Roberts
estimates it will be by 2050) non-Hispanic whites in the aggregate will represent
a minority across the country, as they already are in California, and that there are
"Hispanic advocates" who reject the idea of a single national community and
cultural homogenization as they "seek to transform America as a whole into a
bilingual, bicultural society."[48]

But what Huntington fails to do is to look carefully at the increasing numbers
of studies that indicate that most Mexican Americans are following a course not

unlike those of other economic migrants from across the seas who came in the nineteenth century, drawn to America's shores by opportunities said to abound in the United States. Some of those were also "birds of passage," who moved back and forth, but like so many Mexicans today, any number eventually stayed, learned English and became Americans, even as they retained some significant vestiges of the old culture. Once again, the findings of the NPR/Kaiser/Kennedy School Poll on immigration issues are enlightening.

In questioning some 784 immigrants, the researchers learned that there were sharp differences in their own attitudes and other perceptions of them. For example,

> Immigrants are more likely than nonimmigrants to say that immigrants strengthen the country because of their hard work and talents, rather than be a burden on the country; they are more likely to say immigrants work harder than other Americans, less likely to believe that they take jobs away from Americans. Moreover, the findings clearly show that while immigrants keep some ties to their home country, it is not as much as many believe ... And, perhaps, not surprisingly, children of immigrants have views more like native-born Americans than like those in their countries of origin.[49]

There is little evidence that Samuel Huntington and other prominent critics of immigration in general, and Mexican immigration in particular, were moved by what the immigrants themselves had to say.

When Huntington's opening salvo was first published in the journal *Foreign Affairs,* there were many critical responses. They showed that surveys of Mexican Americans demonstrated a high degree of patriotism, an eagerness to participate in the society and more than a willingness to learn English, as clearly indicated in the work of Richard Alba and Victor Nee. In the recently published *Remaking the American Mainstream: Assimilation and Contemporary Immigration,* the authors point to the fact that in 1990 more than 95 percent of Mexican Americans between the ages of twenty-five and forty-four who were born in the United States could speak English well.[50] In another new book that is far more nuanced than Huntington's, *Impossible Subjects: Illegal Aliens and the Making of Modern America,* Mae Ngai and her colleagues make points similar to those of Alba and Nee. Various contributors to the book explain the reasons for the dramatic increases in border crossings by both legal and undocumented Mexicans.[51] Had Huntington looked at these studies and a number of others, his fears of a pending demographic debacle might have been calmed. But, from the start, he seems to follow that old saying "My mind is made up, don't confuse me with the facts."

But critiques of Huntington's arguments notwithstanding, a difficult question remains: If everyone who wants to come to the United States for whatever reason cannot be allowed to do so, who should be admitted? At a conference held in the late 1980s on "The Acculturation of New Americans," sponsored by the Institute on Pluralism and Group Identity of the American Jewish Committee, one participant, an economist, asked the assembled corps of policy makers—representatives of major volunteer agencies that work with immigrants and refugees, members of several ethnic organizations, and some foundation personnel and academics—a similar question: How many would favor unlimited immigration to the United States?[52] Not one said he or she would. But the experts could not, or would not, say whom they would admit and whom they would exclude.

Some members of minority groups who were at the meeting later commented that most Americans would probably be willing to continue to welcome as many Indochinese as wanted to come, as well as any number of anticommunists from Europe, including Soviet Jews and Pentacostalists, but would balk at large-scale requests from Africans or Latin Americans. They called this "racism," pure and simple. Others, also speaking off the record, argued that it was not racial prejudice per se but political and cultural bias, a preference for those fleeing left-wing dictatorships and those thought to have the skills or the "potential" for developing skills necessary for a modern industrial society.

The issue reached the halls of Congress when, in the last year of the Reagan administration, the Kennedy-Simpson Immigration Bill was introduced. (It was passed overwhelmingly in the Senate, failed in the House, and was resubmitted a year later.) The bill sought to alter certain provisions of the 1965 Immigration Act by including reductions in the family reunification system and the addition of an independent category of some 50,000 visas allocated on the basis of a point system that favored those with high educational levels, professionals over unskilled workers, and English language ability. The bill was denounced by many Hispanic and Asian representatives because of the favoritism shown to English speakers. They also opposed it because it would eliminate visas for married brothers and sisters under what is known the "fifth preference," used mostly by Hispanics and Asians to bring in relatives. Others from all over the world objected to the proposed elimination of "sixth preference" visas, those issued to unskilled workers who are in demand in the U.S. labor market.

Much of the controversy over the proposed legislation reflected deeply felt sentiments in our society. For some there was continuing concern about the changing character of American culture (being directly linked to debates about Americanization and bilingualism), a feeling—later to be spelled out in detail by Samuel Huntington—that "they" are so different from "us" that things will never be the same, and that a limit has to be imposed on what seems like a threat of inundation. For others, the threat was not that the newcomers were so different but that, whatever they are today, tomorrow they will be too similar: skilled competitors in a society in which ethnic ties remain a primary basis for group cohesion and for social action. The latter sentiment seemed especially to underlie the concerns of those who object to the high rate of emigration from Asia.

Debates about acculturation paradigms aside, as Ellis Cose has noted, "Congress had ended up with a most expansive result—one ensuring that an already steady stream of strange people knocking on America's door would swell into a torrent, heightening not only the potential for ethnic enrichment but also for ethnic turmoil."

The last five words highlight an old and familiar problem that, in recent years, has taken on renewed urgency, that is, finding a way to reconcile diversity—the most recent flow of immigrants contains the largest influx of nonwhites of any time since the peak years of the slave trade—with the renewal of group-based competition and further black alienation so characteristic of the years of the Great Migration and their immediate aftermath.

The recent tensions between new immigrants and old minorities, especially African Americans, in cities across the land are pointed indicators of the sorts of conflicts Cose fears.

The Continuing Dilemma

By the mid-1990s, many African Americans, concerned about those most disadvantaged in the society, found themselves in a paradoxical situation. They claimed that all around them things were improving for members of almost every sector of society save for theirs. And many added that the increasing presence of outsiders were bent on taking a large share of the hard-won entitlements set aside for the American poor. General impressions were corroborated in opinion surveys, which showed that, in general, the majority of those polled at random felt that immigrants get more from the United States through social services and unemployment benefits than they contribute. This sentiment was often expressed most strongly within lower socioeconomic groups.

In June 1995, after extensive research and a careful weighing of all concerns, a Select Commission on Immigration Reform, appointed by the President and chaired by former Congresswoman Barbara Jordan, made a series of recommendations. Among the most significant was to phase down the numbers to be admitted to the United States from the then current average of 750,000 per annum to 500–550,000 over a five-year period. Simultaneously, Congress was urged to alter the "preference system" for admission. Although still stressing family reunification, the commissioners felt priority should go only to spouses and minor children and should no longer be extended to parents of immigrants and resident aliens, nor to collateral kin such as brothers and sisters and, by extension, their families. Part of this was in reaction to mounting anti-immigration sentiment, especially in the six states that had the largest inflow—California, New York, Texas, Florida, New Jersey, and Michigan—and, incidentally, a very large percentage of minorities. But much of it was a value judgment that the stability of families is the most important thing to maintain for newcomers from abroad. Many commentators on inner city youth added that this was as true of the internal migrants such as African Americans who moved north.

Notes

1. Michael Novak, *The Rise of the Unmeltable Ethnics* (New York: Macmillan, 1971).

2. Ralph Levine, "Left Behind in Brooklyn," in *Nation of Nations,* Peter I. Rose, ed. (New York: Random House, 1973), p. 342.

3. See, for example, Ben Halpern, "The Ethnic Revolt," *Midstream* (January 1971), pp. 3–16.

4. Nathan Glazer and Daniel Patrick Moynihan have pointed out that, in many ways, the American ethnic groups are a new social form, having no counterpart anywhere. See *Beyond the Melting Pot,* 2nd ed. (Cambridge: M.I.T. Press, 1970), p. 16.

5. Michael Lerner, "Respectable Bigotry," *The American Scholar,* 38 (Autumn 1969), pp. 606–617.

6. Studs Terkel, "A Steelworker Speaks," *Dissent* (Winter 1972), pp. 12–13.

7. Glazer and Moynihan, op. cit., pp. xxxiv–xxxv.

8. Andrew Greeley, *Why Can't They Be Like Us?* (New York: Dutton, 1971), pp. 13–19.

9. See Lawrence Fuchs, *The American Kaleidoscope: Race, Ethnicity and the Civic Culture* (Middletown: University of New England Press, 1990).

10. See Peter Schrag, *Out of Place in America* (New York: Random House, 1970); and Michael Novak, op. cit.

11. *Ibid.,* p. 290. The reference is to Bob Wyrick, "The Three Worlds of Long Beach," *Newsday* (October 18, 1969), 6w.; *Dissent* (Winter 1972), pp. 278–285.

12. See, for example, Bayard Rustin, "'Black Power' and Coalition Politics," *Commentary,* 42 (September 1966), pp. 35–40; and "The Failure of Black Separatism," *Harpers,* 240 (January 1970), pp. 25–34. See also Orlando Patterson, *Ethnic Chauvinism: The Reactionary Impulse* (New York: Stein and Day, 1977).

13. Harold Isaacs, "The New Pluralists," *Commentary,* 53 (March 1972), pp. 75–79. See also Robert Alter, "A Fever of Ethnicity," *Commentary,* 53 (June 1972), pp. 68–73.

14. Ibid., p. 75.

15. Idem.

16. Andrea Hairston, "Polyrhythm-Wise: No More Bad Guys in Black Hats," Peter I. Rose (ed.), *Professorial Passions* (Northampton, Mass.: Smith College, 1998), pp. 49–58.

17. See Michael Lewis, *The Culture Inequality* (Amherst: University of Massachusetts Press, 1978).

18. See William J. Wilson, *The Declining Significance of Race* (Chicago: University of Chicago Press, 1978).

19. See section "Social Indicators of Black Progress in Vincent Parrillo, *Strangers to These Shores,* 4th ed. (New York: Macmillan, 1993), pp. 379–387.

20. See Michael Lind, "The Radical Center or Moderate Middle," *New York Times Magazine* (December 3, 1995), pp. 72–73.

21. NPR/Kaiser/Kennedy School Poll, *Immigration: Summary of Findings,* as reported in NPR.com, October 7, 2004, pp. 1–4.

22. Ibid., p. 4.

23. Wilson, op. cit.

24. Ibid., p. 1.

25. Ibid., p. 2.

26. See William Julius Wilson, *The Truly Disadvantaged* (Chicago: University of Chicago Press, 1987).

27. See Anthony Gary Dworkin and Rosalind J. Dworkin (eds.), *The Minority Report* (New York: Holt Rinehart & Winston, 2d ed., 1988), p. 125.

28. Idem.

29. Stephen Steinberg, *The Ethnic Myth: Race, Ethnicity, and Class in America* (New York: Beacon Press, 2nd ed, 1989), p. 288.

30. Ibid., pp. 288–289. See also, Stephen Steinberg's more recent study, *Turning Back: The Retreat from Racial Justice in American Thought and Policy* (Boston: Beacon Press, 1995).

31. Peter Kwong, *The New Chinatown* (New York: Hill and Wang, 1987.)

32. Thomas Sowell, *Ethnic America: A History* (New York: Basic Books, 1983).

33. For a testing of these assumptions, see Suzanne Model, West Indian Prosperity: Fact or Fiction?, *Social Problems,* 42:4 (November, 1995), pp. 535–553.

34. Idem.

35. Orlando Patterson, "The Culture of Caution," *The New Republic* (November 27, 1995), p. 26.

36. See Paul Berman, "The Other and the Almost-the-Same," *New Yorker* (February, 1994). Also Peter I. Rose, "Blaming the Jews," *Society,* 31: 6 (October/November, 1994), pp. 35–40.

37. Vernon M. Briggs, Jr., *Mass Immigration and the National Interest* (Armonk, N.Y.: M. E. Sharpe, Inc, 1992).

38. Peter D. Salins, *Assimilation American Style* (New York: Basic Books, 1997).

39. Samuel P. Huntington, *Who Are We?: The Challenge to American Identity* (New York: Simon and Schuster, 2004).

40. John Higham, *Strangers in the Land: Patterns of American Nativism, 1860–1925,* (New Brunswick, NJ: Rutgers University Press, 1953), p. 123.

41. Huntington, p. 4.

42. Ibid., p. 5

43. Idem.

44. Louis Menard, "Patriot Games," *The New Yorker* (May 17, 2004).

45. Huntington, pp. 316–317.

46. John Rowland, "A Connecticut Yankee Speaks His Mind," *Outlook,* 136 (March, 1924), pp. 478–480.

47. Sam Roberts, *Who Are We Now?* (New York: Henry Holt, 2004).

48. Huntington, p. 316.

49. NPR/Kaiser/Kennedy School Poll, op. cit., pp. 4–7.

50. Richard Alba and Victor Nee, *Remaking the American Mainstream: Assimilation and Contemporary Immigration* (Cambridge, MA: Harvard University Press, 2003).

51. May Ngai, Gary Gerstle, and William Chafe (eds.), *Impossible Subjects Illegal Aliens and the Making of Modern America* (Princeton, NJ: Princeton University Press, 2004).

52. See *The Newest Americans,* a report of the American Jewish Committee's Task Force on the Acculturation of Immigrants to American Life, New York: American Jewish Committee, 1987.

Chapter 12

The Meanings of Multiculturalism

Celebration

After a decade of refurbishing, the hundred-year-old immigration facility at Ellis Island was rededicated in 1992. Americans of different backgrounds and from different shores—European, African, Asian, and Latino—came to New York to pay homage to all those things that that portal to America was said to represent: shelter, opportunity, liberty, justice. One person after another extolled the wonders of "the world's oldest democracy"; "our haven in a stormy sea"; "the land of the free"; "the world's only truly multicultural society." It was heady stuff, the sort of imagery that makes one proud to be an American.

Yet social scientists, journalists, and leaders of various minority communities who attended the festivities and many more who heard the speeches on radio or television found the commentary somewhat hyperbolic. They readily acknowledged the fact that there had been remarkable advances in intergroup relations in the century that had just passed, especially the integration of the children and grandchildren of the "tired and poor and tempest-tost" who came through Ellis Island in the years between 1892 and 1954 (the year the center was closed). They pointed to the acculturation of successive waves of newcomers, the sort of process so many foreign observers had noted when they wrote of the marvelous achievement of taking so many disparate Europeans, most of them impoverished and parochial, and making them into good, productive, and participating Americans. They further affirmed that most such people were, today, living proof of the notion that ours is a nation in which hyphens connect instead of separate, where having a name like

Cohen, Cuomo, or Kennedy, Celusniak, Dubinsky, or Papadopoulos, whose fore-bears came through the very same gates at Ellis Island, meant being Americans, too—as American as an Adams or a Cabot, a Bush or a Clinton. And going farther, they recognized and applauded marked successes in the realm of legal rights for all citizens, increased opportunities resulting from campaigns for civil rights and the implementation of affirmative action policies, and growing evidence of greater tolerance among most white Americans toward minorities. But they also reported that just across the harbor—and throughout the land—there were struggles that belied the lofty rhetoric of acceptance, inclusion, and unity. Now, fifteen years later, there still are.

Wretched slums not all that different from those that existed when the reception center was first dedicated still pock the cityscape. These days, however, instead of the babble of German, Italian, Polish, Yiddish, and brogue-heavy English, so confusing and offensive to the ears of many old Americans who felt they were being overrun by foreigners in the late 19th and early 20th centuries, the urban centers resound in Spanish, Chinese, Creole, Vietnamese, Arabic, and Black English. What many of those who speak in such languages and dialects face—racism, poverty, alienation, rivalry with others in similar straits, and envy for those who have managed to es-cape—has a depressing familiarity, particularly to those close at hand.

City councilors, police authorities, social workers, schoolteachers, factory man-agers, storekeepers, journalists, bail bondsmen, welfare mothers, gang members, local residents, and nearby neighbors know that the nation's poorest communities are seething caldrons of competition and intergroup tension, and, to paraphrase Bob Dylan, they do not need outside pundits to tell them that they are boiling over.

There are still "in-groups" and "out-groups." Despite the many reasons to cel-ebrate the success of so many in moving from the margins into the mainstream of American society; despite the growth of a significant middle class in almost every ethnic group, including that of African and Mexican Americans; despite far greater visibility of minorities, and not just those of European background, in positions of power and influence—and celebrity—barriers still exist. Many of these barriers are rooted in a prejudice that is nurtured by institutionalized practices of discrimination, and manifest in persistent scapegoating and differential treatment. And although the effects are evident in many sectors of society and at many levels, those who suffer most are those farthest removed from the arenas of social intercourse between groups, especially the ghetto poor.

In those neighborhoods so geographically close to Ellis Island and the Statue of Liberty and in other parts of urban America such as Washington, D.C., Philadelphia, Chicago, and Los Angeles, as well as in many rural regions, large segments of the population are hardly better off than they were a decade or two ago. In many places they are in worse shape. The plight of too many Puerto Ricans, Mexican Ameri-cans, recently arrived refugees from Haiti and Somalia, and African Americans has been further aggravated by intergroup rivalry, a shortage of jobs, a deterioration of communal structures, a sharp rise in levels and technology of violence, and, in too many circumstances, a growing desperation born of anomic conditions marked by the collapse of social institutions and a holding back on public assistance for healthcare as well as welfare. Without major changes in ways those in positions to influence social conditions act, the outlook for a reversal of fortune is not great. The virus of social entropy, a disease manifest in the breakdown of communal spirit as well as the social structure, is spreading. Many feel that unless means of healing the many affected by it and ways of preventing its further spread are implemented, there will be ever-greater alienation on the part of many who constitute the poorest, weakest elements—*and a great threat to society.* Again, echoes of the dichotomy between "they" and "we." *They* are the folks with the disease; *we* are the ones who will suffer if it is not cured! But what is the cure?

It is not that no one cares about the urban poor. From New Deal days to the present, efforts have been made to address their needs. But few have found the way to effect major changes without doing things that would mean unacceptable alterations in the political economy and/or too much personal sacrifice on their own parts. Even when good intentioned attempts have been made to stimulate change, they frequently have been instigated without full comprehension of their consequences, and then greeted with horror when things seem to go awry.

Aaron Wildavsky once described the risks of such misunderstandings: "Promise a lot; deliver a little.... . Lead people to believe they will be much better off, but let there be no dramatic improvement.... . Feel guilty about what has happened to black people; tell them you are surprised that they have not revolted before; express shock and dismay when they follow your advice."[1]

Revolts have occurred. Some, such as the riots in Watts in the 1960s and in South Central Los Angeles in the 1990s, have been violent and dangerous. Many others have been less raucous but also disruptive, shaking not only the social order but the conscience of the public. The Black Power Movement was one clear expression of such a revolt. Its more recent incarnation, expressed in such singular activities as the Million Man March on Washington a decade ago and the much broader campaign to challenge "Eurocentric hegemony," a central theme of the new multiculturalism, are two others. For the participants in most such activities, there is an underlying theme: a desire to lift the burden of oppression, to take charge of one's own destiny. For the others there is a very direct message, something expressed long ago in Richard Wright's telegraphic admonition "White man, Listen!"[2]

Different Drummers?

Referring to the riots that occurred in South Central Los Angeles in 1992, the black scholar Cornel West offered a thoughtful commentary on the divisions that persist in this society and in the continuation of the "they and we"—or what he calls "us versus them"—mentality that seems, he says, to prevail over a consensus about the common good. West suggested that a dialogue on the real meaning of race in America is long overdue.

> It must begin not with the problems of black people but with the flaws in American society—flaws rooted in historical inequalities and longstanding cultural stereotypes.

How we set up the terms for discussing racial issues shapes our perception and response to these issues. As long as black people are viewed as "them," the burden falls on blacks to do all the "cultural" and "moral" work necessary for healthy race relations. The implication is that only certain Americans can define what it means to be American—and the rest must simply "fit in." The emergence of strong black nationalist sentiments among blacks, especially young people, is a revolt against this sense of having to "fit in."[3]

To many commentators, the kind of revolts West describes are potentially more disruptive than another urban riot. They can also have much more far reaching effects, especially so if led by those

... who can situate themselves within the larger historical narrative of this country and world, who can grasp the complex dynamics of our peoplehood and imagine a future grounded in the best of our past, yet attuned to the frightening obstacles that now perplex us. Our ideals of freedom, democracy and equality must be invoked to invigorate all of us, especially the landless, propertyless and luckless. Only a visionary leadership that can motivate "the better angels of our nature," as Lincoln said, and activate possibilities for a freer, more efficient and stable America.... . Either we learn a new language of empathy and compassion, or the fire this time will consume us all.[4]

The Reverend Louis Farrakhan and his companions who organized the Million Man March on Washington had been acutely sensitive to the feelings of the "landless, propertyless and luckless." Indeed, it was for them, and for the working class and their families that, Farrakhan claimed, black *men* would be marching on October 16, 1995.

Before it was to take place, a number of African American leaders, including some members of "the old elites and voices that recycle the older frameworks," were asked to comment about its significance, especially in light of the fact that it had been called by the controversial Muslim leader, Farrakhan, and that he extended his invitation only to black males. Some, such as Jesse Jackson, said that, despite concerns about the leadership, they would attend—and did. So did a number of others who had attended the integrated March on Washington led by Martin Luther King, Jr., some thirty-two years earlier.

But there were those who refused to participate. Among them, Congressman John Lewis, a former official of the Student Non-Violent Coordinating Committee, who had been beaten almost to death by an angry mob of white racists in the late 1950s. In a lengthy statement Lewis explained the basis of his decision not only to forego the then still forthcoming Million Man March but also to oppose its premise. He began with a reflection on the earlier march that took place in 1963: "In the sea of humanity before me, I saw blacks and whites. Protestants, Catholics and Jews. I saw people in my organization ... wearing buttons with a black hand shaking a white hand—and that became our symbol. We really did believe in integration and in the creation of what we called 'the beloved community.'"[5]

"Thirty years ago I thought we would be further down the road toward an integrated society by now," Lewis said. But he had not given up. Although acknowledging that its general goal of "encouraging African American men to be responsible is sound," he said he wouldn't attend the Million Man March because "it goes against what I have worked for—tolerance, inclusion.... .[6]

After the March a number of those like John Lewis, who had opposed it, had some second thoughts. This included a number of black women as well as many male and female white Americans, especially some who called themselves conservative. (Said one commentator, "Many of the themes of the Million Man March are echoed in Republican rhetoric: family values, self-sufficiency, the power of market economics.)[7] Although decrying the bigotry of the organizer and his message of separation, a number of skeptics now said they recognized the empowering character of so disparate a cross-section of African Americans gathered together to foreswear despair and rededicate themselves to the support of kith, kin, and community. They hoped such efforts would make a difference both in the way African Americans saw themselves and in the views of others.

What they thought was also reflected in the sense of those who were there. David Ruffin, editor of *Focus,* the monthly bulletin of the Joint Center for Political and Economic Studies, reported that for months before he had been getting hints that "something big was building."

> I'd heard expressions of enthusiasm about joining the event from younger men with blue collar jobs who tended to be disconnected from politics. [But] many of the middle-class, college educated men over forty I know had strong reservations about the march, because of the discomfort with its principal organizers or with the fact that women weren't invited....
>
> I predicted ... that most who would show up in Washington on October 16 would be nonprofessional men in their late teens and early twenties who had never been politically active. I was wrong.[8]

David Ruffin's report was accompanied by a statistical profile based on a survey conducted by Howard University and the Wellington Group. In addition to the demographics and the answers to questions about political affiliation and ideology and candidate preference, the study—and Ruffin—revealed that, contrary to the assumptions of many that the "messenger" was the magnet, it was the "message" that energized the participants. Ruffin claimed that "Attending the march was an expression of black unity and a way to affirm what is best among African American men"[9]—a sentiment corroborated by most other participating observers.

Whether intended or not, the March became at once a counter to the Ellis Island jubilee celebration and its functional equivalent. In the first place, it was a closed affair, limited to members of a particular cohort, African American males, rather than the open welcome to all in New York. Yet both gatherings were assertions of pride and purpose: pride in past achievement, calls for further unity. But each was also a symbol of two rather different "takes" on American society, the one showing how far we have come, the other saying how far we have yet to travel. Each was also a reflection on strategies or, perhaps, the "ownership" of strategies for achieving a fair and just solution to America's oldest dilemma: the question of race in a multicultural society.

Table 12.1 Million Man March—A Statistical Profile

Age
18–29 years: 34 percent   30–44: 43 percent   45 and older: 23 percent

Education
Less than high school 5 percent, High school graduate 22 percent, Some college 34 percent, Graduate or professional school 14 percent

Income
Under $24,999: 17 percent $25,000–49,000: 37 percent $50,000–74,999: 23 percent
Over $75,000: 18 percent

Political Party Preference
Democrats 62 percent, Republicans 3 percent, Independents 20 percent, Other 15 percent

Ideology
Liberal 31 percent, Moderate 21 percent, Conservative 13 percent, Nationalist 11 percent, Other 25 percent

Presidential Candidate Preference
Colin Powell 37 percent, Jesse Jackson 23 percent, Bill Clinton 14 percent, Ross Perot 3 percent, Bob Dole 1 percent, None 22 percent

Note: Percentages may not add up to 100 percent.
Source: Howard University Political Science Department and The Wellington Group, a market research firm based in Oaklyn, New Jersey.

Cornel West, John Lewis, and others, including Shelby Steele, Toni Morrison, Angela Davis, Ronald Takaki, Gerald Graff, Stanley Crouch, and Henry Louis Gates, had been drawn into the debates not only about the March, but about the Rodney King verdict, O. J. Simpson's acquittal, the divisions in opinions about both, and some things less "immediate" but far more lasting: the matters of multiculturalism and what came to be known more broadly as "The Culture Wars." Although the conflicts over these latter issues were to take place in the universities, they were not purely academic. To appreciate them, it is important to understand the social topography of the battlefields and the character of the disputed turf—much of it intellectual but all of it highly political.

New Trends on Campus

Two decades after the tumultuous 1960s, colleges and universities that had reeled under the constant strain of political polarization and confrontation seemed quite oblivious to the debates that were still so central to social scientists. In fact, across the country, the onset of the Reagan Era seemed to have signaled a redux of the 1950s and a final break from the 1960s. Group-oriented activism gave way to self-centered personalism characterized best by the materialistic, style-setting "yuppies"—young, urban, professionals. The change was noticeable in course enrollments and the choice of majors, especially in the social sciences. Sociology, which had flourished in the heyday of civil rights and antiwar protest, lost students; economics gained them, and business administration thrived with a new respectability.

In the later years of the Reagan presidency, it was on some of these same campuses that things began to change yet again. According to Shelby Steele, two phenomena led to a heightening of tension and, in many places, even sharper divisions along racial and ethnic lines.[10] The first was the result of the successes of the group rights campaigns of the 1960s and 1970s, which had made even the most elite of universities far more open to the enrollment of individuals from very different backgrounds, far more diverse in student composition than ever before. The second was the result of the additional measures taken to further ensure that the trend toward the integration of the schools did not abate, even when those minorities best qualified to compete were able to go where they wanted. It was not enough to remove the color bar; the affirmative action policies on college and university campuses, though increasingly under attack, were in fact expanded and more carefully monitored.

In spite of the significant increase in the presence of nonwhites (now including many Asians) on campuses—or perhaps because of it—in the middle of the 1980s "race" again became a topic of concern. In some places it was a subject for positive action, most dramatically characterized by coalitional campaigns to demand that regents of public institutions and members of boards of trustees of private ones divest themselves of stockholdings in companies doing business in what was still a white-dominated South Africa.

But in many places it was not apartheid abroad or segregation in their hometowns that brought out the protesters: it was both the social and academic aspects of life on campus. The first had to do with patterns of interaction where students of color sometimes followed the mechanism of minority adaptation known as defensive insulation, while, simultaneously, challenging what they saw as persistent biases in the standard curriculum. (A similar charge was made regarding "sexist biases" and parallel demands were made to revamp courses and programs to address the contributions and roles of women.)

Beginning in 1986, at colleges from New England to California, there were ugly racial incidents ranging from name calling and graffiti writing ("Niggers, Spics, and Chinks: If You Don't Like It Here, Go Back To Where You Came From") to cross burnings and direct physical violence. Minority students, especially African Americans (who were most often the targets), responded with petitions, marches, rallies, sit-ins, and takeovers of administrative offices. One campus observer noted that " ... much of what they were marching and rallying about seemed less a response to [the] specific racial incidents than a call for broader action on the part of the colleges and universities they were attending."[11]

Many who had been involved in or had firsthand memories of the campus turmoil of the 1960s viewed the incidents with a sense of déjà vu, a seeming replay of an earlier scenario. Black students were again making demands: more African American faculty members, more courses on "The Black Experience," more attention to the issue of diversity. (In many places across the country, most notably on the West Coast, these demands were matched by those of Asian and Latino students.) Yet, for all the similarities, there were differences between the protests of the earlier period and the more recent ones.

Those undergraduates involved in the new debates were born after the passage of the 1964 Civil Rights Act. They grew up in an age when racial equality was for the first time enforceable by law. This too was a time when African Americans suddenly appeared on television, as mayors of big cities, as icons of popular culture, as teachers, and in some cases even as neighbors. Today's black and white college students, veterans of Sesame Street and often of integrated grammar and high schools, have had more opportunities to know each other—whites and blacks—than any previous generation in American history. Not enough opportunities, perhaps, but enough to make the notion of racial tension on campus something of a mystery... ."[12]

Shelby Steele suggested that the mystery might be partly explained by recognizing that the new problem became how to live in an atmosphere of assumed equality instead of the old context of presumed, if sometimes challenged, inequality. "On a campus where members of all races are gathered, mixed together in the classroom as well as socially, differences are more exposed than ever."[13] Minority students often found themselves caught on the horns of a dilemma. If they seemed to accept the newfound openness that did exist on many campuses, they were seen by some of their more militant "sisters" and "brothers" as sellouts. But if they maintained a kind of separate existence, in special houses and cultural centers, they would be betraying what had been fought for so diligently in the Civil Rights Era.

At American universities many involved in new movements for group solidarity also wanted recognition and representation. Many of their spokespersons argued that, although they may be engaged in "the politics of difference," their goals were to enhance inclusion and try to alter the structures of society and the character of the universities for the benefit of everyone. In a seeming replay of the demands of those engaged in campus demonstrations in the 1960s, some again began calling for separate facilities for their own group meetings, financial and administrative support for lecturers and other visitors who would present "alternate" views, shifts in departmental and program priorities, and curricular changes that would "begin to neutralize the hegemonic cabal of dead, white males." Included in the newer proposals were those for new courses of study that would include other perspectives and, more pointedly, "the perspectives of others."

Many white students were puzzled by what they perceived as the desire for self-segregation on the part of minority students. Public opinion data clearly indicated that, having grown up in an period when the acceptance of diversity was far more actively promoted than in the past, most were quite prepared to encounter people different from themselves and were far more open to meeting them than many in the minorities believed to be possible. Their suspicions of the latter may have been exacerbated by the tendency of many universities to offer special orientation programs for minority students—programs intending to ease their way into the new environments but that, in some instances intentionally and in others inadvertently, reinforced notions of how different they were from those in the dominant group. In certain cases, first-year students and transfers from other schools were told, often by peer leaders, how to prepare themselves for slurs and snubs, how to organize to fight racism, and the importance of bonding with others in similar straits.

Such activities often proved to be self-fulfilling. Many of those who had come from quite integrated environments but told they would feel alienated, felt alienated. They looked more at examples of negativity and rejection on the part of others (which *were* to be found on many campuses—some quite blatant, others more subtle) than at the much more pervasive, if elusive, signs of acceptance.

The programs to socialize minority students and prepare them for potential hostility had their parallels in the cases of women—white and nonwhite—and of those sometimes called "lifestyle" minorities, especially gays and lesbians.

In the case of all these groups, the deliberations increasingly shifted from social activities to more academic ones, and especially to the character of what was being taught, and how. Sometimes those who belonged to none of the "minority" cohorts called themselves "allies" or some variant and joined forces with them. Students organized to demand some restructuring of the curriculum to make it more inclusive and balanced, to introduce perspectives that, they claimed, had always been over-looked or deliberately underplayed. They sought supporters and faculty advocates among the social scientists who had been the principal partners in the struggle of the 1960s and now those in the Humanities, where many battles in the "culture wars" were to be waged in the waning decade of the twentieth century.

In a forceful essay on the debate over the demands to make core curricula less "Western" and to include in the basic canon the works of minority writers and women, Henry Louis Gates, Jr., suggested that much of the conflict had arisen as new voices with significant representation on the campuses began to challenge what he calls the "antebellum esthetic position … when men were men and men were white, when scholar-critics were white men and when women and people of color were voiceless, faceless servants and laborers, pouring tea and filling brandy snifters in the boardrooms of old boys' clubs."[14] Those leading the campaign to reshape the character of traditional education, challenging the assertions of the new cultural right, began to use the collective strength of newly present groups to assert their critical theories.

Many of the battles were won as colleges and universities adopted policies that led to greater appreciation for the varieties of human experiences and expressions, as, once again, they sought to increase the numbers of minority faculty members and students and devoted more money to the general cause of multicultural education. In a number of places, distribution requirements came to include courses on diversity. Although the civil rights of all was an underlying issue, the main thrust of the new programs and curricular innovations seemed to be on the cultural side, that is, to highlight the contributions of nonwhite minorities in world and American history. Most positive was a shift from a focus on "victimology," or what has been done to this group or that, to a "celebration" of how its strength has been enhanced by certain styles and experiences, and how much others benefit from knowing about this. It was a central part of the new movement called "multiculturalism."

Threat and Promise

As every reader of this book must surely know by now, throughout American history a variety of terms have been used to describe the United States. Many have to do with the *multicultural* character of the country. Even without using the adjective, it was implicit in the images conjured and discussed in earlier chapters: To Whitman, ours is a "Nation of nations;" to Horace Kallen, a "symphony;" to John Kennedy, "a nation of immigrants." More recently, Lawrence Fuchs used the metaphor of a "kaleidoscope" with its multicolored and variegated parts.[15] In each instance, the emphasis was a play on the theme of the motto *E pluribus unum,* "Out of many, one."

Sometime during the past two decades the descriptive adjective "multicultural," by the addition of a short suffix, "ism," was turned into a somewhat different ideology, one that was construed as being far removed from its earlier hyphen-connecting roots. Multiculturalism came to be used by some and seen by many as a term to describe resistance to such traditional views and to offer an alternative. It was in reaction to what was felt to be a failure of integrative pluralism to recognize or appreciate the rich contributions of the widest variety of America's people to the common good.

Some critics saw the neglect of the culture, literature, and music of certain, mainly nonwhite minorities as a clear reflection of persisting racism. And even those who saw less malevolence in what they came to call "Eurocentric biases" noted that, by seeing minorities only as victims, villains, fools, or menaces, those in schools and universities and in the media were still contributing to the perpetuation of stereotypes of many fellow citizens.

The move toward a greater appreciation for the contributions of those of non-European background was nothing new. It has a long history dating back to the Harlem Renaissance in the 1920s when the expression of musical, artistic, and literary forms that were to form the core of the most important yet least credited aspects of what the world knows as "American popular culture" were germinating. It was revived again in the late 1960s with the rise of Black Power and its counterpart, the ethnic consciousness movement, which led to expansion of affirmative action programs and the emergence of cultural centers, departments of Afro-American Studies and of Latino American and Asian American Studies and many related programs on a number of college campuses. The main difference was that, in previous times, the principal rationale of those who pushed for these was to enhance access and to fill the void in their own education. Although there was discussion of the importance of such augmentations of regular offerings, many administrators and traditional faculty members saw them as acquiescence to the militancy of minority students. It was a form of "giving *them* their just due," another good example of "they/we" thinking. Yet, it was effective to the extent that the racial and cultural mix of colleges and universities and many other institutions was greatly expanded.

The more recent campaigns have had a somewhat different focus. And the message is even more complex. Many want multiculturalism to be the instrument of the education and enlightenment of those others who are ignorant of their ways or those of their people, a way of opening the minds of those who have been too narrowly grounded in a single tradition (Western civilization) and "need liberation from their provincialism." Others, from radical feminists to Afrocentrists, go farther, offering not only information but also new ways of thinking and interpreting.

What many multiculturalists have in common is the sense of responsibility to their "sisters" and "brothers"—for seeing that things are changed, the things being assessments of their own pasts and prospects for their own futures. (Here the "they/we" dichotomy may remain but the positions of the sides are reversed!)

Among those who anticipated this new development was Milton Gordon, the sociologist who had written so insightfully about cultural and structural assimilation. Sensitive to the growing frustration of the "never hads" among the urban poor and the tendency of those who claimed to represent them in the political sphere and, even more often on the campus, as long ago as 1981, Gordon predicted there would be a resurgence of demands for group rights and a new "corporate" form pluralism, an alternative to the earlier "liberal" version.[16]

Gordon further argued that deciding which approach to pluralism to adopt, or which path to follow, would become an issue not only for scholars of American culture but for the society as a whole. Resolving this "new American dilemma," as he referred to the problem, "will have much to do with determining the nature, shape, and destiny of racial and ethnic relations in America in the twenty-first century."[17] In the early 1990s, the historian Arthur M. Schlesinger, Jr., angered by what he felt was undermining the liberal agenda on which he had committed much of his work, suggested that the time had already come to make the choice. He posited the dilemma as a challenge to the inclusive trend of American democracy by multicultural separatists. In a lengthy attack against "the ethnicity rage in general and Afrocentricity in particular," Schlesinger saw such movements as serious threats that "not only divert attention from the real needs but exacerbate the problems."[18] "The recent apotheosis of ethnicity, black, brown, red, yellow, white, has revived the dismal prospect that in happy melting pot days American thought the republic was moving safely beyond—that is, a society fragmented into ethnic groups. The cult of ethnicity exaggerates differences, intensifies resentments and antagonisms, drives ever deeper the awful wedges between races and nationalities."[19]

Schlesinger's major thesis, expanded in the last two chapters of *The Disuniting of America,* was that the multiculturalists were the vanguard of those who would reverse the course of history to the point where the country would see itself "as composed of groups more or less indelible in their ethnic character."[20] "Are we," he asked, "to let the *pluribus* overrule the *unum?*"

This question, raised early in the twentieth century by many who, like Theodore Roosevelt, opposed any sort of "hyphenation," was being asked again. Although in the old days the debate was between the "assimilationists" and the "pluralists," it became one between those who wanted to go way beyond the basic premises of the old pluralists and their view of many peoples bound together by a common set of civic and moral values and those who advocated a much more narrowly conceived sense of competing sensibilities. It is not enough to celebrate the diversity of backgrounds, they argued, it has to involve recognition of fundamental differences.

It is hardly necessary to state that members of minority groups, especially nonwhite ones, were then and are still well aware of the difficulty of erasing their "indelible" ethnic character because of the persistence of those who have prevented their full integration. On the contrary, too many feel that they have too often been forced to succumb to others' definitions of their cultures and their conditions. Those who are the most ardent defenders of multiculturalism have noted that Schlesinger and many others in his camp admit that "American history has long been written in the interests of white Anglo-Saxon males" but seek a kind of absolution for whatever sins have been perpetrated by such biases by noting their own solid liberal credentials and the fact that they rarely fail to discuss slavery, the harsh treatment of native peoples, and the exploitation of immigrants.

Historian Ronald Takaki, a leading figure in the movement to broaden the horizons of all Americans through multicultural education, points out that such a "discussion on racial oppression is perfunctory and parsimonious," and that such writers still devote the bulk of their attention to the defense of traditional approaches—and stances.[21]

What happens, Takaki asks, when minority peoples try to define their own histories and conditions? To Schlesinger and other opponents, whatever they called themselves, those who attempt this are seen as subversive particularists. Those opposed to the wide-ranging array of people grouped together as "multiculturalists" often argue that *they* cannot be trusted, for *they* will be ethnocentric, telling lies, exaggerating things in their own favor. Just imagine, they say, "When cohort membership becomes the *sine qua non* of identity and power, extremists will claim that Columbus was an intruder, not a discoverer; that Jefferson was a participant in activities that denied the very spirit of the Declaration of Independence; and that FDR was a racist!"

This is clearly a counter to those assumptions that "since only we know what's good for them, only we can assess their reality," the kind that reminds those with a different sense of history than, say, Schlesinger's, of Jules Feiffer's pointed commentary on an earlier stage of the struggle for access and recognition by African Americans and other minorities. One of his cartoon characters, a white, presumably liberal man appropriately dressed in suit and buttoned-down shirt, says to his clone, "Civil rights used to be so much more tolerable until the Negroes got into it."[22]

Writing about the alchemy of race, civil rights, and the legacy of racism, Patricia Williams puts this sentiment in poignant perspective. Speaking of "something as rich, soulful and sonorously productive as black depression," she said,

> It may be different when someone white is describing need.... black needs suddenly acquire the sort of stark statistical authority that lawmakers can listen to and politicians hear. But from blacks, stark statistical statements of need are heard as strident, discordant, and unharmonious. Heard not as political but only against the backdrop of their erstwhile musicality, they are again abstracted to mood and angry sounds.... For blacks ... the battle is not deconstructing rights, in a world of no rights; nor of constructing statements of need, in a world of abundantly apparent need. Rather the goal is to find a political mechanism that can confront the denial of need.[23]

Schlesinger and others of his persuasion argue that any acceptance of the demands of the multiculturalists is the first step in a slippery slope leading the country toward its ultimate disintegration. This extreme view is not widely shared. However, the issue on which they focus, often spoken of as the "strain toward balkanization," and its many ramifications are being debated in many places today.

The debates tend to center on three often overlapping issues: the meanings and relevance of multiculturalism; what should be taught and what belongs in the "literary canon;" and the relationships between civil rights and individual liberties, most clearly expressed in discussions of "political correctness" and academic freedom.[24]

In her presidential address "On Difference," presented to the Modern Language Association in 1990, Catherine R. Stimpson touched on all these issues but commented mainly on various reactions to the upsurge of interest in multiculturalism. Among those she cited was the concern by many of its practitioners that it would substitute "emotion for reason," a variation on the theme that has long pervaded attitudes to minorities. Others supportive of the move will not stay the full course and "will satisfy themselves with academic reform and not take on the harder task of social change." Then, though cautioning against "the indulgence of romanticizing one's own group and demonizing others,"[25] she spoke of those on whose behalf many battles in the culture wars were being waged. "For still others, with whom I am in much sympathy, multiculturalism promises to bring dignity to the dispossessed and self-empowerment to the disempowered, to recuperate the texts and traditions of ignored groups, to broad cultural history."[26]

With some notable exceptions, the stances of the antagonists in all the debates on multiculturalism and the related topics are not only philosophically significant, they are also sociologically interesting, for they are frequently related to group membership (meaning, in the instance, class, status, power, gender, age, and, especially, ethnic/racial group membership). Not surprisingly, those who have become successful, particularly but not exclusively the old white ethnics and their children, favor what Gordon called the liberal approach—which Diane Ravitch called "pluralistic multiculturalism" as opposed to a more "particularistic multiculturalism"[27]—and see the other one less as a means of enhancing the richness of the society than as the vehicle for its disintegration. On the other hand, those who are still on the outside, who have suffered discrimination generally greater than that ever conferred upon the others, want to use collective action to satisfy a desire for acceptance on their own terms. W. E. B. Du Bois's famous statement about having two warring souls in one body (first referred to in Chapter 6) and stating that "one ever feels his twoness, an American, a Negro," is followed with a desire: "He simply wishes to make it possible for a man to be both a Negro and an American, without being cursed and spit upon."[28]

If African Americans can achieve this still relevant twin goal, then the marches in the streets and messages conveyed in classrooms will have been triumphant. The victories will be theirs but they will also be those of a society in which what George Frederickson calls the peculiarly American "arrogance of race"[29] will have been finally put to rest.

Song of Myself

Throughout this book on racial and ethnic relations in the United States, there has been an emphasis—some critics might say an undue emphasis—on the plight of African Americans. In Chapter 5, there is a long section on "unique Americans";

in Chapter 8, responses of African Americans are used to illustrate "Reactions to Discrimination"; in Chapter 10, on "Pride and Protest," it is *Black* Pride and *Black* Protest that are highlighted. Although the topic is "Multiculturalism," this chapter also focuses more on the disputes between those in the dominant groups and African Americans than on others. The reason for this distinction is based on a fundamental truth: *Tocqueville was right.*

A quarter of a century before the Civil War, Alexis de Tocqueville predicted that, even with the emancipation of the slaves, the racial situation in the United States would be a continuing source of domestic unrest. Writing in the 1830s, Tocqueville expressed the fear that the majority of whites would never overcome their views of the innateness of their own superiority and that the majority of blacks would never lose their enmity for the humiliation and suffering they had experienced.[30] Tocqueville claimed that what we now call "racism" would "perpetually haunt the imagination of Americans, like a painful dream."[31]

Some seventy years later the African American leader W. E. B. Du Bois claimed that "race" would be *the* problem of the twentieth century. The Swedish observer Gunnar Myrdal, writing in the middle of the Second World War, a war in which the racist policies of the Third Reich threatened to wipe out an entire people and nearly succeeded, claimed that "the Negro Problem" was America's main dilemma.[32] And just a few years ago, looking back over all that his people had been through, and all they had achieved in persistent struggles against the inequities of institutional racism and various forms of segregation, the widely recognized "Dean of Black Historians," John Hope Franklin, sadly concluded that "race" is still our number one domestic problem as we face the new millennium. He was correct. Now, nearing the end of the first decade of the twenty-first century, although there have been renewed signs of progress, most evident in the greater integration of government offices, universities, and workplaces, the legacy of slavery lingers on.

Blacks remain apart and their destinies are still too much in the hands of others. Nathan Glazer has recently written, "Thirty years of effort, public and private, assisted by antidiscrimination law and a substantial rise in black earnings, have made little effect on this pattern."[33] The pattern to which he refers is the one rooted in slavery and the caste-line of harsh segregation that is different from that even of other "colored" minorities.

> For Hispanics and Asian Americans, marked in varying degrees by race, it is largely a matter of choice, their choice, just how they will define their place in American society. We see elements in these groups who, in their support of bilingual education and other foreign language rights, want to establish or preserve an institutional base for a separate identity that may maintain some resistance to the forces of assimilation.... . But the difference that separates blacks from whites, and even from other groups "of color" [that] have a [unique] history of discrimination and prejudice in this country is not to be denied.[34]

It is owing to this history that Glazer, long critical of efforts to pay special attention to African Americans, now believes controlling more of their own destinies to be "the most powerful force arguing for multiculturalism and for resistance to the assimilatory trend of American culture and American society."[35]

What has been missing most for too many African Americans have been options freed from those hat-in-hand dependencies that allow them but grudging entry to the big, white world.[36] Now many resisters to such a form of assimilation, are, in fact, trying to assert alternative means to their goals. The motivation for their actions, and the language of their spokespersons who articulate it, are reminders of Hillel's famous phrases relating to the plight of marginalized European Jews.

> If I am not for myself, who will be for me?
> [But] if I am only for myself, what am I?
> And, if not now, when?

What is striking is that despite considerable disputes about tactics, most who are trying new paths see their independent courses ending not in separate societies, perpetuating the idea of "two nations," but as fully participating members of one nation. Indeed, many feel an almost religious sense of a double mission: improve the lot not only of those for whom they claim to speak but all who are "luckless." Many firmly believe that the latest moves involving self-examination (using words like "atonement," "reassessment," and "redemptive acts"), communal dialogue and public debate, and various forms of collective action, even quite strident ones, may succeed in serving to lead them out of the conundrum and into the society on their own terms. The musings of the great American poet, Walt Whitman, in "Song of Myself," will then have renewed and special meaning.

> I am of old and young, of the foolish as much as the wise
> Regardless of others, ever regardful of others,
> Maternal as well as paternal, a child as well as a man,
> Stuff'd with the stuff that is coarse and stuff'd with the stuff that is fine,
> One of the Nation of many nations, the smallest the same and the largest the same.
> Of every hue and caste am I, of every rank and religion.
> I resist any thing better than my own diversity.[37]

Notes

1. Aaron Wildavsky, "Recipe for Violence," *New York* (May 1, 1968), p. 36.

2. Richard Wright, *White Man, Listen!* (Garden City, N.Y.: Doubleday, 1957).

3. Cornel West, "Learning to Talk of Race," *The New York Times Magazine* (August 2, 1992), pp. 24, 26.

4. Idem.

5. John Lewis, "Why We Marched in '63," *Newsweek* (October 23, 1995), p. 33.

6. Idem.

7. Howard Fineman, "Grappling with Race," *Newsweek* (October 23, 1995), p. 32.

8. David C. Ruffin, "Inside the Million Man March," *Focus* (October/November, 1995), p. 7.

9. Idem.

10. Shelby Steele, "The Recoloring of Campus Life," *The Atlantic* (February 1989), pp. 47–55.

11. Ibid, p. 47.

12. Ibid, p. 48.

13. Idem.

14. Henry Louis Gates, "Whose Canon Is It, Anyway?" *The New York Times Magazine* (February 26, 1989), pp. 44–45.

15. Lawrence Fuchs, *American Kaleidoscope: Race, Ethnicity and the Civic Culture* (Hanover, N.H.: University of New England Press, 1990).

16. Milton M. Gordon, "Models of Pluralism: The New American Dilemma," in Milton M. Gordon (ed.), *America as a Multicultural Society. The Annals of the American Academy of Political and Social Science,* 454 (Mar. 1981), pp. 187–88.

17. Idem.

18. Arthur M. Schlesinger, Jr., *The Disuniting of America: Reflections on a Multicultural Society* (Knoxville, TN: Whittle Communications, 1991), p. 2.

19. Ibid., p. 58.

20. Ibid., p. 2.

21. Ronald Takaki, "Battleground of Meeting Ground?" in Peter I. Rose (ed.), *Interminority Affairs in the U.S. Today: The Challenge of Pluralism. The Annals of the American Academy of Political and Social Science,* 530 (November 1993), 115.

22. The Jules Feiffer cartoon, from Robert Lantz, Candida Donadio Literary Agency, Inc., appears with permission in Peter I. Rose, *They and We,* 2nd ed. (New York: Random House, 1974), p. 79.

23. Patricia Waters, *The Alchemy of Race and Rights* (Cambridge: Harvard University Press, 1993), p. 152.

24. See Paul Berman, edition, *Debating P.C.: The Controversy over Political Correctness on College Campuses* (New York: Dell, 1992).

25. Catharine R. Stimpson, "On Differences," in *Debating P.C.,* op. cit, p. 57.

26. Ibid., p. 45.

27. Diane Ravitch, "Multiculturalism: E Pluribus Plures," *The American Scholar,* Summer, 1990, as reprinted in *Debating P.C.,* op. cit. pp. 271–298.

28. W.E.B. Du Bois, *The Souls of Black Folk* (1903), as reprinted in Three Negro Classics (New York: Avon Books, 1965), p. 2.

29. George Frederickson, *The Arrogance of Race: Historical Perspectives on Slavery, Racism and Social Inequality* (Middletown, CT: Wesleyan University Press, 1988).

30. See Peter I. Rose, introduction to Peter I. Rose, Stanley Rothman, and William J. Wilson (eds.), *Through Different Eyes: Black and White Perspectives on American Race Relations* (New York: Oxford University Press, 1973), p. v.

31. Alexis de Tocqueville, *Democracy in America,* Henry Reeve text revised by Francis Bowen (New York: Vintage Books, 1945), 2:391–92.

32. Gunnar Myrdal, *An American Dilemma* (New York: Harper, 1944).

33. Nathan Glazer, "Is Assimilation Dead?," in Peter I. Rose (ed.), *Interminority Affairs in the U.S. Today: The Challenge of Pluralism. Annals of the American Academy of Political and Social Science,* 530 (November, 1993), 135.

34. Ibid., pp. 135–136.

35. *Idem.*

36. See Mary Waters, *Ethnic Options,* (Berkeley: University of California Press, 1990).

37. Walt Whitman, "Song of Myself" from *Complete Poetry and Selected Prose* (edited by James E. Miller) (Boston: Houghton Mifflin, 1959).

Epilogue

Throughout the pages of this book, the focus has been on the nature of conflict and competition based mainly, if not exclusively, on social definitions of race and ethnicity, concepts grounded, often as not, on misperceptions of others. The "they versus we" motif has been a constant in a volume that touched on many subjects—prejudice, discrimination, actions, reactions—all couched in a framework of a "humanistic sociology," a sociology that demands both rigor in the assessment and analyses of social issues and empathy for those involved. This duality underscores the entire enterprise: learning about root causes of intergroup tension and current problems; getting to know *all* the players, those in positions of dominance and those called minorities—and those often caught in the middle; coming to terms with one's own values while learning "to see ourselves as others see us." This last idea, succinctly conveyed in the Kipling poem quoted in the beginning of Chapter 6 says it all.

> If you cross over the sea,
> Instead of over the way
> You may end by (think of it!) looking on We
> As only a sort of They.

What the poet said is rather easy to grasp intellectually. But to internalize such a sentiment and make it truly a part of one's own worldview, is quite another thing. In many ways it is the hardest lesson that those of us who conduct research and teach about intergroup relations try to convey.

When I first started teaching courses on "Ethnic Minorities in America," I was convinced that the only way to really come to grips with this conundrum was through direct involvement. You had to leave the ivory towers and go into the streets, becoming, as it were, at once a participant and an ethnographer. But I soon learned that one doesn't need to leave the classroom to at least start "crossing over the sea."

Over the years, that realization was reinforced on innumerable occasions, but never quite so dramatically or poignantly as one day a few years ago.

Two days earlier, I had told my students "the next time we meet we will be discussing integration." I began that next session by asking them what *they* thought the concept meant.

An African American sophomore spoke up immediately. "Well," she said, "speaking as a black woman ... "

Before she could finish her sentence, a white student interrupted. "Forgive me, but I'm sick and tired of having every comment by some of those here prefaced by the line 'Speaking as a black woman.' I don't begin every sentence with 'Speaking as a white woman!'"

I started to intervene when an angry voice boomed out of the back of the room. "You don't have to!"

The tension was palpable. Most of the black students were clearly upset; so, it appeared, were many of the other nonwhites in the class. The target of the sharp rebuke sat there stoic but clearly shaken. Most of the other white students looked almost as uncomfortable.

Although sharper than most, what we had all just witnessed was not, to me, an unusual exchange. But, somehow, I was especially dispirited by it that day.

Once things had calmed down a bit, I tried to use the incident itself as a basis for a conversation about what had just happened. It was tough going in the beginning but, once the ice was broken, it proved to be one of the best discussions we had all semester. Nearing the end of the period, I again asked if anyone could offer an explication of the term "integration." There was a pregnant silence.

Perhaps, I thought to myself, I've pushed them too hard and they need a breather. Then, with the hands on the clock moving toward the end of the 50–minute hour, a rather shy white student who had always seemed very engrossed but rarely spoke in class said she thought she could define it.

"When she," pointing to the black student who had first spoken out, "can do the things I take for granted, then we will have integration."

A simple truth—and a fitting coda.

Index

Hindus, 115
Hispanics, 80, 82-88, 85
  affirmative action, 221-22
  and census designation, 111
  and class subordination, 240
  enrolled in college, 17
  in Florida, 38
  increase in population of, 248-49
  as linguistic minority, 245
  place in society, 267
  social profile of, xii
  See also Latinos
Hitler, Adolf, 56, 132, 158
Hmong, 81
Hollinger, David, 11
Holmes, Oliver Wendell, 171
Holocaust, 171-72
Holsey, A. L., 188-89
home ownership, 162
homosexuals, xiii, 5, 262
Hong, Sung Chick, 146*n*13
hooks, bell, 107
Horton, Willie, 233
housing, discrimination in, 162-63, 166
Howard University, 258
Hraba, Joseph, 63
Hughes, Langston, 107, 187
humor, and discrimination, 154-58
Hungarians, 57, 63
Huntington, Samuel P., 5, 14, 85, 246-50
Hurston, Zora Neale, 107
Hussein, Saddam, 235, 237
Hutus, 172
Hyman, Jerry, 148*n*43

identity, 108
  American, 247
  denial of, 190-91
  ethnic, 228
  national, 247
  occupational, 228
  politics of, 221, 247
  pride in, 185-86
  and redress, 203-4
Ignacio, Lemuel, 79
Il Mezzogiorno, 57
immigrant model, 104
immigrants and immigration, xii, 53, 98
  adjustment problems, 100
  Chinese, 73-74

debate concerning, 243-51
Germans, 55-56
hardships of, 60-61, 86, 255-56
historical perspective of, 201-3
illegal, 83-84
Irish, 53-55
Jews, 64-68
Muslims, 68-70
quotas for, 63
restrictive legislation concerning, 62-64, 64, 97
role of women immigrants, 18
sentiments of, 227-28
total number by country of birth, 58-59*t*4.1
views of, 227-28, 238-39, 249
visas, 63, 64, 250
vs. settlers, 14
See also migration; *specific nationality*
Immigration Act of 1891, 62-63
Immigration Act of 1965, 250
Immigration and Nationality Act of 1952, 63
Immigration Quota Act of 1921, 63
Immigration Reform Act of 1965, xii, 48, 73, 76, 78
Immigration Restriction League, 63
Indian Reorganization Act of 1934, 34-35
Indians. *See* Native Americans
Indochina Immigration and Resettlement Act of 1975, 64
Indochinese, 80-82, 255
industrial societies, 10
Institute for Government Research, 34
Institute on Pluralism and Group Identity, 249
institutionalization, 18
institutional racism, 16, 165, 240, 241
integration, 6, 46-47, 101-2, 193-94, 195
  and accommodation, 100-102, 206-7
  and amalgamation, 99-100, 194, 195
  Arkansas, 159
  bus rides, 209
  campaigns for, 204
  education responses to, 160-61
  and Eurocentricity, 94-102, 256, 263
  opposition to, 213
  study of, 271
  vs. diversity, 108
  vs. social separation, 108-10, 167
  white ethnics and nonwhite minorities, 102-4

About the Author

Peter I. Rose is a sociologist and writer. He is Senior Fellow of the Kahn Liberal Arts Institute and Sophia Smith Professor Emeritus of sociology and anthropology at Smith College. He has served as a visiting professor at a number of American universities, including Clark, Wesleyan, the University of Colorado, UCLA, Yale, and Harvard, as a resident fellow at Stanford and Oxford, Fulbright professor in the United Kingdom, Japan, Australia, and Austria , and visiting scholar in China, Israel and Italy. A frequent visitor to and lecturer in The Netherlands, he received the University Medal from the University of Amsterdam in 1994 and continues to serve as a consultant with University College Utrecht and the new Roosevelt Academy, both affiliates of Utrecht University.

Author of a recent memoir, *Guest Appearances and Other Travels in Time and Space,* in addition to *They and We,* his other books include *The Ghetto and Beyond, The Subject Is Race, The Study of Society, Seeing Ourselves, Strangers in Their Midst, Nation of Nations, Americans from Africa, Through Different Eyes, Mainstream and Margins, Working with Refugees, Tempest-Tost, Professorial Passions,* and *The Dispossessed: An Anatomy of Exile.*